Real
Estate
Finance

# Real
# Estate
# Finance

**William M. Shenkel**
College of Business Administration
Department of Real Estate
The University of Georgia

American
Institute of
Banking

American
Bankers
Association

**Library of Congress Cataloging in Publication Data**

Shenkel, William Monroe, 1923–
    Real estate finance.

    1.  Real estate business — United States — Finance.
I.  Title.
HD1375.S358        332.7'2'0973        76–44519

Second Printing,
June 1977

0572

Printed in the
United States of America

# Contents

|  |  | Foreword | vii |
| --- | --- | --- | --- |
|  |  | Preface | ix |
| Chapter | 1 | An Overview of Real Estate Credit | 1 |
|  | 2 | Private Property Rights and Mortgage Lending | 20 |
|  | 3 | Sources of Mortgage Credit | 41 |
|  | 4 | Mortgage Financing by Commercial Banks | 66 |
|  | 5 | Mortgage Instruments and Characteristics | 79 |

v

| | | |
|---|---|---:|
| *Chapter* **6** | Federal Assistance in Mortgage Markets | 101 |
| **7** | Financing Single Family Dwellings | 137 |
| **8** | Condominiums and Cooperative Apartments | 162 |
| **9** | Financing Multiple Family Dwellings | 187 |
| **10** | Financing Industrial Property | 207 |
| **11** | Financing Agricultural Property | 224 |
| **12** | Land Development Loans | 245 |
| **13** | Shopping Center Mortgages | 268 |
| **14** | Mortgage Credit Analysis | 288 |
| **15** | Construction Loan Administration | 316 |
| **16** | Mortgage Collection Policies | 335 |
| **17** | Mortgage Portfolio Administration | 359 |
| **18** | Real Estate Investment Yields | 375 |
| | *Appendix to Chapter 18* | 394 |
| | Glossary | 397 |
| | Index | 407 |

# Foreword

Housing and real estate finance are big business for America's commercial banks, and provide them with an opportunity to serve the vital needs of individuals, businesses, and the whole economy. For these reasons the American Institute of Banking, an educational division of the American Bankers Association, has published this book.

Banking's total commitment to housing includes residential mortgage loans, mobile home loans, residential construction and land loans, home improvement loans, investment in securities that directly or indirectly support housing, and loans to other financial institutions for housing purposes. In addition, there are loans to contractors, building suppliers, and to other businesses engaged in housing construction, servicing, and supply.

Researched and written in close cooperation with the Housing and Real Estate Finance Division of the American Bankers Association, this book replaces *Home Mortgage Lending*, which was published in 1963.

The Institute is especially indebted to the author, Dr. William M. Shenkel. We also extend our gratitude to Roger B. Hawkins, Director, and G. Paul Carr, Assistant Director of the Association's Housing and

Real Estate Finance Division, for their major participation in the book's development.

This book is written from a commercial bank perspective, and is intended to help bankers gain a broad overview of real estate finance. It should be useful as a reference source and learning tool for all bankers interested or involved in housing and real estate finance, whether they are practitioners, readers, researchers, or students; whether they attend AIB classes, take AIB correspondence courses or attend schools, workshops, and seminars sponsored by the American Bankers Association.

RUDOLPH R. FICHTEL, Director
American Institute of Banking
American Bankers Association

# Preface

This book represents a survey of real estate finance and serves a two-fold purpose: first, it explains real estate vocabulary, techniques, and regulations for those with virtually no mortgage experience, and second, it presents leading financing techniques for the more experienced mortgage personnel.

The book's 18 chapters are grouped into three broad divisions: institutional arrangements; specific property types; and administrative tasks. The first six chapters cover institutional arrangements governing real estate finance. Beginning with an overview of real estate credit, the text includes a chapter on terms commonly used in real estate and mortgage lending, and continues with an explanation of mortgages and their characteristics. After completing the first six chapters, the reader should have an understanding of how commercial banks operate in mortgage markets.

The next seven chapters refer to more practical subjects. In this part of the text each chapter relates to a specific type of property. These chapters include illustrations showing how mortgage lenders analyze both borrower credit and real estate as mortgage security. Current examples illustrate the vocabulary associated with each property type and special analytical techniques encountered in mortgage lending.

The latter part of the text, the last five chapters, deals mostly with administrative tasks. Material has been assembled to concentrate on credit analysis, mortgage collection policies, and mortgage portfolio administration. The chapter on construction loan administration is drawn from the experience of mortgage lenders who have developed a fairly uniform system of administering construction loans. The last chapter will appeal mainly to those specialists responsible for analyzing investment yields. And, while the chapter and its appendix introduce fairly complex investment calculations, the availability of computers makes most of these techniques feasible among commercial banks.

The forms exhibited throughout the text are those now being used by the various agencies. However, because of the evolving regulations concerning federal anti-discrimination laws, students may anticipate some changes and should check twice before using the forms for anything other than broad illustrative purposes.

In large measure, this writing task has been a group project. Chapter content, arrangement, and organization have been reviewed by members of the Real Estate Finance Committee, American Bankers Association, who made many invaluable suggestions for the final manuscript. In this respect the contributions of Dr. Robert P. Cavalier, AIB's former Director of Education, and Roger B. Hawkins, Director of ABA's Housing and Real Estate Finance Division, have proven most helpful, Their personal attention to this project has guided text preparation from the very beginning. In addition, the assistance rendered by Mr. G. Paul Carr, Assistant Director of the Housing and Real Estate Finance Division, has enabled the author to present the latest and most accurate version of real estate financing rules, regulations, and methods. And finally the quality of the text has been materially improved by the work of Mr. Kevin J. Holland, who reviewed and edited the manuscript.

It should be added that members of the Housing and Real Estate Finance Committee of the American Bankers Association have individually reviewed chapters in their area of specialization. The book would be incomplete without their assistance.

In addition, staff members of several federal agencies have reviewed the material for accuracy with respect to the many laws and regulations governing real estate finance. The Federal National Mortgage Association, and Federal Housing Administration and members of the Department of Housing and Urban Development have been particularly cooperative in checking and contributing illustrative material.

A special debt of gratitude is due Dr. John T. Masten, Jr., Professor of Banking and Finance, University of Georgia for his initial guidance in the project. Further grateful appreciation is extended to members of the author's research staff. Of special note is the work of Mr. Ali Mansour, Ph.D. candidate, College of Business Administration, University of Georgia, who assisted in the research for this book. Mr. Clayton M. Weibel, a graduate student also at the College of Business, University of Georgia, worked diligently as a research assistant in verifying text material. Finally, the book benefits from the careful work of the manuscript typist, Mrs. Sue Hoy. Her outstanding attention to detail improved the quality of the text.

While the author has benefited from the assistance of many individuals, possible errors, omissions, or other shortcomings are the sole responsibility of the author.

*October, 1976*                                          WILLIAM M. SHENKEL

# Chapter 1

# An Overview of Real Estate Credit

Real estate plays a dominant role in the national economy. As a scarce resource, land must be allocated among the most efficient uses as required by social and economic needs. A changing and shifting population, new technology, growing shortages, and environmental issues raise new concerns over the financing, planning, and operation of real estate assets.

In this new environment, real estate finance assumes increasing importance. Financial institutions active in mortgage financing are largely dependent on the orderly flow of savings into mortgage markets. The flow of funds is subject to considerable variation as the result of monetary policy that varies the interest rate and the availability of funds for mortgages.

There are a number of reasons for the variation in funds for mortgages. On the one hand some savings institutions must comply with unique laws that regulate their investment in mortgages. On the other hand, numerous federal agencies intervene in mortgage markets, first, to encourage new housing, or new communities and, second, to subsidize certain borrowers. Compounding these developments are numerous state and federal laws that govern institutions that invest in mortgages.

1

To develop these points, we will first identify the role of real estate and its financing in the national economy. Next it is certainly worthwhile to review the flow of funds into savings institutions and eventually into mortgages. And finally, an explanation of the secondary mortgage market will help to clarify the main problems facing a mortgage department.

## The Role of Real Estate Finance

To understand how real estate finance affects our national economy, it is necessary to consider the relative importance of real estate. Data of 1968 show that the value of tangible assets in the United States amounts to $3,079 billion. Of this total, structures and land account for *73.1 percent*—almost three-fourths—of the total tangible wealth in the United States. Vacant land equals some *23.2 percent* of all national wealth. Other tangible assets are represented by equipment, inventories and consumer goods.

The value of structures accounts for approximately one-half of all non-land tangible assets. Residential structures, currently accounting for *22.2 percent* of all total reproduceable assets, almost equals the total value of the land. The financing of approximately $682.7 billion of residential structures (in current dollars—1968) creates a continuous business for institutions that specialize in supplying long-term mortgage credit.

Consider next, privately owned non-residential properties (1968), accounting for almost 10 percent of the total reproduceable assets in the United States ($288.7 billion). These assets, primarily represented by commercial and institutional properties, equal almost one-half the value of all residential structures in the United States. Farm buildings, showing a value of $50 billion, add to the demand for loanable funds. Indeed, the value of private farm land in the United States totals five percent of all tangible wealth in the United States.

These details are shown in Table 1.1 and illustrated in Exhibit 1.1. The table shows that total tangible assets are divided between structures, equipment, and land. In fact, because most of the national wealth is placed in structures and land, much of the intangible wealth, primarily stocks and bonds, credit instruments and other paper wealth, is based mainly on the value of land and buildings. Though equipment and inventories show a large absolute volume, they are relatively small compared to real estate assets. By considering the contribution of real estate resources to other aspects of the economy, the role of real estate finance assumes even greater importance.

2

**Exhibit 1.1**
**Total Tangible Wealth in the United States**

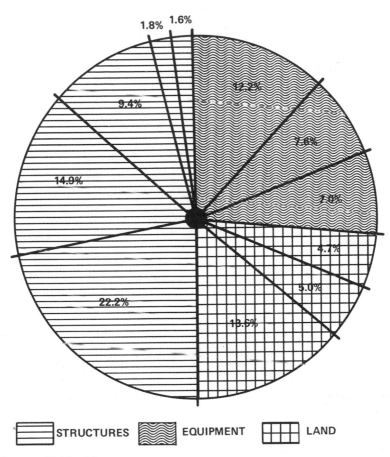

1.8%  1.6%

12.2%

9.4%

7.6%

14.9%

7.0%

4.7%

5.0%

22.2%

13.6%

|▤| STRUCTURES    |〰| EQUIPMENT    |⊞| LAND

Source: Table 1.1.

## Real Estate as a Source of Income

Since real estate occupies a predominant position relative to total national wealth, it may be expected that the real estate industry plays an important role as a source of income. Direct real estate activities including real estate brokerage offices, mortgage companies, real estate management offices, real estate appraising and similar operations, in recent years, have amounted to almost *8 percent* of total national income. By considering banking and finance, insurance and real estate, about *11 percent* of the annual national income arises from businesses related to real estate.

3

**Table 1.1**
**Total Tangible Wealth in the United States, 1968**

| Type of Asset | Dollar Value (in billions) | | Percent of Total | |
|---|---|---|---|---|
| Total Value of Structures | | | | |
| Nonfarm: | | | | |
| Public non-residential ...... | $459.8 | | 14.9% | |
| Institutional ............... | 55.7 | | 1.8 | |
| Residential ................ | 682.7 | | 22.2 | |
| Other private non-residential .. | 288.7 | | 9.4 | |
| Farm structures ............ | 50.0 | $1,537.0 | 1.6 | 49.9% |
| Equipment and Inventories | | | | |
| Business equipment ......... | 377.0 | | 12.2 | |
| Consumer durable goods ..... | 233.8 | | 7.6 | |
| Inventories ................ | 216.2 | $ 827.0 | 7.0 | 26.9% |
| Land | | | | |
| Private farm land ........... | 152.6 | | 5.0 | |
| Private nonfarm land ........ | 418.6 | | 13.6 | |
| Public land ................ | 144.2 | $ 715.4 | 4.7 | 23.2% |
| Total Tangible Assets .......... | | $3,079.4 | | 100.0% * |

* Total may not add to 100.0 because of rounding.
Source: U.S. Bureau of Census, *Statistical Abstract of the United States: 1975* (96th edition), Washington, D. C., 1975. Page 473.

Many authorities would include contract construction as part of the real estate industry. According to this view, 15 percent of the national income originates from finance, insurance, real estate, and construction activities. Few industries have such an impact on national income. Consequently, real estate financing and its development affect other components of the national income. The leverage created by this activity strongly affects other sections of the economy.

### The Significance of Real Estate Debt

Census Bureau data of 1974 show that public and private debt totals some $2,777 billion. Of this amount, public debt accounts for approximately 23.2 percent of all debt in the United States.

| | Total Debt in U. S. (in billions) | Percent of Total |
|---|---|---|
| Public Debt | $ 643 | 23.2% |
| Private Debt | 2,134 | 76.8 |
| Total | $2,777 | 100.0% |

In recent years, the total mortgage debt outstanding has exceeded the federal national debt. A more detailed review of private debt holdings provides an insight into mortgage activity.

**Table 1.2**
**Total National Private Debt, 1974**

| Type of Debt | Amount (in billions) | Percent of Total |
|---|---|---|
| Corporate Debt ................ | $1,254 | 58.8 |
| Farm Debt .................... | 87 | 4.1 |
| Mortgages .................... | 520 | 24.4 |
| Commercial and Financial ....... | 83 | 3.9 |
| Consumer .................... | 190 | 8.9 |
| Total | $2,134 | 100.1 |

Source: U.S. Bureau of Census, *Statistical Abstract of the United States: 1975* (96th edition), Washington, D. C., 1975. Page 473.

**Exhibit 1.2**
**Total Private Debt in the United States, 1974**

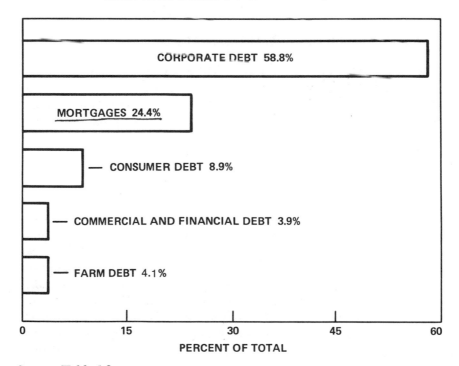

Source: Table 1.2.

As shown in Table 1.2, corporate debt accounts for the larger proportion of private debt, recently amounting to 58.8 percent of all private debt. Note also that total mortgage debt of $520 billion accounts for approximately *one-fourth of all national private debt* held in the United States. This total greatly exceeds the outstanding commercial and consumer debt. These data reveal most pointedly that mortgages serve as a significant source of investment for financial institutions.

## Mortgages Held by Institutions

Financial institutions are highly dependent on mortgages as a source of investments. Over the preceding five years (1970-74), commercial banks have absorbed approximately 15 to 17 percent of total mortgages outstanding. Their total share has exceeded mortgages held by mutual savings banks, United States agencies, and life insurance companies. Only mortgages held by savings and loan associations exceed the mortgages held by commercial banks. Typically, the associations hold about one-third of total mortgages outstanding. Life insurance companies have decreased their mortgage holdings relative to other institutions over the past five years (1970-74) —decreasing from 20.2 to 16.5 percent.

## The Flow of Funds into Real Estate Mortgages

Now suppose we examine the way in which savings flow into the mortgage market. An illustration of how savings are drawn into the mortgage market is suggested by Exhibit 1.3. The annual gross national product—the market value of all goods and services produced in the economy in one year—goes into one of four categories: foreign investment, government expenditures, consumption, and savings which are equal to private investments.

The foreign investment component refers to the amount of annual gross national product invested in foreign countries as a result of changes in the balance of trade. Ordinarily this is a minor component of the gross national product. A certain amount of gross income is spent by government agencies on buildings, public works, defense expenditures and the like. The amount of income going to consumption expenditures, namely, food, shelter, and other consumer goods accounts for the third component of expenditures. The balance of the gross national product goes to savings. In the most recent year, savings accounted for 14.9 percent of the gross national product. These savings may be invested in income earning assets such as government bonds, corporate bonds, and mortgages.

**Exhibit 1.3**
**The Flow of Savings into the Mortgage Market**

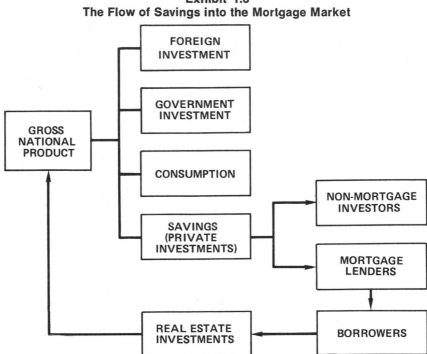

In short, lenders in the business of making mortgages must compete with other non-mortgage investments. When interest rates on mortgages decline to a noncompetitive level with the return earned on, say, government bonds, lenders not only have a smaller volume of funds but the available mortgage funds are loaned at a higher rate of interest. The long-term mortgage borrower, in turn, must compete with other borrowers. If mortgage borrowers are unwilling to pay the market rate of interest as partly determined by the yield on non-mortgage investments, they are unable to compete for the relatively short supply of savings.

Assuming, however, that the mortgage borrowers are successful in competing for funds, they invest mortgage money in existing or new construction. The money invested in new building construction (single family dwellings, commercial, industrial and farm buildings) creates jobs and income for the building industry, which in turn adds to the gross national product. Thus, the flow of savings in the mortgage market describes a circle in which a certain proportion of the gross national product goes into savings which are invested partly in mortgages. Mortgage money invested in new construction, in turn, creates additional income which adds to the gross national product and consequently additional savings.

Exhibit 1.4
Mortgage Origination

## STAGE 1. BUILDING CONSTRUCTION

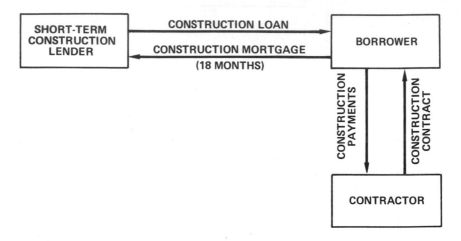

## STAGE 2. CONSTRUCTION COMPLETED

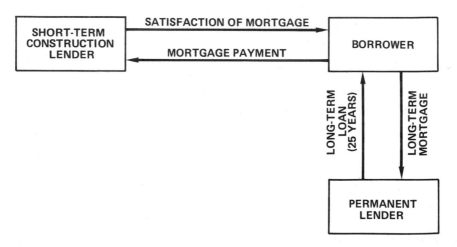

## Mortgage Origination

Before the mortgage loan is approved, a complex series of relationships is established between the short-term lender, the borrower, the contractor, and the permanent lender. See Exhibit 1.4.

Starting with stage one, shown in Exhibit 1.4, assume that the borrower negotiates a contract for a new building. With the plans in hand, the borrower then turns to a short-term lender who specializes in construction loans—quite frequently a local bank. The bank, upon approval of the building plan, credit of the borrower and other financial-legal arrangements, advances a short-term loan, permitting the borrower to finance a new building.

Typically, the borrower has purchased a site from his own personal funds. With approval of the construction loan, the contractor is induced to start construction, receiving payments periodically during stages of construction. The lender is protected because he never finances more than the value of the total construction outstanding. Providing the building is constructed according to contract requirements, the building is then eligible for a long-term mortgage, say 25 years.

At this stage the borrower turns to the permanent lender who deals in long-term mortgages on well secured real estate from qualified borrowers. The permanent lender, after complying with mortgage loan procedures, advances funds to repay the construction lender. The short-term construction lender releases his interest by filing a satisfaction of mortgage agreement in local public records pursuant to applicable state laws which, in effect, gives the permanent lender a first mortgage that has priority over other mortgages. According to the terms of the loan the borrower repays the mortgage at a specified interest over the mortgage term.

In this way, the construction loan allows the borrower to construct a new building, which in its completed form, serves as security for a long-term loan. In the usual case the borrower secures a commitment from the permanent lender to finance the building (say, over 25 years) provided it is completed according to building specifications. Hence, the short-term construction lender is assured of repayment of the construction loan when the contractor completes construction.

The above procedure describes a conventional loan in the simplest of terms. If federal agencies assist in the financing, the procedure is much more complex. Indeed, even with a conventional loan the borrower and lender are intimately involved in the secondary mortgage market. The importance of this market deserves additional explanation.

## A Brief Overview of Secondary Mortgage Markets

In Exhibit 1.5, note that the *primary mortgage market* refers to that segment of the market in which mortgages are originated. Consequently, the primary mortgage market relates only to the originating borrower and the initial lending institution. Banks are among the many originators of mortgages along with savings and loan associations, life insurance companies, and mutual savings banks. In contrast to these primary market relationships, which before 1938 constituted the only mortgage market, the secondary mortgage market provides liquidity for holders of long-term mortgages.

### Exhibit 1.5

### An Illustration of the Primary and Secondary Mortgage Markets

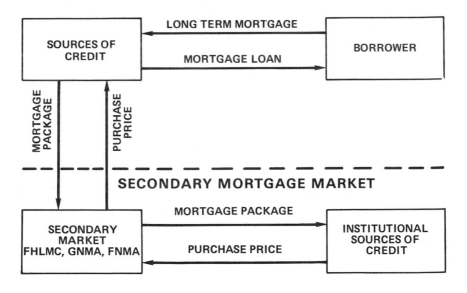

The *secondary mortgage market* refers to the market for existing mortgages which are bought and sold from mortgage originators. This market has no direct relationship to the mortgage borrower. In this sense mortgages are bought and sold much as stocks and bonds are exchanged freely in the open market. In the secondary mortgage market there is only one difference: the market exists only between the mortgage originators and secondary market agencies.

## Secondary market agencies

Initially, the <u>Federal National Mortgage Association</u> (FNMA), which is commonly referred to as Fannie Mae, was <u>organized to provide a</u> <u>market for FHA insured mortgages.</u><sup>& VA guaranteed</sup> Thus, long-term lenders, faced with a shortage of funds, could exchange FHA insured mortgages for cash through FNMA.

More recently the <u>Government National Mortgage Association</u> (GNMA), commonly referred to as Ginnie Mae, was directed <u>to pro-</u> <u>vide a market for government subsidized mortgages</u>—mortgages which are administered under the Department of Housing and Urban Development for various subsidized mortgages. <u>The Federal Home Loan</u> <u>Mortgage Corporation</u> (FHLMC), operating under the Federal Home Loan Bank Board which regulates nationally chartered savings and loan associations, <u>also may buy and sell qualified mortgages that are</u> <u>not insured by FHA or guaranteed by the Veterans Administration.</u> More recently, <u>FNMA has also been authorized to buy and sell conven-</u> <u>tional mortgage loans.</u>

Turning again to Exhibit 1.5, note that the sources of credit, which could be a local bank, may arrange a mortgage package consisting of mortgages in a certain locality, value bracket, age of house, and mortgage maturity which may be sold to one of the secondary market agencies. These agencies in turn (depending largely on national monetary conditions) hold the mortgages in their portfolio or sell mortgage packages to other institutions such as pension funds, insurance companies, and other investors attracted to mortgage yields.

Thus, starting from the initial decision of the borrower to negotiate a long-term mortgage, a chain of events is established that gives mortgages much of the liquidity and yield characteristics of other investments. The successful operation of real estate credit depends on the orderly operation of the secondary mortgage market, though the borrower is not directly affected by its operation. Indeed, the secondary mortgage market has encouraged the flow of funds into real estate mortgages by providing for a ready market for mortgages comparable to other types of investments, i.e., corporate stocks, bonds, and government securities.

## Indicators of mortgage flows

To show how mortgage funds operate in the market, suppose we differentiate between different measures of mortgage flows. See Exhibit 1.6. Assume that a borrower applies for a new mortgage from a local lender, i.e., a commercial bank. The new mortgage pledges real estate

11

## Exhibit 1.6

## Indicators of Mortgage Flows

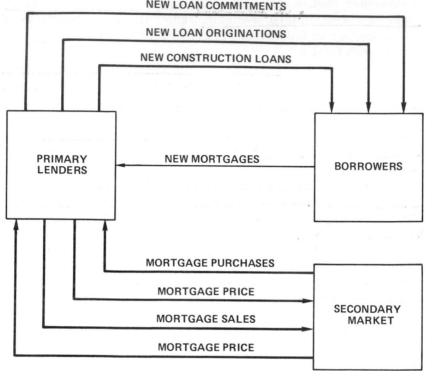

as security to the originating lender. In this respect the lender may engage in three different types of operations. First, the primary lender may grant a *new construction loan*—a temporary loan usually not extending more than 60 months. Second, a lender in the market for a long-term mortgage may make a *new loan commitment,* i.e., 25 years, 9 percent interest, based on a maximum loan equal to 75 percent of the appraised value. The borrower may be granted a new construction loan and a long-term commitment from the same lender. However, typically, two lenders will be encountered: one for the new construction loan and another for the long-term loan. Third, suppose that the building is completed. The primary lender may then *originate a new loan,* an exercise of his new loan commitment.

Therefore, in measuring the volume of mortgage loan activity these three series are highly significant. To provide information on the current market, the Department of Housing and Urban Development issues a monthly report on loan activity. In this report the new loan commitments are given for residential, multifamily, construction, and long-term loans. Included in this report are commitments made by FNMA and GNMA.

Another segment of the market covers secondary mortgage operations. Here the primary lenders have the options of selling or purchasing mortgages. At any given time, depending on credit needs, primary lenders and secondary market agencies are active in the sale and purchase of long-term mortgages. By measuring activity in both the primary and secondary markets, lenders have a fairly current indicator of lending activity.

It should be noted that the Department of Housing and Urban Development's monthly reports show mortgage activity (as shown in Exhibit 1.6) by type of lending institution and type of loan, i.e., construction loans, long-term loans, and mortgage commitments. They are arranged to show the volume of mortgages on new property, existing property, and for the current month compared to the comparable month of the preceding year. The importance of these operations in the secondary market warrants additional review.

## Operations of the Secondary Mortgage Market

Historically, commercial banks have been reluctant to invest in long-term mortgages because of their lack of liquidity. The concentration of short-term borrowers and a dependence on checking account deposits required that banks have ready access to cash to meet any unusual seasonal and cyclical demands. With the FHA insured mortgages and later with the *Servicemen's Readjustment Act of 1944*, which introduced the Veterans Administration guaranteed (VA) mortgage, banks were induced to advance funds on long-term mortgage loans. While the insurance or guaranty reduced the risk of loss, lenders required a means of converting mortgages to cash in periods of monetary restraint. The agency that eventually assumed this role for FHA and VA loans was the Federal National Mortgage Association (FNMA). Commercial banks, probably more than most financial institutions exclusive of mortgage bankers, are dependent on the orderly operation of the secondary mortgage market.

The impetus for a national secondary mortgage market was provided by the Reconstruction Finance Corporation Mortgage Company established by a 1935 act of Congress. Among other responsibilities, this company was authorized to purchase mortgages insured by the Federal Housing Administration but only for dwellings with more than four units. The success of this program led to the creation of FNMA which assumed the role of purchasing and selling mortgages insured by FHA. Mortgages guaranteed by the Veterans Administration were added to their list of authorized purchases and sales in 1948.

In certain periods of rising interest rates, FNMA has operated virtually as the sole source of mortgage funds for government-insured and guaranteed loans. For example, if lenders expect interest rates to rise, they are reluctant to place money in fixed interest mortgages and face the possibility of a decrease in the value of their mortgage holdings. This danger was removed by a commitment from FNMA to purchase at some set figure a lender's mortgage portfolio during a stated period. The lender would then have the option of disposing of mortgages, which carried a fixed interest rate, to FNMA if interest rates were more attractive on non-mortgage securities.

Also, by withholding commitments (which prevailed between 1950 and 1953), FNMA restricted the flow of funds going into FHA and VA mortgages. Without FNMA commitments, high interest rates would lead to heavy mortgage discounts and a general withdrawal of funds from FHA and VA mortgages.

In 1954 FNMA was reorganized specifically to provide assistance to the secondary market for home mortgages. With a *shortage of loanable funds,* FNMA *purchases* mortgages thereby supplying capital which may be invested in new mortgages. In periods of easy credit and an active mortgage market, FNMA *decreases purchases* or *sells* mortgages to absorb funds that would ordinarily be placed in mortgages. In this way FNMA largely controls the flow of funds into government-insured and guaranteed mortgages.

Beginning in 1968, the operation of the secondary mortgage market was affected by two changes: (1) the transfer of FNMA from a government operation to a private operation; and (2) the organization of a new corporation, government owned and operated—the Government National Mortgage Association (GNMA). In this year FNMA extended secondary operations to include conventional mortgages. A parallel development was created to buy and sell conventional mortgages issued by savings and loan associations and banks. The agency assuming this role is the Federal Home Loan Mortgage Corporation (FHLMC), which is empowered to establish a secondary market for conventional mortgages. These institutions have provided an effective means of guiding savings into long-term mortgages.

14

## Federal National Mortgage Association

The intent of the 1968 legislation creating the reorganized FNMA was to convert the secondary mortgage operation to a government-backed private corporation. The new charter authorized the sale of preferred stock to the U.S. Treasury and common stock to private investors. Preferred stock could be retired from capital surplus. The sale of common shares was limited to sellers of mortgages to the association. They are also permitted to raise funds through the sale of credit instruments.

In 1976, FNMA stands prepared to purchase approved mortgages from lenders who qualify as eligible sellers. Their most recent report (issued in February, 1976) qualifies FNMA as the largest single private purchaser of residential mortgages in the United States. The $31.9 billion net mortgage and loan portfolio for the year 1975 represents housing for almost 2.4 million families.

Banks participating in FNMA operations and sellers must be qualified as— 1. experienced in making real estate mortgages;
2. a business enterprise that maintains a network of not less than $100,000 in assets approved by FNMA; and
3. an organization that employs appraisers, underwriters, and attorneys approved by FNMA.

Close observers have noted that these provisions establish a new market to expand local mortgage-lending capacity. Even the small banks will be able to accommodate the home-buying customer with mortgage funds. In this respect commercial banks will not be limited by statutory provisions that limit the total amount of outstanding real estate loans in relation to capital, savings, and time deposits. In addition, banks will be able to maintain an inventory of mortgages at flexible levels which may be easily changed by selling surplus mortgages to FNMA. As a seller of mortgages, banks generate additional revenue by continuing to service FNMA purchased mortgages.

Furthermore, operations of FNMA have the effect of creating more uniformity in mortgage loan contracts. Underwriting procedures tend to be more standardized by lenders in observing uniformity in mortgage loan documentation. Such documentation includes common title reports, appraisals and documentation procedures. These are believed essential steps to encourage the orderly flow of savings among geographic areas most in need of funds.

## Government National Mortgage Association

Under provisions of the 1954 act, FNMA was required to support special housing assistance programs and to liquidate mortgages acquired

15

under earlier programs. Legislation in 1968 established GNMA as a separate government corporation with responsibilities for these two main responsibilities. According to GNMA—

> The Association operates in three major areas. Under its *Special Assistance Function*, an activity previously performed by Fannie Mae, GNMA purchases certain types of mortgages to fulfill two statutorily-mandated objectives: (1) to provide support for types of housing for which financing is not readily available, such as housing for low-income families, and (2) to counter declines in mortgage lending and housing construction. [Emphasis supplied]
>
> (*Annual Report*, Government National Mortgage Association, 1975). p. 7

The special assistance program refers to mortgages that are not marketable under subsidized housing programs and that must be supported by GNMA when directed by the President or by legislation. Mortgages falling in this category have limited appeal to the private sector because of limited borrower credit, location, or because of adverse economic conditions. Thus, special assistance applies to financing cooperative housing, housing for military personnel, and low and middle income housing programs falling under special FHA or VA programs.

As an additional means of mortgage market support, the 1968 Act authorized GNMA to administer a *new Mortgage-Backed Securities Program* which would increase liquidity in the secondary mortgage market and attract new sources of financing into residential loans. Ginnie Mae guarantees the timely payment of principal and interest on securities based on pools of Government-backed mortgages and issued by private mortgage institutions. The GNMA guarantee is backed by the full faith and credit of the United States.

The second operation refers to *mortgage pools* resulting from the new Mortgage-Backed Securities Program. In practice certificates are issued which are backed by a portfolio of mortgages falling in one of the special assistance programs (FHA, VA, or Farmers Home Administration (FmHA)). Providing the originating lender and the mortgages qualify, the lender applies to GNMA for permission to establish a mortgage pool and issue certificates against the pool of pledged mortgages. To gain approval, mortgages must meet certain standards with respect to the type of property, interest rates, and loan maturity. Mortgages forming the pool must not be issued more than one year before the GNMA commitment. Upon approval, GNMA guarantees the certificates. The certificates are then issued to the original lender on the mortgage in proportion to the share of the mortgage pool purchased.

The original issuer of certificates services the loans and passes interest and principal payments to certificate holders.

Holders of certificates may include savings and loan associations, savings banks, credit unions, pension funds, commercial banks, insurance companies, corporations, partnerships, or individuals. With this device GNMA attracts capital to the mortgage market by guaranteeing the payment of interest and principal on certificates which are backed by approved mortgages. At the same time the holder of the certificate is relieved of mortgage servicing responsibilities.

Yet another plan combines features of GNMA and FNMA, known as the *Tandem Plan*. Sponsors of non-profit housing projects using this plan first secure a commitment from GNMA to buy mortgages at par after completion of construction. At the same time FNMA agrees to purchase a given amount of mortgages at current prices. When the mortgage is sold to FNMA at the market price, GNMA pays the difference between the face value of the mortgage and the going, usually discounted, market price.

The advantage of this plan is the leverage afforded GNMA. By paying for only the discount, more funds are available than if GNMA were to hold the entire mortgage in their portfolio. In essence GNMA guarantees the discount, which sponsors of special assistance housing projects probably could not afford.

Finally, under its Management and Liquidation Function, Ginnie Mae assumed responsibility from FNMA for managing the portfolio of federally owned mortgages.

This third function which is relatively unimportant to the current mortgage market is a carry over from Reconstruction Finance Corporation operations.

## The Federal Home Loan Mortgage Corporation

Authorized in 1970, FHLMC (or The Mortgage Corporation) was established by the Federal Home Loan Bank (FHLB) with powers similar to FNMA. The FHLB serves federally chartered savings and loan associations in much the same way as the Federal Reserve Board serves federally chartered banks. The purpose of FHLB was to develop an effective secondary market in which mortgages would compete for capital on an equal basis with other types of investment. The Corporation is authorized to purchase and sell federally insured guaranteed loans in addition to conventional loans. Their purchase program concentrated on the following four mortgage packages:

1. Conventional loans.
2. Conventional, multiple family, fixed constant forward commitments.

17

3. Participation in conventional mortgages.
   a) Loans on multiple family dwellings.
   b) Loans on mixed single family and multiple family dwellings with a maximum of 50 percent invested in multiple family loans.
4. FHA and VA home mortgages.

The innovation introduced by FHLMC relates to the maximum constant forward commitment. This refers to loan commitments at a fixed price allowing the yield to vary, in effect, shifting the cost of changing interest rates to FHLMC. In contrast, the secondary operation of FNMA is based on a stable rate with a varying mortgage price. This latter arrangement has the effect of placing the burden of interest rate changes on the person selling the mortgage.

To explain further, the mortgage constant refers to the monthly mortgage instalment required to retire one dollar at a given interest rate and loan maturity. Multiplying this monthly instalment by 12 gives the annual mortgage constant. Thus, the mortgage constant gives the constant dollar amount that must be paid to amortize the mortgage. The same constant may apply to mortgages that vary in their terms: For example, a high interest rate mortgage with a long maturity, say for 30 years, may produce the same constant prevailing for a shorter-term mortgage with a considerably lower interest rate.

By basing the commitment on a maximum constant, the borrower is assured that his mortgage payments will not rise above the maximum, constant commitment. In practice the constant is established on the basis of market rates on the date the commitment is issued and a 22 year amortization period. Commitments are limited to a maximum of five million dollars per transaction and delivery of loans within 24 months. As the lender delivers the mortgage, the amortization schedule is increased to 30 years. FHLMC reserves the right to impose the effective interest rate on the day they accept the loan up to the point of the maximum constant based on the 30 year amortization schedule.

In short, the builder in accepting a commitment knows the exact amount of his loan and the maximum monthly payments. Therefore, when the loan is presented to FHLMC the amortization period will be extended to 30 years if the market interest rate has increased; or if interest rates have declined, the borrower may extend the amortization rate to 30 years and reduce his monthly payments.

Apparently FHLMC has competed fairly successfully for loanable funds. At the end of the first three years of operation more than 2.6 billion dollars in mortgage loans were held in its portfolio. During this period some 900 million dollars of mortgages were sold. Of the 2.6

billion purchases, approximately 800 million were held in conventional loans. The balance consisted of FHA and VA guaranteed loans.

It is fairly clear that development of secondary mortgage markets removes the former stigma that mortgages lack liquidity. Commercial banks, providing they conform to standard procedures common to secondary mortgage markets, may compete for the best quality mortgage loans. The main problem is to adapt mortgage loan policy that meets the needs of the individual institution. This latter conclusion seems supported by other legislation recently liberalizing mortgage financing for national banks.

# Chapter 2

# Private Property Rights and Mortgage Lending

Underwriting mortgages calls for a detailed knowledge of borrower credit. Mortgage personnel deal continually with such financial aspects of long-term loans as the credit analysis of the borrower; the personal motivation and attitude towards debts; the past payment record and the like. Loan decisions require judgments on the stability of income, an evaluation of financial assets and, in the case of businesses, a review of past profit and loss statements and balance sheets.

It is equally clear that the mortgage underwriter must have more than a casual knowledge of the real estate security. There are circumstances in which the lender looks to the real estate asset as loan security. To this extent the mortgage underwriter must determine the marketability of specialized types of real estate. Judging the real estate security in a single family dwelling represents one of the more complex problems facing the lender. The more technical aspects of condominiums, multiple family projects, and special purpose properties such as industries, farms, and shopping centers is a case in point.

There is one other area deserving of additional study, namely, real property rights important to the mortgage lender. Some familiarity with real estate instruments and property rights associated with conveyance documents, and the growing effect of public land use controls on property values warrant additional review. In the latter case considerable import is attached to the new environmental controls administered on federal and state levels. These public controls tend to affect the cost of development, the time of compliance, and the potential use of real estate. Consequently, it is difficult for the mortgage lender to avoid an evaluation of property rights and land use regulations in arriving at a lending decision. For this reason mortgage personnel should review ownership interests, real estate conveyance instruments, and public rights in real estate including examples of how environmental legislation affects private property development.

# Ownership Interests

It should be emphasized that the system of land titles in the United States was largely carried over from English law which can be traced to feudal times. As a consequence it is common to describe ownership interests as either representing freehold estates or less than freehold estates. The various forms of land title are included in the freehold estates while leases, easements, and other partial interests in real estate fall under the less than freehold classification.

## Freehold Estates

Property owners may convert their freehold estates, which are of uncertain duration, to estates of inheritance or estates not of inheritance. In the first instance, the owner has title during his life which may be passed on to his heirs. Estates not of inheritance include various forms of *life estates* in which title continues only during the life of a person identified as the person whose life determines the duration of the title.

### Estates of inheritance

Under the feudal system in England, a fief was a grant from the king to tenants who usually held the grant or fief over their lifetime. At the discretion of the king, the fief, later known as a fee, was conveyed to the tenant "and his heirs and assigns forever" which converted the estate to one that could be inherited. Today the most absolute form of legal ownership is termed the fee simple estate or in some areas called the fee simple absolute. The term "simple" means that the owner holds title without restrictions or encumbrances on the title.

The owner of the fee simple estate has the right of *exclusive possession*, the right of *quiet enjoyment*, and the right of *disposition*. Under

21

the latter right he may sell, give, or pass title to his lawful heirs. Holding the right of exclusive possession, an owner of the fee simple estate may borrow on the property, control entry on his land, and even collect damages from people who wrongfully trespass against his property. In short, the owner of the fee simple estate has the exclusive right of possession giving him as complete control as possible under our system of ownership.

The right of *quiet enjoyment* refers to the legal right to holding possession without disturbance because of defects in title. A holder of the right of quiet enjoyment has the right to use land in any manner consistent with local laws. The owner is entitled to the proceeds of the land; the owner may devote land to personal use and is entitled to collect rents from tenants. In acquiring the fee simple estate, the owner has the right of holding possession without disturbance because of any defects in title.

The right of *exclusive possession*, held by the owner of the fee simple estate, allows the owner to use the property over his life, to sell all or part of his interest and, subject to statutes prohibiting certain forms of discrimination against others, the owner may sell by any means available. The right may be transferred by will upon death. And, only operation of the law, namely, failure to pay property taxes or other liens, or the taking of private property for public use, will cause the owner to lose his ownership interest.

The fee simple interest, while representing the maximum ownership legally available, is subject to the right of others. It is well established that certain governmental powers restrict private ownership rights. Under the inherent *police powers* of the state, meaning state, local, and federal government, property rights may be regulated in the public interest. In addition, under *eminent domain*, private property may be taken for public use upon payment of the market value of the property taken and the government also has the right of *taxation*. Furthermore, if a property owner dies without a will and he has no legal heirs, title will revert to the state under the power of *escheat*. This latter right provides that upon the owner's death with no will or heirs, ownership will be vested, temporarily at least, in someone. Property may not be left without an owner under our system of private property.

Most of us are aware that private property must be used so as not to cause a nuisance to neighbors. Common law governing nuisance prevents the property from being maintained in an unsafe, unsanitary condition. So while the fee simple absolute provides for maximum control of the property, it is subject to both public and private restrictions.

Attention is also directed to two variations in fee ownership: the fee simple determinable and the fee subject to condition subsequent.

22

These differences in the fee ownership explain why mortgages are not approved without verification of the title, title insurance or other means of validating an ownership interest before loan approval.

*(1) Fee Simple Determinable.* A fee simple determinable terminates upon the occurrence of a known event. Suppose a property owner conveys land to a church "so long as" the land is used for church purposes. The conveyance language specifies a fee simple title as long as the land is used for church purposes. If the church abandons the site, the fee simple interest *automatically* terminates and title reverts back to the grantor (original owner) or his heirs. Under a fee simple determinable, title automatically reverts back to the owner without further action. The mortgage on such an estate should not be approved until a legal opinion is rendered on the possible consequences of ownership termination.

*(2) The Fee Subject to Condition Subsequent.* If the fee simple owner transfers property to a church under this form of ownership, the new owner acquires virtually the same possessory and use rights of the fee simple determinable. The language identifying this interest will usually read "on the condition that" with an added statement that the original owner may repossess the premises. In short, the fee simple subject to condition subsequent continues until the original owner takes action to repossess the premises. As differentiated from the fee simple determinable, which automatically terminates at the occurrence of some event, this title requires two conditions for termination of title: (1) the stated event must occur, i.e., the church has abandoned the site, and (2) the original owner must take steps to reenter and repossess. Without this latter step, the fee simple subject to condition subsequent continues even though the original terms of conveyance have been broken.

### Estates not of inheritance

Mortgage lenders are faced with various forms of life contracts and certain other legal estates provided by state statutes. While state law is controlling, certain types of titles are universally recognized in their general form. For the present purpose, it is important to distinguish between the various forms of life contracts, and those legal estates provided by statute governing the interests of married persons called dower, curtesy, tenancy by the entireties, and community property.

**(1) The Ordinary Life Estate.** The owner of the fee simple estate may convey an interest in an ordinary life estate by giving all rights of use, enjoyment, and possession to some person for a specified term measured by the life of the person receiving the estate or even some other person. Upon death of the person whose life measures the estate, the life estate automatically terminates. Such an estate may be created by the express wish of the owner by deed or by will. For example, if **A** transfers a life estate to **B** during **B's** life with the provisions that the estate is to revert to **C** upon **B's** death, **C** holds the *remainder* and he is known as the remainderman or the reversioner.

The designated life serves as a time clock measuring duration of the estate. Technically the life estate, measured by the life of a party other than the grantee, is known as an estate *pur autre vie*.

A person holding a life estate is referred to as the *life tenant*. See Exhibit 2.1.

## Exhibit 2.1

### Ordinary Life Estate

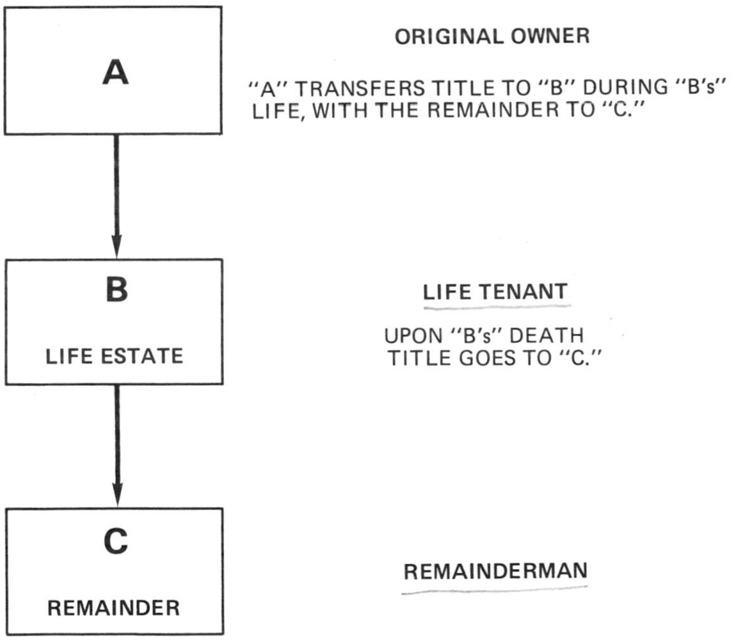

**A**

**ORIGINAL OWNER**

"A" TRANSFERS TITLE TO "B" DURING "B's" LIFE, WITH THE REMAINDER TO "C."

**B**

**LIFE ESTATE**

**LIFE TENANT**

UPON "B's" DEATH TITLE GOES TO "C."

**C**

**REMAINDER**

**REMAINDERMAN**

In some states, the life tenant has an interest that may be mortgaged, but the mortgage lender may have no security if the life tenancy terminates upon the death of the designated person. And, like a borrower with a mortgage, the life tenant must not commit undue waste or otherwise subject the property to permanent injury. Even changing the use of the property or demolishing buildings or subjecting the property to a use that prevents the remainderman from accepting the property in an unchanged condition is prohibited. The life tenant is directed to pay taxes, maintain the property, and undertake repairs necessary to preserve property value. In some states the life tenancy automatically terminates if the life tenant violates these restrictions.

(2) **Legal Life Estates.** Note that the ordinary life estate must be created by some express act of the owner—a deed or a will. The legal life estates on the other hand are created by operation of the law. State law provides for certain interests of the spouse that arise during the marriage. Lending officers in states with these legal life estates must insure that married parties join in the execution of deed and mortgage instruments. A brief review of the legal life estates prevailing among the different states shows the importance of reviewing documents for signatures of married parties. The more common provisions deal with curtesy, dower, tenancy by the entireties and community property.

The right of *curtesy*, though varying among the states of Alabama, Arkansas, Hawaii, North Carolina and others, gives the widower an estate for life in all real estate owned by his wife in her own name during the marriage, provided there is a valid marriage and the birth of a living child during marriage. The estate terminates on divorce or death of the husband. A curtesy interest cannot be defeated by the wife's transfer of her property during her lifetime unless her husband joins in the transfer. Thus, mortgage and title documents in states providing for curtesy require that the husband sign conveyance documents to extinguish rights of curtesy. Depending largely on state law and individual circumstances, a wife executing a conveyance instrument which passes title to her real estate without her husband's signature may jeopardize the title because of the subsequent exercise of curtesy rights.

In certain states, the surviving wife has a *dower* interest in real estate acquired during marriage. Under the common law, the surviving widow is generally entitled to a life estate in one-third of the real estate held by her husband in his own name during the marriage. This right may be either *inchoate* or *consummate*. The former refers to the anticipated interest a wife has in land acquired during marriage which cannot be terminated by the husband or by his will. Without a release of the wife's interest, it is said that a wife with a dower interest holds a contingent interest of an inchoate dower.

At the husband's death, the surviving wife assumes all rights and obligations of a conventional life estate tenant. In some states, the surviving wife has the right to take a proportion of the husband's entire estate, including personal property or real estate in place of the dower interest. Where dower prevails, the dower right may be released by the wife joining the husband in executing real estate conveyance instruments. On the death of the husband, the widow has a consummate interest not only in the real estate owned by the husband at the time of death but in all real estate owned during marriage in which she did not release her dower right. The dower estate may also terminate by divorce, death of the wife, or election of the wife to accept an alternative share of the husband's estate in lieu of the dower interest.

*Tenancy by the entirety,* as in Florida, treats property conveyed to a husband and wife as a single estate. Though neither party owns an individual interest in the property, they both own the whole property. This concept parallels the common law interpretation that the husband and wife own property as one person which is terminated by death at which time the surviving spouse emerges as the sole owner. Divorce converts tenancy by the entirety to joint ownership, without the right of survivorship.

Mortgage lenders are aware that property held in this form is not subject to a debt against only one of the parties. Moreover, one of the parties may not transfer his or her interest to another, as joint conveyance is required. Finally, neither party may pass this estate to heirs by will.

*Community property,* a concept evolved from early Spanish and French law, is found in many of the Western and Southwestern states. Community property is liable for debts of either spouse but the main difference is that each spouse has the right to dispose of his or her undivided interest in community property by will. Without a will, the surviving spouse assumes title by intestate succession.

Where community property rights are effective, care must be taken to differentiate between *separate* property and *community property.* Separate property is owned by either spouse at the time of marriage or acquired during marriage by inheritance, will, or gift. Separate property is owned independently from any interest of the other spouse unless it is commingled with community property. In contrast, community property assumes that the husband and wife share equally in all property acquired during marriage, i.e., community property. Mortgage and other documents involving community property must include signatures of both spouses. No conveyance instrument or contract is valid without signatures of the husband and wife where a community property interest is involved.

Some states provide for *homestead rights,* another type of formal life contract. The importance of homestead to the lender lies in the protection the homestead provides the head of a household against certain types of creditors. Generally the homestead must be declared and filed in the local county office in a form required by state statute. That portion of the property designated as a homestead is protected from public sale to satisfy certain creditors.

In some instances the homestead is limited to a maximum dollar claim, i.e., $15,000 in California. Some states like Florida limit the homestead to an area: 160 acres of rural property, or one-half acre for a homestead located within an incorporated city. The head of the household who has the right to file a homestead is often defined to include a married woman as head of the family. The possibility of a homestead right again calls for a careful legal interpretation that may affect loan security.

## Less Than Freehold Estates

To the long-term lender less than freehold estates have importance with respect to leases: an interest in real estate conveyed over time. As shown in Exhibit 2.2 an owner who executes a lease to a tenant creates two new estates: the leased fee and the leasehold interest. The owner then becomes the *lessor* while the tenant who acquires the leasehold interest assumes the role of the *lessee*. Leases may assume many different forms, i.e., the short-term leases, long-term leases, which may extend to 99 years, and leases in which the owner leases land to a tenant who constructs a building on the site (a net ground lease).

**Exhibit 2.2**

**Leased Fee and Leasehold Interests**

| LEASED FEE<br>INTEREST | LEASEHOLD<br>INTEREST | 2 estates |
|---|---|---|
| OWNER OR<br>LESSOR | TENANT OR<br>LESSEE | |

**FEE SIMPLE ESTATE**

A lease conveys the exclusive right to possession, use, and enjoyment for a limited time which the tenant acquires in return for payment of rent and for meeting other obligations of the lease. Compared to fee ownership, in which future use rights are acquired in perpetuity for a lump sum payment (the purchase price), the tenant pays rent periodically as he uses the property. At the end of the lease, the property reverts to the owner who then holds the fee simple estate. It is possible for the tenant to mortgage the leasehold interest or for the lessor to mortgage his leased fee interest.

27

The mortgageable interest depends largely on the type of freehold estate created by the lease: an estate for years, a tenancy at will, a tenancy from period to period or a tenancy at sufferance. These interests assume the greatest value if the lease creates an estate for years.

*Estate for years* greatest value owner gives up use & enjoyment but retains right to dispose.

A lease that continues for a definite period of time creates an estate for years. Legally the time may be virtually for any period, a month, a year or a number of years. In this case, the lease must have a definite beginning date and termination date at which time the lessee must vacate. With a known lease term, the leased fee or leasehold assures value for the lessor or lessee according to terms of the lease, the market rent at the time of valuation, and the capitalization rate used to convert rights of the parties to a capital interest. A mortgage loan on either the leased fee or leasehold interest would require an estate for years.

*Tenancy at will* can be terminated at will of either party

Suppose a lease, which provides for monthly payment of rent, terminates on December 31. Before the lease is terminated, let us assume also that the owner amd tenant agree that the tenant may continue to occupy the premises after December 31 provided he continues to pay the monthly rent of $500. In this instance, the term of the tenancy is uncertain; it may be terminated at the will of either party. Consequently, a tenancy at will is an estate that may be terminated at the will of the lessor or lessee. Termination is generally exercised by the giving of proper legal notice as required by state statute. For example, a tenancy at will providing a month-to-month tenancy typically requires a 30 day or 45 day written notice by either party. Statutory requirements will specify the time, form of notice, and method of service. Because of the uncertain tenancy, a tenancy at will has limited value; it would not provide security for a long-term loan.

*Tenancy from period to period*

A tenant who occupies an apartment under an agreement providing for a monthly rent of $200 illustrates this type of tenancy. It continues from period to period as agreed upon by the owner and tenant. The tenant may continue to occupy the premises on a month-to-month basis for an indefinite period. Like the tenancy at will, this estate has little economic value.

*Tenancy at sufferance*

This estate covers the tenant who originally entered the premises lawfully under a valid lease and holds over after the lease terminates without permission of the owner. The tenancy at sufferance creates no estate for the tenant; the tenant has no rights in law because he continues to use the premises without the express consent of the owner. The tenancy at sufferance continues unless the owner consents to continued possession or takes action to repossess. The only difference between this tenancy and a trespasser is that the tenant at sufferance gains lawful possession with the consent of the owner though he continues to hold unlawfully. Such a tenant holds no interest in the premises, and no notice to terminate a tenancy at sufferance is required. There is no economic interest to mortgage, convey, or assign to others.

## Easement Rights

Up to this point it has been demonstrated that the owner of a fee interest has several options: the owner may sell an entire interest, convey the interest in the form of a life estate, or grant the possession and use over the limited time, i.e., execute a lease. Moreover, the owner has the right to convey only partial interests in the estate, for example, the sale of subsurface rights (mineral, oil, coal rights) or the right to use air space over the surface. An easement demonstrates a partial conveyance: it covers the right to use real estate for a specific purpose.

Frequently, there is no economic purpose served in acquiring a fee simple estate for only a right-of-way. Thus, public utilities acquire easements giving them the right to use land for the construction and maintenance of electric power transmission lines, or oil and gas pipelines. In these instances, the fee owner continues to use property subject to the easement. The complications arising from easements suggest the importance of title investigation. A mortgage lender may be unaware of existing easements and their effect on property use and value solely by physical inspection. A brief description of easements shows their relative importance to property owners and mortgage lenders.

If the easement relates to a right-of-way, two estates are created: the *dominant estate* and the *servient estate*. For example if **B** grants a 40 foot right-of-way to **A** who benefits from the easement, **A** holds the dominant estate while **B** holds the *servient* estate. See Exhibit 2.3. If the easement is valid, executed by a proper instrument, **A**'s right is said to "run with the land." **B**'s interest may not be transferred free of the easement. That is, if **B** transfers his ownership to **C**, **C** must observe the rights of **A**, the holder of the dominant estate. An easement that runs with the land constitutes an *easement appurtenant*.

## Exhibit 2.3

## Right-of-Way Easement Showing the Dominant and Servient Estates

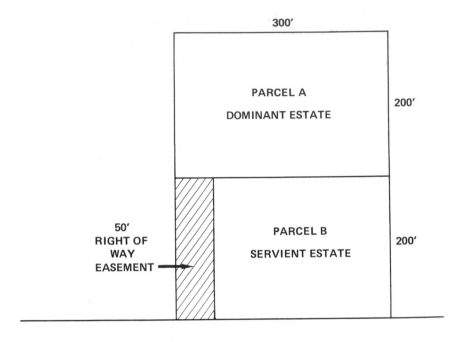

PUBLIC ROAD

In practice, easement deeds are executed with all the formality of other real estate documents. In a pipeline easement for example, the owner conveys—

> . . . *an easement for a pipeline right-of-way with the right to construct, maintain, inspect, identify, operate, protect, replace, repair, change the size of and remove a pipeline and appurtenances, including markers for the transportation of liquids, gases, solids, or mixtures of any or all thereof, upon and along a route to be selected by grantee, said right-of-way being. . . .*

Such an easement typically will further provide that the pipeline company has the right of access to the pipeline, over the owner's land to maintain the right-of-way clear of trees, undergrowth and brush. The owner is restricted from constructing buildings on the pipeline right-of-way without written permission. The title of the owner is affected by the clause identifying an easement of appurtenance: "These shall be covenants running with the land and shall be binding on grantors, their heirs and assigns."

An easement that does not run with the land is called *easement in gross,* which is a personal right only between the grantor and grantee. Such an easement cannot be assigned, conveyed, or inherited, and it does not create dominant and servient estates. Referring to the earlier example, if **B** transfers his property to **C** subject to an easement in gross, **A** must negotiate directly with **C** to re-establish the personal right to use land of **C,** i.e., an easement in gross.

In property development, land use may be affected by easement established by *prescription.* Hence, it is not always possible to identify an easement by search of public records. In most states if certain conditions have been met, an easement will be established if the land has been used (1) adversely to the property owner, (2) openly and notoriously, and (3) continuously for the statutorily defined time.

If the owner has granted permission to use the land, no easement by prescription is created, since it arises only if the interest is adverse, i.e., without permission of the owner. The open and notorious requirement must be such that the owner would know of the hostile use by inspection. The time required to establish an easement by prescription varies: 10, 15, or 20 years depending on state law.

The possibility of an easement right calls for both an inspection of the property and legal interpretation. An unknown right of access may be expensive to litigate or even prevent certain types of development. Overhead or underground rights-of-way similarly restrict the construction, use and development of property and therefore its value.

## Real Estate Conveyance Instruments

While passing judgment on real estate documents is the responsibility of lawyers, it is worthwhile to understand the need for proper signatures, witnesses, and procedures followed in processing loan applications. The rights of parties to a conveyance document often depend on the type of deed. While the terminology and specific requirements vary among the states, they follow a fairly common pattern.

### Types of Deeds

A deed is a written instrument that transfers an interest in real estate. To be enforceable, a deed not only must conform to contract law, but it must include elements unique to real estate transactions. Requirements of enforceable deed include:

1. Instruments conveying an interest in real estate must be in writing;
2. The deed must identify a competent grantor and a grantee;
3. The deed must include proper words of conveyance;
4. The deed must describe the land conveyed;
5. The deed must have proper signatures; and
6. The deed must be delivered and accepted.

The first requirement renders oral agreements unenforceable. A written deed generally may not be amended orally. Accordingly, parties to a deed must reduce their entire agreement in writing. The grantor must be legally competent. For example, corporate officers must have legal authority to transfer corporate property. A legally appointed guardian must act for a minor. Moreover, the deed is not enforceable if it transfers an interest to a fictitious grantee or one who does not exist. The statutory words of conveyance identify the type of deed and are specified by state law. The land must be described in definite terms: a legal description must be sufficiently precise to remove all questions of the land conveyed. Street addresses, though under certain circumstances adequate for enforceability, are usually insufficient for this purpose. Consideration, defined as a promise or a sacrifice of one party, must be present for enforceability. The signature of the grantor is required. In the case of married couples it is necessary to extinguish rights arising from community property, dower, and curtesy by requiring signatures of both husband and wife as grantors.

Even with these requirements, the deed is not enforceable until it has been delivered and accepted by the grantee. In some circumstances, the act of recording the deed in a public office or the services of an escrow agent—a third party who acts on instructions of the seller according to the escrow agreement—may constitute delivery. A properly signed deed may not transfer an interest if it may be established that the deed was not delivered and accepted.

In most states, deeds, though known by different names, include the warranty deed, the special warranty deed, quit claim deeds, bargain and sale deeds, and certain other deeds for special purposes.

## Warranty deeds

The warranty deed stands out from other conveyances since the grantor or seller in conveying title makes certain promises or covenants to the buyer. While these promises seldom are stated in the deed itself, by statute it is implied that the seller includes all covenants of a statutory warranty deed. The conveyance words identifying a warranty deed are usually words such as "grant and convey, convey and warrant, or grant and release" as specified by statute. With the proper words of conveyance, the warranty deed usually implies the following five covenants:

1. The covenant of seizin;
2. the covenant of quiet enjoyment;
3. the covenant against encumbrances;
4. the covenant of further assurances; and
5. the covenant of warranty of title.

*[handwritten margin note: doctrine of after acquired title if grantor says he is going to convey a certain title, & doesn't have it, but then does attain it, it goes to grantee.]*

The buyer of the property may act against the seller if any of the covenants are violated. For instance, the covenant of seizin represents a promise by the seller that he or she is seized or possessed of the real estate described and that he or she has the right to transfer title. If the seller violates this promise, the buyer may sue under a warranty deed for violation of the covenant of seizin.

The warranty deed includes a promise that the owner is entitled to the peaceful use of property, free of claims by other persons not mentioned in the deed. A third party, previously unknown, who claims title would entitle the buyer to sue the seller for violation of the covenant of quiet enjoyment.

Claims or other debts not identified in the deed break the covenant against encumbrance. For in a warranty deed, the seller promises to protect the buyer from any lien, debt, mortgage, or easement not identified in the deed.

Title is further protected by the covenant of further assurance that requires the seller to obtain further documents necessary to give the seller title. Failure to obtain the right signature to extinguish dower would be a violation of this covenant. Any defects in title may be remedied by executing other conveyance documents while under this covenant.

The last covenant means that the seller promises to defend title against all claims of persons contesting the title. Expenses of defending a contested title remain the responsibility of the seller under a warranty deed.

## Special warranty deeds

A special warranty deed includes warranties of title, but, they apply only for acts occurring during the grantor's ownership. This deed is used if the seller is unwilling to make warranties for events occurring while the property was not under personal control. Defects in the title occurring before the seller's ownership must be remedied by previous owners who have executed a warranty deed.

## Quit claim deeds

Only the grantor's interest in the real estate described is transferred by a quit claim deed. The grantor makes no promises or warranties of title. He may even have no interest in the real estate described as indicated by the conveyance language common to a quit claim deed: "remise, release, and forever quit claim." The seller makes no promise that he has an interest in the property; the deed transfers only the interest he has, if any.

The main use of the quit claim deed is to release defects in title. A spouse who mistakenly failed to sign a conveyance document may be asked to execute a quit claim deed, as may a minor of age, on property owned during the minority. Corporations that transfer property without the proper authorized signature may release any claim that they may have with this document.

## Bargain and sale deeds

The key conveyance words provided by statute identifying this deed typically read "grant, bargain and sell." While the seller conveys the land and not an interest as in a quit claim deed, there is no warranty of title though there is an implied assumption that the seller has possession and title.

## Specialized deeds

Certain other deeds are commonly encountered that are adapted to a specific purpose. Among the more frequently encountered instruments are executor's deeds, the sheriff's deed, correction deeds, and trust deeds. It should be noted also that certain states use a different vocabulary in referring to commonly recognized deeds. Thus, a grant deed in California is similar to the special warranty deed. In Georgia, a security deed substitutes for a warranty deed and mortgage. In this instance, the security deed conveys title by warranty deed that secures a debt and at the same time transfers power of attorney to a lender who is authorized to sell property upon default of a debt. The security deed avoids a time-consuming and costly mortgage foreclosure.

Executor deeds are used by court appointed executors who operate under court supervision. Property, which must be sold, and which was formerly owned by a deceased person who left no will, will be conveyed by an executor's deed. Usually the full price must be stated with the executor warranting title only against his acts. No other warranties are included in the executor deed.

It will be appreciated that mistakes in deeds are awkward to correct. Documents are placed on public record and even if they are amended, properly initialled and signed, over time questions arise as to their authenticity. A preferred alternative calls for a *correction deed* that states that the deed corrects a deed of a certain date between a named grantor and grantee filed and identified in a designated public record. To be enforceable, the correction deed must meet the legal elements required of other deeds.

A *sheriff's deed* is encountered in foreclosure procedures. Lenders who foreclose on a mortgage must follow statutory requirements that may eventually lead to a public sale. Conveyance at a public sale will be under a sheriff's deed (or its equivalent) that conveys title but includes no warranty or representations of any kind. Buyers purchasing foreclosed property must assume the risks of possible title defects.

An instrument useful in mortgage finance authorized in states such as Arizona and California is the *trust deed*. Under this arrangement, a borrower conveys title to a third party, a trustee, who holds the title for the benefit of the lender who is identified as the beneficiary of the trust. The trust deed includes terms common to the long-term mortgage. If the borrower defaults on terms of the trust, i.e., failure to make mortgage payments, the lender (beneficiary) notifies the trustee who then takes steps comparable to a mortgage foreclosure for the benefit of the lender. In this manner the trust deed eliminates the more lengthy mortgage foreclosure procedure.

## Public Land Use Controls

After passing on the legal aspect of ownership interests and their conveyance, lenders and the property owner face the impact of growing restrictions on land use. The restrictions include the customary local land use controls following from the exercise of the police power in addition to environmental controls exercised at all levels of government. In fact, some communities have reached the point of incorporating no growth or limited growth policies. Growth policies are a means of controlling population density.

Clearly, it is no longer possible merely to secure a building permit and a first mortgage and proceed with construction. The mortgage lender and developer face legal requirements. For the present purpose it is deemed helpful to cover the general plan, the zoning ordinance, building and other codes and, in addition, the new environmental, ecological controls. According to one view, these controls are subordinate to the general plan.

## The General Plan

The general plan represents a statement of local community goals covering the physical development of the community in the light of social, economic, and political objectives. Administered on a municipal, county, or regional basis, the general plan provides guidelines to allocate public and private land for recreational, public, commercial, and residential and industrial uses. In some states the general plan (comprehensive or master plan) is required for every community; it is a means of coordinating public and private agencies and it provides for a continual review of land use and related planning issues.

Ideally, the plan would be adapted to local needs: the promotion of tourism in southern California and Florida; the hardware industry in New Britain, Connecticut; or manufacturing in Detroit, Michigan. To this end, the master plan incorporates a detailed study of physical characteristics of a community, the economic base—those activities in which people earn their living—and a social survey, i.e., population characteristics such as education, age level, household size, per capita income and the like. In a sense, the master plan is an inventory of community facilities available for promotion of community goals. With these data in hand, local land use controls tend to implement the master plan.

## Zoning Ordinances

Historically, zoning ordinances, which are justified under the right of government to regulate land use in the public interest, convenience, health and safety, have dealt with three issues: land use districts, building bulk and height, and minimum property standards. The first function relates to the division of the community into land use districts. Consequently, property zoned for single family use may not be used for an apartment, a store or industrial building. Typically, this is the only land use district that is restricted to a single use. Commercial districts, confined to various types of retail uses, usually allow commercial land uses "and all other uses in the preceding district." Certain industrial districts have the same feature. The consequence of multiple uses, allowing for mixed property uses, limits the desirability of space for a particular use.

For example, an owner of property zoned for a retail store usually has the option of using the property for residential purposes, with the result that the district becomes a mixed residential and commercial district. Organized industrial districts, shopping centers, and controlled subdivisions are a means of providing for exclusive land use—reserving land use for harmonious, mutually attractive uses.

The second issue falling under the local zoning ordinance, bulk and height regulations, control population density. Such controls take the form of limiting the height of buildings, e.g., 140 feet in Washington, D.C., or 45 feet in Palm Springs, California. Or, the ordinance may restrict the maximum floor area permitted for a given land area. For instance, an apartment house zoning may restrict development to one apartment unit per 2,000 square feet of land area. Still another means of providing for open space relates to building set-back requirements— a minimum building front yard set-back from the street line, side yards, and rear yards.

These regulations restrict development and, therefore, the potential value of property. In general higher land use density leads to higher property value. Though land use controls of this type are socially desirable, it will be realized that density controls place limits on building construction and tend to limit potential property income.

The zoning codes provide minimum standards in that a residential area may be restricted, for example, to buildings of not less than 1,000 square feet of floor area or to residential lots of at least 6,000 square feet. Public land use controls of this type have been criticized on grounds they exclude low and middle income groups. An ordinance that requires a minimum lot area of 6,000 square feet for every single family dwelling effectively eliminates families that cannot afford the minimum land area. For this reason, developers often turn to large scale developments with deed and subdivision restrictions that give more flexibility in planning. Planned unit developments covering several thousand acres—Irvine project in California or Columbia, Maryland—are examples in which land use controls provide for community needs under an integrated plan of development: residential, commercial, and industrial land use that must conform to architectural and land use requirements compatible with the community standard.

## Building Codes

Building codes, representing another exercise of the police power, provide for safe buildings by establishing minimum standards of construction and materials. According to the International Conference of Building Officials, building codes "provide minimum standards to safeguard life or limb, health, property and public welfare by regulating and controlling the design, construction, quality of materials, use and occupancy . . . of all buildings and structures . . . ." Enforcement is provided by the permit system. Construction is legally permissible only after a permit has been issued by the local jurisdiction.

*Housing codes*

Minimum housing standards established under a housing code may restrict the number of persons legally permitted in a dwelling, provide for minimum maintenance, sanitation facilities, ventilation and lighting standards. Hence, building plans and specifications must conform to local codes and ordinances directed to protecting the public health and safety.

# Environmental Controls

With over 70 percent of the population concentrated in metropolitan areas and with 2,000 acres converted daily from rural to urban use, social and economic objectives have been directed to sound land use practices that minimize pollution. At the present time, it is estimated that over one-third of all counties with populations of over 400,000 have citizen and environmental commissions to evaluate the effect of land use development on the environment. Congress has enacted several new laws that affect land use practices. The main environmental controls include:

> *The National Environmental Policy Act of 1969*
> *The Clean Air Act Amendments of 1970*
> *The Federal Water Pollution Control Act Amendments of 1972*
> *The Coastal Zone Management Act of 1972*
> *The Flood Disaster Protection Act of 1973*

These relatively new environmental controls have changed the emphasis on land use controls from a pre-regulation type characteristic of zoning, housing, and building codes, to a *case by case* review of land use projects. The review method allows numerous regulating agencies to monitor community and environmental impacts. Project developers subject to these environmental controls must prepare environmental impact statements that include an evaluation of the total effect of land development.

The change in emphasis is largely a consequence of the National Environmental Policy Act of 1969 (NEPA).

## The National Environmental Policy

NEPA established a policy "which will encourage productive and enjoyable harmony between man and his environment; to promote efforts which will prevent or eliminate damage to the environment and biosphere and stimulate the health and welfare of man. . . ."

NEPA relates only to federally funded projects—it requires federal agencies to make a full disclosure of all federal agency actions that have a significant impact on the environment. It has been reported that 23 states have enacted similar legislation. In a few states, such as California, the environmental impact review requirements apply to privately sponsored projects.

The most important feature of NEPA is that it requires an environmental impact statement for every federal action. Those actions with a significant projected impact on the human environment require the preparation and approval of an environmental impact statement (EIS) before the action can be taken. Section 102(2)(c) addresses five concerns:

1. The probable environmental impact of the proposed action.
2. Any adverse environmental effects which cannot be avoided upon implementation of the proposal.
3. Alternatives to the proposed action.
4. The relationship between local short-term uses of man's environment and the maintenance and enhancement of long-term activity.
5. Any irreversible and irretrievable commitments of resources which would be involved in the proposed action, should it be implemented.

At the state level developers have criticized the delays and the costs of complying with the state EIS requirements. In California, an environmental impact study relating to a 500 unit, single family subdivision, costs an estimated $25,000. One rather large scale developer in Newport Beach, California, has prepared a 13 page checklist to guide procedures in processing environmental impact studies.

## Air Quality

Under the Clean Air Act Amendments of 1970 each state is given primary responsibility for achieving and maintaining air quality within its borders. Federal grants up to two-thirds of the cost of planning, developing, establishing, and improving air quality programs are available to the states. The Clean Air Act also requires publication of a list of air pollutants which are considered to affect the public health. The Environmental Protection Agency (EPA) continually monitors air quality at some 247 air quality control regions, and air pollutants must conform to standards issued by EPA.

## Water Quality

The Federal Water Pollution Control Act Amendments of 1972 control the chemical, physical, and biological quality of water. At the present time it is a national goal to eliminate the discharge of pollutants into navigable waters by 1985; to provide for the protection and propagation of wild life and for water recreation by July 1, 1983; and to prohibit the discharge of toxic pollutants in toxic amounts. Federal assistance is available to local governments to improve water quality.

## The Management of Coastal Zones

By the Coastal Zone Management Act of 1972, Congress defined a coastal zone measured from the shore line to a point necessary to control shore lands that have a significant impact on coastal waters. California has enacted a similar act controlling real estate developments affecting coastal waters.

Both the federal and California acts require the preparation of management programs governing land use in coastal areas. The management program must preserve or restore designated areas for purposes of conservation, recreation, ecological, and aesthetic values. Consequently, land use developments in the coastal zones require a permit which is issued only after a planning review. Thus, the coastal zone restrictions increase costs of development, lengthen development time and eliminate projects that do not conform to environmental standards.

## Flood Disaster Protection Act of 1973

The Flood Disaster Protection Act of 1973 requires that state or local land use controls be adopted in those areas identified by the U.S. Department of Housing and Urban Development (HUD) as flood prone or mudslide areas. The controls adopted must meet the minimum federal requirements for a community to participate in the flood insurance program that is administered by the Federal Insurance Administration (FIA).

If after one year of being identified as a flood prone area, a community fails to participate in the insurance program, then no federal grants or federally insured or guaranteed financial assistance will be available within the flood prone area. This restriction applies to new financing and refinancing by banks and savings and loan institutions.

The mortgage lender must look to compliance with these environmental controls in addition to evaluating financial feasibility.

# Chapter 3

# Sources of Mortgage Credit

The supply of long-term mortgage credit largely depends on the flow of savings into financial institutions. The institutions accounting for the bulk of mortgage investments include commercial banks, savings and loan associations, mutual savings banks, and life insurance companies. Less important sources include pension funds, real estate investment trusts, individuals, and certain government direct loan programs. While each institution supplies mortgage credit, it will be realized that each pursues its own special function in promoting the interest of shareholders or depositors. Moreover, the extent of their regulatory restraint varies: Some operate under state charters, others under federal charters, and still others have relatively few lending restrictions.

The impact of government policies and the welfare of the economy alter the flow of savings into these institutions quite differently. In addition, mortgage investment policies vary widely during periods of prosperity and recession. An understanding of the objectives of these main financial institutions sets the stage for assessing the role of commercial banks and federal intervention in mortgage markets.

# Savings and Loan Associations

In contrast to other financial institutions, savings and loan associations were formed specifically to encourage home ownership. For the most part their regulations and policies are still directed to this singular goal. More recently they have actively promoted thrift in their local communities, primarily to secure funds for new home mortgages. The central idea of the savings and loan association is to pool individual savings in the community for the purpose of financing local home ownership. For the most part, regulations require that they confine direct lending on dwellings within 100 miles of the home or branch office. Savings and loan businesses may not be judged by the same tenets applying to commercial banks; basically, savings and loan associations operate as specialized, essentially mutual, financing institutions to finance home ownership.

It should be noted that savings and loan associations are treated differently under the federal corporate net income tax relative to commercial banks. Though, like commercial banks, savings and loan associations are subject to the federal corporate income tax law (since 1951), they are allowed taxable deductions not permitted by other financial institutions. Before calculation of net income, associations may deduct additions to bad debt reserves to a maximum of 12 percent of their savings balances. Tax legislation of 1969 restricted deductible additions to a loan loss reserve of not more than 40 percent of net income. This lower allowance, decreased from 60 percent, is being phased in over a ten year period which began in 1970.

In this respect savings and loan associations have experienced problems unique to their industry. The more important problems center around three issues:

1. They must attract a sufficient net inflow of savings to meet local home financing needs.
2. To meet their objectives, the cost of home financing (i.e., interest rates) must be kept as low as possible.
3. They must work to provide the greatest mobility of loanable funds for housing purchases.

Because demand for housing tends to be concentrated in growth areas, and because savings are concentrated in metropolitan areas, loanable funds must be sufficiently mobile to allow the transfer of excess capital in one area to other areas of housing shortages and lack of loanable funds. A review of their historical development shows how these problems have been met.

## The Early Development of Savings and Loan Associations

The present orientation of associations may be traced to British building societies that were copied in colonial times. The first known building association, organized in 1831 in Frankford, Pennsylvania, served as the pattern for savings and loan associations of today. Initially, members subscribed to shares on which they paid on a monthly basis. When the association accumulated $500 from share payments, members submitted bids for these funds to purchase or build a home. Every shareholder was entitled to a loan as funds permitted. Loans were based on careful appraisals with a shareholder required to purchase insurance on property financed by the borrowers.

Subsequent organizations formed in Brooklyn, New York (1836), and South Carolina (1843), started a trend so that by 1880 associations had been established in every state. At this time associations were voluntary, unincorporated, and operated with virtually no public supervision. As the last member repaid his loan, the organization typically went out of business, since it had served its purpose.

New York initiated the regulation of these associations in 1875 by requiring annual reports of condition. Starting in 1892, they were inspected by the Superintendent of Banks. All but two of the states provided for the regulation of savings and loan associations by 1931. Associations reached their numerical peak of 12,804 in 1927; since that time the number has declined to a current total of 5,102.

## Developments Since 1932

Like commercial banks, savings and loan associations lost ground in the Great Depression of the 1930s. They were faced with an unusual high rate of withdrawals and delinquent mortgages. Mortgage foreclosures increased from an average of 75,000 a year before the Depression to 273,000 in 1932. The Depression experiences introduced new legislation that has guided the growth and development of S&Ls to the present time.

The present Federal Home Loan Bank System (FHLBS) was established in 1932, primarily to establish a credit reserve for member associations comparable to the functions of the Federal Reserve System which served similar needs of commercial banks. It is governed by a three member board appointed for four-year terms by the President with Senate consent. The board serves as the regulatory authority over federally chartered savings and loan associations. It operates through 12 regional banks. The regional banks raise capital through the compulsory purchase of stock by member savings and loan associations equal to one percent of the unpaid principal of home loans held in their portfolio, or $2,500, whichever is greater. Each home loan bank is separately incorporated, and managed by its own board of directors.

In operation, member associations may borrow from their home loan bank to meet requirements of withdrawals or advances to make mortgage loans. Advances to member banks are limited to a portion of their savings balances.

All federally chartered savings and loan associations are required to be members of the Federal Home Loan Bank System. Mutual savings banks and state chartered associations and insurance companies may join, provided they conform to FHLBS rules and regulations. While the prime purpose of the FHLBS is to provide a central credit facility to member institutions, it serves as a secondary source of money in meeting unusual withdrawal demands. It also attracts capital to institutions by issuing loans in large denominations which are sold to financial institutions—including commercial banks. In this way, money is channeled from financial markets to the savings and loan industry. An additional purpose is to stabilize residential construction and financing under unfavorable monetary or financial conditions. For instance, in 1969, the system issued a large volume of obligations to support a record number of advances to member associations. By this method the board permitted members to continue making mortgages in a period of tight money and limited savings growth.

## Mortgage Loan Activity

By the end of 1975 federally chartered savings and loan associations numbered 2,060 which held 56.7 percent of the total assets of all savings and loan associations. State chartered institutions, numbering 3,042, accounted for some 43.3 percent of total assets. True to their origins, associations concentrate on residential property. A comparison of their mortgage loans with other institutions is shown in Table 3.1. Note that of the total volume of mortgage loans outstanding at the end of 1975, $250.7 billion, approximately 90 percent was invested in residential mortgages. S&Ls are a relatively minor source of mortgages on commercial and farm properties.

It may be expected that because of this concentration, savings and loan associations are the largest single supplier of mortgages on single family dwellings. A comparison of savings and loan participation, in terms of number of residential mortgages, is shown in Table 3.2. Considering mortgages on one-to-four family dwellings only, the data show that the savings and loan associations are the main source of financing for these properties. By the end of 1975, some $447.6 billion of mort-

**Table 3.1**
**Mortgage Loans Outstanding by Type of Lender and Type of Property,**
**December 1975**
(Billions of Dollars)

| | *Residential Properties* | | | | | |
|---|---|---|---|---|---|---|
| *Lender* | *One-to-Four Family* | *Multi-Family* | *Total* | *Commercial Properties* | *Farm Properties* | *Total Mortgage Loans* |
| Savings and Loan Associations .. | $225.3 | $25.4 | $250.7 | $ 28.0 | | $278.7 |
| Commercial Banks ............ | 76.6 | 6.6 | 83.2 | 45.5 | $ 6.4 | 135.1 |
| Mutual Savings Banks ......... | 46.0 | 17.7 | 63.7 | 13.3 | 0.1 | 77.1 |
| Life Insurance Companies ...... | 17.7 | 19.9 | 37.6 | 45.0 | 6.8 | 89.4 |
| Individuals and Others ......... | 23.5 | 11.5 | 35.0 | 19.1 | 18.1 | 72.2 |
| TOTAL.. ................ | $389.1 | $81.1 | $470.2 | $150.9 | $31.4 | $652.5 |

Source: *Federal Reserve Bulletin,* March, 1976, p. A42.

gages were outstanding on one to four-family, non-farm homes. Savings and loan associations accounted for 50.3 percent of mortgages falling in this category, totalling some $225.3 billion. The next closest institutions were commercial banks that held $76.6 billion of outstanding mortgages on one to four-family dwellings at the end of 1975.

**Table 3.2**
**Volume of Mortgages Outstanding on 1-to-4 Family**
**Dwellings by Type of Lender**
**December 1975**
(000 Omitted)

| *Lender* | *Amount of Mortgages* | *Percentage Distribution* |
|---|---|---|
| Savings and Loan Associations .............. | 225,332 | 50.3% |
| Commercial Banks ......................... | 76,616 | 17.1 |
| Mutual Savings Banks ...................... | 45,698 | 10.3 |
| Life Insurance Companies .................. | 17,692 | 4.0 |
| Federal Agencies .......................... | 58,436 | 13.1 |
| All Others ................................ | 23,539 | 5.3 |
| TOTAL ................................. | 447,583 | 100.1% |

Source: *Federal Reserve Bulletin,* March, 1976, p. A42.
Note: Totals do not add to 100% due to rounding.

45

## Effects of Disintermediation

Savings and loan associations are unusually vulnerable to changes in monetary policy. The outflow of savings from savings and loan associations and commercial banks to higher earning stocks and bonds has been termed *disintermediation.* This refers to the shift that savers make in withdrawing savings deposits for direct investment in stocks and bonds and other higher paying assets.

In the years prior to 1960, savings associations planned on about half the increase in savings of families and individuals. After 1960, the share of savings going to savings and loan associations began to decrease. The decrease was more marked in 1966 as the Federal Reserve instituted a tight monetary policy. As open market interest rates increased, savers shifted savings from associations to open market investments, causing a drop in deposit growth. For example, the recovery started in 1970 was halted by a sharp increase in short-term interest rates in mid-1973. The net savings flow among associations dropped from $32.7 million in 1972 to $20.5 million at the end of 1973.

Part of the explanation for declining deposits lies in the change in the competitive yields on savings and loan deposits compared to yields paid by commercial banks. For instance, the average yield on a savings deposit in 1958 was 3.38 percent, some 1.17 percentage points above comparable rates paid by commercial banks. This competitive position was reversed as banks increased rates on time savings deposits. Another step in this direction was taken by the Federal Reserve Board in July, 1973, in approving a four-year maturity, minimum balance of $1,000 with no interest rate ceiling. The ceiling on these deposit certificates was later placed at 7.5 percent by the Federal Reserve Board. The commercial banks' share of personal savings increased from *43.4 percent* in *1972* to *59.2 percent* by 1973. The continued participation of savings and loan associations in mortgage financing depends on the extent to which they attract deposits which may be invested in long-term mortgages.

At this point it is appropriate to show the effect of Regulation Q—a regulation first published by the Federal Reserve System in 1933 which established the maximum interest rate paid by commercial banks on time and savings deposits. At the time it was believed that excessive interest rate competition for deposits undermined the soundness of the banking system. With the passage of the Interest Rate Adjustment Act of 1966, the return paid on savings by the associations was controlled by the Federal Home Loan Bank Board. This legislation had the effect of decreasing interest rate competition between savings and loan associations and commercial banks. At this writing, federally insured savings and loan associations may pay an interest rate of 0.25 percent higher on passbook savings than the rate paid by commercial banks.

With the lowering of allowable rates paid depositors the tendency is for savings deposits to decrease. If deposit rates under Regulation Q are increased, time deposits appear more attractive than competing, highly liquid, short-term financial instruments such as Treasury bills. Or to put it differently, when market rates of interest rise above the Regulation Q ceiling, depositors are encouraged to shift funds away from commercial banks and savings and loan associations. Accordingly, many observers believe that Regulation Q increases instability in the mortgage market.

## ② Mutual Savings Banks

Mutual savings banks are primarily thrift institutions. Concentrated in the Northeastern portion of the United States, they operate exclusively under state charters. Since they have few geographic lending restrictions, they are an important supplier of mortgage credit nationally and are heavy purchasers of federally insured and VA guaranteed home mortgages. Also, like the savings and loan associations, they are highly vulnerable to monetary policies that increase interest rates. A brief review of mutual savings bank operations shows how they serve specialized functions not found in other financial institutions.

### Early Development

Mutual savings banks began with a philanthropic group of 25 individuals who each contributed ten dollars to a fund and then personally volunteered to perform the necessary clerical bank services. This initial undertaking in 1816, called the *Philadelphia Savings Fund Society,* grew to an institution with a $200,000 deposit total by 1821. In the 40 years between 1820 and the Civil War, savings banks were well established in the Northeastern states. During this period they continued to operate as thrift institutions, investing deposits in public securities and real estate mortgages. After the Civil War, savings banks continued to expand primarily in the Northeastern part of the United States reaching a peak of 666 banks by 1875. Approximately 80 percent of the present number of savings banks were organized by this time.

After the 1920s, savings banks dramatically increased their holdings in real estate mortgages. At this time railroad securities became less attractive and yields in mortgages increased with a history of relative safety. The standard rate on mortgage loans was six percent compared to a five percent yield on bonds. At the onset of the 1930 depression savings banks were caught by prevailing optimistic loans on high appraisals which were encouraged by rising costs and real estate prices. Subsequent losses on mortgage portfolios ranged from 10 percent to 16 percent in the 1930s causing banks to shift into government obligations at the expense of new mortgage lending.

## Current Development

At the end of World War II savings bank deposits grew from $15.3 billion in 1945 to $109.8 billion at the end of December 1975. With this growth of deposits, banks also held large quantities of government securities that were liquidated to make mortgage loans. In this favorable environment, savings banks invested approximately 75 percent of their total assets in mortgages. The expansion was concentrated in FHA and VA loans.

By 1964 some 40 percent of the mortgage loans were out of state. Approximately three-fourths were in non-savings bank states. As a result savings banks became important sources of government insured and guaranteed loans throughout the United States. At the end of the second quarter of 1975, mortgage loans constituted 64.9 percent of total assets. Their total mortgage holdings increased from $4 billion at the end of World War II to $77.1 billion at the end of December, 1975. This portfolio is concentrated in mutual savings banks located in the middle Atlantic and New England states. Approximately seven-eighths of their total number are located in five states: Massachusetts, New York, Connecticut, Maine and New Hampshire.

In terms of mortgage debt outstanding, mutual savings banks hold approximately 10.4 percent of total mortgages outstanding. See Table 3.3. While this proportion of mortgages held by savings banks has ranged from 10.4 percent to 13.7 percent since 1945, these figures do not show the importance of mutual savings banks in total holdings of FHA and VA loans.

For example, Table 3.4 indicates that among the financial institutions, mutual savings banks tend to invest more heavily in these types of loans. At the end of 1975, some 34.7 percent of their mortgage portfolio was placed in FHA and VA loans. This total far exceeds the proportion held by commercial banks, savings and loan associations, and life insurance companies. In addition, they share with savings and loan associations a concentration in residential property—some 82.6 percent of mortgages held by mutual savings banks are invested in residential property.

## Table 3.3
## Mortgage Debt Outstanding, by Type of Holder, Selected Year-End Dates, 1945–1975
(In millions of dollars)

| End of year | Total | Mutual savings banks | Commercial banks | Savings and loan associations | Life insurance companies | Federally sponsored credit agencies | Real estate investment trusts | Pension funds | All other holders |
|---|---|---|---|---|---|---|---|---|---|
| | | | | (In millions of dollars) | | | | | |
| 1945 | 35,536 | 4,208 | 4,772 | 5,376 | 6,636 | 1,035 | — | 18 | 13,491 |
| 1950 | 72,817 | 8,261 | 13,663 | 13,657 | 16,102 | 952 | — | 177 | 20,004 |
| 1955 | 129,988 | 17,457 | 21,004 | 31,461 | 29,445 | 1,583 | — | 639 | 28,399 |
| 1956 | 144,452 | 19,746 | 22,719 | 35,729 | 32,989 | 2,390 | — | 844 | 30,035 |
| 1957 | 156,519 | 21,169 | 23,337 | 40,007 | 35,236 | 3,553 | — | 1,123 | 32,094 |
| 1958 | 171,767 | 23,263 | 25,523 | 45,627 | 37,062 | 3,468 | — | 1,478 | 35,346 |
| 1959 | 190,818 | 24,992 | 28,145 | 53,141 | 39,197 | 4,410 | — | 1,981 | 38,952 |
| 1960 | 206,845 | 26,935 | 28,806 | 60,070 | 41,771 | 5,467 | — | 2,751 | 41,045 |
| 1961 | 226,317 | 29,145 | 30,442 | 68,834 | 44,203 | 5,700 | — | 3,456 | 44,537 |
| 1962 | 248,620 | 32,320 | 34,476 | 78,770 | 46,902 | 5,898 | — | 4,118 | 46,136 |
| 1963 | 274,268 | 36,224 | 39,414 | 90,944 | 50,544 | 5,371 | — | 4,832 | 46,939 |
| 1964 | 300,126 | 40,556 | 43,976 | 101,333 | 55,152 | 5,715 | — | 5,816 | 47,578 |
| 1965 | 325,752 | 44,617 | 49,675 | 110,306 | 60,013 | 6,801 | — | 7,070 | 47,270 |
| 1966 | 347,417 | 47,337 | 54,380 | 114,427 | 64,609 | 9,354 | — | 8,427 | 48,884 |
| 1967 | 370,245 | 50,490 | 59,019 | 121,805 | 67,516 | 11,131 | — | 9,086 | 51,198 |
| 1968 | 397,496 | 53,456 | 65,696 | 130,802 | 69,975 | 13,293 | 230 | 9,429 | 54,614 |
| 1969 | 425,333 | 56,138 | 70,705 | 140,232 | 72,027 | 17,764 | 1,107 | 10,200 | 57,160 |
| 1970 | 451,742 | 57,948 | 73,275 | 150,331 | 74,375 | 23,598 | 3,219 | 11,107 | 57,889 |
| 1971 | 499,767 | 61,978 | 82,515 | 174,250 | 75,496 | 29,926 | 5,763 | 10,768 | 59,071 |
| 1972 | 564,825 | 67,556 | 99,314 | 206,182 | 76,948 | 36,602 | 10,607 | 9,954 | 57,662 |
| 1973 | 634,954 | 73,230 | 119,068 | 231,733 | 81,369 | 47,000 | 15,100 | 9,400 | 58,054 |
| 1974 | 688,652 | 74,920 | 132,105 | 249,293 | 86,234 | 61,900 | 16,000 | 9,400 | 58,800 |
| 1975p | 741,547 | 77,249 | 136,186 | 278,693 | 89,358 | 74,600 | 13,400 | 9,800 | 62,261 |

p—preliminary.
Source: *1976 National Fact Book of Mutual Savings Banking* (New York: National Association of Mutual Savings Banks), p. 53.

49

**Table 3.4**
**Percentage Distribution of Mortgage Holdings of Main Types of Financial Institutions, by Type of Loan and Property, December 31, 1975**
(In percent)

| | Mutual savings banks | Com- mercial banks | Savings and loan associations | Life insurance companies |
|---|---|---|---|---|
| **By type of loan** | | | | |
| FHA | 18.7 | 7.6 | 11.0 | 21.2 |
| VA | 16.0 | 3.8 | | 10.4 |
| Conventional and other | 65.3 | 88.7 | 89.0 | 68.4 |
| TOTAL | 100.0 | 100.0 | 100.0 | 100.0 |
| **By type of property** | | | | |
| Residential | 82.6 | 60.9 | 89.8 | 41.8 |
| 1- to 4-family | 59.6 | 56.6 | 80.6 | 19.7 |
| Multifamily | 23.0 | 4.3 | 9.1 | 22.1 |
| Nonresidential | 17.3 | 34.4 | 10.2 | 50.7 |
| Farm | .1 | 4.7 | — | 7.6 |
| TOTAL | 100 0 | 100.0 | 100.0 | 100.0 |

Source: *1976 National Fact Book of Mutual Savings Banking* (New York: National Association of Mutual Savings Banks), p. 54.

The preference for federally underwritten mortgage loans lies in the VA guarantees and FHA insurance that give out of state mortgages liquidity. As a purchaser of mortgages in out of state locations, mutual savings banks are attracted by the safety and liquidity afforded to out of state loans which are not under their immediate control. However, since the mid 1960s conventional loans and residential properties have been favored. Private mortgage insurance, that gives conventional loans more liquidity, and the improved secondary market facilities for conventional loans allow these loans to be sold in the open market. The growing complications of the FHA programs have encouraged further conventional mortgage financing.

## Competition for Savings

As thrift institutions, mutual savings banks share with other institutions the risk of deposit withdrawals in response to changing monetary conditions. When it is realized that between 60 percent and 70 percent of total savings in the economy are generated by individual consumers, total deposits for mortgage lending vary with changes in total personal saving. As deposit interest rates become less attractive, the total flow of funds into savings accounts may be expected to decrease.

Consequently, the savings flow into mutual savings banks generally declines in periods of monetary restraint, and increases in periods of stable or declining short-term interest rates. This record was shown in the deposit gains of 1971 and 1972 when savings accounts yielded competitive interest rates. The decline in deposits occurred in 1959, 1966, 1969, and 1973, and was intensified by competition for savings and inflationary pressures.

These developments have been explained by regulations on deposit interest rates. As federal ceilings were applied to thrift institutions in 1966, deposits were withdrawn in favor of high yielding securities. In mid-1973, certificates of deposits carrying no ceiling in interest rates with maturities of four years or more were offered by commercial banks and savings institutions. Ceilings were placed on such deposits in November 1973 imposing a 7.5 percent and 7.25 percent ceiling on such accounts held in savings institutions and commercial banks.

## Life Insurance Companies    *no emphasis on residential loans*

As mortgage investors, life insurance companies enjoy certain competitive advantages not found in savings institutions. Probably, their most distinguishing feature is the predictability of funds available for investment. Because their investment income is derived from insurance premiums and because their expenditures can be predicted from mortality tables, life insurance companies seek investments that protect shareholders and stockholders. They are given considerable flexibility in placing mortgages since they are controlled only by state regulations that give life insurance companies considerable laxity in the type of mortgages selected and their geographical location.

**Table 3.5**
**Distribution of Assets of U. S. Life Insurance Companies**
(000,000 Omitted)

| Year | Government Securities | Corporate Securities Bonds | Stocks | Mortgages | Real Estate | Policy Loans | Misc. Assets | Total |
|------|------|------|------|------|------|------|------|------|
| 1965 ...... | 11,908 | 58,244 | 9,126 | 60,013 | 4,681 | 7,678 | 7,234 | 158,884 |
| 1966 ...... | 11,396 | 60,819 | 8,832 | 64,609 | 4,885 | 9,117 | 7,797 | 167,455 |
| 1967 ...... | 11,079 | 64,687 | 10,877 | 67,516 | 5,187 | 10,059 | 8,427 | 177,832 |
| 1968 ...... | 11,096 | 68,310 | 13,230 | 69,973 | 5,571 | 11,306 | 9,150 | 188,636 |
| 1969 ...... | 10,914 | 70,859 | 13,707 | 72,027 | 5,912 | 13,825 | 9,964 | 197,208 |
| 1970 ...... | 11,068 | 73,098 | 15,420 | 74,375 | 6,320 | 16,064 | 10,909 | 207,254 |
| 1971 ...... | 11,000 | 79,198 | 20,607 | 75,496 | 6,904 | 17,065 | 11,832 | 222,102 |
| 1972 ...... | 11,372 | 86,140 | 26,845 | 76,948 | 7,295 | 18,003 | 13,127 | 239,730 |
| 1973 ...... | 11,403 | 91,796 | 25,919 | 81,369 | 7,693 | 20,199 | 14,057 | 252,436 |
| 1974 ...... | 11,965 | 96,652 | 21,920 | 86,234 | 8,331 | 22,862 | 15,385 | 263,349 |
| 1975 ...... | 14,582 | 106,755 | 28,259 | 89,358 | 9,634 | 24,389 | 16,107 | 289,084 |

Source: Compiled from *Federal Reserve Bulletins.*

In Table 3.5, the participation of life insurance companies in mortgages is compared to their investment in other assets. While the proportion of assets in mortgages is 30.9 percent of their total investment portfolio, the volume of activity in selected mortgages is relatively high compared to other institutions. More recently, insurance companies have decreased their holdings in residential properties and concentrated more heavily in mortgages on commercial properties.

## Table 3.6
## Types of Mortgages Owned by U. S. Life Insurance Companies
(000,000 Omitted)

| Year | Farm | Nonfarm F.H.A.[1] | Nonfarm V.A. | Nonfarm Conventional | Total |
|---|---|---|---|---|---|
| 1947 ........... | $ 895 | $ 1,398 | $ 844 | $ 5,538 | $ 8,675 |
| 1950 ........... | 1,327 | 4,573 | 2,026 | 8,176 | 16,102 |
| 1955 ........... | 2,273 | 6,530 | 6,074 | 14,568 | 29,445 |
| 1960 ........... | 2,982 | 9,290 | 6,901 | 22,598 | 41,771 |
| 1961 ........... | 3,170 | 9,949 | 6,553 | 24,531 | 44,203 |
| 1962 ........... | 3,400 | 10,518 | 6,395 | 26,589 | 46,902 |
| 1963 ........... | 3,792 | 11,160 | 6,401 | 29,191 | 50,544 |
| 1964 ........... | 4,304 | 11,935 | 6,403 | 32,510 | 55,152 |
| 1965 ........... | 4,823 | 12,538 | 6,286 | 36,366 | 60.013 |
| 1966 ........... | 5,240 | 12,852 | 6,201 | 40,316 | 64,609 |
| 1967 ........... | 5,569 | 12,672 | 6,122 | 43,153 | 67,516 |
| 1968 ........... | 5,801 | 12,469 | 5,954 | 45,749 | 69,973 |
| 1969 ........... | 5,773 | 12,271 | 5,701 | 48,282 | 72,027 |
| 1970 ........... | 5,649 | 12,001 | 5,394 | 51,331 | 74,375 |
| 1971 ........... | 5,601 | 11,336 | 5,004 | 53,555 | 75,496 |
| 1972 ........... | 5,678 | 10,512 | 4,660 | 56,098 | 76,948 |
| 1973 ........... | 5,996 | 9,740 | 4,402 | 61,231 | 81,369 |
| 1974 ........... | 6,321 | 8,600 | 4,200 | 67,137 | 86,258 |
| 1975 ........... | 6,576 | 8,200 | 4,000 | 69,259 | 88,035 |

[1] Includes mortgages insured under the Canadian Housing Act; in 1973 these amounted to $532 million.
Source: Compiled from *Federal Reserve Bulletins.*

Table 3.6 indicates that the volume of mortgages in FHA and VA mortgages has decreased annually since 1967. The growth of nonfarm conventional mortgages from $5.5 billion in 1947 to $69.2 billion in the fourth quarter of 1975 reflects the growing preference for commercial investments, i.e., large scale apartments, shopping centers, and the like. Apparently the cost of underwriting and servicing a small residential property per unit is greater than the same costs associated with multiple family, hotel and other types of commercial and industrial loans.

Insurance companies that do not maintain a branch mortgage office work through loan correspondents who are given advance commitments on the amount of mortgages that may be placed with the insurance company at a given maturity and interest rate. Correspondents originate the loan, and document the loan proposed for presentation and approval by the investing insurance company. Such correspondents may represent numerous insurance companies and other lenders so that at any given time a potential borrower may place a loan according to the specific needs of an individual lender at a given time.

Insurance companies tend to be highly competitive with other mortgage lenders partly because of the lack of federal supervision over investment policy. For instance, state regulations usually restrict the amount of the mortgage to some stated percent of the appraised value, typically $66\frac{2}{3}$ percent to 75 percent. Most states do not establish appraisal standards that are uniformly applied and enforced. Consequently the insurance companies tend to favor borrowers with unusually strong credit ratings. In other words, a borrower with an excellent credit rating, with a record of good performance on similar projects, and with a project in which the expected net income will more than cover mortgage payments is a good prospect for securing a relatively high loan to value ratio—though on paper the loan will be based on the legally approved 75 percent of the appraised value.

As price inflation has progressed, insurance companies observed developers earning substantial capital gains and high returns on their capital investments. To guard against the erosion of the rate of return because of progressive inflation, most companies now require a minimum rate of return on their mortgages, consistent with market rates, in addition to a percent of the *owner's return on equity—a 25 percent share* is not uncommon. Or in other instances, insurance companies have negotiated for a share of the equity, with funds supplied by the insurance company and with management and development expertise supplied by the project sponsor.

*equity kicker*

*nat'l & state banks cannot take SBIC & MESBIC can !*

*normally taken in form of stock hedge against inflation*

## ④ Commercial Banks

Commercial banks are actively competing for a greater volume of mortgage business. Not only have monetary conditions changed to encourage greater mortgage participation, but the institutional framework in which commercial banks operate favors increasing long-term mortgage credit. Their increasing share of time deposits permits commercial banks to seek a greater share of mortgage business. In addition, commercial banks fill a gap in communities that have virtually little access to savings and loan associations, mutual savings banks, or the advantage of long-term mortgage funds from insurance companies and other institutional investors. A long series of events have led to lending policies calling for greater activity in mortgage markets.

## Early Mortgage Activity

It must be remembered that commercial banks, operating before the Federal Reserve Act of 1913, operated in an environment of recurring financial panics. Before the Federal Reserve System, commercial banks depended largely on demand deposits as a source of loanable funds. Because demand deposits fluctuated widely over the business cycle and seasonally, banks tended to invest in short-term loans.

In these circumstances mortgages appealed to commercial banks in that mortgages were usually granted on a term basis—three to five years—with no amortization and with annual interest payments. Since the mortgages were callable, they were considerably more liquid than the conventional long-term amortized mortgage of today.

Yet speculative excesses in real estate construction and the recurrence of mortgage defaults and the following deflation of real estate values prejudiced banks towards residential mortgages. This sentiment was expressed in the National Bank Act of 1863 which gave no authority for national banks to engage in mortgage lending. Even though some state chartered banks were permitted to make such loans, bank policy usually limited participation in the mortgage market.

By the end of the nineteenth century, stability in real estate and prices gradually led state chartered banks to participate in long-term lending. The growing inequality between national and state chartered banks was corrected by the Federal Reserve Act of 1913 which allowed national banks to make mortgage loans on improved farmland. In 1916 the authority was broadened to cover one-year loans on urban properties. Successive relaxation of restrictions on mortgage lending continued until 1927 when national banks could make residential mortgage loans up to five years with a maximum 50 percent loan-to-value ratio. From 1927 to 1929 national banks increased non-farm real estate loans by some 45 percent.

As commercial banks weathered the 1930 depression, they suffered widespread default in home mortgage loans. This experience led to fundamental changes in mortgage finance which were brought about by the *National Housing Act of 1934. First,* under this act, eligible home mortgages could be exchanged for government guaranteed bonds in the event of default. *Second,* the act required that insured mortgages (FHA) be fully amortized. Mortgage lenders, including banks, could then look towards repayment of loans as a source of capital in

## Table 3.7
## Savings Classified by Source, Selected Years, 1920–1975
(in millions of dollars)

| End of year | In millions of dollars | | | | | Percentage distribution | | | | |
|---|---|---|---|---|---|---|---|---|---|---|
| | Total | Mutual savings banks | Commercial banks | Savings and loan associations | Credit unions | Total | Mutual savings banks | Commercial banks | Savings and loan associations | Credit unions |
| 1920 | 17,100 | 4,806 | 10,546 | 1,741 | 7 | 100.0 | 28.1 | 61.7 | 10.2 | * |
| 1930 | 34,364 | 9,384 | 18,647 | 6,296 | 37 | 100.0 | 27.3 | 54.3 | 18.3 | .1 |
| 1935 | 27,029 | 9,829 | 12,899 | 4,254 | 47 | 100.0 | 36.4 | 47.7 | 15.7 | .2 |
| 1940 | 30,578 | 10,618 | 15,403 | 4,322 | 235 | 100.0 | 34.7 | 50.4 | 14.1 | .8 |
| 1945 | 53,026 | 15,332 | 29,929 | 7,365 | 400 | 100.0 | 28.9 | 56.4 | 13.9 | .8 |
| 1950 | 70,086 | 20,002 | 35,200 | 13,992 | 892 | 100.0 | 28.5 | 50.2 | 20.0 | 1.3 |
| 1955 | 109,032 | 28,113 | 46,331 | 32,142 | 2,446 | 100.0 | 25.8 | 42.5 | 29.5 | 2.2 |
| 1960 | 170,546 | 36,343 | 67,079 | 62,142 | 4,982 | 100.0 | 21.3 | 39.3 | 36.4 | 2.9 |
| 1965 | 302,770 | 52,443 | 130,754 | 110,349 | 9,224 | 100.0 | 17.3 | 43.2 | 36.5 | 3.1 |
| 1966 | 321,930 | 55,006 | 142,904 | 113,949 | 10,071 | 100.0 | 17.1 | 44.4 | 35.4 | 3.1 |
| 1967 | 359,205 | 60,121 | 163,433 | 124,548 | 11,103 | 100.0 | 16.7 | 45.5 | 34.7 | 3.1 |
| 1968 | 389,775 | 64,507 | 181,322 | 131,661 | 12,285 | 100.0 | 16.6 | 45.5 | 33.8 | 3.2 |
| 1969 | 393,444 | 67,086 | 177,029 | 135,589 | 13,740 | 100.0 | 17.1 | 45.0 | 34.5 | 3.5 |
| 1970 | 439,218 | 71,580 | 205,794 | 146,322 | 15,522 | 100.0 | 16.3 | 46.9 | 33.3 | 3.5 |
| 1971 | 513,232 | 81,440 | 239,246 | 174,188 | 18,358 | 100.0 | 15.9 | 46.6 | 33.9 | 3.6 |
| 1972 | 593,426 | 91,613 | 273,504 | 206,731 | 21,578 | 100.0 | 15.4 | 46.1 | 34.8 | 3.6 |
| 1973 | 661,963 | 96,496 | 314,376 | 226,518 | 24,573 | 100.0 | 14.6 | 47.5 | 34.2 | 3.7 |
| 1974 | 729,887 | 98,701 | 360,709 | 242,959 | 27,518 | 100.0 | 13.5 | 49.4 | 33.3 | 3.8 |
| 1975p | 822,849 | 109,873 | 393,885 | 286,043 | 33,048 | 100.0 | 13.4 | 47.9 | 34.8 | 4.0 |

*Less than .05 per cent.
p — preliminary.

Source: *1976 National Fact Book of Mutual Savings Banking* (New York, New York: National Association of Mutual Savings Banks), p. 46.

55

addition to deposits. *Third,* bank participation in FHA insured mortgages was encouraged by the provision that restrictions as to maturity and maximum loan-to-value ratios would not apply for FHA loans.

Without FHA or VA guaranteed mortgage loans, amortized conventional loans could have maximum loan-to-value ratios of 75 percent of the appraised value and a maximum maturity of 20 years. Such conventional loans could not exceed capital and surplus or 60 percent of savings and time deposits, whichever was greater. In 1964 amendments to the Federal Reserve Act permitted banks to make home loans up to 80 percent of the appraised value, amortized over a maximum of 25 years. Later rules allowed national banks to make real estate loans up to 70 percent of time and savings deposits or 100 percent of capital and surplus, whichever is greater. The relaxation of these rules with 1974 legislation is covered in Chapter 4.

## Commercial Banks Since World War II

A prime factor in projecting mortgage activity of commercial banks relates to the flow of savings to commercial banks. Immediately after World War II, banks worked off their excess liquidity held in the form of government bonds to the point that they were short of loanable assets. Their demand deposits had not grown in proportion to the economy. To increase their volume of savings, banks began to aggressively market certificates of deposit and passbook savings (time deposits).

For example, Table 3.7 shows that the flow of savings from 1974 to 1975 held by commercial banks increased some 9.2 percent ($360.7 billion to $393.9 billion). Total savings in the selected media shown in Table 3.7 increased by 12.7 percent in the same year. In absolute amounts, commercial banks increased their net gain in savings by $33.2 billion in 1975 compared to $11.2 billion for mutual savings banks and $43.1 billion for savings and loan associations.

As shown in Table 3.2, commercial banks hold approximately 17.1 percent of mortgages on 1-4 family dwellings. Commercial banks increased their holding of mortgage loans outstanding to $76.6 billion by the end of 1975 compared to $74,758 million in 1974. Trends that favor mortgage expansion in commercial banks include the following developments:

    ✓ 1. A continuing growth in time deposits that allow for greater volume of long-term mortgages.

    ✓ 2. The creation of a secondary market for conventional loans through FNMA and other outlets.

    ✓ 3. Legislation that has liberalized mortgage restrictions formerly imposed against nationally chartered commercial banks.

These changes will be detailed in the succeeding chapter.

In contrast to other institutional mortgage lenders, commercial banks tend to specialize in certain types of loans. First, they make direct loans to the borrower. These policies range from the small town bank that constitutes virtually the only source of mortgage money in the area to the larger communities where mortgage loans are made to long-standing customers who participate in other short-term credit business. The record shows also that commercial banks sponsor real estate investment trusts that provide long-term credit for customers without usual bank mortgage restrictions. Banks also invest money from trust accounts in mortgages, if mortgages conform to the trust agreement. Such funds are held for long periods of time and are attracted to long-term loans.

Construction loans, which are granted for terms six months to eighteen months and sometimes up to 60 months, are provided to builders who construct buildings that are later eligible for long-term financing from other lenders. Commercial banks, which rank first in construction lending among all financial institutions, assume the higher risks and earner higher rates of interest for administering short-term construction loans, which are later converted to long-term, amortized mortgages. The details of construction loans are reserved for separate chapter treatment. Because banks operate in a local community with available resources in money and personnel, they can advantageously operate in this market.

Though not directly replacing mortgages, commercial banks participate in operations of mortgage bankers who originate and place the mortgage with a long-term lender. To provide working capital for the "warehousing of mortgage loans," mortgage bankers turn to commercial banks for a line of credit. Typically the mortgage banker will pledge a block of mortgages and securities for cash to arrange a loan. As mortgages are closed, they are sold to private investors supplying cash to pay the commercial bank for their warehousing operation. This is a form of intermediate credit granted to a mortgage banker that packages mortgages for institutional investors.

## ✳ ⑤ Mortgage Bankers

Financial institutions organized to originate and service mortgage loans for long-term investors are termed mortgage bankers. Typically they are incorporated and are subject to a minimum of federal or state supervision. They range from a one man office to large corporations that have offices in many cities. They are closely tied to the commercial bank industry in that they rely on short-term bank credit to finance their operations. Some states require mortgage bankers to be licensed, but in most respects, they are subject only to audit by companies with which they do business.

Unlike other institutions, the mortgage banker operates on an advance commitment from a financial intermediary such as an insurance company, pension fund, or other supplier of credit. With this advance commitment to buy mortgages at a stated interest rate, maturity, type of property and location, they are able to secure short-term credit from commercial banks. With the knowledge that they may market loans of a given type, the mortgage banker solicits real estate brokers and builders who are in the market for credit. A mortgage banker will appraise property, and assemble other documents for approval by a potential purchaser. In that the mortgage banker works with an inventory of loans under process, he must look to commercial banks for working funds. For example, a mortgage banker may have a commitment by a lender to buy a block of mortgages, 9.5 percent interest, 25 year maturity on multiple family projects up to five million dollars in a selected metropolitan area. While the loans are being processed and assembled, the mortgage banker must use his own cash in anticipation of selling the mortgages to the lender. In the meantime he is dependent on commercial banks for short-term borrowing which will be repaid when the mortgages are assembled, approved, and sold to an investor.

In return for his service, the mortgage banker collects an origination fee charged to the borrower and a servicing fee paid by the lender for loan collection or other administrative services associated with managing a mortgage portfolio. It is important to realize that mortgage bankers are not regarded as separate financial institutions in the sense of a savings and loan association or commercial bank. Rather, they operate with funds from other institutions. They are concentrated in the capital shortage areas of the south and west, though they are found in other states. To this extent, they help distribute mortgage capital from capital surplus areas to capital shortage areas.

Some mortgage bankers specialize in FHA or VA mortgages since they are readily marketable. With the Federal National Mortgage Association, the mortgage banker has a ready market for this type of mortgage. Other mortgage bankers prefer to specialize in income properties working through advanced commitments of national insurance companies or other suppliers of long-term credit.

Generally mortgage bankers concentrate on four types of loans:

1. Loans on single family dwellings insured by FHA or guaranteed by VA and committed for purchase by a long-term lender by a specific date.
2. Loans on single family dwellings insured by FHA or guaranteed by VA that are unsold and committed for later purchase.
3. First construction mortgages given by builders to the mort-

58

gage banker and repledged to the commercial banker in return for a loan to the mortgage banker for relending to a builder who constructs dwellings eligible for FHA or VA loans.

4. Loans secured by a first mortgage on land given by the land owner and builder to the mortgage banker and repledged to a commercial bank.

Loans by the commercial bank usually fall in two categories: First, short-term loans with a maturity of 60 days to 180 days secured by FHA insured and VA guaranteed loans, committed for purchase within the maturity date of the note by a recognized institutional lender. The second type of loan extends over nine months or two years and is secured by a commitment for purchase by a permanent investor by a long-term, forward commitment.

In the first instance the loan is similar to a commercial bank loan to finance business inventories. Such loans are necessary because a mortgage banker, operating with limited capital, requires a loan to carry the mortgage while mortgage loan documentation is assembled and transmitted to the permanent investor. A commercial bank gives considerable weight to the credit analysis and the form and nature of the permanent purchase commitment of the recognized institutional lender.

In dealing with mortgage bankers, it is essential to differentiate between the types of commitment common to the industry. The *take-out* commitment is a binding letter of agreement from a permanent investor to a mortgage banking company agreeing to purchase prior to a specific time at a designated price on a group of mortgages of a designated location, subject to the approval of the credit of the borrower and other mortgage loan documentation. Because of the close working relationship between the mortgage banker and his correspondent (the permanent lender), mortgage bankers are familiar with the underwriting requirements of investors so that they may properly document the mortgage. With a close working relationship between the mortgage banker and his permanent lender, the commercial banker regards the commitment as firm and binding.

The *allocation commitment* is used by a permanent lender through a long-standing relationship with a valued mortgage banking company. The allocation commitment letter merely states that the investor will purchase within a specific period of months a certain volume of given mortgages at a given price at a specific location. Technically, the investor may reject loans because of deficiencies in location, size, design or credit of a borrower and the amount and terms of a mortgage. However, in practice, the mortgage banker is sufficiently familiar with underwriting requirements of his permanent investor so that the rejection rate is normally quite nominal. Such commitments are held in high regard by the experienced mortgage banking company and, though there may be some rejections, the alternative sources of credit usually enable the banker to sell rejected loans elsewhere.

√ The *stand-by purchase commitment* is used in periods of monetary restraint. It is called a stand-by commitment because it is really not intended to be utilized unless absolutely needed. For example, a builder may proceed with an apartment house project during a period of tight money when most lenders have withdrawn from the market. If the project is feasible, the builder may secure a stand-by commitment from a mortgage company or other source of funds at above market interest rates for a period longer than the average construction loan, say up to three to five years. The builder will pay a premium for the commitment letter. With this above market stand-by commitment, the builder may obtain a construction loan to proceed with the project.

The builder in this instance will obtain sufficient funds to construct a building and an adequate time to secure occupancy so that he may obtain a more reasonable long-term loan from other sources. If he obtains loans at the market rate, he forfeits his commitment fee of 2 to 4 percent of the loan. The take out commitment is regarded as a preferred substitute to the speculative house loan.

It should be added that lenders ordinarily charge a commitment fee from the mortgage company refundable at the time the commitment is exercised. For example, a lender may charge a mortgage company a commitment fee of one percent on a ten million dollar commitment which would require a hundred thousand dollar deposit by the mortgage company. At the end of six months, the end of the commitment term, if only eight million dollars of the commitment is exercised, the mortgage banker would forfeit $20,000, the unfilled portion of the commitment fee.

## Other Financial Sources

A group of miscellaneous sources accounting for a percentage of total loans outstanding include pension funds, real estate investment trusts, individuals, and direct loan programs sponsored by various lending agencies. Among these groups, pension funds stand as the most important since some of the larger funds are under management by commercial banks. Recent innovations in secondary mortgage markets give bankers an opportunity to introduce pension and trust funds to high yield mortgages.

## ⑥ Pension Funds

Simply stated, a pension fund is accumulated and managed over the working life of individuals to provide income during retirement. This special role requires pension fund administrators to weigh security heavily over yields. Unlike life insurance companies and thrift institutions, they are under no pressure to maximize yields for their constituents. The preference to minimize costs of administration has led pension funds to invest mostly in high grade stocks and bonds. Because they are exempt from income taxation, they make the decision purely on investment principles irrespective of tax consequences.

Regulations on their investment are largely free of the restraints imposed on other financial institutions. The Employee Retirement Income Security Act of 1974 (ERISA) requires that the fiduciary of a pension plan discharge his duties solely in the interests of plan participants and beneficiaries. Trustees must exercise the care, skill, and diligence which men of prudence would exercise in conducting a similar enterprise. Further, trustees must diversify the investments of the pension plan so as to minimize the risk of large losses, unless under the circumstances it would be clearly unwise or imprudent.

Pension funds trace their origin to colonial times; and, by 1950 their total assets amounted to $11.7 billion. By 1980, assets of private pension funds alone are expected to reach $250 billion, which is above the present asset value of life insurance companies.

While this source would seem suitable for mortgage investments, pension fund trustees have not participated actively in mortgage markets for one or more of the following reasons: (1) Trustees do not have the detailed knowledge or administrative experience in judging mortgage investments. (2) There is no market quotation on mortgages that guides similar decisions which are made for stocks and bonds. (3) Mortgage monthly repayments require reinvestment of principal, raising administative costs not found in the stock and bond market.

Recent developments in mortgage financing minimize some of these objections. By working with mortgage bankers, for example, servicing a block of government insured loans, pension funds may realize the yields which may be above AAA bonds or well secured stock. In other words a mortgage banker would establish the same relationship with a pension fund that is held with institutional investors.

Another factor expected to induce pension funds to invest in real estate mortgages is the availability of the Government National Mortgage Association "pass through" mortgage backed securities. This is an effort to give mortgage investments characteristics of bonds. The security purchased is backed by a specific block of loans guaranteed by the

United States and, in turn underwritten by FHA, VA, or the Farmers Home Administration. As the block of mortgages is submitted to GNMA for review, the agency issues its own guarantee for each package. By purchasing the certificates, investors are relieved of the administration associated with mortgages. Moreover the fund recovers yields on a monthly basis compared to a semi-annual basis typical of bonds.

The limitation of this type of investment relates to the periodic monthly payment of principal which creates reinvestment problems. Yet, the repayment of both principal and interest on a monthly basis may serve as an advantage to some funds. Mortgages secured by the GNMA certificates are federally guaranteed and the certificate itself may be traded on the open market as stocks and bonds, giving mortgages the same liquidity as other financial investments.

Consequently as pension funds utilize these new financial devices and their staff becomes more familiar with mortgage evaluation, they may be expected to invest more funds in long-term mortgages. Even today the pension funds staffed with mortgage personnel are direct lenders in large scale shopping centers, apartment projects, and purchasers of real estate for leaseback to tenants with a favorable national credit rating.

## Real Estate Investment Trusts

An amendment to the Internal Revenue Code effective January 1, 1961 authorized Real Estate Investment Trusts (REIT). Sections 856 to 858 of the Code permitted organization of real estate investment trusts to distribute income to stock holders with exemption from the corporate net income tax. Presumably the investment trust would operate in a manner similar to the mutual funds that enjoyed the same privileges in stock and bond investment. The rationale behind the new law was to attract investment capital into large real estate investments, giving the relatively small investor the advantage of high returns on real estate. Initially, real estate investment trusts were believed to:

1. Pool savings of small investors into a fund which would be available for investment in real estate enterprises. This would give the advantage of relatively high rates of return on real estate investments to the small investor who normally could not participate in real estate projects.
2. The shareholder of a REIT would gain from investment diversification. The trusts would spread their risk over investments which would appeal to individuals who typically could not diversify so extensively.

3. Shares in a REIT may be bought and sold in the open market, giving real estate investments liquidity not available through direct ownership of real estate.

Sponsors of a REIT must qualify under fairly rigid requirements to gain exemption from the corporate net income tax.

1. Ownership must be in an unincorporated trust or association managed by at least one trustee, with transferable certificates of beneficial interest or shares, and ordinarily taxable as a domestic corporation.
2. There must be at least 100 beneficial owners.
3. The trust must not be a personal holding company.
4. The trust may not hold property primarily for sale to customers in the ordinary course of business.
5. It must elect to be treated as a real estate investment trust.
6. At least 90 percent of the income must come from real property rentals, dividends, interests, or gains from the sales of security or real estate.

The law further requires that at least 75 percent of the trust income must be directly attributable to real property with another 15 percent derived from real estate or any other source from which a regulated investment company would derive most of its income, i.e., interest and dividends. In addition, not more than 30 percent of the gross income could come from short-term gains on security sales (less than six months), or gains from sale of real estate held for less than four years.

Real estate investment trusts tend to specialize in one of three main groups: short-term mortgage trusts, equity trusts, and long-term mortgage trusts. The sponsorship of real estate investment trusts by large financial institutions has led to combinations of these three forms which are known as hybrid trusts. Investment experience and financial operation of these trusts vary considerably between these groups.

**Short-Term Mortgage Trusts.** Initially, mortgage trusts concentrated in long-term, FHA insured and VA guaranteed loans. To realize higher yields they also participated in short-term construction loans. As interest rates increased in 1966 they decreased originations of FHA and VA loans, since yields in these mortgages with fixed interest rates declined. After 1968 some real estate investment trusts revised their portfolio to include construction and development and short-term first mortgage loans. These trusts, specializing in short-term loans, prefer to invest in construction loans, short-term first mortgage loans and to some extent FHA insured or VA guaranteed first mortgage loans. The larger financial institutions have created these trusts to supplement long-term mortgage operations.

**Equity Trusts.** Trusts that emphasize rental income prefer investments in equity—either outright ownership or subject to long-term mortgages. Their general appeal to the investor lies in income tax depreciation allowances that are passed through to shareholders. Trusts that hold income property for later sale also anticipate gains from appreciation of property values.

**Long-Term Mortgage Trusts.** These trusts are primarily organized to grant loans over a period of 10 to 30 years. They negotiate for not only the market rate of interest but for equity participations and other arrangements calling for bonus interest payments; for example, a share of gross income, or a percentage of capital gains in event of a sale and the like. Typically, an investment trust will raise capital by the sale of stock, and secure bank credit at a lower interest rate than the anticipated rate on long-term mortgages.

Though started on an optimistic note, recent experience has shown that real estate investment trusts have been burdened with an unusual number of "unproductive" loans. Their return on assets decreased in some instances to nominal rates of one or two percent in 1974. Observers have predicted that losses of REITs would lead to more conservative asset and liability management policies. The failure experienced by REITs to realize their optimistic projections follows from (1) lack of competence in real estate analysis held by established financial institutions such as life insurance companies, commercial banks, and other institutions; (2) The unpredicted rise in the prime interest rate in 1974 which gave negative cash flows to trusts trading on thin equity; (3) an oversupply of investment properties which were built with relatively high construction loan interest and building costs; and (4) high management fees by REIT managers. With these conditions corrected, real estate investment trusts will probably continue to absorb part of the significant demand for financing real estate.

## Individuals and Other Credit Sources

Though constituting a relatively small portion of total mortgage credit outstanding, it must be recognized that individuals participate in mortgage financing. They range from wealthy individuals who regularly invest capital to secure high rates of return on well secured investments to individuals financing family projects. In still other cases individuals enter the mortgage market by accepting a second mortgage to expedite the sale of property. This is a device supplementing first mortgage loans granted by institutions to accommodate the purchaser who has limited cash for equity payments. In this instance, the motive of the seller is to expedite the sale and not to participate in mortgage markets.

Individuals advancing mortgage credit must observe the same state regulations governing usury, foreclosure laws, and truth-in-lending legislation. In that individuals are free from the regulations governing financial institutions, they play an important role since they are more flexible in supplementing institutional credit. This is particularly true where a purchase and sale is partly financed by the seller.

# Chapter 4

# Mortgage Financing by Commercial Banks

It seems worthwhile to review the early development of mortgage lending for national banks. Much of our lending authority may be understood in the light of historical precedent. Next, it is deemed advisable to review national bank lending authority in the light of recent legislation. With this background information, a discussion of mortgage instruments will aid in the understanding of commercial bank mortgage operations.

## Early Development of Mortgage Lending for Banks

Before the *National Bank Act of 1863,* commercial banks commonly financed the purchase and construction of real estate. However, recurrent monetary crises, and repeated land speculation with their consequent boom and bust periods discouraged commercial banks from investing in mortgages. Frequent mortgage foreclosures and real estate price fluctuations made mortgages too risky for commercial banks. As a result, the National Bank Act of 1863 prohibited national banks from mortgage lending. Though at the same time some state chartered banks

66

were permitted to invest in mortgages, more conservative banks did not engage in large-scale mortgage lending.

The competition between the more liberally regulated state chartered, and nationally chartered banks, and the growing stability of the real estate market led to pressures to equalize mortgage lending opportunities between state and nationally chartered banks. Accordingly, in 1916, a broadening of the Federal Reserve Act of 1913 authorized national banks to engage in one-year loans on urban properties. By 1927, amendments to the act permitted commercial banks to make residential loans up to 50 percent of the appraised value. Mortgage terms were limited to five years. The heavy defaults in mortgages during the 1930 depression led to mortgage lending reforms. Many of the mortgage lending practices observed by commercial banks today resulted from experience gained in the 1930 depression.

The *National Housing Act of 1934* was responsible for introducing mortgage lending as it is practiced today. Commercial banks participated more heavily in mortgage lending in that banks and other lenders could exchange government guaranteed bonds or cash for foreclosed mortgages. The latter provision protected financial institutions from costly foreclosures and considerably reduced the risk of lending on long-term mortgages.

Probably the most significant change was the provision for *amortized mortgages*. In place of the existing practice of paying mortgage interest payments over a term loan, amortized mortgages set aside a portion of each mortgage payment towards repayment of principal. Subsequent mortgage payments are calculated on the remaining balance. Thus, with the amortized mortgage, each payment tends to reduce the amount owed. To the borrower, this method of amortization led to the periodic reduction of debt and the eventual debt retirement. While to the lender, each contribution to the principal reduced the risk of mortgage lending. Ideally, the retirement of debt would be more rapid than depreciation on the real estate offered as security for the loan.

Another factor attractive to commercial banks was the exemption of government insured mortgages from restrictions relating to loan maturity and loan-to-value ratios. Generally, loan-to-value ratios and the length of the mortgage were far more liberal for government guaranteed or uninsured mortgages. These provisions of the National Housing Act of 1934 allowed commercial banks to compete more actively with other lenders for government guaranteed mortgages.

Successive amendments permitted commercial banks to lend on government insured loans (Federal Housing Administration) and guaranteed home mortgages (Veterans Administration) without regard to statutory restrictions governing commercial bank mortgage lending.

Generally on these loans, banks were permitted to grant mortgage loans without regard to restrictions governing loan-to-value ratios, the length of the loan, or the total amount of mortgages held. Formerly, loans not insured or guaranteed by the federal government could not exceed 75 percent of the appraised value and were restricted to a debt not exceeding 20 years. Moreover, loans not guaranteed or insured by the federal government formerly could not exceed capital and surplus or 60 percent of savings and time deposits, whichever was greater. Comparable regulations affected state bank mortgage lending, though practices among the states varied.

Another trend favoring commercial bank mortgage lending concerns construction lending. Construction loans provide real estate credit over a short term, typically 12 months to 18 months, but legally permissible to a 60-month maximum, giving builders and other investors funds to construct buildings that qualify for long-term mortgages. Financial institutions generally may not grant long-term loans on vacant land or unfinished buildings. Commercial banks with their local experience and with available short-term funds have tended to specialize in this area of mortgage financing.

In other respects commercial banks fulfill a very special role in mortgage credit. Commercial banks serve credit requirements of a large group of borrowers—farmers, businesses, consumers, producers, and public agencies. Hence, the lending portfolio must be highly flexible to meet current demands of a wide variety of borrowers. In periods of high mortgage yields and credit shortages, commercial bank lending supplements the more specialized agencies and institutions that invest heavily in real estate mortgages. In fact, mortgages are ideally suited to that part of the portfolio that must earn a stable long-term return. Thus, banks currently are prepared to meet the demand for more mortgage credit because of new legislation and the growing credit needs of the community in which mortgage lending occupies a significant part.

It will be recalled that commercial banks are absorbing an increasing share of savings. The increase tends to be placed in time deposits. For this reason alone, it would be expected that mortgage lending by commercial banks would tend to increase. The evidence confirms this expectation.

Data in Table 4.1 reveal that total mortgages held by commercial banks increased from $49,675 million in 1965 to $135,125 in 1975—an eleven-year increase of 172.0 percent. Total mortgages outstanding over the same period increased by only 127.5 percent (from $326,000 million, 1965, to $741,659 million, 1975).

**Table 4.1**
**Mortgage Debt Outstanding by Commercial Banks: 1965–1975**
(in millions of dollars)

| Year | Residential | Nonfarm | Farm | Total[a] |
|------|-------------|---------|------|----------|
| 1965 ......... | $32,387 | $14,377 | $2,811 | $49,675 |
| | (65.2) | (28.9) | (5.9) | (100.0) |
| 1966 ......... | 34,867 | 16,366 | 3,138 | 54,380 |
| | (64.1) | (30.1) | (5.8) | (100.0) |
| 1967 ......... | 37,642 | 17,931 | 3,446 | 59,019 |
| | (63.8) | (30.4) | (5.8) | (100.0) |
| 1968 ......... | 41,433 | 20,505 | 3,758 | 65,696 |
| | (63.1) | (31.2) | (5.7) | (100.0) |
| 1969 ......... | 44,573 | 22,113 | 4,019 | 70,705 |
| | (63.0) | (31.3) | (5.7) | (100.0) |
| 1970 ......... | 45,640 | 23,284 | 4,351 | 73,275 |
| | (62.3) | (31.8) | (5.9) | (100.0) |
| 1971 ......... | 52,004 | 26,306 | 4,205 | 82,515 |
| | (63.0) | (31.9) | (5.1) | (100.0) |
| 1972 ......... | 62,782 | 31,751 | 4,781 | 99,314 |
| | (63.2) | (32.0) | (4.8) | (100.0) |
| 1973 ......... | 74,930 | 38,696 | 5,442 | 119,068 |
| | (62.9) | (32.5) | (4.6) | (100.0) |
| 1974 ......... | 81,640 | 43,375 | 6,028 | 131,043 |
| | (62.3) | (33.1) | (4.6) | (100.0) |
| 1975 ......... | 83,237 | 45,537 | 6,351 | 135,125 |
| | (61.6) | (33.7) | (4.7) | (100.0) |

[a] The proportion of mortgages held in each category is shown in percentage terms within parentheses.
Source: Compiled from *Federal Reserve Bulletins*.

Note also that the composition of the mortgage portfolio is undergoing change. The proportion of mortgages in single and multiple family dwellings declined from 65.2 percent (1965) to 61.6 percent (1975). The proportion of nonfarm loans (mostly commercial) increased over the same period.

Although not shown in Table 4.1, the proportion of residential mortgages represented by FHA and VA loans has *decreased* dramatically. Of the $32,387 million residential mortgages held by commercial banks in 1969, approximately $10,400 million or 32.4 percent were FHA or VA loans. By 1974, their volume decreased to $9,800 million or only 13.1 percent of all residential mortgages.

Another way to review commercial bank mortgage activity is to look at the annual percentage increase in mortgages outstanding. See Table 4.2. In only two years since 1965, has the annual increase in mortgages outstanding been less than 7.6 percent. In five of the last ten years, the annual increase was over ten percent; in years 1973 and 1974 the annual increase was 19.9 percent and 10.9 percent; the comparable figures for total mortgages outstanding in the United States are 12.4 percent and 8.2 percent. In 1975 these trends were reversed: commercial banks increased their total mortgages outstanding by only 2.3 percent.

**Table 4.2**
**Total Mortgages Outstanding by Commercial Banks Showing the Annual Percentage Increase**
(in millions of dollars)

| Year | Mortgages Outstanding | Annual Percentage Increase |
|------|------------------------|-----------------------------|
| 1965 | 49,675 | — |
| 1966 | 54,380 | 9.5 |
| 1967 | 59,019 | 8.5 |
| 1968 | 65,696 | 11.3 |
| 1969 | 70,705 | 7.6 |
| 1970 | 73,275 | 3.6 |
| 1971 | 82,515 | 12.6 |
| 1972 | 99,314 | 20.4 |
| 1973 | 119,068 | 19.9 |
| 1974 | 132,105 | 10.9 |
| 1975 | 135,125 | 2.3 |

Source: Compiled from *Federal Reserve Bulletin,* March, 1976, p. A42.

## National Bank Lending Authority

This trend is expected to continue for another reason: The legal environment covering mortgage lending has been changed markedly by the *Housing and Community Development Act of 1974.* This act, effective August 22, 1974, amended Section 24 of the *Federal Reserve Act,* which controls mortgage lending activity by national banks. The amendment has the following three-fold effect on mortgage loan activities of banks: *First,* it broadens lending authority with the result that national banks may invest a greater share of bank assets in real estate loans. *Second,* the act authorizes banks to grant loans on real estate formerly ineligible for mortgage credit. *Third,* lending authority was liberalized on loans already authorized. This legislation will not only encourage national banks to be increasingly active in mortgage markets, but, the more liberal provisions place greater responsibility on bank personnel who administer mortgage credit. A brief review of mortgage procedures shows the extent of these changes. See Exhibit 4.1 for a summary of these changes.

## The Increase in Available Mortgage Funds

The immediate effect of the Housing and Community Development Act of 1974 made additional funds available for real estate loans. Formerly, federally chartered banks could not grant real estate loans in excess of the greater of (a) capital stock paid in and unimpaired, plus unimpaired surplus funds, or (b) 70 percent of total time and savings deposits. Under the 1974 act, the aggregate limit on total real estate loans may equal 100 percent of time and savings deposits. Or, if greater, real estate loans may equal capital stock paid in and unimpaired plus the amount of unimpaired surplus funds. Bank policy permitting, a greater supply of long-term loanable funds is potentially available to the national bank.

A related measure reclassifies construction loans, under certain circumstances, as nonreal estate loans. For instance, a construction loan on a residence or a farm building with a maturity of less than nine months qualifies as a nonreal estate loan, and, therefore, qualifies for discount as commercial paper with the Federal Reserve. The construction loan must have a firm takeout agreement effective upon completion of the building by an approved lender. In essence, qualified construction loans will be treated as commercial paper and will not be included in the aggregate amount that may be legally invested in real estate loans.

With the exception of loans on residential or farm buildings, construction loans were permitted only with a take out commitment. Even prior to then, construction loans were limited to a maximum term of 60 1974 months. In contrast, construction loans on buildings may amount to 75 percent of the appraised value with no take out commitment and no statutory limit on maturity if the loan qualifies as a real estate loan. If a construction loan term is 60 months or less, the 75 percent loan-to-value ratio may be exceeded with a firm take out commitment. However, no take out commitment is necessary for loans on residential or farm buildings.

Any real estate loan guaranteed or insured by the National Housing Act, or backed by the full faith and credit of the United States or a state housing agency, is exempt from the aggregate limitation controlling the maximum amount of real estate loans. Banks have the option of increasing real estate loans under this provision. The former regulation was more restrictive in the type of state guarantees acceptable.

Similar provisions relate to other long-term mortgages if the loan is secured by the borrower's general credit standing or other collateral. Such loans may now be regarded as nonreal estate loans, and potentially increase the capital available for mortgages. The same provisions

71

# Exhibit 4.1

## 1974 Amendments to Section 24 of the Federal Reserve Act

**I. The Increase in Available Mortgage Funds**

| | *Former Law* | *1974 Amendment* |
|---|---|---|
| (1) Aggregate Amount That May Be Invested In Real Estate Loans | Greater of capital stock paid in and unimpaired plus the amount of its unimpaired surplus fund of 70% of its time and savings deposits. | Classed as commercial loans and are subject to an aggregate limit (including any construction loans voluntarily classed as commercial by the bank) of 100% of capital and surplus. |
| | | Greater of capital stock paid in and unimpaired plus the amount of its unimpaired surplus fund or the amount of the bank's time and savings deposits. |
| | | Loans secured by other than first liens may not exceed in the aggregate 20% of the capital stock and surplus of the association and loans which are insured or guaranteed are not included in the aggregate amount that may be invested in real estate loans or real estate loans secured by other than first liens. |
| (2) Discounting Construction Notes as Commercial Paper | No provisions. | Notes representing construction loans on residential or farm buildings and having maturities of not more than nine months and with valid take-out are eligible for discount as commercial paper. |
| Construction Loans | Not considered real estate loans but as ordinary commercial loans—not permitted without a take-out except for residential or farm buildings. Maximum term 60 months. Aggregate amount may not exceed 100% of paid-in and unimpaired capital plus 100% of unimpaired surplus fund. | Loans to finance the construction of improvements to real estate may be made in amounts up to 75% of appraised value, without a take-out commitment and with no statutory limit on maturity and still qualify as a real estate loan if secured by a lien on the real estate. Construction loans may also be made in amounts in excess of 75% of appraised value, provided that the maturity is 60 months or less and there is a firm take-out commitment by a financially responsible lender. No take-out is neces- |

sary for loans financing residential or farm buildings. The bank has the option of classing construction loans, which qualify as real estate loans under the statute, (i.e. not more than 75% of appraised value and secured by a valid lien on the realty) as either real estate loans or commercial loans. Other construction loans as described above are classed as commercial loans and are subject to an aggregate limit (including any construction loans voluntarily classed as commercial by the bank) of 100% of capital and surplus.

(3) Guaranteed Loans

Exempts from amortization maturity and loan to value requirements loans insured by U.S. under the provisions of Sec. 8 of Title I, Title II, Title VI, Title VII, Title IX of the National Housing Act or insured by Sec. of Agriculture pursuant to Title I of Bankhead-Jones Farm Tenant Act of 1949, Sec. 203b of National Housing Act and loans at least 20% guaranteed by VA

Extends exemption from aggregate limitation to all loans insured under the National Housing Act or guaranteed by HUD and certain other types of loans when the guarantee is backed by the full faith and credit of the U.S.

Exempts loans fully guaranteed or insured by a state or state authority for the payment of which the faith and credit of the state is pledged.

Extends exemption to cover any agency or instrumentality thereof provided the faith and credit of the state is pledged.

Loans insured pursuant to Sec. 203b of National Housing Act or at least 20% guaranteed by the VA are not included in determining the aggregate amount invested in real estate loans.

(4) Exempt Loans Classed as Commercial Loans

Where borrower looks to repayment relying primarily on borrower's general credit standing and forecast of income.

This exemption is continued and expanded to cover loans secured by assignments of rents under a lease.

| | Former Law | 1974 Amendment |
|---|---|---|
| | Loans to established industrial or commercial business in which the S.B.A. participates on an immediate or deferred basis. | No changes. |
| | No provisions. | Loans secured by real property and a firm take-out exists to advance the full amount of the loan within 60 months. |
| (5) Loans Secured by Real Estate and Non-Real Estate Collateral | By Comptroller's ruling only amount by which the loan exceeds the value as collateral of such other security is considered a loan upon the security of real estate. | Comptroller's ruling is incorporated in law. |
| II. New Loans Permitted | | |
| (1) Lien Requirements | First lien only except in abundance of caution situations. | First and junior liens permitted. Bank's lien when added to the amount of prior liens may not exceed the respective proportions of appraised value as provided. Aggregate of junior liens may not exceed 20% of capital and surplus. |
| (2) Loans on Unimproved Real Estate | Not permitted. | Permitted—may not exceed 66⅔% of value. |
| Loans on Improved Real Estate | 90%—loan to value ratio 30 years maximum term. | Improved with offsite improvements such as facilities consisting of streets, water, sewers and other utilities—loans permitted up to 75% of value.  Improved with a building or buildings—loan may not exceed 90% of value with a maximum term of 30 years. |
| (3) Basket Provision | No provisions. | 10% of amount that may be invested in real estate loans may be invested in real estate loans that do not comply with the limitations and restrictions in this section. The aggregate amount of non-qualifying loans must be included in the maximum aggregate amount allowed for real estate loans. |

*[handwritten annotation: Cannot lend more than 10% to anyone person.]*

## III. Existing Loan Authority Extended

### (1) Amortization

If loan is not in excess of:

1) 50% and 5 years no amortization required,

2) 66⅔% and 10 years installment payments sufficient to amortize:
   a) 40% of loan by 10th year,
   b) entire principal of loan by 20th year,

or

   c) entire principal by maturity,

3) 66⅔% and 20 years installment payments must be sufficient to amortize:
   a) entire principal of loan by 20th year

or,

   b) entire principal by maturity.

Loan in excess of either 66⅔% or 20 years must be fully amortized by maturity.

No amortization required unless the loan exceeds 75% of value or the property is improved by a 1-4 family dwelling. If the loan exceeds 75% of value or the property is improved with a 1-4 family dwelling minimum instalment payment sufficient to repay the loan within 30 years are required.

Maximum payout schedule is 30 years with no requirement that the loan be fully amortized by maturity if the term is less than 30 years.

### (2) Forest Tract Loans

Loans could not exceed 60% of fair market value of timber, lands, and improvements. Maturity limited to 3 years unless amortized.

Bank's loans together with prior liens may not exceed 66⅔% of value of timber, lands, and improvements. Maturity limited to 3 years except that maximum maturity may be 15 years when installment payments are sufficient to amortize the loan within a period of not more than 15 years and at a rate of at least 6⅔% per year.

Amount of such loans may not exceed 50% of capital and surplus and are to be included in aggregate limits for all real estate loans.

75

*considered non-real estate*

apply to loans secured by the tenant's interest in long-term leases which assign rents to the bank in cases of default. Loans guaranteed by the Small Business Administration fall in the same category.

A final point worth noting is that a former comptroller's ruling, which considered only that portion of a loan in which the value exceeded collateral as a real estate loan, is now incorporated as part of the law.

## New Loans Permitted

Banks were among the financial institutions generally prohibited from making loans secured by less than a first lien. A commercial bank may now make loans on subordinate or *junior liens* if the combination, say, of the first mortgage and the second mortgage, does not exceed the appraised value. Further, the total of junior liens and second mortgages (and other loans subordinate to a first mortgage) must not be more than 20 percent of capital and surplus. Consequently, if a proposed borrower offers a second mortgage as security, and the project is otherwise feasible, the bank may in effect finance part of the equity. To the extent that the other financial institutions do not have this privilege, banks may be highly competitive for such loans, providing the risk is acceptable.

Historically, institutional lenders, including banks, have not encouraged loans on vacant land because of speculative land prices and the uncertainty over real estate values. Usually, banks place such loans in a high risk category. Today, loans by national banks on vacant land are permitted provided they do not exceed 66⅔ percent of value. If the land is improved with offsite improvements, for example, streets, domestic water, sewers or utilities, the loan may extend up to 75 percent of value. Similarly, if the land has a building under construction, the 75 percent ratio complies with the new law.

✳ Still another section of the Housing and Community Act, called the *Basket Provision*, allows 10 percent of the total invested in real estate loans to exceed the limitations and restrictions of the amendment restrictions. This latter provision gives banks flexibility in granting real estate loans on property that does not conform to allowable limits. Presumably, the financial circumstances and judgment of the bank officials would be controlling.

## Existing Loan Authority Extended

National banks now have considerably more leeway in varying the *amortization schedules* of mortgage loans. No amortization now is required unless the loan exceeds 75 percent of the appraised value or the property is improved by a one to four-family dwelling; also, instalment payments must be sufficient to repay the loan in 30 years. Although mortgage loans in excess of 30 years are not permissible, loans of less than 30 years have no requirement that the loan be fully amortized by maturity.

The effect of these provisions permits more flexibility in arranging repayments. Borrowers, who have limited present income but a favorable projection of income in later years of the loans, may have payment schedules more nearly conforming to their ability to service the loan. For example, consider a newly qualified medical doctor who is entering a medical practice. During the early years of his practice, he would probably have less ability to service a loan compared to his projected income in five or more years later. The same reasoning applies to properties such as apartment structures, shopping centers, new residential developments, and the like.

On *forest tracts*, loans previously could not exceed 60 percent of fair market value of the timber, land and improvements with the loan limited to a three year maximum, unless amortized. Today, the bank loan on timber tracts, including prior liens, must not exceed 66⅔ percent of the value with a maturity limited to three years unless amortization over a 15 year term returns the principal at the rate of 6⅔ percent a year. Total timber tracts falling under these provisions must not exceed 50 percent of capital surplus, and must fall within the aggregate limit applying to real estate loans.

## Continued Prudence and Careful Evaluations

Policy on mortgage lending by national banks has been explained by the Comptroller of Currency who stated:

> National bankers are reminded that the above liberalizing amendments were adopted by the Congress on the assumption that bankers today possess expertise in the real estate lending field and that there was no longer a necessity for all of the prior detailed statutory requirements in the particular area of lending. The statute therefore contains *minimum* standards of prudence and is not in any way meant to suggest actual loan terms. Each real estate loan officer is expected to continue to examine each prospective credit individually and to tailor each loan with due regard to banking prudence as well as the borrower's needs and capabilities.
>
> (*Banking Bulletin* 74-4, dated September 9, 1974)

Clearly, bank participation in mortgage finance will increase. The increase, however, will be made with a clear recognition of the special characteristics of mortgages and its security, the real estate.

## Related Financing Activities

Because commercial banks serve total credit needs of the community, they actively support housing and other real estate developments beyond the direct placement of mortgages. The development of new communities requires heavy investment in municipal utilities, hospitals, schools, and other public facilities. And some of the more prominent ways in which commercial banks indirectly participate in real estate development deserve mention.

Other invest-ments.

(1) Consider, for example, the investment of commercial banks in securities issued to finance mortgages. Though not listed as real estate mortgages, banks that purchase securities issued by the many federal agencies provide funds for the real estate industry. The purchase of securities issued by agencies such as the Federal Home Loan Bank Board, the Government National Mortgage Association, the privately owned, the Federal National Mortgage Association, and others, provides money that is used directly to finance real estate mortgages. It has been reported that investments by commercial banks in housing related securities amounts to over $10 billion annually.

(2) Consider next the securities issued by cities, towns, counties and other local governments to finance transportation facilities, schools, water, sewer and other utility systems. Such funds are used to support local real estate developments with the issue of bonds and securities repaid from local revenues and taxes. In this way banks supply capital necessary for housing and other real estate projects.

(3) Mobile home financing, while not classed as a real estate loan, in reality is a method of financing low-cost housing. It has been reported that mobile homes represent the only conventionally available low-cost housing for some 40 percent of the families earning less than $8,000 per year. Commercial banks currently finance more than 50 percent of all mobile homes. Indeed, commercial banks have more flexibility in financing mobile homes than other institutions that are largely restricted to real estate mortgages.

(4) It is also true that banks lend to other financial institutions that are active in the real estate market. Included in this list would be savings and loan associations, mortgage bankers, life insurance companies, and real estate investment trusts. Financial institutions seek funds from commercial banks to meet seasonal credit demands and to provide temporary financing of mortgage originations.

(5) A related activity includes loans to building contractors, suppliers and the many other businesses engaged in housing, construction, services and supply. The financing of businesses active in the real estate industry emphasizes further the vital role that banks play in supporting the market for real estate.

Chapter 5

# Mortgage Instruments and Characteristics

Loan personnel must know basic mortgage instruments and the various types of mortgages to effectively communicate with clients and others. An explanation of mortgage and real estate characteristics indicates why definite administrative, legal, and financial procedures have been specifically developed for mortgage loans.

## Mortgage Instruments

Simply stated, a mortgage is an instrument that pledges real estate as security for a debt. The debt is evidenced by a personal promise to pay as stated in the promissory note or bond. Without a debt, there can be no mortgage. In some instances, the promissory note will be included with the mortgage and appears as one instrument. Though mortgages have no certain form, each mortgage must have a common set of elements to be legally enforceable. See Exhibit 6.1, Chapter 6, for an example of a mortgage instrument.

## Elements of a Mortgage

In one sense a mortgage is a specialized contract which must have all requirements of an enforceable real estate contract. Though mortgages tend to be specialized and have special clauses, it is generally agreed that the form of a mortgage must include certain essential elements:

1. The mortgage must be in writing.
2. The mortgagor (borrower) and mortgagee (lender) must be legally competent. *must always be present*
3. √ There must be a clause creating the mortgage.
4. √ The debt must be identified with terms of payment clearly stated.
5. The property pledged by the mortgagee should be legally described.
6. √ The borrower should warrant title and he must have an interest which is mortgageable.
7. √ Foreclosure provisions in the event of default should be stated.
8. The mortgage must be properly executed, witnessed or acknowledged.
9. The mortgage must be delivered and accepted.

Mortgages must conform to the general rule that real estate conveyance instruments must be in writing to be enforceable. This rule, falling under the Statute of Frauds, specifies that real estate contracts, leases for more than one year, deeds, mortgages and other like documents must be in writing. While oral contracts may be valid between two parties, without written evidence conveyance documents would be unenforceable in a court of law.

The competency of both parties to a mortgage document is another item common to enforceable contracts. Thus, a minor has no legal authority to mortgage property without the consent of a legally appointed guardian. To give another example, a corporate officer may not pledge property of the corporation to a mortgage unless he is granted authority by the corporate charter, action of the board of directors, or by-laws of the corporation. Experienced lenders dealing with corporations require evidence of authority to execute real estate documents.

Some of the other elements of mortgage clauses are unique. For instance, the mortgaging clause in some states may actually convey the property with words such as "grants and conveys," or in other states the mortgaging clause would be satisfied by the word, mortgages, e.g., John Jones mortgages to the National Bank.

Ordinarily, the monthly payment, interest rate and maturity of the mortgage would be stated in the mortgage document. The legal de-

*Raines does not use the rate of interest. He just says "interest to be paid" w/ usuary, might make contract unenforcable*

scription common to deeds and other conveyances should describe the property pledged. It is also important to state the ownership and interest subject to the mortgage such as a leasehold interest (the interest of the tenant), or the fee simple estate subject to easements, rights of way, or other interests. This clause clearly defines the property to be pledged and subject to foreclosure.

In addition to these requirements some states require promises that are a mandatory part of the mortgage. For instance, the mortgagor or borrower may be required to agree to protect the property mortgaged for the benefit of the lender and make other promises with respect to payment of the debt. It is common for the borrower to promise to pay taxes, assessments, and other utility liens and protect the property from harm.

In other respects, mortgages must be signed, witnessed or acknowledged according to state statutes. In some states witnesses are necessary to the validity of the mortgage. Even with proper signatures, witnesses and acknowledgment, the mortgage may not be enforceable unless it is delivered voluntarily and accepted by the lender. The mortgage, with its promissory note or bond, is held by the lender until the mortgage is satisfied. Mortgages are regarded as a form of intangible personal property and may be bought and sold as other properties subject to ownership. The mortgage should be recorded.

## Rights of the Mortgagor  *Borrower*

Both the mortgagor and the mortgagee have rights partly defined by covenants (promises) of the mortgage or defined by statute. Generally, rights common to both estates center on the rights of the borrower to redeem the property in the event of default and the right of the lender to foreclose the property.

### Equity of redemption  *All states have this.*

It is generally true that the borrower retains the right of ownership. He has the right of possession, use and enjoyment of the real estate. Depending on his interest he may lease, sell, or transfer the properties subject to the rights of the lender. However, if the borrower defaults in his payment schedule, the lender has the right to foreclose according to the terms of the mortgage and state law. In this event the borrower possesses the right to recover the property mortgaged upon payment of obligations due the lender plus costs and expenses borne by the lender in executing a foreclosure suit and sale. This right, termed the equity of redemption, may be exercised at any time before the foreclosure sale.

*Statutory right of redemption*   ~~28~~ states have this

In some states borrowers have the right to redeem the mortgaged property *after* the foreclosure sale which is referred to as the statutory right of redemption. In at least one state the statutory right of redemption continues for two years after the foreclosure sale. Lenders operating under this rule stand the risk of losing title during the statutory redemption period. This tends to increase risks, cloud the title, and prevent the lender from recovering his debt. States with the restrictive statutes are less likely to attract out of state mortgage funds from institutional lenders.

both can be waived in advance by owner in Deed of Trust.

*Prepayment privileges*

The mortgagee normally incurs considerable expense in processing mortgages. Because these costs are undertaken in anticipation of receiving interest over the mortgage term, the mortgagee will define circumstances in which the borrower may repay the debt prior to maturity. Frequently, the lender will impose a penalty if the borrower prepays before maturity. Arrangements vary from prepayment privileges limited to a certain percentage of the principal, to penalties based on a percentage of the principal effective only for prepayments during the first few years. Prepayment penalties protect the lender from borrowers who may wish to refinance the property at a lower rate of interest.

## Rights of the Mortgagee   Lender

The rights of the lender depend on rights of foreclosure which are treated in greater detail in a succeeding chapter. For the present purpose it is deemed relevant to review acceleration clauses, assumptions, and the right of assignment.

### Acceleration clauses

Technically, a borrower is in default if he misses a single payment. Depending on the individual circumstances, the lender may not initiate foreclosure procedures until the loan is 60 or more days in default. To give the lender options in protecting the loan principal, the acceleration gives the lender the right to the full amount of the principal immediately if the mortgagee is in default. For instance, a borrower who has made payments for two years on a 30 year mortgage must return the entire principal if the acceleration clause is enforced. Without this clause the lender could demand only the amount of defaulted payments, since the balance of the debt was not due and payable. To recover the debt, in this case the lender would have to initiate a series of foreclosure suits to recover each individual payment over the life of the debt.

In practice the acceleration clause is enforced only after the lender has exhausted all other remedies. In the event of the property abandonment or negligence, the acceleration clause helps the lender protect his security by exercising the option of foreclosing on the entire debt.

It should be added that the acceleration clause may be exercised not only for nonpayment of the debt but for other defaults on the part of the borrower. The defaults could include nonpayment of real estate taxes, failure to purchase insurance when it is required by the mortgage, or failure of the borrower to protect the property from waste and damage.

## Assumption of mortgages

It is to the advantage of the purchaser to acquire property with an existing mortgage that has more favorable terms than terms common to new mortgages. For example, suppose Jones offers to buy Smith's property for $45,000, by paying $10,000 cash and assuming an existing mortgage with a remaining balance of $35,000. Under these circumstances most lenders restrict the right of the buyer to assume an existing mortgage. Such rights are justified on grounds that the lender has the right to approve the credit of the buyer who assumes an existing loan. Indeed, the lender may charge an assumption fee for changing records, undertaking a credit investigation, and incurring other expenses of approving a new borrower. Mortgage terms may include provisions for levying assumption fees.

In the case of an existing loan which is accepted by a new buyer, two options are available. The buyer who acquires a new property with an existing loan may buy *subject to* or *assume* an existing mortgage. If the buyer buys subject to the existing mortgage, he is not personally liable for the unpaid debt. In this case the lender may foreclose on the property but he may not sue the new borrower under the promissory note. Again there is no personal liability on the part of a buyer who purchases subject to an existing mortgage. The lender may seek recourse only against the property and not against the person.

The alternative is presented if the buyer *assumes* an existing mortgage. In this event, most lenders require that the borrower/seller transfer personal liability for a mortgage under a written agreement to the other party who intends to assume the obligation.

In some states the purchaser is personally responsible only if he executes and acknowledges an outstanding mortgage debt which he personally assumes and agrees to pay. It should be added that unless the original borrower is released, the lender may sue against the original borrower and subsequent parties who have agreed to assume the obligation. This step would be taken if the proceeds of the foreclosure sale would be insufficient to pay the outstanding debt. In this instance the lender would file a deficiency judgment against the borrower—a judgment that recognizes his personal obligation to pay the debt.

*Assignment of mortgages* should be recorded.

Because a mortgage is a form of intangible personal property, it may be transferred or assigned by the lender without permission of the borrower. In fact it is this right that gives mortgages a degree of liquidity important to institutional lenders. The person to whom the assignment is made, the assignee, acquires all rights of the original lender. The borrower should be given notice of the assignment indicating where the mortgage payments should be sent and to whom future payments are to be made. The assignment should be recorded.

## Recording Mortgages

Recording is the act of placing a document on public record. In most states, a county official such as the Recorder of Deeds or other county or township official is designated to accept documents for recording. Recording is accomplished by filing a reproduced copy of the document in a public file which is listed alphabetically by the name of the buyer, seller, borrower, or lender.

In general, the act of recording is not necessary to make a mortgage or other instrument legally enforceable. Yet, in the case of a mortgage, the act of recording protects the lender from claims of subsequent parties. The protection lies in the assumption that recording the mortgage constitutes "constructive" notice to the world that the mortgage exists for all to review and examine. The priority of liens is based generally on the order of acceptance for recording. For example, an unpaid creditor who records a lien against real estate after a first mortgage is accepted for recording has a lien subordinate to the holder of the first mortgage.

For this reason, lenders are careful to record mortgages immediately after their execution. In fact, to guard against prior claims of mechanics and materialman liens, lenders advancing funds for new construction make certain that the mortgage is recorded before construction commences; thereby insuring that first mortgages have prior claims against subsequent lien holders such as unpaid contractors, laborers, and suppliers.

It is generally true that holders of junior liens, i.e., second mortgages, that are recorded and executed without knowledge of the holder of the senior mortgage, acquire priority over the unrecorded first mortgage. Similarly, other judgments against property that the borrower owns may take precedent over unrecorded mortgages, even though the mortgage lien precedes other judgments. In other words, the public is put on notice to determine the nature of the interest held by parties who record real estate documents.

## Other Legal Aspects

The requirements of the states vary in the interpretation and administration of mortgages. States that vest title of the mortgaged property with the mortgagee are termed *title theory* states. Most states treat the mortgage as a lien against the title held by the mortgagor. These states are called the *lien theory* states.

### Title theory states

Under the title theory concept, the terms of the mortgage place the title in the name of the mortgagee. In the event of default the lender is given the right to dispossess the borrower. Although the borrower retains visible possession subject to a mortgage, he retains possession only as long as he is not in default.

### Lien theory states

With the exception of Arkansas and Missouri, states west of the Mississippi treat the mortgage as a lien against title held by the borrower. The lender gains neither title nor right of possession to the property mortgaged. Unless the borrower voluntarily surrenders property after a default, the lender may acquire possession only after proceeding under foreclosure statutes. Here it is assumed that the lender is not the owner and has no rights of possession until the ownership is determined by foreclosure sale and the equity of redemption or statutory rights of redemption have expired.

## Types of Mortgages

Mortgages tend to be specialized instruments that vary according to the purpose of the mortgage and the purpose of payment. It is common to differentiate between conventional mortgages, and those mortgages insured or guaranteed by FHA or VA. The latter classification is helpful in interpreting mortgage statistics and identifying mortgages that do not have characteristics of the conventional loan. Some mortgages may have features of several classifications.

## Mortgages Classified by Purpose

While a mortgage may cover more than one type of classification, it is worthwhile to explain the specialized vocabulary associated with different kinds of mortgages.

### Open-end mortgages    not used

The open-end mortgage is a privilege granted by the lender, usually for a loan on a one family dwelling, to borrow additional money under terms of the original mortgage. Suppose, for example, during the fifth year of a mortgage with 20 years remaining, a borrower wishes to add a swimming pool or an additional bedroom. If he has an open-end mortgage, he may borrow at the same interest rate, increasing his repayments by relatively small additional amounts.

The alternative would be to secure a home improvement loan repayable over five years at a higher interest rate. This would require a second mortgage and possibly endanger the ability of the borrower to service the first mortgage. Some borrowers may look to the open-end mortgage as a relatively inexpensive way to raise capital for other family emergencies, such as medical care or educational expenses.

### Blanket mortgages

The blanket mortgage covers more than one parcel of real estate. To raise necessary funds, a borrower may pledge several parcels of real estate as security for a single loan. Typically, however, the blanket mortgage is a device to finance new subdivisions. To finance utilities, land development, and other associated costs of a new subdivision, a blanket mortgage may constitute a lien against all subdivided lots. With a blanket mortgage, it is customary to include a clause that releases title to a particular house or lot if the seller pays a proportion of the lot value to the original land owner. As individual houses are sold, a separate loan is executed to the new buyer and part of the proceeds of this loan (and down payment) are used to pay the blanket loan covering all lots of the subdivision. The new buyer secures a document releasing his house and lot from the blanket mortgage which covers the remaining unsold lots.

## Package mortgages

Custom dictates that certain types of personal property are included in the sale of a single family dwelling. It is not uncommon to include automatic washing machines, dryers, refrigerators, or other applicances and personal property in the mortgage. For instance, a $300 appliance included in a 30-year, 8½ percent mortgage would increase monthly payments by only $2.31. Purchasers with limited cash assets may prefer the slight monthly increase to a cash outlay of several hundred dollars for appliances. The alternative would be to purchase appliances under consumer instalment credit, which may range from 10 percent to 20 percent in simple interest.

## Purchase money mortgages   buyer to seller

The purchase money mortgage is often granted by a seller who is willing to accept part of the price in the form of a mortgage from the buyer. In most states the purchase money mortgage does not include a promissory note and is secured only by the real estate and not the personal promise of the buyer. If the buyer finances the purchase with a first mortgage from an institutional lender, the purchase money mortgage is usually subordinate to the prior claim of the first mortgage lender. Since the mortgage does not include a promissory note, institutional lenders seldom loan on purchase money mortgages.

## Participation mortgages

For some properties it is desirable to spread the risk among several lenders. Large commercial projects, shopping centers, community development loans and the like may be financed with a mortgage in which more than one lender loans money secured by a single mortgage. The participation agreement governs the share assumed by each lender. This procedure is also followed if institutional lenders are legally restricted in the amount of real estate loans they may make, or if they wish to diversify their risks geographically or by property type.

## Wraparound mortgages

The wraparound mortgage serves a purpose if (1) an existing property is subject to a loan of relatively low interest payments, and (2) the borrower wishes to borrow more money. Given an existing loan financed under relatively low interest rates, a second lender may be willing to advance a new mortgage based on the current property value

Thisway → 2nd lender knows if mortgagor is in default

by loaning the difference between the principal of the new mortgage and the principal of the outstanding first mortgage. The second lender then assumes the mortgage payments of the existing mortgage, making payments from the payments of the borrower on the new mortgage. The second lender keeps the difference between the payment on the old mortgage and the new mortgage.

In this example, the originator of the wraparound mortgage, the second lender, actually holds the second mortgage which has an effective yield higher than the going rate on new mortgages. The borrower, in turn, usually gains additional financing at a lower rate than he would by refinancing because he retains the low market interest rate of the original mortgage.

### Construction mortgages

These mortgages, actually a form of interim financing, are dealt with in greater detail in a separate chapter. For the present it should be emphasized that construction loans are granted at relatively high interest rates compared to long-term financing; they are relatively short-term— typically 12 to 18 months; funds are advanced only as the building under construction reaches certain stages of completion. Because they require considerable local administrative experience, they appeal to local financial institutions such as commercial banks and mortgage bankers.

## Mortgages Classified by Type of Payment

Mortgage lenders have a wide range of mortgage plans tailored to meet special needs of borrowers. The variety of payment plans range from interest payments only, postponing principal repayment to a future lump sum payment, to plans that shift principal repayment to the later years of the mortgage. The essential problem is to select that mortgage payment plan best adapted to the property pledged as security and to the financial status of the borrower.

### Term mortgage

Though infrequently used today, the term mortgage was the typical payment plan before the 1930 depression. The term was usually limited to three to five years with the principal due in its entirety at the end of the term. The borrower paid interest on a quarterly, semi-annually, or annual basis. For example, a $5,000 mortgage with a five year maturity might call for a semi-annual interest payment of $225 with repayment of principal at the end of five years. Frequently, lenders were expected to renew the loans at the end of the term, although this was optional on the part of the lender.

The term mortgage had limitations in that the loan was of relatively short term; it provided for no periodic payment of principal; and it placed an unusual burden on the borrower since the principal payment was due in a lump sum. Default on the principal payment at the end of the term constituted grounds for foreclosure. The amortized mortgage overcomes these objections.

## Amortized mortgages

Amortized mortgages provide for the periodic repayment of principal. Ordinarily, each payment includes interest and principal payments, though in some types of mortgages principal payments are postponed during the initial years. Amortized mortgages usually take one of two forms—variable payment, or level payment—though variations in these plans are common.

The *variable payment mortgage,* which is the least common plan, calls for a constant payment to principal. To determine mortgage payments, the lender and borrower must agree on the amount to be applied to principal with each payment; the annual interest rate; and the frequency of payments. For example, to repay a $5,000 five year loan, 9 percent interest over five annual payments, it may be agreed that the principal will be retired with five, $1,000 annual payments. The first mortgage payment would be then $1,450 (see Table 5.1).

### Table 5.1
### Amortization by a Variable Payment Mortgage

| End of Year | Principal Repayment (Constant) | Annual Interest .09 | Annual Mortgage Payment | Remaining Balance |
|---|---|---|---|---|
| 1 | $1,000 | $ 450 | $1,450 | $4,000 |
| 2 | 1,000 | 360 | 1,360 | 3,000 |
| 3 | 1,000 | 270 | 1,270 | 2,000 |
| 4 | 1,000 | 180 | 1,180 | 1,000 |
| 5 | 1,000 | 90 | 1,090 | 0 |
| Total | $5,000 | $1,350 | — | — |

Note that with a constant principal repayment the portion paid to interest decreases over the life of the loan. This makes the total payment relatively high during the early years of the mortgage compared to later years. This feature accompanied by a varying payment either

89

monthly, annually, or other basis decreases the popularity of this amortization plan.

Under the *level payment* amortization plan mortgage payments are constant, but, the amounts accruing to principal and interest vary with each payment. The monthly payment is determined by calculating the amount of money required to amortize $1.00, given the number of payments and the annual interest rate. Mortgage amortization schedules are based on the formula for the *instalment of one*.

$$\frac{1}{a\overline{\rceil}_{n}} = \frac{i}{1 - \dfrac{1}{(1+i)^n}}$$

The above formula gives the amount necessary to amortize $1.00. Assume for example that $1.00 must be repaid in annual instalments, including interest and principal, under a mortgage interest rate of 8 percent. The amount necessary to amortize $1.00 over five years would be equal to

$$\frac{1}{a\overline{\rceil}_{5}} = \frac{.08}{1 - \dfrac{1}{(1+.08)^5}}$$

$$= .250456$$

In other words, a payment of $0.250456 at the end of the year for five years would repay $1.00 with interest on the remaining balance calculated at 8 percent annually. To illustrate the allocation of mortgage payments under the level payment amortization plan, consider the amortization of a loan $3,992.71 over five years (annual payments) at an 8 percent interest. Table 5.2 shows how these payments are treated.

**Table 5.2**
**The Amortization of $3,992.71, Five Years, Eight Percent Interest**

| End of Period | Instalment to Amortize | Principal | Constant Annual Payment | Interest on Remaining Balance | Principal Repayment | Remaining Balance |
|---|---|---|---|---|---|---|
| Beginning of Period 1 | — | | — | — | — | $3,992.71 |
| 1 | .250456 × | $3,992.71 | $1,000 | $319.42 | $680.58 | 3,312.13 |
| 2 | .250456 × | 3,992.71 | 1,000 | 264.97 | 735.03 | 2,559.10 |
| 3 | .250456 × | 3,992.71 | 1,000 | 204.73 | 795.27 | 1,763.83 |
| 4 | .250456 × | 3,992.71 | 1,000 | 141.11 | 858.89 | 904.94 |
| 5 | .250456 × | 3,992.71 | 1,000 | 72.39 | 927.61 | −22.67 |
| | | | | | | (rounding error) |
| Total | — | — | $5,000 | $1,002.62 | $3,997.38 | — |
| | | | | | (−4.67 rounding error) | |

Note that in the instalment to amortize $1.00, .250456 is multiplied by the amount of the loan, $3,992.71. The product of this calculation gives the constant annual mortgage payment. At the end of the first year, the lender is entitled to an 8 percent return on the loan of $3,992.71 which is $319.42. By deducting the interest from the constant annual payment, the balance, $680.58, is then allocated to repayment of principal.

At the end of the second year, the remaining balance, $3,312.13 earns an interest of $264.97. This means that in the second year some $735.03 is allocated to principal, reducing the remaining balance by this amount. This process is repeated until the five $1,000 payments are made: $1,002.62 in interest and $3,992.71 in principal (see Table 5.2).

Note that in the initial periods the proportion payable in interst is relatively high; the proportion of the constant payment payable against the outstanding principal increases over the life of a loan. For instance, a mortgage of $40,000 payable monthly over 30 years (360 payments) at an annual interest of 9 percent would call for a monthly payment of $321.84—$300 payable in interest and $21.84 payable in principal (first payment only).

The amortized level payment loan tends to reduce risk to the lender to the extent that principal repayments offset depreciation of the property over its economic life. The borrower in turn looks to the principal repayment as a form of savings. In the event of sale he has an opportunity to recoup his principal repayments, assuming no price changes or unusual property depreciation. Moreover, the borrower benefits from the reduction in interest payments as the loan is reduced with each payment.

## Partially amortized mortgages

The amortized mortgages noted above provide for repayment of principal by the maturity date. Mortgages that partially amortize principal provide for the principal repayment down to a given amount with a lump sum payment of the remaining principal at the date of maturity —a balloon mortgage. In practice the principal payment is seldom made since the partial amortization increases equity to the point that the property qualifies for refinancing under a fully amortized loan.

The effect of the balloon mortgage is to reduce the amount of monthly payment without reducing interest rates and without extending loan terms beyond legal maximum limits. This type of loan accommodates the borrower with an improved credit position in later years of the mortgage, e.g., a professional with an income that increases annually.

Commercial property such as shopping centers and apartment house projects may also be refinanced in this manner if the lender anticipates a minimum cash flow during the early years of project life and a more favorable cash flow as the project benefits from local economic growth.

### Flexible payment mortgages

Flexible payment mortgages (FPM), allow initial monthly payments below those required by a level payment, amortized mortgage. For example, the mortgage payment may be based on interest only up to five years with full amortization effective in the sixth year. Such a plan, depending on the initial interest rate and the length of the loan, may produce monthly payments from 5 percent to 25 percent below the level payment, amortized mortgage.

To illustrate, consider a mortgage of 9 percent and a loan of 20 years. If the borrower applies for a $30,000 mortgage under these terms, he would require a monthly income of $1,350, assuming that the mortgage payment does not exceed 20 percent of income. Under a flexible payment mortgage with interest only payable over the first five years, the required monthly income would be reduced to $1,125 or $225 below the income required for an amortized mortgage. To put it differently, with an income of $1,125 per month a buyer could qualify for a 9 percent 20 year mortgage of $25,000. With a flexible payment mortgage, he could qualify for a loan of $30,000.

### Variable rate mortgages

Savings institutions active in the long-term mortgage market are faced with a dilemma: During periods of rising interest rates they must live with high short-term interest rates paid to depositors. At the same time, they are burdened with relatively low rates earned on long-term mortgages. Their ability to pay depositors higher interest depends mostly on their income from long-term mortgages. While the interest rate on new mortgages may be raised to legal and maximum rates, their incomes are based on the *average yield* earned on total mortgages outstanding, which under the present assumptions were negotiated when interest rates were lower.

If, however, savings institutions are unable to pay higher short-term rates comparable to bond yields (or, for example, on Treasury bills) depositors may withdraw their savings deposits. The variable rate mortgage tends to counteract the flow of funds from savings institutions.

Under the variable rate mortgage, by agreement, mortgage interest may change according to some index. The index must not be under control of the lender and it must be available to the public such as the rate of interest on government bonds, the prime interest rate charged by banks, or the consumer price index. Some lenders have preferred to base variable rates on the interest prevailing on three- to five-year Treasury notes, or the Federal Home Loan Bank Board interest rate series. The Federal Land Bank, which has issued variable rate mortgages to finance rural houses, bases the rate largely on rates charged on the sale of their bonds.

If the index adopted as a reference point increases, then mortgage rates rise by a similar proportion. In this way the higher interest on mortgages allows savings institutions to pay depositors a higher return on savings and effectively decreases the loss of deposits to other competing investments. By the same token a decrease in the index would lower interest rates on mortgages with the consequence that depositors would also earn lower interest dividends. In this manner it is held that variable rate mortgages minimize the boom and bust characteristics of the housing market.

Without the variable rate mortgage, in periods of declining interest rates, the borrower may prepay the loan (depending on mortgage terms) and refinance under more favorable interest rates. The lender, on the other hand, assumes the final risk for he must continue to accept mortgage payments on long-term below market interest rates.

Variable rate mortgages have not been widely adopted in states that impose restrictive statutory ceilings on interest rates. Some states, such as California, have imposed additional restrictions on variable rate mortgages: (1) variable rate mortgages must be flexible downward in the same way they are flexible upward; (2) increases in interest rates are restricted to one quarter of one percent semi-annually; (3) the borrower has the right to prepay the mortgage within 90 days of a notice of a change in interest rates without penalty; (4) the interest rate cannot be changed more than 2.5 percentage points over the life of the loan; and (5) amortization may be increased to 40 years at the option of the buyer without increasing existing monthly payments.

## Other Finance Instruments

To overcome the restrictive foreclosure laws, some states have created substitutes for the mortgage and its associated promissory note. Financially the results are very similar, though the legal implications of these instruments tend to reduce the risk of loss in the event of default. The most popular device used in at least ten states and the District of Columbia is the trust deed. The security deed used in Georgia is actually a substiute for a mortgage and not a deed conveyance instrument.

*Trust deeds* ~~Tennessee~~

In place of the two-party relationship of the mortgagor and the mortgagee in the usual mortgage agreement, the trust deed requires a three-party agreement: the borrower becomes the *trustor,* the lender becomes the *beneficiary* of the trust and the third party operates as the *trustee.* Under this arrangement, the borrower conveys title to the trustee which is held "in trust" as security for the lender, the beneficiary of the trust.

The terms of the trust call for principal and interest payments and other covenants common to a mortgage. When the debt is satisfied the trustee is instructed, according to the terms of the trust, to reconvey title to the borrower. If the debt is in default, the lender notifies the trustee who is instructed to foreclose and sell the property at a public sale for the benefit of the beneficiary. The proceeds of the sale, after legal and other costs are satisfied, are divided between the borrower (the trustor), and the lender (the beneficiary), as their interests appear.

Compared to the mortgage foreclosure procedure, the trust deed considerably shortens the foreclosure period. For example, in California, a defaulting mortgage borrower has a statutory redemption period of one year after the foreclosure sale during which he may remain in possession of the property. Under these circumstances the lender is unable to gain clear title to property pledged as security until the statutory period expires.

**Exhibit 5.1**

**A Diagram of a Three-Party Trust Deed**

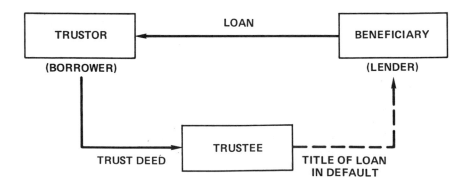

In contrast to a mortgage foreclosure, a California borrower who defaults on his obligation under a trust deed starts the following action: (1) The lender (the beneficiary), notifies the trustee of the default. (2) The trustee notifies the borrower of this default and records a copy of the notice of default. (3) At the end of three months the trustee must publish a notice of sale in a newspaper of general circulation. (4) After a minimum of 21 days between the first notice of sale, the property may be sold at foreclosure. Hence, it is possible for a lender to secure clear title on foreclosed property three months and 21 days after the notice of default. Exhibit 5.1 diagrams the relationships found in a three-party deed trust.

*Security deeds*

For the same reasons that trust deeds have been used as a substitute for mortgages, the security deed, which is used in Georgia, substitutes for a warranty deed and mortgage. The security deed is really a financial device representing a deed executed to secure a debt in the form of conveyance by warranty deed. The security deed includes the following provisions: (1) A statement that the deed secures payment of a stated debt. (2) The deed establishes a power of attorney authorizing the purchaser or his assigns to sell the property upon default of the loan and to apply the proceeds to satisfy the debt. (3) A statement that upon full payment of the debt, the grantee or his assigns will cancel the deed or reconvey the property to the grantor.

Upon satisfaction of the debt, the security deed becomes null and void. In sum, these provisions represent a warranty deed given to a creditor who holds the power of sale in the event of default without proceeding under the more time consuming and costly mortgage foreclosure procedures.

## General Characteristics of Mortgages

The technicalities governing mortgage-lending arise from a combination of legal and economic characteristics. The mortgage lender must observe numerous state and federal laws governing mortgages in general. Moreover, various financial institutions themselves are governed by a special set of laws dealing with real estate credit. As a result, mortgage lending calls for highly skilled personnel and a set of regulations and practices that must be followed in every detail with the advice of bank counsel being obtained in specific instances. The more relevant characteristics, because of their overwhelming importance to mortgage administration, deserve special mention.

## Usury Laws

Many states, under the pressure of protecting distressed borrowers, have enacted laws providing for interest rate ceilings. Such legislation is rationalized in the belief that interest rate ceilings protect the borrower from exorbitant interest rates. However, as these laws are applied to mortgages, many authorities contend that the end result is more harmful than beneficial. Since mortgage capital tends to be concentrated nationally among the more populous states; namely, the financial capitals of the Northeastern states, these institutions tend to lend money among states providing for the highest rate of return in the light of investment risks.

Hence, it is argued that states with below-market usury rate ceilings discriminate against borrowers. Financial institutions tend to place surplus funds in states that have the least interest rate restrictions. To this extent, borrowers living in communities with restrictive usury laws, must compete for a smaller supply of loanable funds. In this way, usury laws decrease the flow of savings among states with interest rate ceilings.

## Interest Rates on Government-Insured and Guaranteed Loans

Congress establishes the maximum interest rate that may be charged for government-insured and guaranteed loans. In periods of rising interest rates and credit shortage, mortgages subject to these restrictions are discounted. For example, a mortgage with a fixed interest rate of 9 percent, 25 years, $30,000, may be discounted by five points (1 point is equal to 1 percent). This means that a lender would advance $30,000 less five percent of the face value of the mortgage to the borrower— $28,500. In these circumstances the lender advances $28,500 but receives a return based on the face value of the mortgage, $30,000. The discount gives him another source of income. If the mortgage is held for three years, i.e., the property is sold and refinanced, the lender earns an additional return of $500 per year ($1,500/3). In effect, the shorter the time the mortgage is outstanding, the higher the rate of return on the loan.

Assume, for example, that the 25-year mortgage amortized monthly provides for a 9.25 percent interest rate. If the loan is held to maturity and is discounted by five points, the lender earns 9.9 percent interest. If the loan is prepaid in ten years, the effective rate of return increases to 10.09 percent. Mortgage tables have been prepared giving the effective rate of return for different combinations of mortgage terms and discount points.

96

## Mortgages Subject to Loan-to-Value Ratios

Risks associated with real estate investment have led to legislation that restricts long-term mortgages to a maximum percentage of the appraised value. To illustrate, property appraised for $50,000 may legally warrant only a 75 percent loan or a maximum loan of $37,500. Prudent judgment, credit availability, portfolio and yield policies, may justify an even lower loan-to-value ratio.

For each mortgage loan granted, two decisions must be made: (1) Does the prospective loan conform to legal restrictions covering the maximum loan allowable? (2) Is the proposed loan economically justified in view of the present value of the property appraised? As a rule, borrowers tend to be more optimistic and negotiate for the highest possible loan-to-value ratio. The lender in contrast favors the lowest possible loan-to-value ratio. In other instances, loan-to-value ratios may be varied according to the risk associated with the property mortgaged, the interest rate yield, and the availability of credit. Even with favorable projections, the loan-to-value ratio must not exceed the maximum legal ratio.

## Credit of the Borrower

A real estate mortgage pledges real estate as security for a loan. The loan itself is evidenced by a promissory note or other evidence of indebtedness which, in effect, is based on the *personal promise* of the borrower to repay the loan as negotiated. In this respect, the mortgage lender looks to the individual credit of the borrower as further security for the loan. In this instance, the loan assumes characteristics of any other loan except that credit is granted for a long-term period. Mortgages are then characterized by a very careful review of borrower credit, his past repayment record, competence, and financial ability.

## Real Estate Valuation

Because the mortgage pledges real estate as security, a value must be placed on real estate as the basis of the loan. The lender then faces all of the complex problems associated with estimating real estate value: For income property, the estimate of gross income, expenses of operation, capitalization rates; and for residential property, neighborhood trends, the condition of the property and many other factors. Ordinarily these issues must be resolved by trained personnel experienced in judging local real estate values.

## Mortgage Foreclosure Regulations

Mortgage foreclosure laws, which vary widely between states, may affect the decision of lenders to grant loans. Under the laws of most states, the borrower who defaults on a mortgage has a specific time in which to make good his default before the lender exercises his right of foreclosure. For example, after being served with a notice of default, borrowers in Connecticut and Vermont have a set time ranging up to four months in which to redeem property.

In still other states after foreclosed property is sold at a public sale, the borrower is given an additional period (called the statutory right of redemption), to gain full possession of the property by remedying the default and paying certain legal and court costs. States that follow this procedure add to the risk of a long-term mortgage. For example, a lender is prevented from securing full title to the mortgaged property without first instituting foreclosure procedures and waiting for the statutory period of redemption to expire. In the meantime, vandalism, property depreciation, neglect, and a long-standing vacancy adds further to the risk of loss.

# Characteristics of Mortgage Security: Real Estate

Real estate has many unique features not found in such personal property as automobiles, home appliances, or stocks and bonds. It is these features which are responsible for the regulations governing mortgage lending and controlling investments in mortgages by financial institutions. A review of the main differences in real estate relative to other types of assets explains why specialists in real estate finance must learn the requirements of a mortgage operation. The most noteworthy characteristics may be summarized in five points.

1. Real estate is relatively indestructible.
2. Real estate is immobile.
3. Real estate markets are highly stratified.
4. The supply of real estate is relatively fixed in the short run.
5. Real estate is subject to continual modification.

## Indestructibility

To be sure buildings are destroyed by fire and action of the elements, but, relative to other types of property, real estate is long lasting and durable. Consequently, because of its durability it serves as an excellent security for long-term loans. Indeed, a properly maintained building may last over several generations, and, if the building is modernized at periodic intervals, it may serve as security for several mortgages over its economic life.

The indestructibility of real property is not without certain disadvantages. A structure improperly placed or economically unjustified may not be easily destroyed. Thus, blighted neighborhoods and obsolete buildings tend to depreciate surrounding property. However, given favorable growth trends, the indestructibility feature encourages long-term financing.

## Immobility

The immobility of real estate stresses the importance of real estate decisions. Building a 100-unit apartment where such a unit is uneconomical causes losses to the developer, the lender, and the borrower. No one benefits from an inappropriately designed real estate project. A surplus of apartment units in St. Petersburg, Florida, will not relieve housing shortages in New York City. Or, on a local basis, an oversupply of $50,000 to $75,000 houses in the northern part of the city will not meet the market demand for $35,000 to $45,000 houses in the southern part of the community. Real estate operators are not able to move their product to more profitable markets. Consequently, the mortgage lender faces the risk of financing an asset which may prove to be an uneconomical investment in a specific location.

## Stratified Markets

There is no general real estate market. Instead developers consider, for example, the housing market as a local market adapted to the needs of a specific neighborhood. Accordingly, there is a market for new houses in the local community for four-bedroom, three-bath houses and yet another market in another section of the same community for three-bedroom, one-bath houses.

Since real estate markets are subdivided by property type, location, age of property, and value groups, the mortgage analyst must judge mortgage risk for a specific locality. And, because of this characteristic, it is difficult to secure information on the demand and supply of local real estate. In this sense real estate markets may not be interpreted with market information available to buyers and sellers of agricultural products or even common stocks or government bonds.

## Short Run Supply

The time required to develop a new subdivision from the initial land negotiation to the sale of the last single family dwelling usually extends over several years. Or because of the local economic conditions, new housing may be demanded in the short run but the supply may not be increased until several months have passed. Therefore, it is claimed that the relatively fixed supply of real estate leads to short-run price distortions in land, housing rents, and real estate prices. This is another area in which market conditions must be carefully evaluated when judging loan security.

## Modification

As land use changes from agricultural to residential use, from multiple family to office use, and from other less extensive uses to intensive uses, property values substantially change—and to laymen, often unpredictably. Therefore, a structure that seems ideally suited to the site when it is newly built may turn out to be uneconomical for use as the neighborhood changes to more intensive commercial and industrial uses.

This characteristic requires that the mortgage specialist observe growth trends that indicate the possibility of modification. A mortgage placed on a shopping center may show outstanding performance over the first five years, but with the modification of competing space from an agricultural to a shopping center use, the older mortgage may stand in default because of the new competition. This factor introduces risks that must be compensated by lending techniques not found in other types of lending.

# Federal Assistance in Mortgage Markets

Since the 1930 depression, the role of federal agencies in mortgage markets has steadily increased. The reorganization of the Federal National Mortgage Association from a government agency to a private agency, beginning in 1968, and the development of a secondary market for conventional loans further increased the flow of funds into mortgages. These changes have been sufficiently marked to affect institutional lenders and borrowers alike.

## The Impact of Federal Programs

Available data show that at the end of 1975 federal and related agencies own $89,073 million mortgages outstanding, amounting to 12.0 percent of total mortgages outstanding. Of the total mortgages held by federal agencies, approximately 65.6 percent represent 1-4 family dwellings. If multiple family projects are added to this total, some 80.2 percent or approximately four-fifths of mortgages held by federal agencies are for residential properties.

The importance of federal intervention is suggested by Table 6.1 which lists mortgages held by federal agencies and FNMA, 1970–1975. It

**Table 6.1**
**Mortgage Debt Outstanding by Type of Holder: 1970–1975**
(In millions of dollars)

| Type of Holder | 1970 | 1971 | 1972 | 1973 | 1974 | 1975 |
|---|---|---|---|---|---|---|
| Federal National Mortgage Association ........ | $15,502 | $17,791 | $19,791 | $24,175 | $29,178 | $31,824 |
| GNMA Pools ............. | 452 | 3,154 | 5,815 | 9,109 | 13,892 | 21,257 |
| Government National Mortgage Association .... | 5,222 | 5,323 | 5,113 | 4,029 | 4,846 | 7,438 |
| Federal Home Loan Mortgage Corporation .... | 357 | 964 | 1,789 | 2,604 | 4,586 | 4,987 |
| Farmers Home Administration ................ | 767 | 819 | 837 | 1,200 | 1,600 | 2,000 |
| Federal Housing and Veterans Administration .. | 3,505 | 3,389 | 3,338 | 3,476 | 4,015 | 5,004 |
| Federal Land Banks (Farm only) ............. | 7,187 | 7,917 | 9,107 | 11,071 | 13,863 | 16,563 |
| | $32,992 | $39,357 | $45,790 | $55,664 | $72,380 | $89,073 |

Source: *Federal Reserve Bulletin,* March, 1976, p. A42.

will be observed that the Federal National Mortgage Association accounts for a greater share of the agencies listed in Table 6.1—$31,824 or 35.7 percent of the current total. The next most significant agency is represented by Government National Mortgage Association pools accounting for $21,257 million of total mortgages outstanding. If the purchases held by the Government National Mortgage Association are added ($7,438 million), holdings of the Government National Mortgage Association represent 32.2 percent of mortgages listed in Table 6.1 ($28,695 million). The two agencies, FNMA and GNMA, together account for only two-thirds of mortgages held by federal agencies. The Federal Home Loan Mortgage Corporation in the five years of its operation has increased its mortgage portfolio substantially each year. The other specialized agencies, the Farmers Home Administration and the Federal Land Bank, though important in rural and farm areas, are less significant in comparison to other federal agencies. In recent years the mortgages insured or guaranteed and held by the Federal Housing Administration and Veterans Administration have shown a nominal increase, from $3,505 million in 1970 to $5,004 million at the end of 1975.

## The Federal National Mortgage Association

The secondary mortgage operations of FNMA have evolved from a series of changes that started with emergency legislation of the 1930s.

With FHA introducing a standardized procedure for qualifying the mortgage, the mortgagor, and the dwelling, the stage was set for a nation-wide market for government insured loans. However with FHA loans, an instrumentality was needed to purchase government insured mortgages from institutions that originated mortgages.

To fulfill this need, in 1935 the Reconstruction Finance Corporation *result of Depression* established the RFC mortgage company "To assist in the re-establishment of a national mortgage market." Originally confining purchases to loans for new construction and loans on apartment houses, hotels and office buildings, RFC later contracted with FHA to purchase FHA-insured mortgages on residential housing. The purchase of VA-guaranteed mortgages was authorized in 1946.

## The Origin of FNMA

Subsequent events indicated that the RFC Mortgage Company would not have sufficient funds to meet mortgage demands in the housing industry. To meet this need the Federal National Mortgage Association was chartered in 1938. Beginning in 1950 FNMA transferred from the RFC to the Housing and Home Finance Agency—the predecessor of the Housing and Urban Development Department. Legislative revisions, in 1954, separated FNMA secondary mortgage activity into three operations.

1. Privately financed secondary market operations for residential mortgages.
2. Special assistance functions operated exclusively for government with government borrowed funds. This latter function was to support various housing programs sponsored by FHA.
3. Management and liquidating functions for the government account to liquidate and manage mortgages acquired before 1954.

Attention is especially directed to the first principal activity: support of secondary mortgage operations. Here FNMA was specifically directed to "provide supplementary assistance to the Secretary for home mortgages by providing a degree of liquidity for mortgage investments thereby improving the distribution of investment capital available for home mortgage financing. . . . " In other words FNMA was required to purchase mortgages within the range of market prices for a given class of mortgages. The philosophy of FNMA operations was expressed by directives that required mortgage purchase prices and sale prices "effected only at such prices and on such terms as will reasonably prevent excessive use of the corporation's facilities. . . ." In all of these activities this portion of FNMA was intended to be self-supporting.

These directives assumed that secondary mortgage operations were activities that could be guided by the private not the public sector. This goal was finally achieved in the 1968 reorganization.

### The FNMA Charter Act of 1968

*[handwritten: Control by govt : 5 board mem appt by prez / secty Hud / borrow from Treasury]*

Under the Housing and Urban Development Act of 1968, FNMA assumed its present status as a private corporation. The new charter provided for a 15 member board of directors, ten elected annually by stockholders and five appointed by the President of the United States. Its operations are administered by the board elected president who acts as chief executive officer.

Although a private organization, the corporation is regulated by the federal government through the Secretary of Housing and Urban Development. The Secretary is empowered to examine and audit the books of the corporation.

To finance the purchase of mortgages, FNMA depends largely on borrowed capital. And, although FNMA is authorized to issue short-term discount notes to buyers of commercial paper with maturities ranging from 30 to 270 days, its principal method of borrowing is *[handwritten: full faith & credit]* through the issuance of debentures *[handwritten: notes]* which are longer-term obligations —1 to 25 years. To supplement private borrowing, FNMA is also authorized to borrow from the U.S. Treasury, which is permitted to purchase up to $2.25 billion of FNMA obligations. The Treasury has not exercised this option, but it serves as an important potential source of capital if funds cannot be raised privately. Other funds are gained by the official requirement that sellers of mortgages to FNMA are required to buy FNMA stock. A line of credit of $400 million by a group of banks provides additional flexibility in the event of adverse financial conditions. In 1970, the corporation also issued stock available for sale to the public increasing the FNMA capital base by some $50 million. Earnings from fees, income from investments, and sales of its portfolio supply additional sources of capital.

### The Current Role of FNMA

The current role of FNMA is best understood by reviewing operations of the private mortgage market. With this background, steps that FNMA takes under conditions of monetary restraint and credit ease indicate how FNMA provides for a constant flow of mortgage funds.

*The mortgage credit market*

The central problem of the mortgage market arises from cyclical shortages of mortgage funds that affect thrift institutions equally. In periods of tight credit, savings available for mortgage lending decline among the main thrift institutions. At the same time mortgage lenders, with considerable portfolio flexibility, shift to higher yielding security markets during periods of tight credit. The purpose of a secondary market facility is to mitigate cyclical mortgage credit.

Mortgage funds for residential mortgages tend to be concentrated among thrift institutions, commercial banks, mutual savings banks, and savings and loan associations. Historically, they have accounted for 70 to 80 percent of total residential financing. Life insurance companies, which are highly yield conscious, tend to shift funds from mortgages to security markets as yields on mortgages decline relative to other assets.

Compounding these difficulties are the imperfections inherent in mortgage markets: First, the *need* for mortgage funds tends to be concentrated in developing areas like the South and the far West. Second, the *supply* of capital concentrates in financial centers of the Northeastern states. The discrepancy between capital availability and capital need has created a demand for the specialized services of the mortgage banker who originates loans in capital shortage areas for out-of-state investors with surplus funds.

The mortgage bankers are highly dependent on a secondary mortgage market. They originate loans and sell mortgages to institutional buyers, securing income in origination fees and fees for servicing a mortgage portfolio. Because they have little capital (mortgage bankers do not accept deposits), they are dependent on interim financing and the ready sale of blocks of mortgages to private or government investors who operate exclusively in the secondary mortgage market. Because of the improved secondary market in conventional FHA and VA loans, large scale investors such as pension funds are less dependent on mortgage banker operations.

### Periods of tight credit

During periods of tight credit, yields on financial securities increase. With restrictions on interest payable to depositors, savings flow from the thrift institutions to open market investments. While the savings in thrift institutions decline, other institutions with investment alternatives such as commercial banks, mutual savings banks, and insurance companies, transfer funds to nonmortgage investments. This leaves mortgage bankers and others who rely on the secondary market for permanent mortgage placement short of funds. In recent times the Federal National Mortgage Association has served as the traditional source of secondary market capital.

Suppose, for example, that a mortgage banker originates a mortgage. While he may secure short-term bank financing, eventually he must sell the mortgage to an investor so he may raise funds to finance additional mortgage originations. Hopefully, he sells to commercial banks, mutual savings banks, insurance companies, pension funds and the like. If these sources are unavailable, he may turn to FNMA, though he must pay a fee for the commitment from FNMA. Because of the commitment fee, the mortgage banker prefers to sell to other private investors. Consequently, FNMA may be regarded as a residual supplier of funds in the private mortgage market.

*Periods of credit ease*

If in the judgment of policy makers, credit conditions encourage an excess flow of funds into mortgage markets, FNMA may act to minimize the flow of funds going to mortgages by selling its portfolio. Sales are induced by manipulating the price of mortgages. By selling, FNMA absorbs funds that would normally flow into the private mortgage market. In this way FNMA tends to smooth out peaks in the cycle of mortgage activity.

## FNMA Operations

A review of FNMA operations bears out the prime role that FNMA plays in evening out the cyclical availability of mortgage credit. After the 1954 charter, purchases by FNMA reached $648 million by the end of 1956. Under the tight credit conditions of 1957, the new corporation purchased $1 billion in new mortgages. The following year sales exceeded purchases. With the restrictive credit conditions that began in 1959, FNMA again increased its portfolio to over $850 million, which was almost 9 percent of single family mortgage money. In the next three years FNMA again became a consistent seller of mortgages. By 1965 FNMA purchased heavily to offset tight credit conditions.

Under the extreme credit conditions of 1966, FNMA purchased over $2 billion worth of mortgages, almost doubling their portfolio in one year. By this move FNMA accounted for some 13 percent of home mortgages in 1966. Continued heavy purchases in 1967, 1968, and 1969 increased FNMA's portfolio to $16 billion, and then doubled to $32 billion by the end of 1975. In 1970 FNMA accounted for 25 percent of home mortgage financing, but only 7 percent in 1973, the year of FNMA's record $7 billion in purchases, reflecting a much higher increase in total mortgages outstanding.

## GNMA Programs Administered by FNMA

Under present law the Secretary of HUD by regulation may require "that a reasonable portion of the corporation's mortgage purchases" be related to the housing needs of low and moderate income families. Such purchases may be undertaken to provide a reasonable economic return to the corporation. Current programs in FNMA accomplishing these purposes include various types of tandem agreements with GNMA.

*Program 16*

This program includes only mortgages insured under FHA. Under Section 235 (j), which subsidizes lower income families in buying dwellings or cooperative housing, projects underway are eligible for FNMA commitments at the same price applying to nonsubsidized FHA commitments and purchases. If the GNMA has made a commitment to purchase these mortgages at a higher price, GNMA underwrites the loss.

*Program 17*

The two programs insured by FHA, calling for rent subsidies (Section 221(d)) or mortgage interest subsidies (Section 236), are purchased by FNMA under a price formula determined by taking the greater of (a) prices for the multifamily standby, or (b) the current over-the-counter price. FNMA has established a preferential price 2.75 percent above its regular price of the first $1 billion of such mortgages purchased in any one year.

*Program 18*

This program provides an interest subsidy to low and moderate income families purchasing single family dwellings (Section 235). Prices charged by FNMA on Program 18 mortgages produce yields equivalent to the average yield obtained by FNMA at the current four month free market auction.

*Program 19*

A relatively unimportant program in terms of volume, Program 19 provides for the purchase of multiple family mortgages insured by FHA and certified by HUD as part of an Operation Breakthrough prototype project. Pricing policies of Program 17 and 18 also apply to this program.

*Program 20*

This program covers both one to four family and multiple family mortgages in GNMA. FNMA accepts the assignment of these mortgages from GNMA at the prices comparable to regular FHA commitments.

*Programs 21 and 22*

Initiated in 1971, these programs give added support to FHA-VA housing mortgages. They are designed to support the market price of these
mortgages in periods of tight credit by supporting above market commitment prices by GNMA. To encourage the private purchase of these
mortgages, GNMA agrees to sell commitments to the commitment
holder at a price below the price at which GNMA has agreed to pay.
FNMA serves only as the administrator and warehousing source. The
price subsidy is assumed by GNMA.

## Government National Mortgage Association  *controlled by HUD*

*acquire $$ thru appropriations of US Govt  ① provide support for low & moderate income ho*
*② help FNMA reduce cyclical change in mortgage fu*

The main activity of GNMA in seeking new sources of mortgage credit *availabit*
lies in the authority of GNMA to issue guaranteed "pass-through"
mortgage backed securities. First initiated in 1970, these securities were
directed to pension and retirement funds for private placement. The
guarantee of the full faith and credit of the federal government was es-
sential to attract state and municipal retirement funds into the mortgage
market. The security, though backed by mortgages, eliminated the docu-
mentation and paper work involved in a series of individual mortgages.

### Security Regulations     *" guarantee corporation "*

Institutions participating in the GNMA guaranteed pass-through
securities must comply with certain basic regulations. (Mortgage
backed securities are especially attractive to pension funds which have
been growing at an annual rate of 12 percent and are expected to ex-
ceed the total assets of traditional mortgage lenders.) At the time pass-
through securities were issued, pension funds invested less than 5 per-
cent of their assets in mortgages. Regulations are tailored to compete
with bonds and other securities that require no servicing facilities or
servicing costs. The main regulations may be summarized in six points.

(1) Any FHA mortgagee or joint group of mortgagees in good stand-
ing and possessing a net worth of not less than $100,000 are eligible. In
no case must the net worth exceed $250,000. Any state or local govern-
ment or instrumentality may also qualify.

(2) The mortgage pool backing securities must be originated no
more than 12 months before the date of issue and must total at least
$1 million.

(3) To guard against the outflow of dollars from thrift institutions,
the original securities were offered in minimum amounts of $50,000
with additional increments to be offered at $10,000. In 1970 the mini-
mum offering was limited to $25,000.

(4) Securities pay interest rates equivalent to the VA or FHA mortgages less a servicing fee calculated at $\frac{1}{2}$ percent lower than the interest rate on the underlying mortgage. While final yield terms are negotiated between issuer and the investor, security prices are adjusted to produce competitive yields.

(5) The issuer services all mortgages that comprise the pool and is responsible for making payments to the investor.

(6) Theoretically, the securities could be issued for as long as 20 years. But since 20 and 30 year mortgages are subject to prepayment, both issues are of shorter duration.

With the adoption of these regulations, the first securities were placed with three New Jersey pension funds early in 1970 issued by Associated Mortgage Companies of Washington, D.C., and New York City. The $2 million pool consisted of FHA and VA single family dwelling mortgages amortized from 20 to 30 years. An average yield of $8\frac{1}{2}$ percent and a contract rate of 8 percent was carried by the pool. Securities were issued at a price of 94.75 producing an effective yield of 8.5 percent if held to maturity, or 8.75 percent if prepaid in 12 years.

## Types of Securities

The issue of securities authorized by GNMA may be the "straight pass-through," or the "fully modified" security. Under the straight pass-through security, the amortized interest and principal is passed straight through from the borrower to the investor less servicing costs of $\frac{1}{2}$ percent. In the event of delinquencies, funds are not available and are not passed through.

The fully modified pass-through security guarantees a fixed monthly payment of amortized principal and interest. The principal is determined by an amortization schedule for the entire mortgage pool while interest is computed on the unpaid principal balance. Mortgages in default are processed by the issuer by paying the principal balance to the investor and adjusting the payment schedule accordingly. The issuer in turn, turns to FHA-VA foreclosure procedures. If massive defaults occur, GNMA takes over the pool and takes responsibility for making cash payments to the investor.

## Federal Home Loan Mortgage Corporation Don't worry about!

First authorized by the Emergency Home Finance Act of 1970, the agency has been popularly called "Freddie Mac," although it is officially referred to as The Mortgage Corporation.

Initially the agency held a portfolio of $2.5 billion and outstanding commitments to purchase mortgages of $0.2 billion as of December

1973. The portfolio increased to approximately $4.5 billion by December 1974, with commitments outstanding of $2.4 billion. This substantial increase was aided by a $3 billion Federal Special Forward Program which began in May 1974. The program authorized The Mortgage Corporation to issue forward commitments for conventional home loans at a subsidized rate of 8.75 percent for a term up to one year. The portfolio again increased in 1975 to approximately $5 billion, 65 percent of which consisted of conventional mortgages. This relatively modest increase in the portfolio followed because The Mortgage Corporation in 1975 sold more than $1 billion in conventional mortgage-backed instruments.

The Mortgage Corporation purchases conventional home mortgages under two programs: The *Home Loan Program* and the *Class B Participation Program*. Under the first plan, loans are purchased outright in groups totalling at least $100,000 and not more than $5,000,000. In the latter program, undivided interests of 50 to 85 percent in a pool of loans are purchased with a minimum contract of $100,000 and a maximum of $5,000,000. At the present time no mortgage may be included in either program above $55,000. These mortgages may be on one to four family dwellings, including units in condominium or planned unit development projects. Also in 1975, The Mortgage Corporation, as agent for GNMA, purchased $1.2 billion of mortgages under the GNMA/FHLMC Conventional Home Mortgage Program. The Mortgage Corporation will continue to purchase mortgages under this program through November 1976 and approximately $700 million of commitments were outstanding in mid-1976.

The yield at which The Mortgage Corporation purchases mortgages under both programs is quoted as a *required net yield* to The Mortgage Corporation. Sellers add an additional servicing fee to The Mortgage Corporation's net yield, and receive the amount of interest on each mortgage that is in excess of The Mortgage Corporation's required net yield. If The Mortgage Corporation, for example, quotes a yield of 9.5 percent, then the home mortgage rate (coupon rate) would be 9⅞ percent (assuming a ⅜ percent service fee).

The Mortgage Corporation sells mortgages principally by means of Mortgage Participation Certificates (PCs) and Guaranteed Mortgage Certificates.

## Mortgage participation certificates

PCs are sold each business day through The Mortgage Corporation's five regional offices in Arlington, Va., Atlanta, Chicago, Dallas, and Los Angeles, in denominations of $100,00, $200,000, $500,000 and $1 million. Each PC represents an undivided interest in conventional mortgages individually underwritten and previously purchased by The Mortgage Corporation. PCs were first sold in 1971 and more than $1.4 billion worth were sold through 1975. PCs qualify as mortgage investments for certain tax and regulatory purposes applicable to thrift institutions.

In short The Mortgage Corporation supports a secondary market in PCs by acting as transfer agent and registrar; PCs are freely transferable. The Mortgage Corporation passes through to each certificate holder every month a pro rata share of the principal payments collected on the mortgages in the underlying pool, including prepayments, and interest on the outstanding balance. The corporation guarantees the timely payment of interest at the certificate rate and the full return of principal regardless of the status of the underlying loans.

### Guaranteed mortgage certificates

GMCs are sold through a selected group of securities dealers managed by the Office of Finance of the Federal Home Loan Bank System. Each GMC represents an *undivided interest* in conventional residential mortgages individually underwritten and previously purchased by The Mortgage Corporation. Structured to meet the needs of investors who do not traditionally invest in mortgages, GMCs return principal once a year in guaranteed minimum amounts regardless of the status of the underlying mortgages. Interest is paid semiannually.

GMCs are sold in fully registered form in initial principal amounts of $100,000, $500,000 and $1 million. The first two issues of GMCs, totaling $500 million, were sold in 1975. In February 1976, $200 million in GMCs were issued at 8.55 percent.

In sum, three agencies participate in secondary mortgage market operations: FNMA, GNMA, and The Mortgage Corporation. Their programs relate to conventional loans at market rates of interest, subsidized programs with conventional loans, and VA and FHA loans which include market rate and subsidized mortgages. The regulations governing loans that qualify, the maximum interest rate, the term maximum loan-to-value ratios, and commitment terms vary under each program. For convenience, these programs are summarized in Table 6.2.

## Federal Housing Administration

Like many of the other institutions operating in the mortgage market, the Federal Housing Administration has undergone a change in philosophy and operation since its formation under the National Housing Act of 1934. Indeed, the early policies of FHA had a permanent im-

# Table 6.2
# Secondary Mortgage Market Programs

*Conventional Loans: Market Rate Programs*

| | Qualifying Loans | Maximum Mortgage | Term | Maximum Loan/Value | Maximum Age | Commitment Period | Rate at Which Purchased | Fees | Servicer's Fees |
|---|---|---|---|---|---|---|---|---|---|
| Mortgage Corp. 60-day whole loan | Conventional new or existing 1-family, condo, or 2- to 4-family homes within same state as lender or 100 miles of lender's principal office. | $55k up to 90%. $40k over 90%. Higher for 2- to 4-family. Second mortgages permitted. | up to 30 years. | 80% without private mortgage insurance (PMI). 95% with PMI on amount over 75%. | No Limit | Mandatory delivery within 60 days after purchase contract acceptance. | Yield set periodically by FHLMC. See Thursday WSJ. | .5% for non-members only originating bank's fee approximately 2%. | Same as Participation |
| Class B Participation | Same type of housing as above. Also, up to 50% of amount of pool may be multifamily. FHLMC buys 50-85% undivided interest in pool. | $55k up to 90%. $40k over 90%. Higher for 2- to 4-family. Second mortgages permitted. | up to 30 years. | 80% without private mortgage insurance (PMI). 95% with PMI on amount over 75%. | No Limit | Mandatory delivery within 60 days after purchase contract acceptance. | Yield set periodically by Mortgage Corp. See Thursday WSJ. | .5% for non-members only originating bank's fee approximately 2%. | Spread between interest rec. on mtgs. and required net yield. |
| FNMA 4 mos | New and existing conventional, 1-family detached, or condominium with project commitment approval. | $55k up to 90%. $40k over 90%. No second mortgages allowed. | up to 30 years. | 80% without private mortgage insurance (PMI). 95% with PMI on amount over 75%. 90% limit for condos. | 1 year | 4 mos. Optional delivery | Determined by free market system auction for conventional mortgages. | .5% for home loans, and for condo loans not delivered. ⅛% additional for condo loans when delivered. .01% additional if competitive bid. $1500 for condo project approval originating bank's fees approximately 2%. Stock subscription of ¼% of commitment. | ⅜% |

112

| 1 year | New and existing conventional, 1-family detached or condominium with project commitment approval. | $55k up to 90%. $40k over 90%. No second mortgages allowed. | up to 30 years. | 80% without private mortgage insurance (PMI). 95% with PMI on amount over 75%. 90% limit for condos. | 90 days | 1 year. Optional delivery; convertible to free market system yield.* | Determined periodically by FNMA for conventional mortgages. Convertible to FMS yield.* | .51% for home loans not delivered. .5% additional for home loans when delivered. ⅜% for condo loans when delivered. $1500 for condo project approval, new construction; origination; originating bank's fees approximately 2%. Stock subscription of ¼% of commitment. | ⅜% |
|---|---|---|---|---|---|---|---|---|---|

### Conventional Loans: Subsidized Programs

| GNMA/ Mortgage Corp. and GNMA/ FNMA | Conventional, 1-family completed since 10/18/73. However, 10% may be existing homes. No condominiums. | $42k. No second mortgage allowed. | 25 to 30 years. | 80% or up to 95% with PMI. | Subsequent to date of commitment contract. | 12 mos. Optional delivery. Extendable for 3 mos. | Commitment rate determined monthly according to government's cost of borrowing. Initially 8½%, then 8¼%, 8%, and 7¾%. | 1.01% nonrefundable commitment and processing fee. 1½% loss reserve and marketing fee at closing. Originating bank limited to: 1 point commitment fee half by builder; 2 points origination fee at closing/half by buyer. No nonmember fee. | ⅜% |
|---|---|---|---|---|---|---|---|---|---|

* Commitment may be converted to free market system average yield at any time after 4 months. Whole balance must be converted and will expire 4 months later or at end of regular commitment period, if sooner.

*FHA and VA: Market Rate and Subsidized Programs*

| FHA/VA Single | Qualifying Loans | Maximum Mortgage | Term | Maximum Loan/ Value | Max- imum Age | Commit- ment Period | Rate at Which Purchased | Fees | Ser- vicer's Fees |
|---|---|---|---|---|---|---|---|---|---|
| Mortgage Corp. | FHA/VA. New 1- to 4-family pri- mary homes and condominiums within 100 miles of an office of the lender. | FHA limit. $50k for VA. | Must comply with FHA or VA requirements. | | No Limit | Mandatory de- livery within 60 days after pur- chase contract acceptance. | Price set pe- riodically by Mortgage Corp. See Thursday WSJ. | Fee set by Mortgage Corp. (½ %) for non- members only. | ⅜ % |
| FNMA 4 mos. | New and existing FHA/VA. 1- to 4- family homes and condominiums. | FHA limit. $50k for VA. | Must comply with FHA or VA requirements. | | 1 year | 4 mos. Option- al delivery. | Determined by free market system auction for FHA/VA mortgages. | ½ % for home loans and for condominium loans not de- livered. .01% additional if competitive bid, originating bank's fees ap- proximately 2% stock sub- scription of ¼ % of com- mitment. | ⅜ % |
| 1 year | New and existing FHA/VA. 1-to 4- family homes and condominiums. | FHA limit. $50k for VA. | Must comply with FHA or VA requirements. | | 90 days | 1 year. Option- al delivery; convertible to free market system yield.* | Determined pe- riodically by FNMA for FHA/VA mort- gages; conver- tible to free market system yield.* | .51% if loan not delivered. .5% additional for home loans when delivered. Originating bank's fees ap- proximately 2%. Stock sub- scription of ¼ % of com- mitment. | ⅜ % |

114

GNMA

| Program | Eligible properties | Loan amount / rate | Loan requirements | Commitment origination | Commitment period | Delivery / yield | Fees | Pass-through rate |
|---|---|---|---|---|---|---|---|---|
| | FHA and VA, 1- to 4-family homes and condominiums. | | Must comply with FHA or VA requirements. | | | Discounted to provide yield necessary to market the pool. | .04% annually for straight pass-through. .06% annually for modified pass-through. $500 application fee. | .375% straight pass-through. .44% modified pass-through. |
| Special Assistance (tandem) #22 | FHA and VA, 1- to 4-family homes and condos, new or completed within 15 mos. before commitment and never owner-occupied. | $33k at 7¾% or 8%. $38k at 8¼% an extra $2.5k is allowed for 4 BR units. | Must comply with FHA or VA requirements. | Originated after commitment. | 1 year. Extendable for 3 mcs. for extra ⅛% fee or unused commitment. | 98% at applicable interest rate. | .51% commitment and processing fee. 2% discount (indicated at left) when delivered. Originating bank's fees approximately 2%. | ⅜% |

* Commitment may be converted to free market system average yield at any time after 4 months. Whole balance must be converted and will expire 4 months later or at end of regular commitment period, if sooner.

Source: Reprinted with permission from *Real Estate Review*, Summer 1975, Volume 5, Number 2, Copyright 1975, Warren, Gorham, and Lamont, Inc., 210 South St., Boston, Mass. All Rights Reserved. The table has been adjusted slightly to reflect review comments received from The Mortgage Corporation.

pact on the mortgage industry. FHA set the stage for an orderly real estate mortgage market by introducing standard mortgage underwriting practices. The contributions of FHA in this direction may be summarized in the following points:

* 1. FHA introduced the monthly payment amortized mortgage, providing for the periodic repayment of principal. The amortized mortgage became the industry standard replacing the term mortgage.

* 2. FHA substituted a single high loan-to-value ratio mortgage for a high equity, first and second mortgage combination— with lower interest costs.

* 3. By establishing minimum standards of construction for FHA insured houses, FHA reduced the risk of lending money on single-family dwellings.

* 4. FHA introduced standard appraisal procedures with the result that lenders looked more to the value of real estate and less to the borrower's credit as loan security.

* 5. Standard procedures were introduced to judge mortgage risks, including the interaction of borrower credit and real estate in relation to mortgage terms.

The combined effect of these procedures stabilized mortgage interest rates nationally and provided for the flow of mortgage money from capital surplus areas to areas of capital shortage. Practices introduced by FHA have become common mortgage underwriting procedures.

Initially, the Federal Housing Administration was viewed as a temporary device to increase employment in the building trades. The principle of insurance was covered by Title 1 of the act which provided for home improvement loans for five years, and by Title 2 which provided for long term, amortized mortgages. Subsequent statutory authority under which FHA operates directs the agency "to encourage improvement in housing standards and conditions, to facilitate sound home financing on reasonable terms, and to exert a stabilizing influence in the mortgage market" (Thirteenth Annual Report of the Housing and Home Finance Agency, 1959). The *Housing and Community Development Act of 1974* changed the orientation of housing programs to meet primary objectives of the 1974 Act:

> . . . the development of viable urban communities, by providing decent housing and a suitable living environment and expanding economic opportunities, principally for persons of low and moderate income. . . .

FHA with other federal agencies serve these primary objectives. As a result of the 1974 legislation long established FHA programs have been discontinued and others have gained increased emphasis. A review of FHA policies precedes an explanation of FHA underwriting policies.

116

## Mutual Mortgage Insurance

By the end of the first year of operation, some 8,046 institutions had applied for and received approval as FHA lenders. The long-term monthly amortized mortgage became firmly established. FHA succeeded in shifting mortgage funds from communities with surplus capital to communities with a capital shortage. Construction practices improved, standard appraisal methods were introduced, and minimum property standards were enforced. In 1935, 31 percent of new building permits for one- to four-family structures were for FHA loans. These results were largely due to the mutual mortgage insurance programs.

Under the 1934 Housing Act, mutual mortgage insurance funds provided a pool from which to pay insurance claims. Each mortgage insured by FHA required the borrower to pay an insurance premium of 1/2 of 1 percent of the principal balance outstanding at the time of payment. Such a fund operates to the benefit of the lender who is assured of receiving cash or debentures if the loan is in default. Since 1965 the Secretary of HUD has the option of paying insurance claims in cash or debentures. Currently claims for all single family and several multiple family programs primarily directed toward low to moderate income programs are paid in cash. Claims under most other multiple family programs are paid in debentures. The debentures issued by FHA have a 20 year maturity at an interest rate equivalent to rates on comparable treasury bonds prevailing at the time the mortgage insurance was committed.

In operation, the lender is required to report to FHA all loans which are in default for 60 days. If the default continues for 12 months, the lender is required to institute foreclosure proceedings unless FHA approves an extension. In the absence of renegotiation of the loan, the property is sold at a foreclosure sale. If the amount realized is less than the unpaid balance of the debt, the lender is expected to bid for the property.

*[handwritten margin note: ...day, FHA pays mortgage in lender FHA fore- ...ses.]*

In taking title of the property at foreclosure the lender presents a claim to FHA, transferring title to FHA in return for the debentures or cash equal in value to the outstanding mortgage.

*[handwritten margin note: Total insurance pkg. All principle, interest, costs related to foreclosure. will be covered.]*

## FHA Programs

From a program that insured residential property on a market interest basis, Congress added programs serving special purpose projects and numerous subsidized programs for low and moderate income families. A list of the current programs shows how FHA has changed its emphasis. It is well to remember however, that insurance availability depends upon Congressional appropriations to support the authorized programs.

## TABLE 6.3

## FHA Mortgage Insurance Programs

*Title I*

*Section 2.* (Authorized in 1934)
*Property Improvements.* Insurance of approved lending institutions against loss on loans (usually made without collateral) to alter, repair, improve, or convert existing structures or to build small new nonresidential structures. The insurance protection on an individual loan is limited to 90 percent of the lender's loss on the loan. The maximum loan amount is $10,000 for improving a one-family dwelling or building a nonresidential structure. For improving a multifamily structure, the maximum loan amount is $5,000 per unit, but not to exceed $25,000 altogether.

*Mobile Homes* (Authorized in 1969)
Insurance of approved lending institutions against loss on loans used to purchase mobile home units by buyers intending to use them as their principal residence. The maximum amount of the loan is $12,500 ($20,000 if two or more modules are to be financed).

*Title II*

*Section 203(b).* (Authorized in 1934)
Insurance of mortgages on proposed, under construction, or existing one- to four-family dwellings. The maximum mortgage amounts are as follows: $45,000 on a one-family property; $48,750 on a two- or three-family property; and $56,000 on a four-family property.

*Section 203(h).* (Authorized in 1954)
Insurance of mortgages to finance the acquisition of proposed, under construction, or existing one-family housing by an occupant-mortgagor who is a victim of a major disaster. The maximum mortgage amount is $14,400 and the loan-to-value ratio is 100 percent of the HUD-FHA estimate of property value and closing costs.

*Section 203(i).* (Authorized in 1954)
Insurance of mortgages to finance the purchase of proposed, under construction, or existing one-family housing in outlying areas or farm housing on five or more acres adjacent to a highway. The maximum mortgage amount is $16,200.

*Section 203(k).* (Authorized in 1961)
Insurance of loans to finance the alteration, repair, or improvement of existing one- to four-family housing located outside urban renewal areas. The maximum insurable loan on a single-family structure is $12,000 or up to $17,400 in high cost areas.

*Section 207.* (Authorized in 1934)
Insurance of mortgages used to finance the construction or rehabilitation of rental housing with eight or more units, and on mobile home parks.

118

**TABLE 6.3** *continued*

*Section 213.* (Authorized in 1950)
Insurance of mortgages to finance the construction or rehabilitation of cooperative housing projects consisting of five or more units.

*Section 220.* (Authorized in 1954)
Insurance of mortgages to finance the purchase or rehabilitation of one to eleven family housing and multifamily projects of two or more units located in approved urban renewal areas, concentrated code enforcement areas, and urban areas receiving rehabilitation assistance as a result of natural disaster.

*Section 221(d)(2).* (Authorized in 1954)
Insurance of mortgages to finance the purchase or rehabilitation of low-cost one- to four-family housing for families displaced by urban renewal or other governmental action, and for other low- and moderate-income families.

*Section 221(d)(3).* (Authorized in 1954)
Insurance of market-rate mortgages on unsubsidized multifamily rental and cooperative housing for low- and moderate-income families and families displaced by urban renewal or other governmental action. Eligible sponsors include public, nonprofit, cooperative, builder-seller, investor-sponsor, and limited distribution mortgagors.

*Section 221 (d)(4).* (Authorized in 1959)
Insurance of mortgages for general mortgagors (profit motivated) on multifamily rental housing for low- and moderate-income families, with priority given to those displaced by urban renewal or other governmental action.

*Section 222.* (Authorized in 1954)
Insurance of mortgages on single-family homes purchased for their own occupancy by persons on active duty with the Armed Forces or Coast Guard or serving in the U. S. National Oceanic and Atmospheric Administration who obtain eligibility certificates from the branch of the Service to which they are attached.

*Section 223(a), (b), and (c).* (Authorized in 1954)
Insurance of miscellaneous type mortgages, refinancing of existing mortgages, or insurance of mortgages on specified types of permanent housing sold by Federal or State Governments.

*Section 223(d).* (Authorized in 1961)
Insurance of mortgages to cover the excess of expenses over project gross income incurred during the first two years following the date of completion of the project.

*Section 223(e).* (Authorized in 1968)
Insurance of mortgages used to finance the purchase or rehabilitation of housing located in older, declining urban areas.

*Section 223(f).* (Authorized in 1974)
Insurance of mortgages used to finance the purchase of or to refinance an existing multifamily housing project.

119

**TABLE 6.3** *continued*

*Section 225.* (Authorized in 1954)
Insurance of additional advances under an open-end provision in a mortgage insured under any section of the National Housing Act on a one- to four-family home, when the advances are made to finance repairs or improvements to the property.

*Section 231.* (Authorized in 1959)
Insurance of mortgages on new or rehabilitated housing projects with eight or more units designed for occupancy by elderly or handicapped individuals.

*Section 232.* (Authorized in 1959)
Insurance of mortgages to finance the construction or rehabilition of nursing or intermediate care facilities, or a combined nursing home and intermediate care facility, accommodating 20 or more patients who are in need of skilled nursing home care and/or minimum but continuous care by licensed or trained personnel.

*Section 233.* (Authorized in 1961)
Insurance of mortgages to finance the construction or rehabilitation of single-family housing and multifamily projects that incorporate new or untried construction concepts designed to reduce housing costs, raise living standards, and improve neighborhood design.

*Section 234.* (Authorized in 1961)
Insurance of project and home mortgages on condominiums (a family unit in a multifamily structure or multifamily development of individual houses, and an undivided interest in the common areas and facilities that serve the structure).

*Section 235.* (Authorized in 1968)
Insurance of mortgages coupled with interest reduction payments to enable lower-income families to purchase new or substantially rehabilitated single-family dwellings or condominium units approved prior to beginning of construction or beginning of substantial rehabilitation. This program was included in the overall suspension on January 5, 1973, of the subsidized housing programs, and was reactivated, with major revisions, in January 1976.

*Section 236.* (Authorized in 1968)
Insurance of mortgages on rental and cooperative projects coupled with interest reduction payments to make possible lower rents, within the financial reach of low- and moderate-income families, including the elderly or handicapped. This program was included in the overall suspension on January 5, 1973, of the subsidized housing programs. Except as necessary to meet bona fide commitments which cannot be met under the Section 8 Lower Income Housing Assistance program, commitments for additional projects will not be made under the program.

*Section 237.* (Authorized in 1968)
Insurance of mortgages used to finance the purchase of new, existing, or substantially rehabilitated single-family homes by low-income families who, for reasons of credit history, irregular income patterns caused by seasonal employment, or other factors, are unable to meet normal FHA credit requirements.

**TABLE 6.3** *continued*

*Rent Supplement Program.* (Authorized in 1965)
Insurance of mortgages on new or substantially rehabilitated rental housing coupled with a rent supplement paid to the private project owner. Assistance covers the difference between the tenant's payment and the market rental, but may not exceed 70 percent of the market rental. This program was included in the overall suspension on January 5, 1973, of the subsidized housing programs. Except as necessary to meet bona fide commitments which cannot be met under the Section 8 Lower Income Housing Assistance program, commitments for additional projects will not be made under this program.

*Section 240.* (Authorized in 1968)
Insurance of mortgages for homeowners to purchase fee simple title to property which is held under long-term leases and on which their homes are located.

*Section 241.* (Authorized in 1968)
Insurance of supplemental loans for alterations, repairs, additions, or improvements to any multifamily housing project financed with an FHA-insured mortgage. Loan proceeds may be used to finance the purchase of equipment to be used in the operation of a nursing home or group practice facility.

*Section 242.* (Authorized in 1968)
Insurance of mortgages to finance the construction or rehabilitation of private non-profit and proprietary hospitals, including major movable equipment.

*Section 244.* (Authorized in 1974)
Coinsurance of mortgages by HUD and FHA-approved private lenders, whereby losses will be shared in the event of default on a 90%-10% basis, respectively. Mortgagees will also be compensated with a portion of premium income commensurate with the extent of risk exposure which they bear on the transaction. In addition, the program provides for the delegation to mortgagees of the evaluation, credit underwriting, and property disposition functions which would otherwise be performed by HUD staff.

*Title VIII*

*Section 809.* (Authorized in 1956)
Insurance of mortgages on homes built for sale to civilian employees at or near research or development installations of the Department of Defense, NASA, AEC, or their contractors.

*Section 810* (Authorized in 1959)
Insurance of mortgages on off-base housing for military or essential civilian personnel of the Armed Services, NASA, or AEC, or employees of contractors thereof. Congressional approval in an annual military construction authorization act is required prior to issuance of a commitment for projects located near military bases.

**TABLE 6.3** *continued*

*Title X* (Authorized in 1965)

Insurance of mortgages to finance the purchase of land and development of building sites for subdivisions or new communities, including water and sewage systems, streets, and other utilities.

*Title XI.* (Authorized in 1966)

Insurance of mortgages to be used to finance the construction or rehabilitation of group practice facilities, including major movable equipment, for group practice of dentistry, medicine, optometry, osteopathy, or podiatry.

*Other Non-insured HUD Programs*
*Section 8.* (Authorized in 1974)
Provides housing assistance payments to permit participating owners, developers and Public Housing Agencies to provide decent, safe and sanitary housing for lower-income families in private accommodations at rents they can afford. The program is designed to promote economically mixed housing through existing, newly constructed, and substantially rehabilitated housing.

*Section 202.* (Authorized in 1959, amended in 1974)
Provides direct loans which may be used to finance the construction or rehabilitation of rental or cooperative housing and related facilities (such as central dining) for the elderly and handicapped.

*Indian Housing.* (Authorized in 1937, amended in 1974)
Provides annual contributions to Indian Housing Authorities to assist in financing the development or acquisition cost of low-income housing projects for Indian families.

*Section 518(a).* (Authorized in 1964)
Authorizes assistance to owners of new one- to four-family dwellings approved for mortgage insurance prior to the beginning of construction, where such dwellings are found to have major structural defects or defects which threaten the structural components of the dwellings.

*Section 518 (b).* (Authorized in 1970, amended in 1974)
Authorizes assistance to owners of existing one- to four-family dwellings when such housing is determined to require correction of structural or other major defects which so seriously affect the use and livability as to create a serious danger to the life or safety of the inhabitants.

Source: Furnished by FHA July 1976.

A review of Table 6.3 clearly indicates that FHA has progressed from an insurance program that initially insured mortgages for the benefit of the lender to a more socially-oriented program. From an orientation directed to reducing the lender's risk, FHA has developed into a series of programs that promote programs considered beneficial to the community interest, i.e., nursing homes, medical clinics, housing for the elderly, subsidized low income programs, and the like. The 1974 Housing and Community Development Act revised these programs materially.

## The Housing and Community Development Act of 1974

The Housing and Community Development Act is regarded as omnibus legislation containing eight subtitles:

| Title Number | Topic |
|---|---|
| I | Community Development |
| II | Assisted Housing |
| III | Mortgage Credit Assistance |
| IV | Comprehensive Planning |
| V | Rural Housing |
| VI | Mobile Home Construction and Safety and Standards |
| VII | Consumer Home Mortgage Assistance |
| VIII | Miscellaneous |

This act not only introduced new programs, it terminated many of the existing programs. Of special interest are the Urban Renewal and Neighborhood Development Program grants that formerly could be used for housing facilities. The Model Cities Program and rehabilitation loans were among the programs terminated. Title IV and VI, since they do not relate directly to mortgage lending, are omitted from this discussion.

*Title I, Community Development*

Loans under the Title I program were consolidated into a system of grants to communities with urgent community development needs. New programs called for a broad range of direct grants which could be used to (1) purchase blighted and deteriorated property, (2) rehabilitate property, (3) restore historic sites, promote urban beautification and conserve open spaces (4) construct public works, and (5) assist in other community development programs.

## *Title II, Assisted Housing*

Title II of the act eliminated some of the former provisions applying to public housing and altered other regulations. Since this public housing does not directly affect mortgage finance, it has less importance to mortgage lenders. It should be added, however, that ownership of public housing by tenants is authorized by sale of projects to tenants under Section VIII. In addition, housing for the elderly comes under Title II, referred by the act as the Section 202 Program that authorizes loans for construction of 202 Projects. These loans are also authorized under the Section 8 program for low and moderate income families.

The Section 202 Program authorized loans made at a rate equal to the Treasury borrowing rate plus allowances for administrative costs and losses. Mortgage insurance is made available for disabled persons and was designed to insure both low and moderate income families.

## *Title III, Mortgage Credit Assistance*

In general, Title III provisions increased mortgage insurance limits while other programs were terminated. The main points under Title III deserve additional comment.

    (1) Section 203 (b) (2) increased maximum insurance limits from $33,000 to $45,000.

    (2) Section 220 (d) (3) increased mortgage insurance limits from $33,000 to $45,000.

    (3) Section 221 (d) mortgage limits increased from $18,000 to $21,600.

    (4) Section 222 (b) mortgage insurance increased from $33,000 to $45,000.

    (5) Section 234 (c) mortgage limits increased from $33,000 to $45,000.

Additionally, the multiple family per unit mortgage limits applying to Section 207 mortgages were increased approximately 30 percent. This applies to Section 213 (b), 220 (d), 221 (d), 231 (c) and 234 (e). Similarly, this section of the act removed former overall maximum project mortgage dollar limits for multiple family, medical clinics, hospitals, nursing homes, and land development programs.

*Section 235 Program.* This program, subsidizing home ownership, was extended for two years only. Minimum down payments were increased to 3 percent of value. Eligibility requirements were changed at the same time.

*Section 236 Program.* This program was also extended for only two additional years. Like the 235 Program, eligiblity income limits were set at 80 percent of the median income for the area.

Other provisions of Title III increased property improvement loans on multiple unit structures from $15,000 to $25,000. Loans were authorized to finance purchase of mobile home lots. Moreover, loan to value ratios were varied for unsubsidized mortgages starting with a 97 percent loan to value ratio for the first $25,000, increasing to 90 percent between $25,000 and $35,000 and to an 80 percent loan to value ratio over $35,000.

Other provisions made minor changes to loans on management cooperatives, assisting multiple family projects, dormitory style housing, group medical practice facilities, and land development. Land development loans could be financed to 80 percent of the estimated value of the land before development and 90 percent of estimated cost of development. Congress authorized extension of unsubsidized FHA programs through June 30, 1977. The Secretary of HUD was given authority to set interest rates to meet the mortgage market through June 30, 1977.

## Title V, Rural Housing

The next significant section important to mortgage lenders deals with the expanded rural housing program. Rehabilitation loans, other loans, grants or combined loans and grants were increased to a maximum of $5,000, with loans of over $2,500 repayable within 20 years. Programs to assist housing of farm labor and self-help housing were authorized at higher funding levels through June 30, 1977.

The Secretary of Agriculture is authorized to insure loans under the Rural Housing Program to low income persons. The act permits assistance payments to owners of rental housing for eligible tenants to a subsidy exceeding 25 percent of income. In addition, the Secretary of Agriculture may make advances from the Self-Help Housing Land Development Fund to recipients of self-help housing grants to establish revolving accounts for purchase of land.

Site loans are authorized to be used by public, private or nonprofit organizations to acquire and develop sites to be sold to families, nonprofit organizations, public agencies and cooperatives eligible for assistance under Title V of the Housing Act of 1949. Rural, low, and moderate income persons are eligible for loans from the Secretary of Agriculture for purchase of condominium units located in rural areas.

## Title VII, Consumer Home Mortgage Assistance

This section of the new act authorized savings and loan associations to make construction loans on the basis of a borrower's general credit rating. The maximum loan amount for single family dwellings has been increased to $55,000. Property improvement loans to be financed from savings and loan associations were increased from $5,000 to $10,000.

## Title VIII, Miscellaneous Authority

Primarily, this title deals with procedural matters and secondary mortgage operations. For instance, it increases the GNMA mortgage limitation from $22,000 to $33,000 with authority to raise the limit to $38,000 in high cost areas. FHLMC and FNMA purchases of older mortgages is limited to a maximum 20 percent limit if a seller of mortgages invests an equivalent dollar amount in residential mortgages within 180 days. National banks, FHL banks and savings and loan associations, as well as credit unions, are authorized to purchase FHLMC securities. Any approved mortgagee is allowed to service mortgage purchased by FHLMC.

Title VIII contains a provision that changes the procedures of institutions participating in federal Flood Insurance programs. The change requires the lending institution to notify in writing a purchaser obtaining a loan in a designated flood-prone area of such flood hazards. The notification must be within a reasonable time in advance of the signing of the purchase agreements, leases or other documents. A community that has made adequate progress toward meeting the one-hundred year flood protection system standard as determined by HUD is eligible for flood insurance under the subsidized premium rate if—

(1) 100 percent of the project cost of flood protection system has been authorized;

(2) At least 60 percent of project cost has been appropriated;

(3) 50 percent of the project cost has been expended; and

(4) The system is at least 50 percent completed.

Finally, it should also be noted that Title VIII of the act prohibits discrimination on the basis of sex in the financing, sale, or rental of housing or the provision for brokerage services. Section 808 of this title amends the National Housing Act to state that—

No Federally related mortgage loan, or Federal insurance, guaranty, or other assistance in connection therewith (under this or any other Act), shall be denied to any person on account of sex; and every person engaged in making mortgage loans secured by residential real property shall consider without prejudice the combined income of both husband and wife for the purpose of extending mortgage credit in the form of a Federally related mortgage loan to a married couple or either member thereof. [Section 527]

## FHA Mortgage Forms

The documentation of an FHA loan application for new projects requires the preparation of 40 to 50 documents. While it is not feasible to review each of these documents, it is relevant to review the main forms used by FHA in processing the more common loans. Because single family dwellings account for the largest number of FHA cases, the emphasis is placed on single family dwellings.

FHA regulates loan maturity, interest rates, prepayment clauses and other mortgage terms. FHA form 9118, Mortgage Note (single family dwelling), includes the acceleration clause and the form for the promissory note that conforms to FHA provisions. See Exhibit 6.1.

Exhibit 6.2 illustrates FHA form 2165M covering a mortgage deed for a single family dwelling. Note that provision 7 is a covenant insuring that the borrower maintain the mortgage premises in good, orderly condition.

### *The mortgage application*

The lender is responsible for completing FHA form 2900-1—the mortgagee's application for mortgage or approval and commitment for mortgage insurance. The form illustrated applies to a single family dwelling. This form, shown in Exhibit 6.3, covers most of the documentation common to typical mortgage application: assets for closing, housing expenses, previous monthly fixed charges, liabilities of the borrower and probable settlement requirements. Methods of analyzing this form are explained in the chapter on mortgage credit.

### *The property appraisal*

Part of the documentation requires the mortgagee's application for property appraisal and commitment for mortgage insurance, FHA form 2800-1. Although this is only a request for an appraisal, the essential information must be complete including a legal description of the property, a summary of construction features and the minimum of financial information. See Exhibit 6.4.

### *Credit analysis*

A credit analysis is necessary to analyze effective income, the future monthly payments and the settlement requirement. The form used for this analysis is shown on page 307 and explained in Chapter 14 which deals with mortgage credit analysis.

# Exhibit 6.1

# FHA Form 9118 Mortgage Note

FHA FORM NO. 9118
Revised March 1971

This form is used in connection
with mortgages insured under the
one- to four-family provisions of
the National Housing Act.

FHA CASE NO.

$

, Indiana.
, 19 .

FOR VALUE RECEIVED, I, or we, jointly and severally, promise to pay to the order of

, the principal sum
of                                                                    Dollars
($                            ), with interest from date at the rate of
per centum (                        %) per annum on the unpaid balance until paid.   The said principal
and interest shall be payable at the office of

in,                                               , or at such other place as
the holder may designate in writing, in monthly installments of
                    Dollars ($                            ), commencing on the
first day of                    , 19    , and on the first day of each month thereafter until the principal and interest are fully paid, except that the final payment of the entire indebtedness evidenced
hereby, if not sooner paid, shall be due and payable on the first day of                    ,     .

In the event of default in the payment of any installment under this note, and if such default is not
made good prior to the due date of the next such installment, the entire principal sum and accrued interest shall at once become due and payable without notice at the option of the holder of this note. Failure to exercise this option shall not constitute a waiver of the right to exercise same at any other time.

All installments of the principal sum and all accrued interest thereon shall bear interest after maturity at the above rate, and attorney's fees.

I, or we, and each of us, whether principal, surety, guarantor, endorser or other party hereto, severally waive the benefit of any valuation or appraisement right as against said debt, and waive demand,
protest and notice of demand, protest and nonpayment.

GIVEN UNDER THE HAND AND SEAL of each party.

_____ [SEAL]  _____ [SEAL]

_____ [SEAL]  _____ [SEAL]

GPO 908.939

128

## Exhibit 6.2

## FHA Form 2165M Mortgage Deed

**STATE OF OHIO**

FHA Form No. 2165M
Revised November 1972

# MORTGAGE DEED
# WITH DOWER

KNOW ALL MEN BY THESE PRESENTS, THAT

of                                                    , County of

and State of Ohio, the Grantor, for and in consideration of the sum of

Dollars ($            ), to him paid by

, a corporation organized and existing under the laws of
, and having its principal place of business at
, Grantee, the receipt of which is hereby acknowledged, does give, grant,

bargain, sell, and convey unto the Grantee the following-described premises, situated in the

of                                                    , County of                                    , State

of Ohio, and bounded and described as follows, to wit:

together with the privileges and appurtenances thereunto belonging, and all the rents, issues, and profits which may arise or be had therefrom; and all the estate, title, and interest of the said Grantor, either in law or in equity, of, in, and to the said premises; to have and to hold the above-granted and bargained premises, with all the privileges and appurtenances thereto belonging, including all heating, plumbing, and lighting fixtures and equipment now or hereafter attached to or used in connection with the said premises, and all the rents, issues, and profits which may arise or be had therefrom, unto the said Grantee, its successors or assigns, forever. And the Grantor covenants that at and until the execution and delivery of these presents, he is well seized of the above-described premises in fee simple, and has good right to bargain and sell the same in manner and form above written, and that the same are free from all encumbrances whatsoever; and that he will warrant and defend said premises, with the above-mentioned appurtenances to the said Grantee, its successors and assigns, forever, against all lawful claim or claims and demands whatsoever.

And, for a valuable consideration, the said                                                    of said
, does hereby remise, release, and forever quitclaim, unto the Grantee all right and title
of dower in the above-described premises.

The conditions of this deed are such that whereas the Grantor has executed and delivered to the Grantee his certain promissory note, of even date herewith, in the principal sum of

Dollars ($            ), with interest from date at the rate of                          percentum (        %) per annum on the unpaid balance until paid, said principal and interest being payable at the office of

at                                                    , or at such other place as the holder may designate in writing, in monthly installments of

Dollars ($            ), commencing on

the first day of                          , 19      , and on the first day of each month thereafter until the principal and interest are fully paid, except that the final payment of principal and interest, if not sooner paid, shall be due and payable on the first day of

Exhibit 6.2 *Continued*

AND WHEREAS the Grantor further covenants and agrees that:

1. He will promptly pay the principal of and interest on the indebtedness evidenced by the said note, at the times and in the manner therein provided. Privilege is reserved to pay the debt in whole or in an amount equal to one or more monthly payments on the principal that are next due on the note, on the first day of any month prior to maturity; *provided, however,* that written notice of an intention to exercise such privilege is given at least thirty (30) days prior to prepayment.

2. In order more fully to protect the security of this deed, he will pay to the Grantee, together with, and in addition to, such payments of principal and interest, the following sums:

*(a)* An amount sufficient to provide the holder hereof with funds to pay the next mortgage insurance premium if this instrument and the note secured hereby are insured, or a monthly charge (in lieu of a mortgage insurance premium) if they are held by the Secretary of Housing and Urban Development, as follows:

(I) If and so long as said note of even date and this instrument are insured or are reinsured under the provisions of the National Housing Act, an amount sufficient to accumulate in the hands of the holder one (1) month prior to its due date the annual mortgage insurance premium, in order to provide such holder with funds to pay such premium to the Secretary of Housing and Urban Development pursuant to the National Housing Act, as amended, and applicable Regulations thereunder; or

(II) If and so long as said note of even date and this instrument are held by the Secretary of Housing and Urban Development, a monthly charge (in lieu of a mortgage insurance premium) which shall be in an amount equal to one-twelfth (1/12) of one-half (½) per centum of the average outstanding balance due on the note computed without taking into account delinquencies or prepayments;

*(b)* A sum equal to the ground rents, if any, next due, plus the premiums that will next become due and payable on policies of fire and other hazard insurance protecting the premises covered hereby, plus taxes and assessments next due on the premises covered by this deed (all as estimated by the Grantee) less all sums already paid therefor divided by the number of months to elapse before one month prior to the date when such ground rents, premiums, taxes and assessments will become delinquent, such sums to be held by the Grantee in trust to pay said ground rents, premiums, taxes and special assessments before the same become delinquent; and

*(c)* All payments mentioned in the two preceding subsections of this paragraph and all payments to be made under the note secured hereby shall be added together, and the aggregate amount thereof shall be paid by the Grantor each month in a single payment to be applied by the Grantee to the following items in the order set forth:

(I) premium charges under the contract of insurance with Secretary of Housing and Urban Development, or monthly charge (in lieu of mortgage insurance premium), as the case may be;

(II) ground rents, taxes, special assessments, fire and other hazard insurance premiums;

(III) interest on the note secured hereby; and

(IV) amortization of the principal of said note.

Any deficiency in the amount of such aggregate monthly payments shall, unless made good by the Grantor prior to the due date of the next such payments, constitute an event of default under this deed. The Grantee may collect a "late charge" not to exceed two cents (2¢) for each dollar ($1) of each payment more than fifteen (15) days in arrears to cover the extra expense involved in handling delinquent payments.

3. If the total of the payments made by the Grantor under subsection *(b)* of paragraph 2 preceding shall exceed the amount of the payments actually made by the Grantee for ground rents, taxes, or assessments or insurance premiums, as the case may be, such excess, at the option of the Grantee, shall be credited by the Grantee on subsequent payments to be made by the Grantor, or refunded to the Grantor. If, however, the monthly payments made by the Grantor under such subsection shall not be sufficient to pay ground rents, taxes, or assessments or insurance premiums, when the same shall become due and payable, then the Grantor shall pay to the Grantee any amount necessary to make up the deficiency, on or before the date when payment of such ground rents, taxes, assessments or insurance premiums shall be due. If at any time the Grantor shall tender to the Grantee, in accordance with the provisions of said note, full payment of the entire indebtedness represented thereby, the Grantee shall, in computing the amount of such indebtedness, credit to the account of the Grantor all payments made under the provisions of subsection *(a)* of paragraph 2, above, which the Grantee has not become obligated to pay to the Secretary of Housing and Urban Development, and any balance remaining in the funds accumulated under the provisions of subsection *(b)* of paragraph 2. If there shall be a default under any of the provisions of this deed resulting in a public sale of the premises covered hereby or if the Grantee acquires the property otherwise after default, the Grantee shall apply, at the time of the commencement of such proceedings, or at the time the property is otherwise acquired, the balance then remaining in the funds accumulated under such subsection *(b)* of paragraph 2 as a credit against the amount of principal then remaining unpaid under said note, and shall properly adjust any payments which shall have been made under subsection *(a)* of paragraph 2.

4. He will pay all ground rents, taxes, assessments, water rates, and other governmental or municipal charges, fines, or impositions, levied upon said premises, or upon the interest of the Grantee in and to said premises, for which provision has not been made heretofore, and in default thereof the Grantee may pay the same; and he will promptly deliver the official receipts therefor to the Grantee.

5. The Grantee, its successors or assigns, shall have the right to pay any ground rents, taxes, assessments, water rents, and other governmental or municipal charges, fines or impositions, which the Grantor has agreed to pay under paragraph 4, above, and to make any payments hereinabove provided to be made by the Grantor in subsections *(a)* and *(b)* of paragraph 2 hereof, and any amount so paid by the Grantee shall then be added to the principal debt named herein and bear interest at the rate set forth in the note secured hereby, payable monthly, from the date of such payment, and be secured by this deed.

6. He will keep the improvements now existing or hereafter erected on the premises covered by this deed, insured as may be required from time to time by the Grantee against loss by fire and other hazards, casualties and contingencies including war damage insurance, in such amounts and for such periods as may be required by the Grantee and will pay promptly, when due, any premiums on such insurance provision for payment of which has not been made hereinbefore. All insurance shall be carried in companies approved by the Grantee and the policies and renewals thereof shall be held by the Grantee and have attached thereto loss-payable clauses in favor of and in form acceptable to the Grantee. In event of loss Grantor will give immediate notice by mail to the Grantee, who may make proof of loss if not made promptly by Grantor, and each insurance company concerned is hereby authorized and directed to make payment for such loss directly to the Grantee instead of to the Grantor and the Grantee jointly, and the insurance proceeds, or any part thereof, may be applied by the Grantee at its option either to the reduction of the indebtedness hereby secured or to the restoration or repair of the property damaged. In event of foreclosure of this mortgage deed, or other transfer of title to the property covered hereby in extinguishment of the indebtedness secured hereby, all right, title and interest of the Grantor in and to any insurance policies then in force shall pass to the purchaser or Grantee.

7. He will keep the mortgaged premises in as good order and condition as they are now, and will not commit or permit waste, reasonable wear and tear excepted.

8. That if the premises, or any part thereof, be condemned under any power of eminent domain, or acquired for a public use, the damages, proceeds, and the consideration for such acquisition, to the extent of the full amount of indebtedness upon this Mortgage, and the Note secured hereby remaining unpaid, are hereby assigned by the Grantor to the Grantee and shall be paid forthwith to the Grantee to be applied by it on account of the indebtedness secured hereby, whether due or not.

9. The Grantor further agrees that should this deed and the note secured hereby not be eligible for insurance under the National Housing Act within _____ from date hereof (written statement of any officer of the Department of Housing and Urban Development or authorized agent of the Secretary of Housing and Urban Development dated subsequent to the _____ time from the date of this deed, declining to insure said note and this deed, being deemed conclusive proof of such ineligibility) the Grantee or the holder of the note may, at its option, declare all sums secured hereby immediately due and payable.

130

# Exhibit 6.2 *Continued*

10. Upon a default in any of the terms of the note secured hereby, or upon a breach of any condition or covenant of this deed, the rents of the real estate herein described shall immediately accrue to the benefit of the Grantee, and such rents shall be immediately payable to the Grantee.

· 11. Upon any default in the note secured hereby, or under this deed, foreclosure proceedings may be instituted, at the option of the Grantee. In any such action, the Grantee shall be entitled, without notice and without regard to the adequacy of the security of the debt, to the appointment of a receiver of the rents and profits of the mortgaged premises and in case of any other suit, or legal proceeding, wherein the Grantee shall be made a party thereto by reason of this mortgage, its costs and expenses, and the reasonable fees and charges of the attorneys or solicitors of the Grantee, so made parties, for services in such suit or proceedings, shall be a further lien and charge upon the said premises under this mortgage, and all such expenses shall become so much additional indebtedness secured hereby and be allowed in any decree foreclosing this mortgage.

12. The Grantee is authorized and empowered to do all things provided to be done by a mortgagee under Section 1311-14 of the Revised Code, and under the Act of the Legislature passed May 27, 1915, 106 Ohio Laws, Pages 522-534, and any amendments or supplements thereto.

Now, therefore, if the Grantor shall well and truly perform all the conditions of this deed, and of the note secured hereby, then this deed shall be void; otherwise, it shall remain in full force and virtue.

The covenants herein contained shall bind, and the benefits and advantages shall inure to, the respective heirs, executors, administrators, successors and assigns of the parties hereto. Whenever used, the singular number shall include the plural, the plural the singular, and the use of any gender shall include all genders.

IN WITNESS WHEREOF, the Grantor (s) ha     hereunto set     hand    , this
day of     , A.D. 19

Signed, acknowledged and delivered in the presence of _____

_____    _____

_____    _____

STATE OF OHIO       )
                    ) *ss:*
COUNTY OF       )

Before me, the undersigned, a                 in and for said State and County, personally appeared the above-named,                Grantor in the above mortgage deed, and severally acknowledged the signing thereof, and that such signing was freely and voluntarily performed, for the uses and purposes therein mentioned.

IN TESTIMONY WHEREOF, I have hereunto signed my name, and affixed my official seal, this         day of     , A.D. 19

_____

_____

The conditions of this mortgage have been complied with, and the same is fully paid, satisfied, and discharged.

_____

The form of this instrument was prepared by the Office of the General Counsel, Department of Housing and Urban Development, and the material in the blank space in the form was inserted by or under the direction of _____ .

# Exhibit 6.3

# FHA Form 2900–1 Mortgagee's Application for Mortgage or Application for Approval and Commitment for Mortgage Insurance

Form Approved
OMB No 63—R1062

| U.S. DEPARTMENT OF HOUSING AND URBAN DEVELOPMENT FEDERAL HOUSING ADMINISTRATION | 2. FHA Case No. |
|---|---|

**1.**
MORTGAGEE'S APPLICATION FOR MORTGAGOR APPROVAL AND COMMITMENT FOR MORTGAGE INSURANCE UNDER THE NATIONAL HOUSING ACT

☐ SEC. 203(b)    ☐ SEC.

**5. MORTGAGEE** - Name, Address & Zip Code    *(Please Type)*

*(Please locate address within corner marks)*

**3. PROPERTY ADDRESS**

**4. MORTGAGORS:**

Mtgor.    Soc. Sec. No.    Sex   Age
Co-Mtgor.    Soc. Sec. No.    Sex   Age

Address

| Married | Yrs. | No. of Dependents | Ages |
|---|---|---|---|
| Co-Mortgagor(s) | | Sex | Age(s) |

*(Check One)*
☐ White *(Non Minority)*    ☐ American Indian    ☐ Spanish American
☐ Negro/Black    ☐ Oriental    ☐ Other Minority

**6.**
MORTGAGE APPLIED FOR ➡

| | Mortgage Amount | *Interest Rate | No. of Months | Monthly Payment Principal & Interest |
|---|---|---|---|---|
| | $ | % | | $ |

**7. PURPOSE OF LOAN** . . .
☐ Finance Constr on Own Land   ☐ Finance Purchase   ☐ Refinance Exist' Loan   ☐ Finance Impr to Exist' Prop     ☐ Other

**MORTGAGOR WILL BE** . .
☐ Occupant   ☐ Landlord   ☐ Builder   ☐ Escrow Commit Mortgagor

| **8.** ASSETS | | | **12.** SETTLEMENT REQUIREMENTS | |
|---|---|---|---|---|
| Cash accounts | $ | | (a) Existing debt (Refinancing only) | $ |
| | | | (b) Sale price (Realty only) | |
| Marketable securities | | | (c) Repairs & Improvements | |
| Other (explain) | | | (d) Closing Costs | |
| **OTHER ASSETS** (A) TOTAL | $ | | (e) TOTAL (a + b + c + d) Acquisition cost | |
| Cash deposit on purchase | | | (f) Mortgage amount | |
| Other (explain) | | | (g) Mortgagor's required investment(e-f) | |
| | | | (h) Prepayable expenses | |
| | | | (i) Non-realty & other items | |
| (B) TOTAL | $ | | (j) TOTAL REQUIREMENTS (g + h + i) | |
| **9.** LIABILITIES | Monthly Payt | Unpd Bal | (k) Amt pd ☐ cash ☐ Other (explain) | |
| Automobile | $ | $ | (l) Amt to be pd ☐ cash ☐ Other (explain) | |
| Debts, other Real Estate | | | (m) Tot assets available for closing (B) (A) | $ |
| Life Insurance Loans | | | **13.** FUTURE MONTHLY PAYMENTS | |
| Notes payable | | | (a) Principal & Interest | $ |
| Credit Union | | | (b) FHA Mortgage Insurance Premium | |
| Retail accounts | | | (c) Ground rent (Leasehold only) | |
| | | | (d) TOTAL DEBT SERVICE (a + b + c) | |
| | | | (e) Hazard Insurance | |
| | | | (f) Taxes, special assessments | |
| TOTAL | $ | $ | (g) TOTAL MTG. PAYT. (d + e + f) | |
| **10.** EMPLOYMENT | | | (h) Maintenance & Common Expense | |
| Mortgagor's occupation | | | (i) Heat & utilities | |
| Employer's name & address | | | (j) TOTAL HSG. EXPENSE (g + h + i) | |
| | | | (k) Other recurring charges (explain) | |
| years employed | | | (l) TOTAL FIXED PAYT. (j + k) | $ |
| Co-Mtgor occupation | | | **14.** PREVIOUS MONTHLY HOUSING EXPENSE | |
| Employer's name & address | | | Mortgage payment or rent | $ |
| | | | Hazard Insurance | |
| years employed | | | Taxes, special assessments | |
| **11.** MONTHLY INCOME | | | Maintenance | |
| | | | Heat & Utilities | |
| Mortgagor's base pay | $ | | Other (explain) | |
| Other Earnings (explain) | | | TOTAL | $ |
| Co-Mtgor base pay | | | **15.** PREVIOUS MONTHLY FIXED CHARGES | |
| Other Earnings (explain) | | | Federal, State & Local income taxes | $ |
| Gross Income Real Estate | | | Prem for $ Life Insurance | |
| Other (explain) | | | Social Security & Retirement Payments | |
| TOTAL | $ | | Installment account payments | |
| | | | Operating Expenses other Real Estate | |
| | | | Other (explain) | |
| | | | TOTAL | $ |

**16.** Do you own other Real Estate ☐ Yes ☐ No   Is it to be sold ☐ Yes ☐ No   FHA mortgage ☐ Yes ☐ No   Sales Price $   Orig Mtg Amt $
Unpaid Bal $   Address   Lender

**17. MORTGAGOR'S CERTIFICATE** -- I ☐ have ☐ have not received a copy of the FHA Statement of Value (FHA Form 2800-6) or Veterans Administration Certificate of Reasonable Value (VA Form 26-1843) showing the estimated value of the property described in this application. Have you sold a property within the last year which had an FHA mortgage? ☐ Yes ☐ No. If "Yes" was the mortgage paid in full? ☐ Yes ☐ No. If "No" give FHA Case Number , buyer's name , property address , original mortgage amount $ , lender's name and address , date of transfer , unpaid balance when sold $ . Did buyer intend to occupy? ☐ Yes ☐ No. Have you ever been obligated on a home loan, home improvement loan or a mobile home which resulted in foreclosure, transfer of title in lieu of foreclosure, or judgement? ☐ Yes ☐ No. If "Yes" attach statement giving full details including date, property address, name and address of lender, FHA or VA Case Number, if any, and reasons for the action. If dwelling to be covered by this mortgage is to be rented, is it a part, adjacent or contiguous to any project, subdivision, or group of rental properties involving eight or more dwelling units in which you have any financial interest? ☐ Yes ☐ No. Not to be rented. If "Yes" give details. Do you own four or more dwelling units with mortgages insured under any title of the National Housing Act? ☐ Yes ☐ No. If "Yes" submit FHA Form 2561. The Mortgagor certifies that all information in this application is given for the purpose of obtaining a loan to be insured under the National Housing Act and is true and complete to the best of his knowledge and belief. Verification may be obtained from any source named herein. *NOTE. The interest rate shown in item 6 is the FHA-VA maximum rate in effect on the date of this commitment and may increase prior to closing unless buyer and lender agree otherwise.

Signature(s) _____ Date _____ 19____

**18. MORTGAGEE'S CERTIFICATE** - The mortgagee certifies that all information in this application is true and complete to the best of its knowledge and belief. Signature _____ Date _____ 19____

FHA FORM NO. 2900-1 Rev 5/75      FHA COPY - FILE IN CASE BINDER

## Exhibit 6.4

# FHA Form 2800–1 Mortgagee's Application for Property Appraisal and Commitment for Mortgage Insurance

| FHA MORTGAGEE NO. *(Please Verify)* | U.s. DEPARTMENT OF HOUSING AND URBAN DEVELOPMENT FEDERAL HOUSING ADMINISTRATION | FHA CASE NO. |
|---|---|---|

| MORTGAGEE'S APPLICATION FOR PROPERTY APPRAISAL AND COMMITMENT FOR MORTGAGE INSURANCE UNDER THE NATIONAL HOUSING ACT | PROPERTY ADDRESS |
|---|---|

☐ SEC. 203(b)  ☐ SEC._____

**MORTGAGEE** Name and Address including ZIP Code  *(Please Type)*
*(Please locate address within corner marks)*

⌐                                                          ¬

This form is a request for an appraisal and a commitment to insure a loan on an individual property.

We cannot process incomplete applications.
Rejecting them is costly.
Please help by giving us well prepared applications.
Keep all entries within alloted spaces.

L                                                          ⅃

Telephone No.

| EXISTING HOUSE ☐ | Name of Occupant *(or person to call if unoccupied)* | | Tel. No. | Key Encl. | ☐ *(If unfurnished)* |
|---|---|---|---|---|---|
| | Mon. & Yr. Completed | ☐ Never Occup. ☐ Vacant | Occupied by ☐ Owner ☐ Tenant at $ | Per Mo. ☐ Furn. ☐ Unfurn. |

**PROPOSED ☐**
**SUBSTAN. REHAB. ☐**
**UNDER CONSTR. ☐**

Builder's Name & Address Including ZIP Code          Tel. No.          Model Identification

☐ Plans.  ☐ First Subm.   Prob. Repeat Cases ☐ Yes ☐ No   ☐ Prev. Proc. as FHA Case No.

Mineral Rights Reserved
☐ No ☐ Yes *(Explain)*

| Utilities: | Public | Comm. | Individual |
|---|---|---|---|
| Water | ☐ | ☐ | ☐ |
| Gas | ☐ | ☐ | ☐ |
| Elect. | ☐ | ☐ | ☐ |

☐ Underground Wiring

|  | | | Sept. Cess Tank Pool |
|---|---|---|---|
| Sanitary Sewer | ☐ | ☐ | ☐ ☐ |

| **SPEC. ASSESS.** Prepayable. $_____ Non-Prepay. $_____ | LOT_____ x_____ ☐ Irr. ☐ Acres_____ Sq. Ft. |
|---|---|
| Int.____% Ann. Pay. $_____ Unpd. Bal. $_____ Rem. Term____Yrs | GENERAL LOCATION: |
| **ANN. R. EST. TAXES $** | **ANN. FIRE INS. $** | **SALE PRICE $** |

### EQUAL OPPORTUNITY IN HOUSING

Federal laws and regulations prohibit discrimination because of race, color, religion, sex, or national origin in the sale or rental of residential property. Numerous state statutes and local ordinances also prohibit such discrimination. In addition, section 805 of the Civil Rights Act of 1968 prohibits discriminatory practices in connection with the financing of housing.

If FHA finds there is noncompliance with any applicable antidiscrimination laws or regulations, it may discontinue FHA business with the violator.

**LEGAL DESCRIPTION** *(Attach one page if necessary)*

**SHOW BELOW:** Shape. location. distance from nearest intersection and street names. Mark N at NORTH point.

Please consider the following TITLE EXCEPTIONS in value:

Please consider the following Equipment in value:

| **LEASEHOLD** | **Ground Rent** *(Per Yr)* $ | Lease is: ☐ 99 years | ☐ Renewable | ☐ FHA Approved | Expires |
|---|---|---|---|---|---|

In submitting this application for a conditional commitment for mortgage insurance, it is agreed and understood by the parties involved in the transaction, that if, at the time of application for a Firm Commitment, the identity of the seller has changed, the application for a Firm Commitment will be rejected and the application for a Conditional Commitment will be reprocessed upon request by the mortgagee.

It is further agreed and understood that in submitting the request for a Firm Commitment for mortgage insurance, the seller, the purchaser and the broker involved in the transaction shall each certify that the terms of the contract for purchase are true to his best knowledge and belief, and that any other agreement entered into by any of these parties in connection with this transaction is attached to the sales agreement.

**BUILDER/SELLER'S AGREEMENT: All Houses:** The undersigned agrees to deliver to the purchaser FHA's statement of appraised value. Proposed Construction: The undersigned agrees, upon sale or conveyance of title within one year from date of initial occupancy, to deliver to the purchaser FHA Form 2544, warranting that the house is constructed in substantial conformity with the plans and specifications on which FHA based its value and to furnish FHA a conformed copy with the purchaser's receipt thereon that the original warranty was delivered to him. All Houses: In consideration of the issuance of the commitment requested by this application, I (we) hereby agree that any deposit or down payment made in connection with the purchase of the property described above, whether received by the undersigned or an agent of the undersigned, shall upon receipt be deposited in escrow or in trust or in a special account which is not subject to the claims of my creditors and where it will be maintained until it has been disbursed for the benefit of the purchaser or otherwise disposed of in accordance with the terms of the contract of sale.

Signature: ☐ Mortgagee ☐ Builder ☐ Seller ☐ Other          19

**MORTGAGEE'S CERTIFICATE:** The undersigned mortgagee certifies that to the best of its knowledge all statements made in this application and the supporting documents are true, correct and complete.

Signature/Title of Mortgagee Officer:          19

**WARNING:** Section 1010 of Title 18, U.S.C., provides: "Whoever, for the purpose of . . . influencing such Administration . . . makes, passes, utters, or publishes any statement, knowing the same to be false . . . shall be fined not more than $5,000 or imprisoned not more than two years, or both."

FHA FORM NO. 2800-1 Rev 5/75

FHA COPY — FILE IN CASE BINDER

## Veterans Administration Guaranteed Loans

Lenders favor VA guaranteed loans because of the early foreclosure settlement practiced by the Veterans Administration. The VA appraises the property then determines if it is advantageous to the government to pay the claim or pay the entire indebtedness. If the last option is selected the VA takes title and resells through local real estate brokers.

Currently the VA guarantee is limited to 60 percent of the appraised value or $17,500, whichever is less. Further, the veteran is prohibited from paying discounts on the mortgage and he is not required to make a down payment. The VA limits loan origination fees to 1 percent of the loan.

A veteran entitled to the full guarantee negotiating for a $50,000 *70,000* loan provides the lender with the equivalent of a 75 percent loan to value ratio of conventional loan—the $17,500 is guaranteed by the VA. In effect, this establishes a loan ceiling among the lenders who regularly place conventional loans at 75 percent of the appraised value.

Veterans are eligible for VA guarantees on (1) single family dwellings, (2) farm homes, which are limited to 50 percent of the original mortgage amount or $40,000 whichever is less. The limit increases if the farm includes accessory buildings which allow the 60 percent, $17,500 limitation, (3) mobile homes based on a $12,000 loan for 12 years; higher allowances are provided for purchase of a mobile home and an undeveloped or developed lot.

## VA Loan Procedures

Before a loan is approved for a VA guarantee, lenders must meet qualifications of the Veterans Administration. For this purpose VA does not require prior approval of the lenders if they are supervised by an agency of the federal government or they are approved by FHA as an approved mortgagee. Other nonsupervised lenders must obtain VA loan approval. Such lenders must file an application for a loan guarantee commitment from VA. Issuance of the commitment permits the lender to process the loan for submission to VA for guarantee approval.

The next step rests with the veteran who must secure a *Certificate of Eligibility* issued by the Veterans Administration. The rules of eligibility depend on service in the armed forces during specified times and the veteran's prior use of the guarantee.

The loan applicant must determine his or her eligiblity for a home loan guarantee. See VA form 26-1880, Exhibit 6.5. The form details service and information detail related to loan guarantee entitlement.

# Exhibit 6.5

## Request for Determination of Eligibility and Available Loan Guaranty Entitlement

Form Approved
OMB No. 76-R0371

| VETERANS ADMINISTRATION | | VETERANS ADMINISTRATION |
|---|---|---|
| **REQUEST FOR DETERMINATION OF ELIGIBILITY AND** | TO | ATTN: Loan Guaranty Division |
| **AVAILABLE LOAN GUARANTY ENTITLEMENT** | | |

NOTE: Please read instructions on reverse before completing this form. If additional space is required, attach separate sheet.

| 1. FIRST - MIDDLE - LAST NAME OF VETERAN | 2. ADDRESS OF VETERAN (No., street or rural route, city or P.O., State and ZIP Code) | 3. DATE OF BIRTH |
|---|---|---|
| | | |

4. MILITARY SERVICE DATA.--I request the Veterans Administration to determine my eligibility and the amount of entitlement based on the following period(s) of active military duty: (Start with latest period of service and list all periods of active duty since September 16, 1940.)

| PERIOD OF ACTIVE SERVICE | | NAME (Show your name exactly as it appears on your separation papers (DD Form 214) or statement of service) | SERVICE NUMBER | BRANCH OF SERVICE |
|---|---|---|---|---|
| DATE FROM | DATE TO | | | |
| 4A. | | | | |
| 4B. | | | | |
| 4C. | | | | |
| 4D. | | | | |

| 5A. WERE YOU DISCHARGED, RETIRED, OR SEPARATED FROM SERVICE BECAUSE OF DISABILITY, OR DO YOU NOW HAVE ANY SERVICE-CONNECTED DISABILITIES?  ☐ YES  ☐ NO (If "Yes," complete Item 5B) | 5B. VA FILE NUMBER  C- | 6. IS THERE A CERTIFICATE OF ELIGIBILITY FOR LOAN GUARANTY OR DIRECT LOAN PURPOSE ENCLOSED?  ☐ YES  ☐ NO (If "No," complete Items 7A and 7B.) |
|---|---|---|

| 7A. HAVE YOU PREVIOUSLY APPLIED FOR A CERTIFICATE OF ELIGIBILITY FOR LOAN GUARANTY OR DIRECT LOAN PURPOSES?  ☐ YES  ☐ NO (If "Yes," give location of VA office involved) | ADDRESS OF VA OFFICE |
|---|---|
| 7B. HAVE YOU PREVIOUSLY RECEIVED SUCH A CERTIFICATE OF ELIGIBILITY?  ☐ YES  ☐ NO (If "Yes," give location of VA office involved) | |
| 8A. HAVE YOU PREVIOUSLY SECURED A VA DIRECT HOME LOAN?  ☐ YES  ☐ NO (If "Yes," give location of VA office involved) ▶ | |
| 8B. HAVE YOU PREVIOUSLY OBTAINED HOME, FARM, CONDOMINIUM OR BUSINESS LOAN(S) WHICH WERE GUARANTEED OR INSURED BY VA?  ☐ YES  ☐ NO (If "Yes," give location of VA office involved) ▶ | |
| 8C. HAVE YOU PREVIOUSLY OBTAINED A VA MOBILE HOME AND/OR LOT LOAN(S)?  ☐ YES  ☐ NO (If "Yes," give location of VA office(s) involved) ▶ | |

| 9. Check only if this is a request for a DUPLICATE Certificate of Eligibility ▶ | ☐ PLEASE ISSUE A DUPLICATE CERTIFICATE OF ELIGIBILITY IN MY NAME. THE CERTIFICATE PREVIOUSLY ISSUED TO ME IS NOT AVAILABLE BECAUSE IT HAS BEEN LOST, DESTROYED OR STOLEN. IF IT IS RE-COVERED, IT WILL BE RETURNED TO THE VA FOR CANCELLATION. |
|---|---|
| I certify that the statements herein are true to the best of my knowledge and belief. | 10. SIGNATURE OF VETERAN                    11. DATE |

**FEDERAL STATUTES PROVIDE SEVERE PENALTIES FOR FRAUD, INTENTIONAL MISREPRESENTATION, CRIMINAL CONNIVANCE, OR CONSPIRACY PURPOSED TO INFLUENCE THE ISSUANCE OF ANY GUARANTY OR INSURANCE BY THE ADMINISTRATOR.**

| THIS SECTION FOR VA USE ONLY | | | |
|---|---|---|---|
| DATE CERTIFICATE ISSUED AND DISCHARGE OR SEPARATION PAPERS AND VA PAMPHLETS GIVEN TO VETERAN OR MAILED TO ADDRESS SHOWN BELOW | TYPE OF DISCHARGE OR SEPARATION PAPERS RETURNED | SIGNATURE AND TITLE OF APPROPRIATE OFFICIAL (If applicable) | STATION NUMBER |
| | | | CERTIFICATE NUMBER |

VA FORM 26-1880, AUG 1975                    *DO NOT DETACH*

---

IMPORTANT — You must complete Item 12, since the certificate of eligibility together with all discharge and separation papers will be mailed to the address shown in Item 12 immediately below. If they are to be sent to you, your current mailing address should be indicated, or if they are to be sent elsewhere, the name and address of such person or firm should be shown in Item 12.

The amount of loan guaranty entitlement available for use is endorsed on the reverse of the enclosed Certificate of Eligibility. This certificate must be returned to the VA at the time a loan application or loan report is submitted.

12. RETURN TO (Enter name and address below dots)

•                              •

[*PLEASE DELIVER THE ENCLOSED PAMPHLETS AND DISCHARGE OR SEPARATION PAPERS TO THE VETERAN PROMPTLY.  THANK YOU.*]

VA FORM
AUG 1975  **26-1880**

Other substantiating documents will include:

(1)  An approved credit report.

(2)  Verification of bank deposits.

(3)  A copy of the contract for sale.

(4)  Verification of employment.

(5)  A certificate of reasonable value.

(6)  Certificate of Eligibility.

(7)  Other documents required by the VA to cover individual problem cases.

On this point it is worthwhile noting that a veteran securing a release of liability selling his house does not necessarily restore his entitlement to the guarantee. Though the veteran may be released from an original loan by the lender, the VA is subject to the guarantee as long as the original loan is outstanding. The VA grants a loan release only if (1) the loan is current, (2) the VA qualifies the purchaser as an acceptable credit risk and (3) the new purchaser assumes the veteran's obligations. Veterans are advised to sell contingent on the VA acceptance of the purchaser and the issuance of a release of liability if a VA loan is assumed. In other respects, VA may restore eligiblity if the original loan is fully paid off and the property disposed of.

## VA Insurance and Direct Loans

Under certain conditions supervised lenders have the option to have veteran's loans insured instead of guaranteed. If the lender selects the insurance option, an account is established in the lender's name in which the VA credits up to 15 percent of each VA loan. In the event of default, the VA reimburses the lender up to the amount of the account or to an amount equal to the maximum guarantee amount whichever is less. With a large portfolio, the effect of the insurance is virtually the same as a guarantee.

*Direct loans* are authorized if the proposed mortgaged property is located in an area where veterans are unable to secure a mortgage from private lenders. The veteran, however, must exhaust opportunities for mortgage credit administered by the Secretary of Agriculture and further prove that mortgage money is unavailable from private lenders. Given these prerequisites, the VA will loan directly for the purchase of a farm, or a residence subject to home qualifications required by the Veterans Administration.

# Chapter 7

# Financing Single Family Dwellings

Mortgages secured by one-to-four family dwellings by the end of 1975 represent 60.3 percent of total mortgage debt outstanding. Of this total, commercial banks hold almost one out of five outstanding mortgages on one-to-four family dwellings· some 17.0 percent of the total. The current mortgage debt on dwellings held by commercial banks, for example, totaling some $76.6 billion, is greater than the current total volume of bank-held consumer instalment credit of $75.7 billion.

These figures assume even more importance since home ownership historically has increased. As the proportion of home ownership grows, financing of single family dwellings will tend to assume even greater significance. The financing of single family dwellings concentrates on three types of loans classified according to the mortgage security. Each type of loan calls for special financing techniques not found in other property types.

The first type of loan covers _new construction._ These loans are based on relatively short-term credit and are secured by land and a building under construction. The construction loan is granted in expectation of a sale with financing of the completed building under a long-term mortgage. The complications arising from construction loans warrant

### Table 7.1
### Multiplier Effects of the Loan-to-Value Ratio

| *Downpayment* *Requirement* | *Loan-to-Value Ratio* | | | | |
|---|---|---|---|---|---|
| | *50%* | *60%* | *70%* | *80%* | *90%* |
| Maximum Dwelling Value: $5,000 Downpayment ....... | $10,000 | $12,500 | $16,500 | $25,000 | $50,000 |
| Maximum Dwelling Value: $2,500 Downpayment ....... | 5,000 | 6,250 | 8,250 | 12,500 | 25,000 |

an explanation in a separate chapter. The second significant type of financing covers the _new dwelling_. The mortgage applies to a new property, usually in a newly developed subdivision, and presents a credit problem quite different from the financing of an existing building. The next important type of property in single family dwelling financing covers the older, existing property. The appraisal problems and the mortgage credit analysis, though they may use the same administrative forms, present unique features complicating the financing problem. To review these points, this chapter concentrates on mortgage risk analysis unique to single family dwellings, special problems encountered in financing plans and case studies to illustrate practical issues in arranging for a single family dwelling mortgage.

The financing of single family dwellings tends to be critical not only because of their relative importance in the mortgage market but because of the effect of financing terms on the demand for housing. Given the market rate of interest, terms of the mortgage have a significant bearing on ability of the borrower to finance real estate.

The first effect relates to the loan-to-value ratio: the lower the downpayment, the more housing may be purchased with a given downpayment. For example, Table 7.1 shows how the purchasing power of a $5,000 and $2,500 downpayment varies as the loan to value ratio is increased from 50 percent to 90 percent. A 50 percent loan enables a person with a $5,000 downpayment to purchase a $10,000 dwelling. With a 90 percent loan and assuming monthly payments may be met, a $5,000 equity would justify a maximum loan of $45,000. Even with an equity of $2,500, the purchasing power increases from $5,000 with a 50 percent loan to $25,000 with a 90 percent loan. Lending policy and regulations governing maximum loan to value ratios bear significantly on the housing market.

The other important effect relates to the variation in monthly payments given a fixed interest rate and given the loan-to-value ratio as the mortgage term is extended. Table 7.2 shows how monthly pay-

**Table 7.2**
**Monthly Payment Variation as the Term of Mortgage Varies:**
**9 Percent Interest**

| *Amount of* | *Mortgage Term in Years* | | | | |
| *Mortgage* | *10* | *15* | *20* | *25* | *30* |
|---|---|---|---|---|---|
| $30,000 | $380.02 | $304.27 | $269.21 | $251.75 | $241.38 |
| $20,000 | $253.35 | $202.85 | $179.94 | $167.83 | $160.90 |

ments vary under a 9.0 percent monthly amortized mortgage of $20,000 and $30,000. It will be readily appreciated that the marketability of real estate is enhanced merely by changing the mortgage from 15 years to 30 years. Under the assumptions of Table 7.2, the monthly payment varies from $380.02 to $241.38 for a $30,000 mortgage. A $20,000 mortgage shows similar variation: Monthly payments of $253.35 for a 10 year mortgage and $160.90 for a 30 year mortgage. Table 7.2 discloses that the monthly payment, with a given interest rate, varies significantly as the mortgage term changes.

As a consequence, the financing of single family dwellings is highly sensitive to the cost of credit and its availability. As the interest rate increases, monthly payments increase to the point that marginal buyers are unable to finance new houses. More seriously as credit demands increase, money tends to flow out of the mortgage market for single family dwellings to other types of loans. Lenders are more reluctant to commit loans on a long-term basis in the face of rising interest rates. To the extent that state usury laws control interest rates on loans to individuals, mortgage credit on single family dwellings tends to be even more restricted. These factors emphasize the problem of evaluating mortgage risks on single family dwellings.

## Evaluating Mortgage Risks on Single Family Dwellings

The two main elements affecting mortgage risks for single family dwellings are the *real estate* placed as security for a loan, and *borrower credit*. Some authorities contend that the uncertainties of the single family dwelling market recommend that greater weight be placed on borrower credit as security for the loan. The alternate view holds that changes in the borrower's financial status over the life of a mortgage justifies greater attention to the marketability of real estate. Both of these views deserve additional explanation.

## The Real Estate Security

The dwelling offered as security for a long-term mortgage will be judged (1) to minimize the possibility of foreclosure, delinquencies, and additional collection expenses and (2) to minimize the financial loss in the event of foreclosure. In the first instance the borrower has little incentive to repay a mortgage if property values decline below the outstanding mortgage balance. To guard against this possibility, the real estate must be evaluated according to its potential marketability.

The last issue relates to the probable market value of the property over the life of the loan in the event the property must be sold under foreclosure procedures. To show these relationships, it is worthwhile to concentrate on factors that lead to a continuing demand for single family dwellings. The discussion on this point will be directed to the valuation of dwellings in a given community. The emphasis lies in the location of the security leading to a critical review of the economic base. The next issue covering marketability is more easily viewed by directing attention to a specific property. This portion of the chapter is directed to the physical analysis of the property mortgaged.

### Economic base analysis

The economic base refers to all economic activities by which people earn their living. It will be appreciated that risks increase for mortgages placed on dwellings in areas mainly dependent upon a single industry. For instance, the risk of financial loss tends to be higher in communities such as Marietta, Georgia, populated by workers in the Lockheed Aircraft plant, or residential districts in South Seattle, Washington, dominated by employment in the Boeing Aircraft Company. Similarly, cities dependent upon the resort industry, such as Palm Springs, California, present unusual mortgage risks. Likewise, New Britain, Connecticut, showing employment dominated by the prefabricated metal industry, falls in the same category.

Technological changes that affect local employment and variations in government contracts are among the factors that may lower dwelling values. This does not mean that loans will not be granted in these areas; it means that the mortgage risk is greater relative to communities with a more diversified economic base. The terms of the loan may be less favorable in high risk communities to offset the greater probability of losses on mortgage foreclosures.

The influence of the economic base on mortgage risk is suggested by variations in unemployment stratified by risk categories. An FHA survey discovered that over one year unemployment varied widely between categories important to mortgage risk.

| Category | Range in Unemployment Rate in Percent | |
| --- | --- | --- |
| | *Minimum* | *Maximum* |
| By states ..................... | 2.0 | 7.9 |
| By occupation ................ | 0.4 | 8.4 |
| By industry ................. | 1.9 | 9.0 |
| By age of worker ............. | 2.8 | 17.3 |

Hence mortgages falling in these categories would vary considerably in their relative degree of risk. The data show that unemployment (and, therefore, the ability to repay a loan) varies by location, occupation and age of worker. Generalizations on the local economy are not satisfactory. Each application must be considered on its own merits.

*Population characteristics*

Housing demand is closely related to population characteristics such as household size, age, and local housing preferences. Not only is the number of households important, but are households increasing or decreasing? Is the trend continuing? Considerable attention should be given household size and the average household income. Other population characteristics assume equal importance: for example, a neighborhood with an older population will have housing needs quite apart from a community dominated by young married couples. Their income and educational level is another factor directly associated with the number of owner-occupied houses demanded and their value.

*Personal income*

Data should be obtained on the level of personal incomes. In large measure this factor determines the ability of a community to support a high level of home ownership. If personal incomes are rising, the risk is less than if personal incomes are stable or even declining. For most metropolitan areas, counties, and cities, this information is readily at hand. For example, Volume I of the ten-year population census includes:

1.  The number of inhabitants is shown by states, urban and rural residents, standard metropolitan statistical areas, urbanized areas, county subdivisions, all incorporated places and unincorporated places of 1,000 or more.
2.  General population characteristics such as age, sex, race, marital status and relationship to head of household.
3.  General social and economic characteristics include nation-

ality and parentage, state or county of birth, Spanish origin, mother tongue, residence five years ago, year moved into present house, school enrollment (public or private), years of school completed, vocational training, number of children, family composition, disability, veteran status, employment status, place of work, means of transportation to work, occupation group, industry group, class of worker and income by family and by individual.

4. Detailed characteristics cover most of the subjects above presented in more detail and cross classifications.

Volume II of the ten-year census of population concentrates on subject reports covering particular subjects, e.g., Ethnic Groups, Migration, Marriage and Living Arrangements, Income, Employment and the like. These data may be supplemented by local reports (and more current personal income data) prepared by state and local agencies. By relating current developments to a knowledge of trend data, estimates can be made on the probabilities of stable or rising personal incomes over the life of the loan.

### Neighborhood analysis

Analysis of the neighborhood is critical to judging mortgage security. The definition of a neighborhood which is accepted by appraisers follows:

> A portion of a larger community, or an entire community, in which there is a homogeneous grouping of inhabitants, buildings, or business enterprises. Neighborhood boundaries may consist of well-defined natural or man-made barriers or they may be more or less well-defined by a distinct change in land use or in the character of the inhabitants. (Byrl N. Boyce, *Real Estate Appraisal Terminology*, Cambridge: Ballinger Publishing Company, 1975, page 147.)

The more stable neighborhoods are found in districts in which properties are highly conforming: conforming according to (1) type of house, (2) size, (3) cost, (4) style of architecture, (5) age, and (6) general state of repair. If the property considered for a mortgage does not measure up to the neighborhood standards or is definitely above the neighborhood norm, careful analysis for the potential demand of the property is required.

Analysis of a particular neighborhood is directed to a single issue: are property values increasing, stable or decreasing? To answer this question, neighborhoods must be evaluated according to certain selected characteristics. To some authorities the neighborhood is controlling. The same house with a similar site may have a higher value in Neighborhood A than in Neighborhood B. Neighborhood characteristics largely determine property values that serve as mortgage security. It is suggested that neighborhood analysis, at the very minimum, cover the following attributes:

(1) *Physical Adaptability.* The neighborhood should be physically *adapted to* single family use. In this respect new subdivision layouts should follow current trends in subdivision development. Street layout should be such that access, width, drainage, and paving should meet community standards. Lots should be roughly alike in size and shape. Public improvements that are suitable for houses falling in the $15,000 to $25,000 value range may be quite inadequate for neighborhoods with houses priced from $50,000 to $75,000. Though this is a judgmental factor, the mortgage risk quite clearly will be affected by the degree to which the neighborhood is physically adaptable to residential purposes.

(2) *Location Analysis. Property values tend to be more secure if the neighborhood in question lies in the path of growth.* Investment in a subdivision which is not in the path of development, though well planned and otherwise satisfactory, will show greater property depreciation relative to other more popularly located neighborhoods.

There is also the effect of surrounding land uses. A subdivision adjoining vacant land may be more risky since there is a greater possibility of encroachments, i.e., incompatible land uses, relative to an established subdivision surrounded by highly conforming property.

Features that contribute to neighborhood stability include proximity to churches, a progressive community government, fair and uniform real estate taxes, community recreational facilities and convenience to a source of stable employment. Attractive home sites compatible with the general neighborhood are other stability factors.

Neighborhoods dependent on public transportation will show a value influence for proximity to mass transit routes. A neighborhood served by superior transportation facilities and convenient access to urban centers will show favorable value trends—other factors remaining equal.

On this point observers have noted that neighborhoods tend to have a limited economic life. A prestige neighborhood of the past may revert to a rental district of today. Though some neighborhoods change slowly—they maintain their status as an upper income district for many years—it is equally true that as neighborhood populations change property values change. Older residents are replaced by younger residents with larger families; a middle income population substitutes for upper income groups who migrate to new subdivisions. Neighborhood populations seldom remain static for very long. A successful subdivision will show value increases over the early years (5 to 10 years). As the neighborhood tends to be fully developed, values tend to stabilize. At some point, the newer and developing subdivisions compete with the older districts so that price increases tend to be observed in the newer, competing subdivisions and start declining in the older districts. Judging mortgage security on the basis of real estate values requires judgments respecting prospects for neighborhood change over the mortgage term.

*(3) Utility Services.* Residential communities are dependent on an adequate water supply, sewerage system, storm drainage, television cable service, natural gas, public transportation, and fire protection. Other services of the neighborhood include local schools and recreational facilities. Not only must these services be available and compatible with the value range of the neighborhood, but they must be competitive with other neighborhoods on a cost-service basis. Again the utility system acceptable for a lower income subdivision of $15,000 dwellings would be unacceptable for an area of $100,000 dwellings. Utility services ideally relate to a range of property values in question.

## Site analysis

The site should be appropriate for the neighborhood. That is, site characteristics compatible with a neighborhood of $50,000 to $75,000 houses would show considerable differentiation relative to a neighborhood of $15,000 to $25,000 houses. Therefore, the site analysis should relate to the property in question and neighborhood environment. In evaluating a site, certain characteristics are common to judging the mortgage security. A review of points to be covered shows the importance of this type of analysis.

*deed restrictions filed w/ Register w/ platt book.* *(1) Land Use Restrictions.* Subdivision regulations, zoning ordinances, deed restrictions and title restrictions fall into this category. Starting with title restrictions, it must be shown to what extent the title is restricted by overhead powerline easements, sewer line rights of way across the property and the like. The owner's right to property use and placement of buildings on the site may lower marketability.

Subdivision regulations, deed restrictions, and zoning controls, though they limit the rights to use the property, generally tend to protect property values. They do not prevent property depreciation; they retard depreciation. For example, controls that provide for a minimum building area of 2,000 square feet or a minimum lot area of 10,000 square feet or height restrictions that prohibit dwellings higher than 45 feet, side yard restrictions and similar regulations require that surrounding property uses conform to local standards. Land use restrictions that insure compatible neighborhoods reduce mortgage risks.

*(2) Physical Site Characteristics.* Under this heading are included such items as the front foot area, the square foot land area, depth of the site, topography and shape. In this regard, it is important to identify physical characteristics that relate to market value. For example, it does not always follow that a site 200 feet wide will have a site value twice that of a 100 foot wide lot. A house constructed in the middle of a 200 foot wide lot in an area of 100 foot wide lots probably shows little added utility for frontage that does not conform to surrounding lots.

The important point is to relate the minimum and typical characteristics of each lot to standards of the neighborhood. Nonconforming features decrease value. On the other hand, additional square foot areas or an additional lot, like excess frontage, may add little to the mortgage security if they are atypical of the neighborhood. Each property must be judged according to how each of these physical attributes affects marketability.

*(3) Surface Characteristics.* Under this category soil suitability is reviewed with regard to drainage, load bearing quality, and in the case of septic tanks, soil permeability. For example, in an area dependent on septic tanks, an improperly constructed drainage field or poor soil characteristics for septic tanks limits marketability.

Attention should also be given to the number and types of trees, the slope of the property as it favors the dwelling site, and landscaping. Generally speaking, a lot sloping downward to the street is more suitable for dwelling purposes than one that slopes downward below street grade. Other unusual rock or granite formations that increase building costs and foundations should be noted. In some neighborhoods, surface run off, flood hazards and slide conditions detract from value and may render the property unsuitable for mortgage financing.

*(4) Surrounding Encroachments.* Considerable attention should be given to the effect of surrounding land uses on a particular property. Value depreciating factors such as proximity to an airport with its noise, or a site that adjoins a retail building causing traffic congestion, noise and unattractive surroundings limit the resale value of dwellings.

Applying these criteria to property proposed for a long-term mortgage calls for conclusions on the affect of surrounding property as it might influence resale. A property constructed on a site near commercial or industrial uses may have a value less than its cost of reproduction. Clearly, the value of the real estate security will be limited by value depreciating factors such as incompatible commercial and industrial buildings, public buildings, traffic congestion, highway or airport noise and like encroachments.

## *Building characteristics*

The description of the building allows the reviewer to judge the general utility of the property for single family use. Appraisals for mortgage purposes provide sufficient descriptive material to cover the following main building features:

1. Exterior material and workmanship—walls, foundation and roof
2. Interior materials and workmanship—floors, interior wall finishes
3. The floor plan—number of rooms, location, size and layout
4. The building equipment—general utility, quality and present condition.

These data will be reported in considerable detail, especially if the mortgage relates to newly constructed buildings. For new properties emphasis will probably be on reproduction costs: the cost new-value will be judged according to the type of construction and building details. The analysis must cover the quality of materials, fixtures, heating and air conditioning equipment, built-in cabinets, interior finishing, and related details. Workmanship should relate to the value class of the property. The higher the value the more evident quality workmanship should be.

In the final analysis, components of the building should create maximum utility. Unusual room size, awkward floor plans, or inadequate equipment for the size of the dwelling such as hot water heaters, heating and air conditioning equipment lower the value for mortgage purposes. In each instance, the description of building features and their condition should be consistent with the depreciation deduction shown on the appraisal form.

## *Valuation data*

The value estimates supporting the loan should include documented cost data showing the cost per square foot and the site value. Actual construction costs of similarly constructed buildings recently built in the same general locality are preferred as documentation. If depreciation is applied to older buildings, justification for the deduction should be made. Sales data analysis, the subject of considerable explanation in appraisal textbooks, provide sufficient detail to enable the mortgage officer to review actual sales of comparable properties in the same or like neighborhoods.

Sufficient documentation should be given to allow value comparisons on a price per square foot. In this way the final value conclusions submitted by the appraiser should provide an objective standard supporting the mortgage application. Each element of the real estate analysis, therefore, presumes that the property has marketability sufficient to recover the outstanding mortgage balance in the event of foreclosure.

## Judging Borrower Credit

Though mortgage credit analysis is covered in a separate chapter, it is worthwhile to cover the steps followed in judging personal credit for underwriting a mortgage on a single family dwelling. This part of the analysis assumes particular importance since experience shows that proper borrower qualification reduces the possibility of foreclosure losses. Again though credit analysis rests on factual material, the experience of the lender must interpret and weigh the importance of credit information. A review of the main points to be covered shows the type of information that serves as the basis for the mortgage approval.

### *The borrower's credit status*

The mortgage submission will include a report from a credit agency which is helpful in reviewing past payment records. Credit references supplementing these data show how the buyer has honored past debts. Personal verification of these sources is recommended to give greater insight into the probability of mortgage repayment. A report of personal assets and liabilities supplement these data. The latter shows that the borrower has sufficient funds to pay the equity, closing costs and incidental costs of acquiring a new dwelling.

Generally speaking, the greater the equity, the greater the loan security. It is reasoned that borrowers have a stronger motivation for home ownership in rough proportion to an increase in their equity. Moreover, with relatively high equities, the borrower is less likely to abandon the mortgage.

Special attention will be given the fixed obligations of the borrower. Included in this category will be instalment credit payments, past debts, and other expenditures related to size of the family.

### *Source of income*

The employment record will show not only the level of income but its source and possibility of its continued duration. Supplemental income from nonrecurring sources should not be considered. Include income that will be effectively earned over the life of the mortgage with reasonable reliability. In the case of married couples, the work record and training experience of both individuals will be considered.

Certain occupations known to be subject to seasonal and cyclical change may render the borrower ineligible. Construction employment, employment in the entertainment-resort industries, and certain types of sales work fall into these categories. Whether the income will justify favorable recommendation depends on local circumstances. Employment verification should be part of this portion of the analysis.

## Housing expenditure patterns

An analysis of the probable cost of operating a single family dwelling shows how much income remains for the mortgage payment after other family expenditures. Such costs should include these items:

> *Acquisition costs*
>> Sales price (cash sale)
>> Closing costs
>> Downpayment
>
> *Monthly costs*
>> Mortgage payments
>> Property taxes, per month
>> Maintenance costs, average monthly
>> Utilities
>>> Water
>>> Electricity
>>> Telephone
>>> Natural gas
>>> Sewerage
>>> Fuel

Such a statement permits comparison of monthly costs of household ownership with past housing expenditures. Usually the transition from rental occupancy to owner occupancy introduces expenses that may not be anticipated by the borrower. There is a tendency to compare the mortgage payment directly to rental payments without adjusting for normal costs of home ownership.

## Rules of thumb

Specialists in single family dwellings rely on several guides to maximum mortgages and monthly payments. They are only guides that are not always followed if circumstances recommend deviation from standard practice. For instance, some lenders recommend that the mortgage should not be greater than two and a half times gross annual income. Another rule of thumb, popular for many years, requires that the maximum mortgage payment on conventional mortgages be limited to 20 percent to 25 percent of monthly income.

These ratios are difficult to apply to groups in different income categories. Generally speaking, the lower the monthly income, the greater the housing expense in proportion to monthly income. As income increases the proportion paid for housing expenses, including mortgage payments, tends to decrease. The borrower's ability to pay the mortgage should rest on borrower circumstances and not solely on fixed and unvarying rules of thumb.

There are other issues recommending departure from rules of thumb. For instance, young professionally trained heads of household may have limited assets but high and rising personal incomes. In these circumstances, the applicant may represent a better mortgage risk than others who fit the prevailing rule of thumb. By the same token, borrowers with a high level of assets and unstable incomes may represent a good mortgage risk if the loan-to-value ratio is lowered. In general, the greater the assets of the borrower, the greater the probability of mortgage repayment.

## Judging the Mortgage Pattern

For single family dwellings, the cost of processing the mortgage application should be minimized and at the same time provide sufficient information to either approve or disapprove the loan. Accordingly mortgage applications on dwellings rely heavily on standard forms. To illustrate these techniques attention is directed to valuation forms common to (1) conventional, nongovernmental, or guaranteed mortgages, (2) the report forms used to appraise dwellings for Veterans Administration guaranteed loans and (3) mortgage analysis forms required by the Federal Housing Administration.

### Conventional Appraisal Report Forms

The data required in Exhibit 7.1 should provide sufficient information for a rational decision on the suitability of a dwelling for mortgage purposes. Note that the beginning part of the appraisal report identifies the property, recites dimensions, details the floor plan, and requires a photograph.

The detail under land, ground, and utilities calls for a personal evaluation in terms of good, fair, and poor. Note also that the section on neighborhood facilities deals mostly with locational factors and judgments respecting conformity of the property under appraisal with surrounding buildings. Data on encroachments, neighborhood trends, vacancies, and similar information are relevant to the analysis of the dwelling.

# Exhibit 7.1

# Appraisal Form for a Conventional Mortgage

RESIDENTIAL APPRAISAL REPORT                                                  File No.

**To be completed by Lender**

| Borrower/Client | | Census Tract | Map Reference |

Property Address

City                                County                State                Zip Code

Legal Description

Sale Price $          Date of Sale          Property Rights Appraised ☐ Fee ☐ Leasehold ☐ DeMinimis PUD(FNMA only ☐ Condo ☐ PUD)

Actual Real Estate Taxes $          (yr) Loan charges to be paid by seller $          Other sales concessions

Lender                                        Lender's Address

Occupant                    Appraiser                    Instructions to Appraiser

## NEIGHBORHOOD

| | | | | | Good Avg. Fair Poor |
|---|---|---|---|---|---|
| Location | ☐ Urban | ☐ Suburban | ☐ Rural | | |
| Built Up | ☐ Over 75% | ☐ 25% to 75% | ☐ Under 25% | Employment Stability | ☐ ☐ ☐ ☐ |
| Growth Rate ☐ Fully Dev | ☐ Rapid | ☐ Steady | ☐ Slow | Convenience to Employment | ☐ ☐ ☐ ☐ |
| Property Values | ☐ Increasing | ☐ Stable | ☐ Declining | Convenience to Shopping | ☐ ☐ ☐ ☐ |
| Demand/Supply | ☐ Shortage | ☐ In Balance | ☐ Over Supply | Convenience to Schools | ☐ ☐ ☐ ☐ |
| Marketing Time | ☐ Under 3 Mos. | ☐ 4-6 Mos. | ☐ Over 6 Mos | Quality of Schools | ☐ ☐ ☐ ☐ |

Present Land Use ___% 1 Family ___% 2-4 Family ___% Apts ___% Condo ___% Commercial

___% Industrial ___% Vacant ___%

Change in Present Land Use ☐ Not Likely ☐ Likely (*) ☐ Taking Place (*)

(*) From _____ To _____

Predominant Occupancy ☐ Owner ☐ Tenant _____% Vacant

Single Family Price Range $_____ to $_____ Predominant Value $_____

Single Family Age _____ yrs to _____ yrs Predominant Age _____ yrs

| Recreational Facilities | ☐ ☐ ☐ ☐ |
| Adequacy of Utilities | ☐ ☐ ☐ ☐ |
| Property Compatibility | ☐ ☐ ☐ ☐ |
| Protection from Detrimental Conditions | ☐ ☐ ☐ ☐ |
| Police and Fire Protection | ☐ ☐ ☐ ☐ |
| General Appearance of Properties | ☐ ☐ ☐ ☐ |
| Appeal to Market | ☐ ☐ ☐ ☐ |

Note: FHLMC/FNMA do not consider the racial composition of the neighborhood to be a relevant factor and it must not be considered in the appraisal.

Comments (including those factors adversely affecting marketability) _____

## SITE

Dimensions _____ Sq. Ft. or Acres ☐ Corner Lot

Zoning classification _____ Present improvements ☐ do ☐ do not conform to zoning regulations

Highest and best use ☐ Present use ☐ Other (specify) _____

| | Public | Other (Describe) | OFF SITE IMPROVEMENTS | Topo |
|---|---|---|---|---|
| Elec. | ☐ | | Street Access: ☐ Public ☐ Private | Size |
| Gas | ☐ | | Surface | Shape |
| Water | ☐ | | Maintenance ☐ Public ☐ Private | View |
| San.Sewer | ☐ | | ☐ Storm Sewer ☐ Curb/Gutter | Drainage |
| | ☐ Underground Elect. & Tel. | | ☐ Sidewalk ☐ Street Lights | Is the property located in a HUD identified Flood Hazard Area? ☐ No ☐ Yes |

Comments (favorable or unfavorable including any apparent adverse easements, encroachments or other adverse conditions) _____

## IMPROVEMENTS

☐ Existing (approx. yr. blt.) 19____ No. Units ____ Type (det, duplex, semi/det, etc.) Design (rambler, split level, etc.) Exterior Walls

☐ Proposed ☐ Under Construction No. Stories

Roof Material _____ Gutters & Downspouts ☐ None Window (Type) _____ Insulation ☐ None ☐ Floor

☐ Storm Sash ☐ Screens ☐ Combination ☐ Ceiling ☐ Roof ☐ Walls

**BSMT**

Foundation Walls _____ % Basement ☐ Floor Drain Finished Ceiling

☐ Outside Entrance ☐ Sump Pump Finished Walls

☐ Crawl Space ☐ Concrete Floor ____% Finished Finished Floor

☐ Slab on Grade Evidence of: ☐ Dampness ☐ Termites ☐ Settlement

Comments _____

## ROOM LIST

| Room List | Foyer | Living | Dining | Kitchen | Den | Family Rm. | Rec. Rm. | Bedrooms | No. Baths | Laundry | Other |
|---|---|---|---|---|---|---|---|---|---|---|---|
| Basement | | | | | | | | | | | |
| 1st Level | | | | | | | | | | | |
| 2nd Level | | | | | | | | | | | |

Total _____ Rooms _____ Bedrooms _____ Baths in finished area above grade

Kitchen Equipment: ☐ Refrigerator ☐ Range/Oven ☐ Disposal ☐ Dishwasher ☐ Fan/Hood ☐ Compactor ☐ Washer ☐ Dryer ☐

HEAT: Type _____ Fuel _____ Cond. _____ AIR COND ☐ Central ☐ Other ☐ Adequate ☐ Inadequate

## INTERIOR FINISH & EQUIPMENT

| Floors | ☐ Hardwood | ☐ Carpet Over ☐ |
| Walls | ☐ Drywall | ☐ Plaster ☐ |
| Trim/Finish | ☐ Good | ☐ Average ☐ Fair ☐ Poor |
| Bath Floor | ☐ Ceramic | ☐ |
| Bath Wainscot | ☐ Ceramic | ☐ |

Special Features (including fireplaces): _____

ATTIC: ☐ Yes ☐ No ☐ Stairway ☐ Drop-stair ☐ Scuttle ☐ Floored

Finished (Describe) _____ ☐ Heated

CAR STORAGE: ☐ Garage ☐ Built-in ☐ Attached ☐ Detached ☐ Car Port

No. Cars _____ ☐ Adequate ☐ Inadequate Condition _____

## PROPERTY RATING

| | Good Avg. Fair Poor |
|---|---|
| Quality of Construction (Materials & Finish) | ☐ ☐ ☐ ☐ |
| Condition of Improvements | ☐ ☐ ☐ ☐ |
| Rooms size and layout | ☐ ☐ ☐ ☐ |
| Closets and Storage | ☐ ☐ ☐ ☐ |
| Plumbing—adequacy and condition | ☐ ☐ ☐ ☐ |
| Electrical—adequacy and condition | ☐ ☐ ☐ ☐ |
| Kitchen Cabinets—adequacy and condition | ☐ ☐ ☐ ☐ |
| Compatibility to Neighborhood | ☐ ☐ ☐ ☐ |
| Overall Livability | ☐ ☐ ☐ ☐ |
| Appeal and Marketability | ☐ ☐ ☐ ☐ |

Effective Age _____ Yrs. Est. Remaining Economic Life _____ Yrs

PORCHES, PATIOS, POOL, FENCES, etc. (describe) _____

COMMENTS (including functional or physical inadequacies, repairs needed, modernization, etc.) _____

FHLMC Form 70 Rev. 9/75          ATTACH DESCRIPTIVE PHOTOGRAPHS OF SUBJECT PROPERTY AND STREET SCENE          FNMA Form 1004 Rev. 9/75

# Exhibit 7.1 continued

## VALUATION SECTION

Purpose of Appraisal is to estimate Market Value as defined in Certification & Statement of Limiting Conditions (FHLMC Form 439/FNMA Form 1004B). If submitted for FNMA, the appraiser must attach (1) sketch or map showing location of subject, street names, distance from nearest intersection, and any detrimental conditions and (2) exterior building sketch of improvements showing dimensions.

**COST APPROACH**

| Measurements | No. Stories | Sq. Ft. |
|---|---|---|
| ___ x ___ x ___ = ___ | | |
| ___ x ___ x ___ = ___ | | |
| ___ x ___ x ___ = ___ | | |
| ___ x ___ x ___ = ___ | | |
| ___ x ___ x ___ = ___ | | |
| ___ x ___ x ___ = ___ | | |

Total Gross Living Area (List in Market Data Analysis below) _____

Comment on functional and economic obsolescence: _____

ESTIMATED REPRODUCTION COST – NEW – OF IMPROVEMENTS:

| | |
|---|---|
| Dwelling _____ Sq. Ft. @ $ _____ | = $ _____ |
| _____ Sq. Ft. @ $ _____ | = _____ |
| Extras _____ | = _____ |
| | = _____ |
| | = _____ |
| Porches, Patios, etc. _____ | = _____ |
| Garage/Car Port _____ Sq. Ft. @ $ _____ | = _____ |
| Site Improvements (driveway, landscaping, etc.) | = _____ |
| Total Estimated Cost New . . . . . . . . | = $ _____ |

Less | Physical | Functional | Economic
Depreciation $ _____ | $ _____ | $ _____ | = $ ( _____ )

| | |
|---|---|
| Depreciated value of improvements . . . . . | = $ _____ |
| ESTIMATED LAND VALUE . . . . . . . . | = $ _____ |
| (If leasehold, show only leasehold value) | |
| **INDICATED VALUE BY COST APPROACH** . . . | $ _____ |

**MARKET DATA ANALYSIS**

The undersigned has recited three recent sales of properties most similar and proximate to subject and has considered these in the market analysis. The description includes a dollar adjustment, reflecting market reaction to those items of significant variation between the subject and comparable properties. If a significant item in the comparable property is superior to, or more favorable than, the subject property, a minus (-) adjustment is made, thus reducing the indicated value of subject; if a significant item in the comparable is inferior to, or less favorable than, the subject property, a plus (+) adjustment is made, thus increasing the indicated value of the subject.

| ITEM | Subject Property | COMPARABLE NO. 1 | | COMPARABLE NO. 2 | | COMPARABLE NO. 3 | |
|---|---|---|---|---|---|---|---|
| Address | | | | | | | |
| Proximity to Subj. | | | | | | | |
| Sales Price | $ | $ | | $ | | $ | |
| Price/Living area | $ | $ | | $ | | $ | |
| Data Source | | | | | | | |
| Date of Sale and Time Adjustment | DESCRIPTION | DESCRIPTION | +(–)$ Adjustment | DESCRIPTION | +(–)$ Adjustment | DESCRIPTION | +(–)$ Adjustment |
| Location | | | | | | | |
| Site/View | | | | | | | |
| Design and Appeal | | | | | | | |
| Quality of Const. | | | | | | | |
| Age | | | | | | | |
| Condition | | | | | | | |
| Living Area Room Count and Total | Total / B-rms / Baths | Total / B-rms / Baths | | Total / B-rms / Baths | | Total / B-rms / Baths | |
| Gross Living Area | Sq.Ft. | Sq.Ft. | | Sq.Ft. | | Sq.Ft. | |
| Basement & Bsmt. Finished Rooms | | | | | | | |
| Functional Utility | | | | | | | |
| Air Conditioning | | | | | | | |
| Garage/Car Port | | | | | | | |
| Porches, Patio, Pools, etc. | | | | | | | |
| Other (e.g. fireplaces, kitchen equip., heating, remodeling) | | | | | | | |
| Sales or Financing Concessions | | | | | | | |
| Net Adj. (Total) | | ☐ Plus; ☐ Minus $ | | ☐ Plus; ☐ Minus $ | | ☐ Plus; ☐ Minus $ | |
| Indicated Value of Subject | | $ | | $ | | $ | |

Comments on Market Data _____

**INDICATED VALUE BY MARKET DATA APPROACH** . . . . . . . . . . . . . . . . . . . . . . $ _____

**INDICATED VALUE BY INCOME APPROACH** (If applicable) Economic Market Rent $ _____ /Mo. x Gross Rent Multiplier _____ = $ _____

This appraisal is made ☐ "as is" ☐ subject to the repairs, alterations, or conditions listed below ☐ completion per plans and specifications.

Comments and Conditions of Appraisal: _____

Final Reconciliation: _____

This appraisal is based upon the above requirements, the certification, contingent and limiting conditions, and Market Value definition that are stated in ☐ FHLMC Form 439 (Rev. 9/75)/FNMA Form 1004B filed with client _____ 19 ___ ☐ attached.

If submitted for FNMA, the report has been prepared in compliance with FNMA form instructions.

I ESTIMATE THE MARKET VALUE, AS DEFINED, OF SUBJECT PROPERTY AS OF _____ 19 ___ to be $ _____

Appraiser(s) _____ Review Appraiser (If applicable) _____

☐ Did ☐ Did Not Physically Inspect Property

FHLMC Form 70 Rev. 9/75     REVERSE     FNMA Form 1004 Rev. 9/75

The next portion of the report permits a comparison of the property appraised with the neighborhood. Estimates of quality are called for in listing different parts of the property including condition of the main building, equipment and extra features. The last part of this report calls for an estimate of the rental value and age of the property, its actual and estimated remaining life.

The valuation section includes data on the reproduction cost new, its depreciation and site value. The cost data are supplemented by the requirement for at least three comparable sales with an estimate of market value from an analysis of comparable properties. The final estimate of fair market value may or may not agree with either the cost or the market value estimate. The remarks section provides for a listing of factors affecting the marketability of the property.

The appraisal form is directed specifically to the mortgage function. For not only is the report directed to the market value estimate, which must be documented, but considerable attention is given to the long run projection of the property as mortgage security. This analysis is taken from an evaluation of the neighborhood and conformity of the property appraised with the neighborhood.

## The Veterans Administration Appraisal Report

Though less data are called for by the Veterans Administration form, this information permits an analysis of the property proposed for the Veterans Administration guarantee of the mortgage. A review of Exhibit 7.2 shows the importance of the neighborhood, the type of construction, neighborhood age, extent of owner occupancy, vacancies, zoning and transition to other uses. The form requires a list of information on utilities and provides for a brief building description. In this case the analysis requires detail on recently sold comparable dwellings, and a section for remarks directed specifically to mortgage analysis. Questions of property comparability, detrimental influences, and the real estate market are a case in point. If depreciation is listed, it must be explained.

In addition the valuation is estimated by the replacement cost less depreciation. The descriptive data and main features of the building support the allowance for depreciation.

## The FHA Rating System

The preceding analysis concentrated on an evaluation of the property and borrower credit. The mortgage pattern refers to an additional element—the mortgage and its relationship to the real estate and the bor-

# Exhibit 7.2
## Veterans Administration Appraisal Form

Form Approved
OMB No. 76-R0231

### VETERANS ADMINISTRATION
### APPRAISAL REPORT

CASE NUMBER

| 1. MAJOR STRUCTURES | A. CONSTRUCTION | B. TYPICAL COND. | C. BUILT-UP | D. AGE TYP. BLDG. | E. OWN. OCCUP. | F. VACANCY | G. ZONING | H. TRANS. TO | 2. NEIGHBORHOOD RACIAL CHARACTERISTICS |
|---|---|---|---|---|---|---|---|---|---|
| NEIGHBORHOOD | | | % | | | % | % | | ☐ ALL WHITE |
| BLOCK | | | % | | | % | % | | ☐ ALL OTHER ☐ MIXED |

**3. STATUS OF PROPERTY**

☐ A. PROPOSED ☐ B. EXISTING, NOT PREVIOUSLY OCCUPIED ☐ C. EXISTING, PREVIOUSLY OCCUPIED ☐ D. ALTERATIONS, IMPROVEM'TS. OR REPAIRS ☐ E. REFINANCING–RESIDENCE OWNED AND OCCUPIED BY VETERAN APPLICANT AS HIS HOME

**4. CONSTRUCTION COMPLETED BEFORE DATE HEREOF**

☐ A. WITHIN 12 CALENDAR MOS. ☐ B. MORE THAN 12 CALENDAR MOS.

5. NAME AND ADDRESS OF FIRM OR PERSON MAKING REQUEST (Complete mailing address. Include ZIP Code)

6. PROPERTY ADDRESS (Include ZIP Code)

| 7. TYPE OF PROPERTY | 8. NO. BLDGS. | 9. NO. LIVING UNITS |
|---|---|---|
| ☐ HOME ☐ FARM ☐ BUSINESS | | |

10. LOT DIMENSIONS

| 11. DESCRIPTION | | | | NO. ROOMS | DINING ROOM | CAR GARAGE | GAS | CEN. AIR COND. |
|---|---|---|---|---|---|---|---|---|
| DETACHED | WOOD SIDING | CINDER BLOCK | SPLIT LEVEL | | | | | TYPE HEAT. & FUEL |
| SEMI-DET. | WOOD SHINGLE | STONE | % BASEMENT | BEDROOMS | KITCHEN | CAR CARPORT | UNDERGRD. WIRE | |
| ROW | ALUM. SIDING | BRICK & BLOCK | SLAB | BATHS | FAMILY RM. | WATER (Public) | SEWER (Public) | ROOFING DESCRIP. |
| CONDOMINIUM | ASB. SHINGLE | STUCCO | CRAWL SPACE | 1/2 BATHS | UTILITY RM. | WATER (Comm.) | SEWER (Comm.) | |
| | BRICK VENEER | STORIES | YRS. EST. AGE | LIVING RM. | FIREPLACE | WATER (Ind.) | SEPTIC TANK | |

| 12. LEGAL DESCRIPTION | 13. TITLE LIMITATIONS INCLUDING EASEMENTS, RESTRICTIONS, ENCROACHMENTS, HOMEOWNERS ASSOCIATION ASSESS., ETC. | 14. TYPE OF STREET PAVING |
|---|---|---|
| | | CURB |
| | | SIDEWALK |
| | | STORM SEWER |

**15. INTERIOR AND EXTERIOR REPAIRS** (Show below ONLY repairs necessary to make property conform with applicable MPR's)

| | $ | | $ |
|---|---|---|---|
| | | | |
| | | | |
| | | | |
| | | | |
| | | | |
| | TOTAL ESTIMATED COST INTERIOR AND EXTERIOR REPAIRS | $ | |

| 16. COMPARABLE PROPERTIES | S. F. AREA | STORY | RMS. | BED RMS. | BATH | CONSTR. | GAR./ CRPT. | AGE/ COND. | PRICE | DATE | FINANC. | EQ. | SUP. | INF. |
|---|---|---|---|---|---|---|---|---|---|---|---|---|---|---|
| SUBJECT PROPERTY | | | | | | | | | | | | | | |
| | | | | | | | | | | | | | % | |
| | | | | | | | | | | | | | % | |
| | | | | | | | | | | | | | % | |

17. REMARKS (Base ther (a) Property comparability; (b) Detrimental influences; (c) Real estate market in community; (d) Highest and best use, (e) Explain depreciation, (f) Building lot, district, violations; (g) Comments on repairs; (h) Comments on any special assessments) (Use supplemental sheet if necessary.)

IS PROPERTY IN A SPECIAL FLOOD HAZARD AREA? ☐ YES ☐ NO

| 18. PROPERTY SHOWS EVIDENCE OF (Check) | 19. ESTATE (Check) | 20. FUTURE ECONOMIC LIFE (Years) | 21. CALCULATIONS |
|---|---|---|---|
| ☐ TERMITE ☐ DRY ROT ☐ DAMP-NESS ☐ SETTLE-MENT ☐ NO EVIDENCE | ☐ A. FEE SIMPLE ☐ B. LEASE-HOLD | MAIN OTHER | MAIN CU. SQ. OTHER |

| 22. DATA | DESCRIPTION | CONDITION | 23. EQUIP. | DESCRIPTION | DEPR. VALUE | 24. OTHER IMPROVEMENTS | DEPR. VALUE | | |
|---|---|---|---|---|---|---|---|---|---|
| ROOF | | | | | $ | | $ | RATE PER FT. | $ |
| FOUND. | | | | | | | | REPLMT. COST | $ |
| BSMT. | | | | | | | | PHYSICAL DEP. | $ |
| FLOORS | | | | | | | | FUNCTIONAL | $ |
| INT. WALLS | | | | | | | | ECONOMIC | $ |
| BATH FINISH | | | | | | | | TOTAL DEP. | $ |
| GUTTERS | | | | | | | | DEPR. COST | $ |
| 25. ANNUAL TAXES | | | | | | | | TOTAL DEPR. COST OF IMPR. | $ |
| GENERAL | SPECIAL | OTHER | | | | | | OTHER IMPR. AND EQUIP. | $ |
| | | | | | | | | LAND VALUE | $ |
| $ | $ | $ | TOTAL | $ | | TOTAL | $ | TOTAL DEPR. COST OF PROP. | $ |

| 26. DOES PROPERTY CONFORM TO APPLICABLE MINIMUM PROPERTY REQUIREMENTS? | 27. ESTIMATE FAIR MONTHLY RENT TIMES RENT MULTIPLIER | 28. CORRELATION |
|---|---|---|
| ☐ YES ☐ NO (If "No" explain in Item 17) | $ × = $ | A. COST APPROACH $ | B. CAPITALIZATION $ | C. MARKET APPROACH $ |

I HEREBY CERTIFY that (a) I have carefully viewed the property described in this report, INSIDE AND OUTSIDE, so far as it has been completed; that (b) it is the same property that is identified by description in my appraisal assignment; that (c) I HAVE NOT RECEIVED, HAVE NO AGREEMENT TO RECEIVE, NOR WILL I ACCEPT FROM ANY PARTY ANY GRATUITY OR EMOLUMENT OTHER THAN MY APPRAISAL FEE FOR MAKING THIS APPRAISAL: that (d) I have no interest, present or prospective, in the applicant, seller, property, or mortgage; that (e) in arriving at the estimated reasonable value I have not been influenced in any manner whatsoever by the race, religion, or national origin of any person residing in the property or in the neighborhood wherein it is located. I understand that violation of this certification can result in removal from the fee appraiser's roster.

| 29. I ESTIMATE "REASONABLE VALUE" | 30. ESTIMATED REASONABLE VALUE | 31. SIGNATURE OF APPRAISER | 32. DATE SIGNED |
|---|---|---|---|
| ☐ "AS IS" ☐ "AS REPAIRED" ☐ "AS COMPLETED" | $ | | |

VA FORM
DEC 1973 **26-1803**

EXISTING STOCKS OF VA FORM 26-1803, NOV 1972, WILL BE USED.

VA FILE COPY 5

153

rower. In studying the interrelationships of these three items, the amount of risk may govern approval or disapproval or modification of the mortgage. It is not likely that a given application will be either approved or disapproved. It is more likely that the lender will adjust the proposed mortgage to the estimate of probable risk. That is, if future values are relatively uncertain, the loan to value ratio may be adjusted downward, say from 25 years to 20 years to account for the added risk. Likewise, questionable borrower credit may call for decreasing the mortgage term or increasing the downpayment.

Though FHA rating grids apply to only FHA insured properties, the analysis illustrates the problems faced by all lenders. The borrower must be rated, the location must be judged, and the value of the property must be in proper ratio to the amount of loan.

## Statistical Tests of the Mortgage Pattern

While the FHA rating system illustrates the relation between borrower, the physical security, and the mortgage, it is based on highly subjective items. By using computers, it is possible to study the experience of mortgage portfolios to predict loan characteristics which have the highest probability of foreclosure or delinquency or slow-paying characteristics. One such study starts with the factors that normally determine the difference between a good or bad loan. The following is a list of items used to judge single family dwelling mortgages and represent items expected to have significance in predicting quality of a loan:

- Ratio of property value to annual income
- Ratio of monthly mortgage payments to monthly income
- Percentage of purchase price provided as downpayment
- Stable annual income
- Number of satisfactory credit references
- Number of family members
- ~~Previous marital experiences~~
- Stability of husband's employment
- Stability of wife's employment [1]

A study of the experience of some 5,104 loans in St. Louis showed that of these characteristics, listed in order of their importance, certain items stood out. The first significant factors associated with slow paying loans was the ratio of the loan to borrower income. As the amount of the mortgage increased, relative to the annual income of the borrower, the more the loan was likely to be in the poor repayment category. A

---

[1] G. K. Rakes, "A Numerical Credit Evaluation Model for Residential Mortgages," *Quarterly Review of Economics and Business*, Vol. 13 (Autumn, 1973), p. 76.

closely associated item was the number of unsatisfactory credit experiences. The larger the number of previous failures to meet credit obligations the more likely that slow repayments resulted. The relative stability of employment was another significant factor that predicted the probability of a "bad" loan.

Though the statistical survey of 5,104 loans shows results that emphasize many of the same factors listed in the FHA mortgage pattern, the data are more statistically valid. Statistical probabilities may be calculated from a loan portfolio with considerably more precision than the more personal type of rating used by the Federal Housing Administration.

### Private Mortgage Insurance (PMI) *serves same function as FHA*
*state-regulated not fed*
*costs less than FHA*

Mortgage lenders—especially commercial banks—have turned to PMI with great enthusiasm. Its popularity started with the 1956 organization of the Mortgage Guarantee Insurance Corporation (MGIC) in Wisconsin. More recently some 13 PMI companies have been authorized among the several states. Their unusual growth is indicated by recent financial data. MGIC had assets totaling $299 million at the end of 1974. Total industry assets grew from $15 million in 1970 to $552 million by 1974. It is estimated that total PMI in force was almost $34 billion at the end of 1974. *Helps establish secondary market for conventional loans*

This growth record was stimulated by the authority of savings and loan associations and commercial banks to make 95 percent loan-to-value loans. In addition, their popularity is partly based on the following advantages of PMI relative to FHA and VA loans:

1. PMI companies do not insure the full amount of a mortgage loan (in contrast to FHA). PMI policies generally limit the insurance company to a maximum of 25 percent of the loan. The obligation is in lieu of paying the full amount of the claim and taking title of the mortgaged property.

2. PMI is cheaper than FHA insurance: the borrower pays approximately one half of the insurance premium relative to FHA. Further, over the life of the loan, the lender may cancel PMI as the loan-to-value ratio reaches a point in which the risk does not justify the expense of PMI.

3. PMI companies are relatively free of government regulations, and the delay frequently associated with government processing of loan applications.

4. Mortgage lenders prefer PMI and high ratio conventional loans that earn relatively high yields. With the acceptabil-

155

ity of PMI loans in the secondary market, lenders have mortgage portifolio flexibility formerly associated only with government insured loans.

Underwriting practices of PMI companies have insured their success: They select only qualified, eligible lenders; they regularly review basic information on individual loans; and they undertake spot checks of local economic factors, lender appraisals and credit reports. Only lenders are approved that have the demonstrated management ability and evidence of observing accepted standards.

As in other mortgage operations, an application for PMI will include:

An application for PMI insurance
A credit report
Verification of employment
The loan application
A property photograph.

Some of the possible reasons for loan rejection might include (1) lack of experience in a new business venture; (2) lack of sufficient job seniority rights; (3) lack of experience because of short time on job; (4) numerous employment changes; (5) unstable sources of secondary income; (6) recent move of the borrower into the area; and (7) employment of a seasonal nature.

In the event of foreclosure the lender must acquire a clear title to recover loss under one of the following options:

1. *100 percent settlement.* The PMI accepts title to the real estate and pays the lender the full amount of the claim.

2. *20 or 25 percent settlement.* The company may elect to pay 20 percent of the claim total or 25 percent in the case of loans exceeding 90 percent of the value and waive any further interest in the property. In the sale of the property the lender may more than cover the loan balance but if there is a loss, it is absorbed by the lender.

3. *Less than 20 or 25 percent settlement.* With PMI company approval, a lender may resell the real estate before submitting a claim. The insurance payment will be equal to the full extent of loss including foreclosure expenses up to a maximum of a 25 percent loss settlement if no sale has been made.

In sum, private mortgage insurance has certain advantages over FHA and VA loans. In addition to the points already made, it should be noted that the insurance premium on PMI varies according to the degree of risk. For example, the premium charged on 10 percent coverage, for loans 80 percent and under, might call for an annual premium of .15 percent the first year and annually thereafter. On 25 percent coverage on a 90 to 95 percent loan, the premium charged might be 1 percent in the first year and one quarter of one percent annually thereafter.

These arrangements vary from the single premium plan of FHA paid by all borrowers regardless of the individual risk. The combination of a relatively high loan-to-value ratio loan with its higher yield and lower costs, and more expeditious processing, largely accounts for the phenomenal growth of PMI and the relatively declining importance of FHA loans. In the case of subsidized mortgages, however, FHA loans offer the only alternative means of financing.

## A Single Family Dwelling Mortgage Application

Conventional loans require sufficient information to judge the borrower's credit, the real estate security and the appropriateness of the proposed loan. Such an analysis includes the following minimum documentation:

1. The loan application
2. Credit report
3. Residential appraisal report
4. Photograph
5. Floor plan sketch
6. Area maps
7. Employment verification
8. Verification of bank deposits
9. Financial statement.

To illustrate, consider the following example of a loan request for $40,000 covering a dwelling appraised at $75,000.

Re: Wilson W. Jones
300 Grape Street
Denver, Colorado
$40,000, 9%—15 years

### LOAN SUMMARY

LEGAL:
Lots 26, 27, 28 and the South one-half ($\frac{1}{2}$) of Lot 25, Block two (2) CAPITAL ANNEX, City and County of Denver, Colorado

LOCATION:
In Denver's most exclusive, luxury type, single family, residential area, zoned R-O and in the price range of recent comparable sales to $80,000. The area is 100% built up and has a "no

157

vacancy" record. Approximately two miles from downtown Denver, with on-the-street public transportation, with 20-minute service. There are several church denominations represented within 4 to 5 blocks and the Cherry Creek shopping center is 4 blocks east. A grade school is 5 blocks distant; a high school with bus transportation is within 14 blocks. This is truly a 100% residential area.

IMPROVEMENTS:

This is a one story, brick, single family residence, completed in 1956. The owner, Wilson W. Jones, designed and supervised the building of this home. In 1954, he purchased the land on which was situated an older residence. Mr Jones then completely razed the older improvements and built the present residence from the ground up. The original cost in 1954 was $26,500 and including that cost, Mr. Jones has records showing a total complete cost of $132,000. The site includes $3\frac{1}{2}$ lots and extensive investigation has disclosed that if any such building sites were now available in this area it would take from $7,000 to $8,000 per lot to purchase them.

This residence is deluxe in every respect, with 7 finished rooms, which includes 3 bedrooms and $3\frac{1}{2}$ baths, a large living room with fire place, 2 large dressing rooms, utility room and large storage room. You will note from the enclosed colored photos showing several of the interior rooms that the design and finish is extraordinary.

At the rear of the house is a large covered terrace of 572 square feet which overlooks a beautiful landscaped garden with a small rotating stream simulating falls. We enclose photos of this garden area, also, Society Column write-ups from two different Sunday Denver Post issues; one dated October 20, 19X1 and one dated July 17, 19X2. There is also a 2-car attached, electric door, brick garage with concrete slab driveway approach. At the rear in the garage area there is a 200 square foot basement, used only for the heating unit and garden equipment storage.

This house is so well arranged and finished with such excellent materials and good taste that Mrs. Jones advised us she easily accomplishes her own house work, calling for outside service only on special occasions. Considering the type of construction, inside and out, we certainly feel that we have used very conservative valuations, and in my own recent appraisal experience, I have found no difficulty in arriving at comparable valuations on local residences having much less to offer.

BORROWER:

Wilson W. Jones, age 60, married to Lottie H. Jones, age 57. They have one son, age 16 years, now in his first year at an eastern engineering college. For the past two years this son has been spending his summer vacations in his father's office, learning some of the practical aspects of the profession. This is a family of many years of engineering background, with Mr. Jones so engaged for the past 26 years. Until his retirement in recent years, Mr. Jones' father was in the same profession with much success. The enclosed credit information and CPA report indicates a continuing successful and remunerative business, with a Dun & Bradstreet report showing approximately $165,000 net worth. In the report of Mr. Joseph M. Andersen, CPA, and under exhibit "C" of such report, you will find the explanation of the good-will valuation at $100,000 and the basis of accounting for it.

LOAN:

The purpose of this loan is to help consolidate two outstanding obligations on the subject property totaling $55,000. With this $40,000 loan, Mr. Jones has arranged for a one year $15,000 personal loan at his bank which he expects to retire in full within the one year term. Of the total $55,000 against the subject property, $37,000 represents a demand loan from an individual with interest at 2% per month. This is surely a definite incentive for this reorganization loan. Based on the $75,000 appraisal, the requested $40,000 loan represents 53.3%.

The loan application was accompanied by a statement of income and expenses showing a net income of over $71,000 for the first 9½ months of the year. This report was supplemented by a statement of the net income over the past five years. In addition the prospective borrower submitted a balance sheet as follows:

August 28, 19___

*Assets* (other than life insurance equities)

| | |
|---|---:|
| Interest in the firm of Wilson W. Jones | $100,000.00 |
| Automobile: 19— Buick Electra 225 (cost) | 5,600.00 |
| Household furniture and furnishings (cost) | 12,276.00 |
| Jewelry | 5,200.00 |

*Liabilities*

| | |
|---|---:|
| Secured loans—90 day loans | 6,435.00 |
| Loans secured by life insurance policies | 4,597.04 |
| Unsecured loans at banks @ $120.00 per month | 1,200.00 |
| Accounts payable | 750.00 |

/S/ Wilson W. Jones
300 Grape Street
Denver, Colorado

This report was supplemented by additional detail furnished by the loan officer.

Estimates submitted by subject on September 25, 19___

| | | | |
|---|---|---|---|
| Cash–Ckg | 2,500 | Due on Note | $ 6,435 |
| H. Hold Furn. | 12,276 | Due on loan | 4,597 |
| Buick | 4,000 | Due on loan | 1,200 |
| RE-Home | 100,000 | Due on bus. accts. | |
| Int. in business | 100,000 | pay | 959 |
| Jewelry | 5,200 | Mtg. on Home | 18,500 |
| Cash value life ins. | 8,000 | Mtg. on R.E. | 37,000 |
| TOTAL ASSETS | $231,976 | NET WORTH | 164,285 |
| | | TOTAL | $231,976 |

The subject is refinancing a home at 300 Grape Street. Loan amount $40,000 conventional loan.

Subject carries life insurance in face amount of $107,500. Cash value $8,000.

### HISTORY

Subject born December 3, 19— in New York. Has been self-employed for 26 years earning $60,000 to $65,000 per year.

### COMMENTS ON NOTE RECEIVABLE: HECTOR J. RYAN

Mr. Jones sold a one fourth interest in his practice to Hector J. Ryan on January, 19___ for $26,492.76. This price was based on a valuation of $100,000 for Good will and $5,971.04 for other assets. The $26,492.76 to be paid by Mr. Ryan in $2,000 instalments due February 1, 19___ and each February 1 thereafter until paid in full. Interest on the unpaid balance to be computed at 8% per annum, payable in five equal annual instalments beginning February 1, 19___.

Mr. Jones and Mr. Ryan terminated their partnership agreement on January 1, 19___. At that time Mr. Jones purchased Mr. Ryan's interest for the same price originally paid by Mr. Ryan, $26,492.76. This price was evidenced by a promissory note payable to Mr. Ryan in instalments, $4,000 on February 1, 19___, $4,000 on February 1, 19___, $4,000 on February 1, 19___ and the balance in instalments of $2,000 on each subsequent February 1 until paid in full. Interest payable at 8% per annum on the unpaid balance. The financial statement shows a goodwill valuation of $28,003.30 on October 14, 19___. This represents the consideration paid as outlined above plus other charges incurred by Mr. Jones in settling with Mr. Ryan.

A Dun and Bradstreet report, a credit report from a local credit agency, appraisal report, title report are additional papers supplementing this application. The loan request follows from the need to consolidate debts of the borrower. Though the borrower is 60 years old and is requesting a 15 year mortgage, his assets and the relatively high amortization rate and fairly low loan-to-value ratio (53.3 percent), justify the loan judged on the basis of the borrower's credit. The loan summary taken from the appraisal report shows that the security is ideally located with a documented market value estimate of $75,000.

Given these facts on the dwelling, the borrower's financial status, and the acceptable mortgage pattern, the loan officer recommended approval.

*condos started in early 1600's in England & Scotland. There called "flats."*

*napoleonic code 1804 first statutory horizontal act*

---

# Condominiums and Cooperative Apartments

*cooperative - multi-dwelling unit and has undivided interest in entity owning bldg wherein that owner entitled to occupy particular apt by lease.*

*condominium - ind. ownership of unit undivided ownership of common area agreement of owners to maintenance & admin of all property.*

*fee simple + joint tenancy in common area*

---

In the simplest terms, a condominium refers to the common ownership of real estate by several individuals, each of whom owns in fee simple a specific portion of the property and holds an individual interest as partial owner of the common elements of the property. Condominium units are the individual spaces within a condominium project owned as individual estates. In multiple family dwellings the fee owner has title and exclusive possession to a multiple family unit and an undivided interest in areas used in common by other joint owners. The common interest is represented by land, hallways, elevators, and other parts of the complex used by other owners. The concept of a condominium, though most common for residential property, also applies to commercial property, offices, and other multiunit developments.

Under condominium ownership, purchasers gain the advantage of high density residential use, as well as the economies and services of a multiple family structure. At the same time they acquire ownership status of fee titles associated with a detached, single family dwelling. Condominium developers see a growing trend toward condominium ownership: in some communities they are the lowest cost form of home ownership available—they especially appeal to young families and the growing number of single households. The resort property, the second home, and the luxury apartment have already gained considerable acceptance in population centers and vacation-resort communities.

In the United States, condominiums were first authorized by legislation which was enacted by Puerto Rico in 1958, and designed to serve an expanding population faced with a shortage of residential land. The popularity of the condominium form of ownership was increased by enactment of Section 234 of the Federal Housing Act in 1961, which authorized Federal Housing Administration insurance on mortgage loans secured by condominium interests in those states which accorded legal recognition to this form of ownership. A model statute prepared by the Federal Housing Administration in 1962 has served as the basis of most of the state condominium enabling acts.

By 1968, the 50 states and the District of Columbia had adopted statutes permitting the horizontal or unit ownership of real property characteristic of condominiums. This new legislation was required in order to obtain uniformity with respect to the establishment, dissolution, and legal documentation of the ["three dimensional"] condominium form of ownership. In a high rise building the owner of the condominium acquires a cubic foot area representing the inside dimensions of his apartment. At the same time he holds the right to use other portions of the structure in common with other owners. State laws in addition permit property taxes to be levied against each condominium owner separately.

To explain the complexities in financing condominium properties, it is helpful to review the legal statutes of the property interest. Next the advantages and limitations of condominiums are compared to other types of mortgage security followed by an explanation of the special procedures required to value a condominium interest. The contrast between cooperative ownerships and condominiums completes this chapter.

## Legal Aspects of Condominiums

The economic value of condominiums and the special problems in their financing are guided by three critical items: (1) the declaration or master deed; (2) the bylaws governing administration, rules, and regulation; and (3) methods of calculating the percentage of common interest held by joint owners.

### Elements of the Declaration

The declaration (or master deed) is an instrument required by statute to be executed and recorded to legally create a condominium. In effect the declaration establishes the fee title to individual units and to the undivided interest in the common elements. This is the document that describes each interest on a three dimensional plane.

The first part of the document includes a plot plan, a floor plan of the building and the location of each apartment unit. The land will be legally described as other fee simple ownerships. The building will be designated and a number will be assigned to each apartment unit. A prorated percentage interest in the common elements will be assigned to each apartment unit. This may be done on the basis of floor space or the proportion that the value of the individual apartment bears to the value of the whole property. For example, Apartment 102 may have a $30,000 value in a project with a total value of $520,000. The undivided interest in common elements would be $\frac{3}{52}$. At the outset, the builder establishes a value for each unit, normally the selling price, which includes the undivided interest in the joint ownership.

A method of allocating the undivided interest in the common elements, common expenses and surplus by the proportionate square footage of each unit is illustrated by a Florida condominium declaration which states:

> Each home owner's percentage share of the Common Elements, Common Expenses, and Common Surplus as set forth at page 49 of this Prospectus, Exhibit 1 (C), has been determined by computing the ratio of the total floor area of each Apartment to the total floor area of all Apartments.

Certain legal requirements provide for repair or rebuilding in case of partial or complete damage to the structure. In this event a clause will typically provide for a majority vote to decide whether the project will maintain its present status or be sold as a whole. Because of the joint ownership, the declaration will provide for an association, the form of management to be organized, and the number of votes allocated to each apartment owner.

The common elements will be identified and other terms will cover definitions and insurance coverage. Provisions will be made for payment of taxes and special assessments and recovery procedures in case of default on the prorated liability for expenses of operation.

## Condominium Bylaws

The bylaws are binding on every condominium owner. These regulations set out the owner's voting rights with respect to the board of directors, which probably will be based on the original investment so that the owner of a four bedroom unit will have a proportionately larger number of votes than an owner of a one bedroom unit. In the preceding example, the purchaser of a $30,000 unit in a $520,000 project would have voting rights equal to 3/52 of all votes. The bylaws will also allocate monthly assessments for maintenance and operating costs on the same percentage of unit value The bylaws will provide for liens in favor of the association to be placed on each unit to insure payment of mainte-nance assessments.

*✱ problem*

Like other fee titles, condominiums may be sold and mortgaged as provided in the bylaws. Prospective buyers must be referred to the board of directors with the amount of the buyer's offer. The board, in many instances, retains the right of first refusal to meet the prospective buyer's offer or the board may approve the sale to the indicated buyer.

The bylaws cover other organizational matters found in most govern-ing organizations; namely, personnel will be designated for maintenance and other provisions will restrict the use of each unit to residential purposes. Bylaws will provide a method of amending or modifying the bylaws.

In essence, the individual holding a condominium has the exclusive ownership and possessory rights in a specific unit. He receives a deed to his unit on which he pays property taxes and utilities. He is responsible for inside maintenance and decoration and his individual mortgage. In addition he pays his pro rata share of the operation and maintenance of the project. The rights of the unit owner are largely delegated by the elected board of directors. A typical set of bylaws covering powers of the board taken from a Florida condominium are shown in Exhibit 8.1.

## Percentage Ownership of Common Elements

The relationship of the value of the unit to the value of the whole property determines the liability of the owner for maintenance, operat-ing charges and property taxes. Initially, the developer in setting the original price of each unit, for example, $50,000 for a one bedroom unit and $70,000 for a two bedroom unit, determines that the more ex-pensive unit will have a larger percentage of ownership in the common elements than the less expensive unit. The ratio of these values to the total value of the property will also determine the pro rata share of op-erating expenses.

In certain other jurisdictions, such as New York, the percentage in-terest in the common elements may be based on the proportion that the floor area of each individual unit bears to the total floor area of the project. The declaration establishes the method of prorating the value of the common elements in other states. Unless otherwise pro-

*percentage of maintenance costs usually equals the percentage of ownership in common area.*

**Exhibit 8.1**

**Condominium Bylaws Covering Powers and Duties of the Board of Directors**

Section 4. *Powers and Duties of the Board of Directors.* All of the powers and duties of the Association shall be exercised by the Board of Directors, including those existing under the Act, the Articles and the documents establishing the condominium. Such powers and duties of the Directors shall be exercised in accordance with the provisions of the Declaration, and shall include but not be limited to the following:

4.1 Make and collect assessments against members to defray the costs of the condominium;

4.2 Use the proceeds of assessments in the exercise of its powers and duties;

4.3 Maintain, repair, replace and operate the Condominium Property;

4.4 Reconstruct improvements after casualty and the further improvement of the Condominium Property;

4.5 Make and amend regulations with respect to the use of the Condominium Property;

4.6 Approve or disapprove proposed purchasers, mortgagees of apartments and those acquiring apartments by gift, devise, or inheritance, or other transfers in accordance with the provisions set forth in the Declaration;

4.7 To enforce by legal means the provisions of the condominium documents including the Declaration, the Ground Lease, Apartment Sub-Lease Agreement, Assignment of Apartment Sub-Lease Agreement, the Articles, these By-Laws, the Rules and Regulations and the applicable provisions of the Act;

4.8 To contract for the maintenance and care of the condominium property and to delegate to such contractor all powers and duties of the Association except as are specifically required by the condominium documents to have approval by the Board of the membership of the Association;

4.9 Pay taxes and assessments which are liens against any property of the condominium other than the individual Apartments and the appurtenances thereto, and to assess the same against the Apartments subject to such liens;

4.10 Purchase and carry insurance for the protection of Apartment Owners and the Association against casualty and liability;

4.11 Pay the cost of all power, water, sewer and other utilities services rendered to the Condominiums and not billed to owners of individual Apartments;

4.12 Retain and hire such other employees who are necessary to administer and carry out the services required for the proper administration of the purposes of this Association and to pay all salaries therefor.

vided in the declaration, some condominiums allow owners to own common elements as tenants in common in equal shares. An issue also arises as to the review of the percentage interest in common elements over the life of the property. The states of Alaska and Washington provide for bylaws that permit periodic reappraisals of apartment units and common areas. Reappraisal would be called for if resales of the property showed changes in the proportionate value of each unit.

## An Evaluation of Condominium Ownership

The rationale of condominium ownership rests on the fact that occupants may retain a multiple family style of living and yet gain the advantages of fee ownership. For this reason, condominium ownership shares certain advantages of owning a single dwelling.

### Advantages of Condominium Ownership

The condominium owner gains the advantage of deducting mortgage interest and property taxes from his income tax. As a renter it is not always clear that these ownership advantages are passed through by the apartment operator in the form of lower rents. To the extent that ownership reduces income tax liability, the condominium owner gains over the comparable renter. Some observers have reported that condominium ownership is 20 percent to 30 percent less expensive than renting comparable space. The saving depends largely on personal income tax rates paid by the condominium owner. Typically, the higher the marginal personal income tax rates paid, the greater the tax advantage of condominium ownership—relative to renting.

The condominium dweller, as a part-owner of a nonprofit association presumably occupies multiple family space on a cost of operation basis. The association, in sharing costs of operation, eliminates the investor's profit—the rate of return on invested capital. A related advantage is that the owner of the condominium gains from professional management which he supervises, controls and administers through his voting rights in the association. The house rules from a representative high rise condominium in Exhibit 8.2 illustrates management policies that tend to preserve amenities of condominium ownership.

If it is assumed that rents will increase as inflation progresses, then ownership status is preferred to rental status. Though costs of operation and rents increase, and all other things remain equal, the value of the condominium building and common elements will probably increase in the same direction. Therefore, the owner of a condominium

Exhibit 8.2

# HOUSE RULES AND REGULATIONS
## OF
## EMERALD ISLE CLUB, INC.

1. The walkways, entrances, halls, corridors, stairways and ramps shall not be obstructed or used for any purpose other than ingress to and egress from the units.

2. The exterior of the units and all other areas appurtenant to a unit shall not be painted, decorated, or modified by any owner in any manner without prior consent of Emerald Isle Club, Inc. (the "Condominium Association"), which consent may be withheld on purely aesthetic grounds within the sole discretion of the Condominium Association.

3. No article shall be hung or shaken from the doors or windows or placed upon the outside window sills of the units.

4. No bicycles, scooters, baby carriages or similar vehicles or toys or other personal articles shall be allowed to stand in any of the common areas, or driveways.

5. No owner shall make or permit any noises that will disturb or annoy the occupants of any of the units or do or permit anything to be done which will interfere with the rights, comforts, or conveniences of other owners.

6. Each owner shall keep his unit in a good state of preservation and cleanliness and shall not sweep or throw or permit to be swept or thrown therefrom, or from the doors or windows thereof, any dirt or other substances.

7. There shall be a $2.00 lock-out charge if the Association is requested to furnish keys for access to a unit owner who has locked himself out.

8. No awnings, window guards, light reflective materials, hurricane or storm shutters, ventilators, fans or air conditioning devices shall be used in or about the unit except as shall have been approved by the Condominium Association, which approval may be withheld on purely aesthetic grounds within the sole discretion of the Condominium Association.

9. Each unit owner who plans to be absent from his unit during the hurricane season must prepare his unit prior to his departure, by:

    (a) Removing all furniture, potted plants and other movable objects from his terrace and balcony; and

    (b) Designating a responsible firm or individual satisfactory to the Condominium Association to care for his unit should the unit suffer hurricane damage. Such firm or individual shall contact the Condominium Association for clearance to install or remove hurricane shutters.

10. No sign, notice or advertisement shall be inscribed or exposed on or at any window or other part of the units, except such as shall have been approved in writing by the Condominium Association, nor shall anything be projected out of any window in the units without similar approval.

11. All garbage and refuse from the units shall be deposited with care in garbage containers intended for such purpose only at such times and in such manner as the Condominum Association will direct. All disposals shall be used in accordance with instructions given to the owner by the Condominium Association.

## Exhibit 8.2 *continued*

12. Waterclosets and other water apparatus in the buildings shall not be used for any purposes other than those for which they were constructed. Any damage resulting from misuse of any waterclosets or other apparatus shall be paid for by the owner in whose unit it shall have been caused.

13. No owner shall request or cause any employee of the Condominium Association to do any private business of the owner, except as shall have been approved in writing by the Condominium Association.

14. Owners of units shall keep and maintain any storage closet, bin or area, which may bo assigned to such owner, in a neat and sanitary condition at all times.

15. No radio or television aerial or antenna shall be attached to, or hung from the exterior of the units or the roofs thereon, and no transmitting equipment shall be operated in a unit.

16. The agents of the Condominium Association and any contractor or workman authorized by the Condominium Association may enter any unit at any reasonable hour of the day for any purpose permitted under the terms of the Declaration of Condominium, By-Laws of the Condominium Association or Management Agreement, if any. Except in case of emergency, entry will be made by prearrangement with the owner.

17. No vehicle belonging to an owner or to a member of the family or guest, tenant or employee of an owner shall be parked in such manner as to impede or prevent ready access to another owner's parking space. The owners, their employees, servants, agents, visitors, licensees and the owner's family will obey the parking regulations posted in the private streets, parking areas, and drives and any other traffic regulations promulgated in the future for the safety, comfort and convenience of the owners. No vehicle which cannot operate on its own power shall remain within the Condominium Property for more than twenty-four hours, and no repair of vehicles shall be made within the Condominium Property.

18. The owner shall not cause or permit the blowing of any horn from any vehicle of which his guests or family shall be occupants, approaching or upon any of the driveways or parking areas serving the Condominium Property.

19. All damage to the units caused by the moving or carrying of any article therein shall be paid by the owner responsible for the presence of such article.

20. No owner shall use or permit to be brought into the units any inflammable oils or fluids as gasoline, kerosene, naphtha or benzine, or other explosives or articles deemed extra hazardous to life, limb or property.

21. The owners shall not be allowed to put their names on any entry of the units or mail receptacles appurtenant thereto, except in the proper places and in the manner prescribed by the Condominium Association for such purpose.

22. The Condominium Association may retain a pass key to each unit. No owner shall alter any lock or install a new lock on any door leading into the unit of such owner without the prior consent of the Condominium Association. If such consent is given, the owner shall provide the Condominium Association with a key for the use of the Condominium Association.

23. Any damage to the buildings, recreational facilities or other common areas or equipment caused by any resident or his guests shall be repaired at the expense of the owner.

24. Owners shall be held responsible for the actions of their children and their guests.

## Exhibit 8.2 *continued*

25. Children shall be allowed to play only in those areas designated for play from time to time by the Condominium Association.

26. Food and beverage may not be prepared or consumed on the common areas, except in accordance with regulations which may be promulgated from time to time by the Condominium Association.

27. Complaints regarding the management of the units and grounds or regarding actions of other owners shall be made in writing to the Condominium Association.

28. Any consent or approval given under these Rules and Regulations by the Condominium Association shall be revocable at any time.

29. The swimming pool and recreational areas are solely for the use of the Condominium residents and their invited guests. Swimming and the use of other recreational facilities shall be at the risk of those involved and not, in any event, the risk of the Condominium Association or its Manager, if any.

30. The regulations governing the use of the swimming pool, pool area and recreational facilities, permitted hours, guests rules, safety and sanitary provisions, and all other pertinent matters shall be in accordance with regulations adopted from time to time by the Condominium Association and posted in the swimming pool area and recreational areas.

31. No bird or animal shall be kept or harbored in the Condominium unless the same in each instance be expressly permitted in writing by the Condominium Association, which permission may be conditioned on such terms as the Condominium Association in its sole discretion deems to be in the best interests of the Condominium as a whole. Such permission in one instance shall not be deemed to institute a blanket permission or permissions in any other instance; and any such permission may be revoked at any time in the sole discretion of the Condominium Association. In no event shall dogs be permitted in any of the public portions of the Condominium unless carried. The owner shall indemnify the Condominium Association and hold it harmless against any loss or liabilities of any kind or character whatsoever arising from or growing out of having any animal in the development. If a dog or other animal becomes obnoxious to other owners by barking or otherwise, the owner thereof must cause the problem to be corrected; or, if it is not corrected, the owner, upon written notice by the Condominium Association, will be required to dispose of the animal.

32. These Rules and Regulations may be modified, added to or repealed at any time by the Condominium Association.

> By Order of the Board of Directors
> of Emerald Isle Club, Inc.

unit may offset the rising cost of housing through the rising resale value of his interest.

Moreover, the financial liability of the condominium occupant for maintenance, operating costs and other liabilities of the association are limited to the stated prorated share as recorded in the declaration. Though this is a continuing personal liability, it is limited to a fixed percentage. In this respect the condominium departs from cooperative ownerships, various partnerships and other joint ownership plans.

The financial advantage lies in the flexibility provided the purchaser of a condominium. He may negotiate mortgage terms according to his circumstances and the bylaws. Also, he can experience capital gains in the resale of his property, which is not a feature of cooperative ownership. Subject only to bylaws, the owner operates much like the fee simple owner of a dwelling unit.

Furthermore, it is more than likely that the condominium occupies an ideal multiple family space. A view location, the convenience of a multiple family site and a prestige neighborhood are common to condominiums. As a member of a housing association, the maintenance of the common elements are provided by the organization. In some of the better designed projects, the occupant benefits from recreational facilities and services not available to the single family owner. Moreover in the owner's absence, the property will be managed and maintained as part of the complex—generally not true of single family dwellings.

## Disadvantages of Condominium Ownership

The disadvantages of condominium ownership are relative to alternative forms of housing. Compared to single family dwellings, for example, the condominium owner has the disadvantage of owning under management control of a board of directors. Monthly carrying charges may increase and the board may dictate the level of maintenance and services contrary to the wishes of the individual. Moreover, some units may not be adequately maintained by individual owners. These disadvantages are offset by the voice the owner has in management of the property as a joint tenant. Maintenance is a problem of any housing neighborhood. Moving into a subdivision also involves a risk that adjoining property owners may not maintain landscaping and dwelling exteriors.

In highly unionized metropolitan areas condominiums face a further disadvantage: namely, maintenance, exterior painting and exterior repairs are often controlled by union contracts with the result that higher costs are incurred relative to single family dwelling ownership. That is, an owner of a single family dwelling has the option of under-

171

taking his own repairs, such as painting and other types of construction, sometimes termed "sweat equity." Or, alternatively, a dwelling owner may defer maintenance indefinitely or undertake maintenance only during prosperous times. As a condominium unit becomes subject to relatively higher repair and maintenance expenses over its life, this factor may result in higher ownership costs for condominiums compared to like costs experienced under single family dwelling ownership.

If the condominium project is not fully sold, it is operated partly as a rental unit. It is not always clear that the interest of renters and their conduct are compatible with ownership status. Observers have also pointed out practical difficulties of collecting unpaid maintenance charges. These usually become a lien second to the mortgage which may be foreclosed as stated in the bylaws.

To the extent that the right of resale of the property is restricted by the required approval of the board of directors, the owner has restricted rights of sale relative to the ownership of a single family dwelling in the usual subdivision. Others have objected to the allocation of voting rights on the basis of prorated shares. Some critics prefer the one unit-one vote principle.

## Mortgage Financing of the Condominium

To be sure, a principal advantage of the condominium relates to the flexibility of financing terms available to the purchaser. From the standpoint of the lender, the unique title status coupled with the method of development adds unusual elements of mortgage risk not found in other ownerships. For instance in a new structure, it is not certain that all units will be sold; the building may revert to rental status. As a precautionary measure, the lender must view the property both as income property and as a group of saleable units subject to a first mortgage.

There is a trend to convert existing rental apartments to condominium status. The complexities in the conversion process introduce still other types of mortgage risks. It is best to consider both cases separately.

### Financing New Units

In promoting a new condominium unit, the developer operates as if he were developing a subdivision of single family dwellings. Financing a new condominium requires procedures that vary from the typical construction loan on a subdivision. Ordinarily, individual units are released from the blanket encumbrance as the property is sold. In the case of a condominium, the developer or sponsor must provide a larger equity and work under special mortgage payout and release methods.

172

*Condominium construction mortgages*

Assuming that the project is appraised as an apartment rental building and as a condominium, construction funds would normally be disbursed after the equity is committed. The building will be completed with periodic payments of the construction loan.

Suppose, however, that, in advance of construction, the prospective buyers negotiate for special features not included in the standard plan. Suppose further that the changes are not paid for at the time the developer approves of changes in specifications. If the lender is not aware of the changes, the cost of these changes may not be covered in the prearranged construction mortgage. To guard against this event, the lender must plan on additional and more frequent inspections and obtain affidavits from the sponsor, architect and unit owners at each payout. The purchaser or sponsor should make deposits to the lender for extra features. Because of the financial flexibility, the lender should review all contracts verifying equity interest and guard against secondary securities not a part of the original construction mortgage and final mortgage takeout commitment.

Sales to a large group of individual purchasers and a single sponsor create other problems if architectural changes and specifications are negotiated. Structural changes and extra features may delay construction, require additional deposits and affect insurance payments and taxes during construction.

Completion bonds binding on subcontractors and general contractors protect the lender from mechanics and materialmen liens. Preferably, payouts would be made to an escrow that reviews individual contracts and guarantees against liens to the time of payout. Even affidavits, though sound legal documents, may not always protect against law suits or unpaid contractors or subcontractors who stop construction.

For larger projects, construction financing may be undertaken by more than one participating lender. In these circumstances it is preferable to form an escrow agreement to arrange for payouts only after inspection, title review and collection of necessary affidavits from contractors and subcontractors. Joint participation of lenders diversifies risks, reduces inspection and examination of liens, and provides for more uniform processing and risk analysis. In the case of the final disbursement, it is advisable to escrow the last payment to avoid disputes over unpaid liens, changes or extra specifications.

There is also the problem of administering individual mortgages on single units. First payouts usually are made after the cost of completing the unit and common areas is estimated. Such an estimate controls the partial payment. In some instances the sponsor uses unit mortgage funds deposited by the purchaser if authorization is obtained from unit owners. The risk of completion is taken by the unit owner in permitting use of his mortgage funds. At least ten states, however, require that the deposits by purchasers be held in escrow by the developer prior to closing to protect these funds from a project failure.

## Mortgage financing techniques

Other factors that reduce lender risk are provisions in the declaration requiring condominium ownership effective only if 51 percent of the units are sold. Failure to reach this point of sale at a stated time automatically requires conversion of the property to a rental project. Finally, the developer-sponsor requires the highest financial responsibility: first, because rules of mortgage financing recommend that the equity be sufficient to complete the common areas and, second, because individual mortgages cannot be placed until the building is ready for occupancy. For instance, the units on the first floor may be completed but are unusable until elevators and other utility systems are in operation. A purchaser or lender or mortgagee advancing funds on a completed unit in an uncompleted building assumes more than the usual mortgage risk.

Experience has also shown that per unit costs of a condominium are higher than similar costs of rental apartments. Condominiums tend to have superior features common to home ownerships; these features are usually lacking in conventional rental properties. Consequently, the capitalized value of the potential net income of a condominium project will generally not equal the summation of individual condominium dwelling values. That is, the amenities of a single family dwelling are more costly so that the capitalized rental value of a house seldom equals its sale price. In condominiums the discrepancy between the sales price and the capitalized value of the rental recommends a higher purchaser equity—a reduction in the mortgage to possibly 65 to 70 percent of the sales price.

There is one other departure in financing a condominium. In a land subdivision, the developer may recapture his cost and builder's profit as homes and developed lots are sold. In a condominium, part of an operating unit is sold as a unit including common elements. The project must be completed before sales receipts return equity, construction loans and profit. Hence the condominium sponsor must hold his equity for longer periods of time.

## Financing Condominium Conversions

The main difficulty in converting a rental project to a condominium lies in the fact that apartment buildings were not constructed for condominium use. The buildings do not have the amenities found in condominiums, they show substantial obsolescence, they are subject to physical depreciation. Moreover their location may not justify condominium status.

Conversions introduce the added problem of dealing with long-standing tenants. To accomplish the conversion, the sponsor must take four steps: (1) Legally establish the condominium entity, (2) physically adapt apartments to condominium use, (3) organize the transition from rental to owner occupancy, and (4) arrange for building operation during the conversion and subsequent condominium management.

A few jurisdictions presently regulate condominium conversions by statute. The sponsor must thus review the state law in order to conform the conversion to any applicable legal provisions.

### *Physical changes*

Sponsors of the conversion of a multi-story rental building first correct for physical depreciation of the roof, the exterior, landscaping of the grounds and provide for rehabilitation of the lobby. For individual apartments, it is not clear that rehabilitation is always economically feasible. There are some compelling issues to resolve before this step is taken.

Developers have reported that 30 to 60 percent of the sales may be expected from the present tenants. Expensive rehabilitation of outmoded apartments may not be desired by these tenants, since the cost may price the units out of their means. Others have reported that the tenants are unwilling to change their life style and expenditure patterns as the result of rehabilitated apartments.

The sale of individual apartments in their present condition tends to shift rehabilitation costs to the tenants; a cost that may not be recovered in sale price. Consider, for example, kitchens that need rehabilitation of floors and walls, new cabinets, drain boards, dishwashers, ranges, overhead fans and the like. Updating the apartments to compete with new condominium units may be prohibitively expensive.

It is also true that the building equipment, the heating system, air conditioning, and electrical system may be quite obsolete compared to new construction. Feasibility analysis would be necessary before such expensive rehabilitation is advised.

Sales records show also that conversion seems more successful if the rental apartments have balconies and patios. Sales records have suffered, in addition, for apartments which are without basement space that can be converted to dead storage and community recreation rooms. Without basements, generally, it is impractical to provide these latter features in existing buildings.

It is also quite true that rental apartments generally lack the amenities of the newer condominiums, i.e., swimming pools, saunas, exercise rooms, tennis courts, off-street and covered parking and other items. Generally, it is not practical to provide these amenities in a conversion unit.

The location dictates the probability of sale. Investors have reported that conversion tends to be less successful in districts dominated by tenant occupancy. The more successful units are in outlying mixed apartment districts. Buildings constructed in the shape of letters (E, H, U) have restricted views which may be acceptable for tenant occupancy, but tend to be rejected by buyers of condominium units who prefer an open air view.

Tenants who occupy buildings during the conversion increase costs not encountered in the new units. Surveys necessary for the declaration are difficult and costly for existing buildings. Dealing with hostile tenants while preparing the required detailed floor plan for each apartment can be time consuming and costly. However, tenants with leases provide an income during the conversion which is not available for the new condominium unit. If the leases are sufficiently staggered, the building will earn income until the end of each lease at which time the apartment may be converted to a sale unit. Lease occupancy during conversion helps reduce holding costs.

Consider, too, the problem of calculating the ownership interest and common elements. One approach calculates the ownership share by using the proportion that the appraised value of each unit bears to the value of the whole condominium. A more objective method uses the proportion that the net saleable square foot floor area of individual units bears to the total net rentable area. In some cases state law will dictate the method to be used.

If the appraisal method is used, there is a problem of dealing with apartments in poor condition relative to rehabilitated units. If the value rule is followed, those units which have been remodeled have higher value and show a distorted proportionate interest in the common elements relative to similar units that have not been rehabilitated.

## Appraising the Mortgage Security

The mortgage security consists of the value of the living area in each unit, and the associated value of the undivided interest in common elements. Though conventional appraisal techniques are used, their application to condominiums calls for a special type of analysis. In the income technique some allowance must be made for the relatively low value found by capitalizing net income. Under the cost method, the valuation data must identify the value of each living unit, the value of the undivided interests in common elements, and the land value. Sale prices must be judged with respect to the effect of (1) the declaration, (2) bylaws, (3) location, (4) services provided each owner, and (5) the amenities unique to each property.

Lending officers are advised to examine the general market acceptance of condominium ownership. While a condominium unit may be acceptable from a legal and physical standpoint, market resistance may stem from misrepresentations by over-zealous sales persons. In other instances, the evidence indicates that condominium agents have not communicated fully with prospective buyers who purchase without knowledge of their potential liabilities to the condominium association and other limitations of ownership rights. Because of these buyer attitudes, a careful review of local condominium marketability may be advised.

Since the amenities of ownership occupy such importance in the condominium, special attention is given to the location and architectural features. Factors associated with the location which deserve special emphasis in condominiums are identified below.

*Location factors*

1. The ground area and the provision for light, air and attractive view.
2. Access to public transportation, highways, expressways, or boulevards which make traveling to work, shopping or to recreation convenient.
3. New or older neighborhoods which have status appeal.
4. Convenience to schools, churches, and other cultural centers which have appeal to condominium owners.

Certainly the locational analysis will cover other points relevant to apartment house valuation, but the record shows that these points deserve added consideration in condominium appraisal. By the same token, architectural features deserve an equally critical review.

*Architectural and construction features*

1. Attractive exterior, appearance and lobby decor.
2. Large and liveable rooms with at least 15 percent more square feet per room than conventional apartment rooms.
3. Large closets with at least one walk-in closet and one storage closet within the common area.
4. An apartment foyer.
5. Swimming pool and recreation room for high rise luxury building.

Construction features are also critical to condominium values.

1. Fireproof and noise-resistant walls between apartments.
2. Individual heating and air conditioning.
3. No more than four apartments to a floor per elevator.
4. Soundproof elevator operation.
5. Refuse depository from each apartment or floor to basement.
6. Open or closed porches depending on location and climate.
7. One bathroom per bedroom plus one powder room for each apartment.
8. Wind and sun resistant windows and frames.
9. Garage facilities of one or one and a half spaces per unit, depending on location.
10. Provision for passenger and service elevators in high rise buildings.[1]

In essence, the criteria applied to condominiums tests the status appeal of the project building. In this process, the appraisal should cite inadequacies observed in the unit under evaluation compared to competitive units. The main sources of depreciation commonly include the following items:

✓ Insufficient closet and storage space
✓ Parking unsuitable for the project
✓ Recreation facilities inadequate for the quality of condominium units
✓ Premises poorly guarded
✓ Poor provisions for noise insulation and privacy
✓ Unattractive exterior design
✓ Inexpensive material and careless workmanship.

It is important to relate these deficiencies to the price level of the condominiums. Though subject to all objections of a rule of thumb, condominium developers recommend $1,000 per unit for recreation fa-

1. Percy E. Wagner, "Analyzing and Appraising Condominium Projects," *The Appraisal Journal,* Vol. 39 (October, 1971), pp. 577–78.

cilities. On this basis, an 800 unit project would justify a much longer list of amenities and recreational advantages relative to a 50 unit project. It will also be recognized that amenities are relative to the price level. Requirements of low income projects will be fairly minimal compared to a 200 unit luxury condominium with prices falling between $50,000 to $70,000.

**Sale Comparisons** ① Market Approach - analysis of comparables, what is similar prop. selling for?

There are certain generalizations that apply to the analysis of condominium sales collected from many projects. Care must be taken to adjust sales prices for differences in legal requirements as dictated by the declaration and bylaws of the organization. Restrictive bylaws limit values if they are unreasonable and nonconforming to typical condominium projects. More importantly, the value of common elements varies for condominium sales taken from different projects. Though two units of 1,000 square feet illustrate similar construction qualities, they may assume quite different values because of differences in the common elements, for example, swimming pools, covered parking, golf course privileges, tennis courts, and the like.

To price units within a condominium, the simplest procedure is to value the whole property and relate the value of individual units including the value of the undivided common elements by the ratio of sale prices to the completed unit. This type of analysis is illustrated for a 90 unit project.

1. Unit number ........................... 89
2. Square foot area ...................... 1,100
3. Selling price .......................... $29,300
4. Total sales prices, 90 units .......... $3,740,000
5. Ratio of selling price of unit to total
   sales prices ....................... .007834

$$\frac{\$\ 29,300}{\$3,740,000}$$

6. Percent interest in common elements ... .007834

This procedure is applicable to new projects in which the developer has estimated the price of individual units and determined the percent interest in the common elements on the basis of the ratio of individual sale prices to the total sales price of all 90 units. It is assumed that the interest in the common element is equal to the proportionate value of each apartment relative to the total value.

A problem arises on resales. In this case it is difficult to relate the price of individual units to an unknown price of all 90 units. In these instances, appraisers rely on the cost technique.

## Table 8.1
## Calculation of the Common Area Interest: Cost Technique

| Living Area | Type Area | Number of Units | Floor Area | Total Area | Percent of Common Area |
|---|---|---|---|---|---|
| 1st floor | A | 6 | 1,170 | 7,020 | .012200 |
| | B | 6 | 990 | 5,940 | .010300 |
| | C | 12 | 890 | 10,680 | .009170 |
| | D | 3 | 730 | 2,190 | .007970 |
| | E | 3 | 990 | 2,970 | .010520 |
| | F | 3 | 1,450 | 4,350 | .015220 |
| 2nd floor | A | 6 | 1,170 | 7,020 | .011179 |
| | B | 12 | 990 | 11,880 | .009378 |
| | C | 9 | 890 | 8,010 | .008348 |
| | E | 3 | 990 | 1,970 | .010109 |
| | F | 3 | 1,450 | 4,350 | .013944 |
| 3rd floor | (same as the second floor) | | | | |

Source: *Guidelines for Appraising Condominiums,* IAAO-Monograph No. 2 (Chicago, Ill.: International Association of Assessing Officers, no date).

## ② The Cost Technique   *try to duplicate structure in today's market*

The main issue in the cost technique is to allocate the value between individual units and the value of common areas associated with that unit. If the ratio is based on floor area, the calculations of Table 8.1 represent the first step in this calculation. In Table 8.1 it will be observed that units are identified by one of six floor plans designated by letters of the alphabet. The second and third floors have the same floor plan.

With this calculation, the living area by the first, second, and third floors show the floor area included in each unit. With the total area of the building determined by actual measurement, the difference is the common area: the hall space, the elevator space, stairwells, storage space, utility areas and the like. A summary of these figures shows the common area proportion.

|  | *Square Foot Area* |
|---|---|
| *Living Area* | |
| 1st floor | 33,150 |
| 2nd floor | 34,230 |
| 3rd floor | 34,230 |
| Total Living Area | 101,610 |
| *Common Area* | |
| Total Area of Building | 129,960 |
| Less Total Living Area | −101,610 |
| Total Common Area | 28,350 |

180

**Table 8.2**
**The Value of Living Area: Cost Technique**

| Living Area | Unit Type | Unit Number | Area | Cost Per Square Foot | Cost Per Unit | Cost Per Type | Total |
|---|---|---|---|---|---|---|---|
| 1st floor | A | 6 | 1,170 | $15.00 | $17,550 | $105,300 | |
| | B | 6 | 990 | 15.00 | 14,850 | 89,100 | |
| | C | 12 | 890 | 15.00 | 13,350 | 160,200 | |
| | D | 3 | 730 | 16.00 | 11,680 | 35,040 | |
| | E | 3 | 990 | 15.40 | 15,246 | 45,738 | |
| | F | 3 | 1,450 | 15.18 | 22,011 | 66,033 | |
| | Total | | | | | | $ 501,411 |
| 2nd floor | A | 6 | 1,170 | 13.79 | 16,134 | 96,804 | |
| | B | 12 | 990 | 13.65 | 13,514 | 162,168 | |
| | C | 9 | 890 | 13.65 | 12,148 | 109,332 | |
| | E | 3 | 990 | 14.65 | 14,503 | 43,509 | |
| | F | 3 | 1,450 | 13.45 | 19,503 | 58,509 | |
| | Total | | | | | | 470,322 |
| 3rd floor | (same as second floor) | | | | | | 470,322 |
| | Total Value of Living Area | | | | | | $1,442,055 |

Source: See Table 8.1.

The next step is to calculate the value of the living area. The cost of reproduction per square foot is determined by normal appraisal procedures. Table 8.2 shows the per unit value by floors for the total living area. Also shown are the values per unit, per type, and the value per floor. The sum of these data give the total value of the living area $1,442,055. Next, it is necessary to calculate the value of the common area allocated to each apartment unit.

Note that Table 8.3 allocates the common area on a per unit basis, depending on the percent of floor area per unit to the total floor area of the project. For example, since Type A units represent 20.73 percent of the total floor area, 327 square feet are allocated to each Type A

**Table 8.3**
**Distribution of Square Feet and the Value of Common Areas**

| Type | Number of Units | Total Area Per Type | Percent of Total Area | Area Per Type | Area Per Unit | Value: $17.00 Per Square Foot |
|---|---|---|---|---|---|---|
| A | 18 | 21,060 | 20.73 | 5,880 | 327 | $5,559 |
| B | 30 | 29,700 | 29.23 | 8,286 | 276 | 4,692 |
| C | 30 | 26,700 | 26.27 | 7,440 | 248 | 4,216 |
| D | 3 | 2,190 | 2.16 | 660 | 202 | 3,434 |
| E | 3 | 8,910 | 8.77 | 2,493 | 277 | 4,709 |
| F | 3 | 13,050 | 12.84 | 3,645 | 405 | 6,885 |

Source: See Table 8.1.

unit. With a $17.00 per square foot reproduction cost, each owner of a type A unit has an undivided interest of the common elements equal to $5,559. The cost technique gives the total value of each apartment unit including the value of the square foot area for each unit in addition to the value representing the prorated value of an undivided interest in the common elements.

An alternate method is to value the cost of the total project and allocate the resulting sum less accrued depreciation to each unit. The value reported per unit would represent the value of the common area and the value of individual unit.

## ③ The Income Technique

The valuation derived by capitalizing net income protects the lender should foreclosure require the lender to convert to rental status. Gross income is based on the rental value of each unit without respect to the sales price as a condominium. Expenses would agree with typical apartment rental operation if the property is treated as an apartment rental project. Elements of common charges would be included in the appraisal shown by functional divisions, primarily, management expenses, reserves for replacement of building equipment, and exterior maintenance.

It is not unusual for capitalized values to be 15 percent to 20 percent below the selling prices of a condominium unit. Appraisal experts point out that tenants are often unwilling to pay the full rental charge for amenities associated with ownership properties. In this respect, condominiums compare to similar experience reported for single family dwellings.

## Cooperative Apartments    *Started by Finnish in late 1800's*

Cooperative ownership of multiple family units dates from the end of World War I. Historically this form of ownership has been favored in cities of Philadelphia, New York, Chicago, Los Angeles, and Southern Florida. Though condominiums have found more acceptance since the early 1960s, cooperative financing is sufficiently different to call for added explanation. *late 1920's  after WWII co-ops came back big.*

In essence the purchaser of a cooperative apartment buys shares in the cooperative representing a pro rata share of the equity interest. With each purchaser supplying the necessary equity, a mortgage is negotiated for financing the project. Monthly charges cover the pro rata share of the mortgage, operating expenses and maintenance charges. The interest of the cooperator-owner is secured by a proprietary lease

*lessee's right under lease arises out of his interest in entity owning building.*

giving the owner exclusive rights of possession to a specific apartment, provided he complies with terms of the lease. While these provisions apply generally, financing techniques vary for conversion of an existing rental apartment to cooperative ownership and for a new structure developed as a cooperative ownership.

## Conversion of an Existing Apartment

A corporation is organized as a cooperative with shares sold to prospective members. The sale of shares provides the equity required to finance an apartment purchase. Each apartment is assigned a charge depending on its location, floor area, and extra features. The charge collected by the cooperative will include mortgage service, operating costs, and maintenance charges. Each tenant-shareholder will be given the right to the exclusive use and possession of a unit under a proprietary lease.

Under this plan the tenant-shareholder has no personal liability in the mortgage. The lender holds the mortgage on the whole property which remains the liability of the corporation. Financing, therefore, is arranged by sale of stock, allocated to each apartment in proportion to the pro rata value of each unit. Charges are related to the proportionate value of each unit, and cover a pro rata share of mortgage service and other operating expenses.

Under the proprietary lease each purchaser has the right to occupy a particular unit typically for 99 years and he has the right to sell his shares subject to the bylaws of the corporation. If the cooperative is financed entirely by the sale of stock, each apartment unit is priced according to its individual value. Expenses of operation are shared in relation to the relative value of each unit. The monthly charge allocated to each tenant-shareholder covers only expenses of maintaining common elements and operation.

## Financing New Developments

The financing arrangement follows the general pattern described for the conversion of an existing building. The main difference lies in the sale of apartments in advance of construction. Downpayments are substantial, 25 percent or more, representing earnest money deposits on a contract for sale. The contract provides for return of the deposit if an insufficient number of units are sold to justify construction. Such projects may be organized with retail stores located on the first floor and with a limited proportion of apartments rented to noncooperative owners.

Typically the cooperative plan provides for ownership in a trust or a corporation. In a trust form, a bank or trust company holds title as trustee with management responsibilities. Trustees will be self-perpetuating and chosen from tenant-shareholders. The trustee in turn will give certificates of beneficial interest to tenant-owners which give them the right to lease a particular unit. Under the corporate type of cooperative, the title and mortgage rests with the corporation owned by the tenant-shareholders. The board of directors and management of the project are determined by the bylaws.

## Cooperative Bylaws

The bylaws restrict the right of a member to transfer his interest in the cooperative. The model form of bylaws drawn by the Federal Housing Administration gives the corporation the option to purchase the interest of a terminating tenant-shareholder.

The bylaws further define the transfer value as

     (1)   the downpayment paid for the membership,

     (2)   improvements installed by the tenant-shareholder,

     (3)   the amount of principal amortized by the corporation on its mortgage indebtedness attributable to the dwelling unit involved as paid by the member. The first three years of principal payment are not included in this computation.

Compared to the condominium plan, tenant-shareholders in an FHA financed cooperative do not benefit from potential capital gains of cooperative ownership. The possible gain accrues to the corporation if it exercise its option. The tenant-shareholder only receives the equity buildup resulting from the share his assessment contributes to the mortgage principal repayment.

In a non-FHA cooperative, members are allowed to seek the highest price on the open market. The original member benefits from the capital gains at the expense of the new member. With these preliminary remarks, it is useful to compare the relative merits and limitations of cooperative ownership, compared especially to the condominium.

## Cooperative Ownership

For the most part the cooperative plan gives the tenant-shareholder most of the advantages and disadvantages found in condominiums. Yet, there are significant differences. They relate mostly to the financial liability of tenant-shareholders as contrasted to the condominium owner.

*Advantages of the cooperative plan*

To repeat, many advantages of the condominium are associated with cooperative ownership: (1) a tenant-shareholder gains the same personal income tax deductibility of his pro rata share of mortgage interest and property taxes. (2) The cooperative owner gains from the more efficient, lower cost operation of a non-profit organization. More efficient operation is expected by reason of lower vacancies, and the elimination of owner-profits. (3) The tenant-shareholder benefits from an operation controlled by occupants—the operation charges are controlled by the tenant. (4) The tenant-shareholder, provided he conforms to the proprietary lease, has similar rights of interior decorating typical of the fee owner.

The greatest advantage lies in the mortgage liability. The individual tenant-shareholders are not personally responsible for the project mortgage. The lender must look to the corporation for final responsibility. Deficiency judgments are not faced by the defaulting tenant-shareholder. His relationship applies to the corporation and not to the lender. The lender, in turn, must look to the project security and assets of the corporation.

*but most lenders will ask for personal signatures*

*Limitations of cooperative ownership*

While the tenant-shareholder escapes personal liability for his pro rata share of the mortgage, this financial aspect is often offset by his position as a shareholder. As part owner he must share his pro rata responsibility for expenses of operation including mortgage payments. Failure of tenant-shareholders to continue their monthly charges places the burden of operation and mortgage payments on the remaining tenant-shareholders.     *impt! must get subordination of lease to mortgage*

*no capital gains advantage*

This financial position contrasts with the liability of the condominium owner who is responsible only for his pro rata share of operating expenses and his own personal mortgage. In this respect a condominium owner has limited liability: the tenant-shareholder has unlimited liability.

The second main disadvantage concerns opportunities for capital gains. In large measure, the condominium owner may buy and sell condominium units as you would buy and sell single family dwellings in a restricted subdivision. In an FHA financed cooperative, benefits of capital gains, however, accrue to the remaining tenant-shareholders and not to the selling shareholder.

In summary, the tenant-shareholder may lose his original investment and shift the final burden on the remaining owners who must pay additional costs of operation. Hence, it will be appreciated that the condominium owner, while gaining the advantage of multiple family operation, avoids the potential financial hazards of cooperative ownership.

## Financing Techniques

The precautions exercised in new developments are followed in mortgages secured by cooperative ownership. The mortgage and promissory note must be recorded before sale of the apartment units. The proprietary lease requires prompt payment of monthly rental charges and pro rata shares of property taxes and other expenses. The proprietary lease will be subordinate to the mortgage. Because the lender must look to the corporation and the project as the sole security for the loan, the lender must reserve the right to audit books of the corporation and check for compliance with individual proprietary leases. If the mortgage is in default, the lender reserves the right to assume all management functions, the right to collect rent and otherwise manage the property.

condo resale can be by equity assumption or new
  financing
co-op cannot refinance the blanket mortgage. Takes
  a higher equity to get in, then, in resale.

*net income is key to viability off loan*
*have to look to earning ability of project*

*net income = gross income - expenses*

# Financing Multiple Family Dwellings

Some authorities regard the underwriting of apartment house property as a highly specialized task. First, the loan rests on a thorough housing market analysis. In this respect mortgage loan approval requires the same critical analysis as that applied to single family dwellings. Secondly, the loan on multiple family dwellings is secured largely by the present worth of net income. This latter point requires judgments on factors common to income property.

To expand on these points, apartment house characteristics, the rental housing market, the net income statement and the more critical issue of investment analysis will be reviewed. Selected illustrations demonstrate techniques of arranging for a mortgage on apartment buildings. While it is the intent to emphasize general principles in financing multiple family dwellings, the growing importance of rent control deserves special comment.

## The Impact of Rent Control

Lending officers confronted by rent controls or their possibility are well advised to consider the effect of rent control on apartment marketability. In this regard it should be noted that rent controls historically have served as temporary war emergency measures. First used during World War I, they regulated rent increases during temporary war-time housing shortages. Similarly, the *Emergency Price Control Act of 1942* initiated rent controls as a part of a system of national wage and price controls. Their gradual termination was provided by the *Housing and Rent Act of 1947,* which, however, permitted states and localities to continue "temporary" emergency rent controls. The state of New York was among the states that substituted state control for federal housing control under the New York Emergency Housing Rent Control Law of 1950. More recently, rent control has been used to offset the effect of inflation on housing tenants.

## Rent Control Rationale

In contrast to earlier legislation, some localities use rent controls as a permanent anti-inflationary measure. In this respect they have a popular political appeal. On this point housing economists have been highly critical of rent control on the following grounds:

1. Rent controls, without corresponding controls over operating expenses, encourage postponement of repairs in housing maintenance. In apartment house operations most expenses are relatively fixed. Property taxes are determined by local government and not by the owner. Likewise, the cost of utilities and labor are not subject to much owner manipulation. Hence, in the face of declining net incomes, repairs and normal maintenance tend to be indefinitely deferred—leading to substandard housing or even total owner abandonment.

2. Rent control tends to decrease the supply of available rental housing. Under reasonably competitive conditions, the price system largely determines the amount of new housing construction. If a rent control lowers net yields on rental housing relative to other investments, new rental housing is rejected for more profitable alternatives. Accordingly, rent control, or its expectation, tends to decrease the supply of new housing.

3. Rent control places the burden of inflation on the property owner. Under rent controls the real costs of inflation tend to be borne by property owners. While tenants on fixed incomes have an equitable case against rising prices, it is not clear that the standard of living should be maintained at the expense of non-tenant groups. If rent controls are opposed without relief to the owner faced with rising operating expenses, the ability to service a long-term loan is seriously jeopardized.

Even though apartment rents may be increased under hardship provisions of the law, rent increases tend to lag behind operating expenses. Rent increase applications tend to increase administrative costs and, if approved, may be inadequate to cover the increase in operating expenses. Consequently, lenders anticipating a long-term financing program for multiple family housing and faced with the prospect of rent control must prepare net income statements that are fairly realistic, because, if net income proves inadequate to service a loan, the lender must foreclose on an uneconomic project—the loan is secured by a liability, not an asset.

## Characteristics of Apartment Houses

It is fairly common knowledge that retail buildings have shifted from downtown centers to shopping centers, and that industrial buildings have moved from railroad industrially zoned corridors to locations in industrial parks and limited access highways. In the same way, multiple family structures have undergone comparable changes—changes that affect the financing, marketability, and location of apartment houses. The classification of apartment buildings helps identify the more significant changes.

### Apartment Types

Probably the most useful classification is based upon the type of construction. Different types of construction are associated with variations in operating expenses, the level of services furnished by management, the type of tenant, and rental income.

For instance, it will be recognized that high rise elevator buildings—defined as buildings with four stories or more with elevators—stand apart from other apartment buildings. They are found in areas of high land value; namely, central locations, apartment house districts of the larger cities, and in resort cities, or prestige locations. Because of the added cost of elevators and associated equipment, these buildings are more likely to be professionally managed. They also provide a wide range of services and usually cater to a select group of tenants. Gross incomes and expense data for high rise elevator buildings should be compared only to buildings of like characteristics.

At the opposite extreme are the low-density garden type apartments. Generally, the low rise apartments consist of buildings of three stories or less on landscaped acreage operated under one management. Such apartments tend to be located on relatively inexpensive, open and attractively landscaped sites convenient to main traffic routes. Income and expense data for garden type structures vary markedly from the operating experience of high rise elevator buildings. In addition, garden type structures appeal to a different group of tenants.

Low rise apartments refer to walk-up buildings and elevator buildings of three stories or less. Most authorities divide these buildings into two groups: buildings under 25 apartment units and buildings with 25 apartment units or more. The classification by size allows for a more accurate comparison of operating income and expenses. The smaller units tend to be owner-occupied and managed. Apartment buildings of more than 25 units, though marginal, may justify professional operation. They differ from the garden type in that apartment units are found in a single building, not a group of buildings. The cost of construction and operation differ as a group from the two preceding classifications.

## Apartment Locations

To judge the potential demand for apartments, a classification by location is often recommended. For this purpose a central location stands out. The high land cost, the convenience to office, retail, and entertainment centers is common to luxury apartments. The market for these apartments is characterized by a high level of services, spacious apartments with numerous building services. Their operating expenses per unit are relatively high.

It is also true that apartments in a central area tend to be dominated by public housing and low rental walk-up buildings. Housing for the elderly tends to concentrate in central locations providing convenient facilities for this market.

The larger cities tend to develop a nucleus of *apartment districts* probably the result of conscious zoning and planning. Partly because of the locational advantages, apartments concentrated in these areas are served by public transportation or located near a limited access highway.

The *suburban apartments* tend to be located on convenient traffic routes, usually on larger acreages with fairly low densities. Their convenience to shopping centers and employment centers make these units more adaptable to family groups. These apartments tend to have a larger number of rooms per unit than more centrally located buildings and also are less subject to obsolescence and depreciation since the buildings usually have a lower average age than other apartments in the older district.

*Intermediate locations* cover apartments not falling in the other groups. Such buildings are on the fringe of retail areas or at the junction of important streets and mass transit facilities.

*Rental structure*

In practice apartment lenders refer to apartments according to tenant income groups. This directs attention to the demand and supply of buildings that meet requirements of upper, middle, and lower income groups. To this list might be added public housing that serves tenants who meet legal qualifications for subsidized housing. Apartments, judged in this way, differentiate between tenants according to their education, occupation, income, and location requirements.

In this respect the services required of apartments show a growing trend to offer more than living space. Professionally managed apartments, in the competition for tenants and to lower tenant turnover, increasingly are providing a growing list of services and amenities for the apartment dweller. Some examples of services observed in apartments are listed below:

| | |
|---|---|
| Private guard service | Sauna |
| Automatic sprinkler system | Playgrounds |
| Soundproofing | Daycare center |
| Extra storage space | Social director |
| Clubhouse | Central air conditioning |
| Swimming pool | Cable TV |
| Golf course | Maid service |
| Exercise room | Linen service |
| Tennis courts | |

The list will probably expand as the competition for tenants increases. The important point is that each apartment house must be designed for the requirements of a specific tenant group. Moreover, an apartment building that does not provide the services and amenities of competing units may face higher vacancies and declining rent levels. In addition to a comparison of rents, special attention must be paid to the services included in the rent. Normally the cost of extra features is shifted forward to the tenant in the form of higher rent. Hence, the monthly rent is directly related not only to the condition of the property and its location, but to the amenities provided by the management.

## Locational Characteristics

The classification of apartments helps to identify minimum locational requirements of apartment buildings. While the points to be covered are common to each apartment, the emphasis given locational advantages tends to be weighed differently in the case of luxury units relative to low income buildings. A brief review of points to cover in evaluating an apartment location reveals the importance of dealing with different types of apartment houses and separate submarkets.

## Access

If automobile transportation is dominant, the location should be convenient to major transportation routes. An associated requirement would be adequate parking space. In areas served by public transportation, this point is minimized in favor of sites near terminal facilities.

## Shopping facilities

Depending on the type of apartment and its tenant preferences, shopping facilities should be reasonably convenient. Apartments constructed for the elderly would have different demands than garden apartments developed primarily for young married couples. In the latter instance, a location near a shopping center within a few minutes driving time would be satisfactory.

## Governmental services

A central location gains from the proximity to libraries, entertainment, churches, public schools, and centers of employment such as office buildings, public buildings, hospitals and the like. Schools and recreational facilities would be more significant to the outlying garden court apartment. In effect, community and governmental services should meet needs of a particular group of tenants.

## Employment centers

Apartment net income will be more stable, vacancies will be lower and tenant turnover will be much less for a location with convenient transportation to main sources of employment. Again this is a relative item, assuming greater importance for low income groups than for middle and higher income groups that have greater mobility.

## Land use controls

The location should be accompanied by regulations compatible with the structure in question. Apartment dwellers, like owners of single family dwellings, demand protection from unattractive, noxious land uses, noise, and nuisances. If the structure adjoins vacant land, subsequent development may encroach on the apartment over its economic life. Land use controls include not only zoning but building codes, housing codes, fire codes and health codes, that provide standards for future land use and maximum use densities. With these points in mind the next problem is to analyze the rental housing market.

*pro forma = expected financial statement*

## The Rental Housing Market

It should be remembered that the mortgage security is based on *antici-pated* income—not the present or past income. An appraisal of the rental housing market should cite historical data from which projections may be made over the early life of the loan. A current description of market relationships is not enough. Trend analysis is more important. The analysis of statistical trends provides an insight into the probable net earnings of the property mortgaged. To review this type of analysis, data concentrate on demand and supply relationships.

### Demand Analysis

The rental housing market consists of a series of submarkets, i.e., rental housing, stratified by income groups, size of household, age groups and location. Consequently, factors affecting the demand for rental apartments should relate to the particular market in question. Such an approach will support a review of population trends.

The immediate question relates to population projections for the market area: a community, a neighborhood, a county, a city, or other relevant market area. Population projections will be derived from population data of preceding years and will suggest how population growth (or decline) will be affected by current market factors. This part of the analysis is fairly critical since population trends and their projection closely affect gross income expectations.

Starting with general population projections, it is relevant to relate household size as it affects the property under review. For example, an area populated by single groups and young married couples will require rental space of a different type compared to an area with a growing elderly population.

In this respect population projections classified by age groups reveal the potential demand for rental occupancy over the economic life of apartments. A growth in the age group important to a particular apartment building tends to reduce mortgage risk and contributes to a favorable loan decision.

Personal income data and its source are helpful in estimating the present and future demand for apartment space. If past data are available, projections of personal income identified by main employment sources help to determine the degree of risk associated with a mortgage application.

For example an apartment complex largely occupied by employees from a local hospital and medical complex with rising personal incomes may represent greater security than a similar building occupied mostly by employees of a military base. In the latter case, the uncertainties of continued government support increase mortgage risks in the absence of other supporting sources of employment. Further, there is a relationship between personal incomes and the rent that may be collected. This part of the analysis helps judge the potential demand for apartments at a stated rental level.

Housing data relate directly to the potential demand for apartment space. First, there is the demand for owner or renter occupancy. A review of census records and local building permits shows trends favoring owner or rental occupancy. Changing characteristics of the population may justify a revision in the ratio of owner and rental housing locally demanded. For new projects, a projection of housing occupancy by these two classifications supports the final conclusion.

## Supply Analysis

While estimates of demand may be reasonably accurate, the analysis of supply is less objective. To be sure, the existing supply may be studied, analyzed and reviewed, and reported in some detail. In a competitive housing market, however, it is difficult to forecast the number of units that will be placed on the market in subsequent years. Competing developers, government credit policy, federal housing programs, and even the local administration of zoning and building codes affect decisions affecting the supply of rental housing.

Yet, these difficulties may be minimized in part by an analysis of the existing supply of rental units. At least such data, while limited for the long run, has considerable significance in the early years of the mortgage. With these qualifications, an inventory of competing rental housing in the area classified by type of tenancy, location, and rental levels seems relevant. For instance, if the rental level and rising vacancies are too low to provide a reasonable return on new apartment construction, then the mortgage appears risky and may be disapproved.

In this regard, current vacancy rates are significant because high vacancy rates lower yields, and if continued, lower rents. Also, vacancies should be related to the type of rental unit and classified by age, location, and rent level. A vacancy rate of 20 percent or more in new units over the last twelve months probably indicates a short-term saturation of the rental housing market.

When analyzing the supply, monthly rents and vacancies should be related to apartment services provided by competing buildings. This type of study would indicate a relative shortage or surplus of apartments constructed for minimum service buildings or of apartments adapted for middle and high income groups. To make this part of the analysis more meaningful, it is worthwhile to explain methods of rental comparison unique to apartment buildings.

## Standards of Comparison

Cost, value, annual rents and operating expenses must be reduced to per unit values. With these standards, comparisons may be made between and among buildings similarly situated. The two main categories of comparison relate to cost-values, and annual rent and operating expenses.

*Cost-Value: New Construction*

*Building*

per square foot

per room

per apartment

*Site Value*

per square foot

per acre

per room

per apartment

*Annual Rent and Operating Expenses*

per square foot of rentable area

per square foot of building area

per room

per apartment

For new construction, building costs are related to the cost per square foot of building area, room, and apartment. Comparisons based on a per room and per apartment basis tend to be less accurate because of variations in room size and the average size of apartments. The latter two comparisons are accurate only for similar type buildings.

The site value expressed in dollars and cents per square foot or acre should also relate to the price per apartment. While the square foot price has some validity, it may be misleading. For example, $5.00 per square foot may seem unreasonable in the light of comparable sales, but if the zoning allows one apartment unit per 1,000 square feet of land in contrast to one apartment for every 2,000 square feet of land, a higher price per square foot might be justified. To put it differently, the economic analysis of the building and comparable properties in the same submarket may reveal that a land value of $1,000 per apartment unit is economic and reasonable. Thus, the more units that may be placed on a given site, the more income may be earned per unit of land value. Expressing apartment site values on a per apartment basis gives greater insight into project feasibility than the sole reliance on per square foot values. For existing properties, it is not always possible to accurately divide value between land and buildings. In this instance, the cost-value is shown per square foot of building area, per room, or apartment including the land value.

Special attention is directed to rental and operating expense comparisons. Current practice favors comparison of these figures on a square foot of rentable area (which is not always obtainable). The next preferred standard is to show rent and operating expense detail according to the square foot area of the building. These figures compensate for variations in room and apartment size. Custom and familiarity with the local market may also show the reasonableness of the rent projection and operating expenses according to per room and per apartment values. These comparisons are demonstrated in later examples.

To make standards of comparison more meaningful, agreement must be reached on definitions. The Institute of Real Estate Management suggests the following definitions.

*Gross Floor Area*

The gross floor area includes all space from outside wall to outside wall, including the living area, corridors, the lobby, stores, offices, garages within the building, basement and public areas, and all floors.

*Rentable Floor Area*

The total square foot area within all individual apartment units, stores, offices, and other rentable space.

*Number of Rooms*

(1) The Dining Room. If the dining room is combined with the living room and is less than 200 square feet, count as one room. If more than 200 square feet list the space as 1½ rooms.

(2) Count the breakfast room as one room if it is more than 100 square feet.

(3) The *kitchen* counts as one room if it is a separate walk-in.

(4) Combined Kitchen Areas: Total area of 105 square feet or less: 1 room, total area of 105-140 square feet: 2 rooms.

(5) Other Areas. Porches, halls, closets and bathrooms are not listed as rooms.

It is further recommended that if 80 percent of the apartments in a building are furnished, the building should be listed as a furnished apartment. A review of income and operating expenses shows how these standards of comparisons are applied to mortgage loan analysis.

## Analyzing Net Income Statements

Calculation of anticipated net income depends on the estimate of the gross possible income, the vacancy allowance, and operating expenses. The resulting net income should be sufficient to cover the proposed mortgage payments. Furthermore, the capitalization of anticipated net income and cash flow analysis provide additional information for financing purposes. Because the net income estimate is critical to the final decision, it deserves more detailed explanation.

196

## Gross Possible Income

The income statement begins with an estimate of the gross income, assuming one hundred percent occupancy for the year. It is not necessarily the actual income received over the most recent year nor is it necessarily taken from the present rent roll. Instead the gross possible income follows from an accurate estimate of the current market rent. Ordinarily this is expressed as an annual and "stabilized" income and is not the result of unusual cyclical variation or seasonal changes. It is further assumed that the building will be operated under typical management.

The gross possible income should be derived from study of current rent received on comparable properties. The rent must apply to buildings of like character offering the same level of services—adjustments should also be made for utilities included as part of the rent. In each locality for a given quality of rental space, there is a market rent level. For example, recent reports of the Institute of Real Estate Management show prevailing gross possible income on unfurnished apartments according to the rent per square foot of gross floor area. These data are shown in Table 9.1.

It will be observed that the gross possible income expressed in dollars per room is the highest for elevator high rise buildings: $806.26. Data of Table 9.1 show further that this ranges downward to $471.32 for the low rise, 12-24 unit buildings. Since room size varies between buildings, a more accurate basis of comparison is shown by the rent per square foot of rentable area. Elevator high rise buildings show the highest level, $3.30 per square foot. Rents per square foot range downward to $2.00 for low rise, 12-24 unit buildings.

Not only should the gross possible income be tested against comparable properties, it should be compared to annual published data of

### Table 9.1
### Annual Gross Possible Income, Unfurnished Apartments, Classified by Apartment Type

| Apartment Type | Average Rent Per Room | Rent Per Square Foot of Gross Area | Rent Per Square Foot of Rentable Area |
|---|---|---|---|
| Elevator High Rise .............. | $806.26 | $2.57 | $3.30 |
| Garden Buildings ............... | 523.36 | 2.22 | 2.49 |
| Low Rise, 25 units and over ...... | 545.22 | 2.19 | 2.54 |
| Low Rise, 12–24 units ........... | 471.32 | 2.00 | 2.38 |

Source: *Journal of Property Management,* Part Two, Vol. 40, No. 4, July/August, 1975, pp. 43, 64, 85 and 119. Consult current reports for the latest data.

the Institute of Real Estate Management. These data are shown in detail by cities and apartments classified as furnished or unfurnished and by age of building. These standards help review net incomes against known properties and local standards. Frequently the gross possible income must be increased over income actually collected because rents of a given building may be partly controlled by lease rentals that lag behind economic rent.

## The Vacancy Allowance

The vacancy allowance includes a deduction for bad debts and collection losses. On occasion apartments experience a gross possible income that exceeds 100 percent occupancy levels. This result occurs because tenants move out before expiration of their lease, forfeiting advance rent payments and damage deposits. Even in these cases, a deduction must be made from the gross possible income to project net income stabilized over the economic life of the property.

Accordingly, vacancy allowances are taken from typical vacancies experienced locally. An allowance of 4 to 7 percent of the gross possible income is typical for metropolitan apartments. Larger vacancies would be projected for buildings subject to seasonal occupancy and to vacancies resulting from changes in personal income, population, or employment. After the deduction for vacancies and bad debts, the resulting gross income is termed the *effective gross income.* Operating expenses are deducted from the effective gross income. *adjusted gross*

## Apartment Operating Expenses

Apartment house profit-loss statements prepared for income tax purposes are not valid for valuation purposes. These statements include annual deductions for depreciation and mortgage interest which are not true operating expenses. When analyzing income producing property, allowance is made for building depreciation—capital recovery is provided in the capitalization process. The conversion of net income to capital value, except in special cases, does not include mortgage interest payments since these are not operating expenses. To include interest expense would give different capital values according to the amount of mortgage interest payments.

The typical income statement is shown in Table 9.2, which starts with the gross possible income. Recall that this figure is derived from anticipated rents as if the property were fully occupied. The vacancy and bad debt expense of 5 percent is considered typical for the property in question.

*probably high for new project. There is long time for renting up.*

## Table 9.2
### Net Income Statement of Crestwood Apartments

*is the gross in line w/ comparable units?*

| | | |
|---|---|---|
| Gross Possible Income | $462,192 | |
| Vacancy and Bad Debts, 5% | —23,109 | |
| *adjusted or* Effective Gross Income *(or ~~net disposable income~~)* | | $439,083 |
| Operating Expenses *not mortgage payments or depreciation* | | |
| * Taxes *taxes due. pre-empt mortgage due) escrow* | $ 51,765 | |
| Insurance | 5,546 | |
| Maintenance and repairs | 5,084 | |
| * Management *what services do they perform?* | 23,110 | *mortgage lender should approve in advance mngmt* |
| Payroll expenses | 30,202 | *contract, often apt* |
| Electricity | 24,034 | *owner forms mngmt* |
| Gas | 8,182 | *co. & rakes $$ off the* |
| Water | 14,790 | *top!* |
| Heating fuel | 15,015 | |
| Administrative costs | 700 | |
| Painting and decorating | 4,160 | |
| Supplies | 600 | |
| Services | 4,000 | |
| * Reserves for replacements *got to be there!* | 25,883 | |
| Other operating expenses | 924 | |
| Total Expenses | —213,995 | |
| Net operating income | $225,088 | |

For a mortgage appraisal the operating expenses are not identical to actual expenses incurred over the preceding year. They represent reasonable projections of expenses expected over the early years of the property. For example, the item "taxes" shown in Table 9.2, may be adjusted for expected changes in the local tax rate or property tax revaluations that may be in process. Similarly, property and liability insurance and maintenance and repairs should be typical for the property under review.

Management expenses should agree with typical management costs for operation of similar property. Even though the income property may be owner-occupied and managed, the management expense is an operating cost common to apartment house operation. The figure given represents economic costs of management by a professional management firm. Similarly the other expenses should conform to operation of similar properties in the community.

Note also that a reserve for replacement ($25,883) is entered on the expense statement of Table 9.2. This allowance provides for the annual cost of replacing lobby furniture, and short-lived equipment in each apartment such as refrigerators, dishwashers, washing and drying equipment and other equipment that has a life of 3–5 years. If apartments are furnished, the allowance would show the annual cost of replacing apartment furniture on a recurring basis.

## Operating Expense Ratios [1]

Certain generalizations will help guide the evaluation of operating expenses. Experience has shown that the older building is more expensive to operate than newer structures. According to the Institute of Real Estate Management, elevator high rise buildings constructed in 1920 or earlier experienced operating expenses before reserves for replacements and depreciation of 61.0 percent of effective gross income. Similar buildings constructed in 1968 and later showed a comparable operating expense of 48.5 percent of effective gross income. Generally speaking elevator type buildings show higher operating costs than garden court and low rise structures.

The record also shows that unfurnished buildings have lower vacancy rates, currently 3.2 percent of gross possible income for elevator buildings, than furnished buildings—4.6 percent of gross possible income. In this regard elevator buildings tend to have lower vacancy rates compared to low rise and garden court apartments.

On a national average, elevator buildings show a higher rent per gross square foot than low rise or garden court buildings. Current reports indicate a rent per square foot of $2.57 while low rise units, 12-24 units, show an average rent per square foot of $2.00.

Allowance should be made for rising rents and operating expenses. For example, the average rent of unfurnished elevator high rise buildings of 15 to 30 years old increased from $686.53 per room to $796.38 per room from 1971 to 1974. Similar experiences were reported by other types of buildings. Though rents have increased, generally speaking they have not increased as rapidly as expenses.

For instance, the operating ratio before reserves for replacements (and not including depreciation) increased for elevator apartments of the same group above from 51.3 percent to 56.5 percent over the last four years. Operating expense ratios classified by age of structure, location, type of building are helpful in comparing experience of a given building with other properties. For example, the records of 33 apartments in Chicago show an operation expense ratio of 57.1 percent. See Table 9.3.

# Investment Analysis

For the present, the capitalization of net income is treated as part of the investment analysis. The method of capitalization assumes property is unencumbered with a mortgage. Moreover, the capitalization process does not account for the tax effects of income property investments.

---

1. For an expanded treatment of this subject refer to the *Journal of Property Management,* Part 2, Vol. 40, No. 4, July/August 1975.

**Table 9.3**
**Average Income and Expenses of High Rise Elevator Buildings**
**Chicago, Illinois**

| Item | Per Room* | Percent of Total | Per Square Foot of Building Area |
|---|---|---|---|
| Gross Possible Rental Income ............... | $325.41 | 92.3 | $2.84 |
| Miscellaneous Other Income ............... | 22.53 | 2.5 | .08 |
| Gross Possible Total Income ............... | 894.64 | 100.0 | 3.12 |
| Less Vacancies & Delinquent Rents ........... | —27.82 | —3.1 | —.11 |
| Effective Gross Income .................... | $866.82 | 96.9 | $3.02 |
| Expenses | | | |
|   Total Payroll Expenses ................... | 93.22 | 10.4 | .34 |
|   Supplies ............................. | 7.33 | .9 | .03 |
|   Painting & Decorating (interior only) ........ | 26.48 | 3.0 | .09 |
|   Maintenance & Repairs (interior only) ....... | 43.52 | 4.9 | .15 |
|   Services ............................. | 10.21 | 1.2 | .04 |
|   Miscellaneous Operating Expense .......... | 9.47 | 1.1 | .04 |
|   Electricity ............................ | 23.37 | 2.6 | .08 |
|   Water .............................. | 7.59 | .9 | .03 |
|   Gas (excluding heating fuel) .............. | 6.76 | .8 | .03 |
|   Heating Fuel .......................... | 45.51 | 5.1 | .16 |
|   Management Fees ...................... | 41.66 | 4.7 | .15 |
|   Other Administrative Expenses ............ | 21.17 | 2.4 | .08 |
|   Insurance ............................ | 9.93 | 1.1 | .03 |
|   Real Estate Taxes ...................... | 173.03 | 19.3 | .60 |
|   Other Taxes .......................... | 2.30 | .3 | .01 |
| Total All Expenses ........................ | $516.26 | 57.7 | $1.81 |
| Net Operating Income ..................... | $350.77 | 39.2 | $1.21 |

Source: *Journal of Property Management,* Vol. 40, No. 4, July/August, 1975, p. 32.
* Totals may not add to 100 percent since individual items are averages of reported data which are not complete for each case.

For this reason attention is directed next to cash flow analysis which is used by a more sophisticated investor. It will be shown that mortgage financing constitutes an important element in cash flow analysis. Finally, the apartment house mortgage and characteristics of income and its capitalization are subjected to financial ratio analysis. Each of these three techniques of analysis helps to judge the feasibility of a mortgage loan proposal.

## The Capitalization of Net Income    See Notes! Don't try to understand this.

With the net operating income in hand (before depreciation), a capitalization rate must be selected to convert net income to a capital

201

value. Most authorities recommend that the capitalization rate should be taken from two possible sources, the band of investment technique or the market. The method of converting income to capital value for the present purpose uses the building residual method.

## The band of investment

The band of investment is a method of weighting the return on interests in real estate according to their importance:

| Property Interest | Percent of Total | Rate of Return (in percent) | Weighted Rate of Return |
|---|---|---|---|
| First Mortgage .... | 60.0 | 9.0 | 4.5 |
| Second Mortgage .. | 30.0 | 12.0 | 3.6 |
| Equity Interest ... | 10.0 | 20.0 | 2.0 |
| Overall Capitalization Rate ................... | | | 10.1% |

With the first mortgage, representing 60 percent of property value, and a 9.0 percent interest rate, the weighted rate of return is 4.5 percent. A second mortgage of 30 percent of property value and an interest rate of 12 percent gives a weighted rate of return of 3.6 percent. The holder of the equity, taking the greater risk and representing only 10 percent of the property value, requires a 20 percent rate of return. This return weighted by its 10 percent value shows a weighted average of 2.0. By adding the weighted rates of return for respective interests in the property, the overall capitalization rate is some 10.1 percent.

## The market value

The second method of finding the capitalization rate relies on recent transactions of income properties. If the net income is available for these properties, then the capitalization rate may be indicated for several comparable properties.

| | Sale Price | Net Income | Overall Capitalization Rate |
|---|---|---|---|
| 1. | $1,000,000 | $100,000 | 10.0% |
| 2. | 550,000 | 50,000 | 9.1% |
| 3. | 6,525,000 | 541,500 | 8.3% |
| 4. | 3,500,000 | 325,500 | 9.3% |

The above list of apartment house sales shown with their net operating income reveals overall capitalization rates ranging from 8.3 percent to 10.0 percent. The four capitalization rates are not averaged. That rate which is believed most comparable to the property appraised is selected for appraisal purposes. For example, item 4, showing a rate of 9.3 percent, might indicate a capitalization rate of 9.5 percent for the property under appraisal. The 10 percent rate in Sale 1 might be given some weight in arriving at the 9.5 rate.

The next issue is to convert net operating income to market value using the selected capitalization rate. For this purpose, the building residual method is illustrated for the appraisal of a high rise apartment. The property in question has an estimated site value of $365,600 and an estimated building life of 40 years. Under a 9 percent capitalization rate, $32,904 represents a 9 percent return on the value of the land, while income to the building would be capitalized at 9.0 percent plus 2.5 percent for capital recovery of the building, straight line depreciation ($1/40$). With these assumptions the market value under the building residual, straight line capitalization, amounts to $2,038,000.

| | |
|---|---:|
| Net Operating Income .............. | $ 225,207 |
| Less Income to Land | |
| ($365,600 x .090) ................. | — 32,904 |
| Income to Building .................. | $ 192,303 |
| Value of Building | |
| ($192,303/.115) .................. | $1,672,200 |
| Add Value of Land ................. | 365,600 |
| Market Value, | |
| Building Residual ................. | $2,037,800 |
| (Rounded) ..................... | $2,038,000 |

The market value under these assumptions determines the maximum mortgage ratio which would be some percentage of the estimated market value.

## Cash Flow Analysis

Cash flow refers to the amount of money earned after payment of income taxes and annual mortgage payments. Table 9.4 shows how cash flow analysis is calculated for a high rise elevator building. Given the net operating income of $225,207, the annual principal and interest payments are deducted to give a net spendable income of $44,861. Adding the principal payments to this figure gives the net operating income less interest. A negative taxable income of —$57,757 results after deducting the allowable depreciation, in this instance double declining balance. Because of the unusually high depreciation deduction, the owner is not liable for personal income taxes.

In these circumstances, cash flow is equivalent to the net income less principal and interest payments on the mortgage. Note that by adding the tax shelter ($-\$57,757$) to the depreciation $\$121,365$, the effect is to report a net income less interest payments. Subtracting the principal payments then equals the cash flow, which in this case is the net spendable income. This procedure is followed since data are taken from a computer printout that allows for a positive taxable income. With an equity interest of $\$844,464$, the property owner is earning the equivalent of a 26.67 percent return on his equity investment.

The example shows, first, that the net operating income is sufficient to pay annual mortgage payments. Moreover, the property could be quite attractive to individuals subject to high marginal income tax rates, since the $-\$57,757$ could offset taxable income earned from other sources. The point is that investment in real property with favorable financing creates opportunities for generating nontaxable income. Table 9.4 also shows the effect of leverage, using mortgage financing to increase the rate of return on invested capital.

## Financial Ratios

Financial ratios are invaluable to judge project feasibility or to judge the relation of the mortgage to net income. They also provide data for comparison with published reports and comparable properties.

### Table 9.4
### Cash Flow Analysis, First Year

| | | |
|---|---:|---:|
| Net Operating Income ...................................... | | $225,207 |
| Annum Debt Service | | |
| First Mortgage, Principal ........................ | $ 18,747 | |
| Interest ......................................... | 161,599 | |
| Less Principal and Interest .................................... | | —180,346 |
| Net Spendable ............................................. | | $ 44,861 |
| Add Principal ............................................. | | 18,747 |
| | | $ 63,608 |
| Less Depreciation ........................................... | | —121,365 |
| Taxable Income (Shelter) ...................................... | | (—$57,757) |
| Personal Income Tax ........................................ | | 0 |
| Income After Taxes ......................................... | | (—$57,757) |
| Add Depreciation ........................................... | | 121,365 |
| | | $ 63,608 |
| Less Principal First ......................................... | | —18,747 |
| Cash Flow ................................................. | | $ 44,861 |
| Taxable Income/Equity ...................................... | | 0 |
| Cash Flow/Equity ($44,861/$844,464) ......................... | | 5.32% |
| Return on Equity ($225,207/$844,464) ......................... | | 26.67% |
| NOI | | |

204

Table 9.5 lists ratios calculated for an existing apartment building. The *loan ratios* show the relation of the mortgage to the property value and its net income. The loan per unit and the loan per room provide standards to test the reasonableness of the loan in relation to local experience. The first mortgage, expressed as a multiple of gross income, provides a limit for policy purposes. Some lenders restrict loans to mortgages that do not exceed five times the gross income. Expressing the mortgage payment as a percentage of net income shows to what extent net income may fall before net income is insufficient to meet mortgage payments.

A series of *income and expense ratios* shown on a per apartment unit, room and square foot basis allows for a comparison with published reports and experience of other like properties. A section on *valuation ratios* shows the reasonableness of land and building values as they are calculated under the income capitalization technique. The overall capitalization rate of 9.67 percent and the gross income multiplier, i.e., the relation between annual gross income and property value are other tests of appraisal accuracy. In the case at hand, these ratios are believed comparable to like properties.

The assessment ratios are fairly critical. The property taxes are the largest single expense borne by owners of income producing property. Again these ratios can be compared to published reports and data of other properties. The building assessed value shown as a percent of the building value (calculated from the income technique), 34.5 percent, shows that the property is reasonably assessed, assuming the building value is accurate.

If the ratios produced in any of the categories seem unusual or atypical, then the estimate of gross income, expenses of operation, or the capitalization rate may require reexamination. Further, the mortgage amount or the terms of the mortgage may not be compatible with the projected net income. The risk of mortgage financing of apartment buildings is reduced by accurate prediction of expenses, gross income, capitalization rate and by accurate capitalization. Cash flow analysis and financial ratios supplement these main tools of analysis.

There is one further point: in the case of a marginal loan on a multiple family dwelling, the lender has the option—like a loan on a single family dwelling—of reducing risks by insuring the loan with private mortgage insurance. Alternatively, lease insurance may be acquired that guarantees annual income, and in the event of borrower default, pays the mortgage, principal and interest. Thus, in questionable cases, the mortgage may be granted under prevailing interest rates for a relatively high risk loan which is secured by private mortgage or lease insurance.

**Table 9.5**
**Financial Ratios of an Apartment Building**

*Loan Ratios (First Mortgage)*

| | |
|---|---|
| Loan to Value Ratio .................................. | $ .90 |
| Loan per Unit ....................................... | $8,313.95 |
| Loan per Room ...................................... | $2,042.86 |
| First Mortgage as a Multiple to Gross Income .......... | 4.79 |
| Percent of Mortgage Payment to Net Income ............ | 95.79 |

*Income and Expense Ratios*

Gross Possible Income

| | |
|---|---|
| Per Unit ........................................... | $1,737.21 |
| Per Room .......................................... | $ 426.86 |
| Per Square Foot ................................... | $ 2.11 |

Expenses

| | |
|---|---|
| Per Unit ........................................... | $ 737.13 |
| Per Room .......................................... | $ 181.12 |
| Per Square Foot ................................... | $ 0.89 |
| Percent of Gross Possible Income .................... | 42.43 |

Net Income

| | |
|---|---|
| Per Unit ........................................... | $ 883.36 |
| Per Room .......................................... | $ 217.05 |
| Per Square Foot ................................... | $ 1.07 |

*Valuation Ratios*

| | |
|---|---|
| Percent of Land Value to Total Value ................... | 8.04 |

Land Value

| | |
|---|---|
| Per Unit ........................................... | $ 734.44 |
| Per Room .......................................... | $ 180.46 |
| Per Square Foot ................................... | $ 0.89 |

Building Value

| | |
|---|---|
| Per Unit ........................................... | $8,396.23 |
| Per Room .......................................... | $2,063.07 |
| Per Square Foot ................................... | $ 10.18 |

Land and Building Value

| | |
|---|---|
| Per Unit ........................................... | $9,130.67 |
| Per Room .......................................... | $2,243.54 |
| Per Square Foot ................................... | $ 11.07 |
| Gross Rate of Return ................................ | 19.03% |
| Gross Income Multiplier ............................. | 5.26 |
| Overall Capitalization Rate .......................... | 9.67% |

*Assessment Ratios*

| | |
|---|---|
| Taxes Paid per Square Foot of Building Area ............ | $ 0.17 |
| Property Taxes as a Percent of Market Value ............ | 1.52 |
| Property Taxes Paid per Apartment..................... | $ 139.00 |
| Property Taxes as a Percent of Gross Income .......... | 8.01 |
| Total Assessed Value as a Percent of Market Value ....... | 35.25 |
| Land Assessed Value as a Percent of Land Value ........ | 43.82 |
| Building Assessed Value as a Percent of Building Value ... | 34.50 |

# Chapter 10

# Financing
# Industrial Property

*must look to ability of borrower to service mortgage debt*

For mortgage purposes the most inclusive and workable definition of industrial property is the concept introduced by the Industrial Council of the Urban Land Institute:

> Industry is the gainful activity involved in producing, distributing and changing the form of raw materials or of assembling components and parts, packaging, warehousing, and transporting finished products.

While the more inclusive definition includes manufacturing that changes the form of a product, it also includes warehousing and other activities such as truck terminals that distribute goods and services. By the same token airport facilities, packing and crating companies would be classified as industries under this definition as would plants that assemble prefabricated parts. Even the distribution of heavy equipment, air conditioning and refrigeration supplies, laundries and dry cleaning plants are among the land uses that typically require industrial space.

In contrast, zoning codes define industry as necessary to regulate industrial land use districts. As a consequence, the Cook County zoning ordinance of Illinois, for instance, covers regulations that not only include manufacturing but also auto laundries, service stations and the "production, processing, cleaning, servicing, testing, repair or storage of goods, materials, or products . . . and which shall not be injurious or offensive to the occupants of adjacent properties . . . ." Thus, industry for zoning purposes covers virtually all nonresidential and nonretail land uses.

To the Bureau of the Census, most data relating to manufacturing activities, are divided into ten major groups. In this more restricted sense, manufacturing is defined as the mechanical or chemical transformation of inorganic or organic substances into new products. The census definition also includes the assembly of component parts of manufactured products, products manufactured for consumption or products semi-finished as a raw material for further manufacturing. Distribution facilities would be omitted under this definition. Omitted also are many land uses requiring industrial land zoning of the typical industrial zoning ordinance. For the present purpose, the term industrial property refers to the definition as developed by the Industrial Council of the Urban Land Institute.

Financing industrial property is more complex, and some experts claim more interesting, than residential or commercial property. In this type of financing, judging the mortgage pattern calls for special knowledge on industrial location, industrial technology, and a more intensive review of borrower credit. Industrial mortgages on more specialized properties tend to be quite restrictive and unique.

The borrower of funds secured by industrial real estate generally has three options. First, he may negotiate a conventional mortgage. Here the alternatives include combinations of conventional financing and subsidies granted by state, federal and local organizations. A desire to increase local employment leads to subsidies not available to nonindustrial borrowers. The second option refers to a direct loan placement. Loans granted on this basis are secured by credit of the company and not merely the real estate. The last main financing device is a sale leaseback. In each of these options, credit analysis follows the same general outline. For the present purpose, attention is directed to the more relevant issues in judging industrial real estate credit.

## Location Analysis

For industrial property, factors important to location analysis substitute for a study of the housing market for residential property and a study of population and buying power for retail properties. The issue is critically important for industrial loans since it can be most difficult to recover debts secured by industrial real estate. Some properties demonstrate special purpose construction, especially for the original occupant and with limited marketability. Thus, loans on these properties tend to be based on credit of the borrower.

## Industrial Location Requirements

Judging the loan security based on an industrial site requires judgments on industrial site utility. To explain this point, it is convenient to classify industries according to their site preferences, for example, industries that prefer sites near (1) their market, (2) raw materials and (3) labor supply. Add to these categories an expanding group of industries that meet none of these classifications: the so-called footloose industries.

### *Industries oriented to markets*

Market oriented industries include those that prefer sites near their consumers. Manufacturers of beverages, bread, pastry and other perishables such as dairy products, generally cannot be too far removed from their customers. Included also are industries that sell to other industries; namely, producers of components for electrical prefabricators or subcontractors that prefabricate materials for aircraft or that assemble machinery.

An industry oriented to consumer markets tries to lower transportation costs. Typically, such industries add weight in manufacturing—the bottling of beverages is a case in point. In other instances, highly perishable products require a location near the point of consumption. Other industries such as small print shops tend to locate at points convenient for personal contact with customers. It is also true that other goods because of their bulk and relatively high transportation cost must locate near market centers. In illustration, most cities have construction industries that require space near centers of population.

Industries falling into one of these groups judge sites according to how the site allows them to serve their customers. The greater the utility of a site for this purpose, the greater the marketability and the higher the market value.

### *Industries oriented to raw materials*

Industries identified with this group have limited locational choices. The cost of transporting raw materials ties these industries to their source of supply. Typically the processes that lose weight in manufacturing such as furniture manufacture, processing of ore, and cement manufacturing are included in this group. A list of firms using industrial land near raw materials includes grain elevators, cotton gins, as well as food processors, canneries, lumber mills and the like. Industrial sites adapted to this group have little appeal to market-oriented industries.

### Industries oriented to labor

Industries attracted to local labor are concerned with not only the cost but the supply of skilled labor. For example, as textile mills were abandoned in the Northeast, the former textile workers attracted the apparel industry that used local semi-skilled labor. New Britain, Connecticut, is an example of prefabricated metal industry oriented to workers skilled in metal production and tool manufacturing. The aircraft industries of Los Angeles, Wichita, and Seattle, tend to be attracted to the local supply of skilled and professional labor experienced in aircraft work.

### The footloose industries

Technological developments give industries a wider latitude in selecting sites. For instance, automation tends to free industries from specialized labor supplies. By the same token, improved transportation has the effect of increasing the available supply of industrial sites. Air freight facilities widen the market for perishable products and effectively increase the supply of economical industrial sites.

The construction of peripheral highways around central cities, notably the belt highway surrounding Baltimore, Maryland, or Highway 128 around Boston, Massachusetts, or the peripheral highway (I-285) surrounding Atlanta provide access to industrial parks near customers, markets, and suburban labor. Improved highway transportation provides the necessary access to land with room for expansion and parking —and often at a lower cost per acre—while still giving industry advantages of a central location with the amenities of a suburban location.

Consider other observable trends: assembly line production, one story architecture, and the declining importance of railroads. The greater mobility of the so-called footloose industries places increasing emphasis on community factors, cultural advantages, educational resources, climate, available housing, and recreational facilities. Community attitudes are another item weighed heavily in qualifying industrial sites. Judging mortgage security then forces the mortgage analyst to recognize additional changing factors that affect industrial property marketability.

## Industrial Site Requirements

To center on the more significant aspects of industrial site analysis, our examination will include the general types of land available, factors used to judge an individual site and the effect of local industrial zoning. With this background, criteria to judge industrial buildings are offered.

*Judging industrial land*

If you were to select an industrial site, the land under consideration would probably include centrally located sites. Historically, land in central locations— the urban fringe surrounding downtown districts— was established in the late 1800s and before World War I. At this time it was more economical to move goods vertically than horizontally. The dependence on railroads encouraged multiple story construction at the downtown central location. A review of the older established industrial districts shows how industrial land use concentrated around the railroad in industrial corridors. Typically, these areas share certain common characteristics.

(1) *Centrally located industrial sites.* Such land is usually irregularly shaped and relatively expensive. Traffic congestion is common to centrally located areas. While originally located near workers' homes surrounding the urban fringe, such sites are now inconvenient to suburban labor.

Probably the greatest limitation lies in the relative scarcity of land. Space for parking is inadequate and expensive. Off-street truck loading and maneuvering space may not be available, adding further to traffic congestion. Available sites are adversely affected by dilapidated buildings. If relatively high property taxes are still in effect, this is a further limitation of site utility.

Moreover, many of these districts were established before zoning regulations. They reveal mixed areas of commercial and low-quality industrial property and in some areas include walk-up apartments in poor condition.

In favor of central space is its relatively low development cost. The utilities are adequate for the area. Frequently, buildings may be economically rehabilitated to alternative uses. Moreover, the central area constitutes a supply of low-cost space for the small marginal firm. Generally speaking, such districts constitute high mortgage risks; they are declining in utility for industrial purposes and they appeal to a limited group of industrial operations. The demand for this space is pretty much concentrated among industries that must be near customers: small distribution warehouses, industrial services and industries that require low cost space in older buildings, industries that use unskilled labor in heavily populated areas and small industries that are closely dependent on local plants.

*(2) Industrial acreage.* This type of land refers to underdeveloped land in rural, suburban areas surrounding urban centers. In many instances these areas are undergoing a transition from agricultural to urban use. The utility of such land varies markedly from other types of industrial land.

As a rule, industrial acreage is fairly remote from urban centers. In addition, the provision for water and waste disposal, natural gas and electricity may be quite limited. The larger industrial sites, therefore, appeal only to larger organizations that construct their own utility systems. This factor alone considerably narrows the market for industrial acreage.

Industries that have important linkages with other companies tend to avoid outlying locations. Add to this factor the development costs in roads and land preparation. The load bearing quality of the soil must be subject to investigation. If the soil does not have adequate load bearing capacity or it is poorly drained, the utility for industrial use is quite limited.

Offsetting these limitations is the relatively low land cost per acre. In this respect the land value must be sufficient to offset higher transportation and development costs. Probably the main attraction is availability of large sites permitting plants to isolate their operations from adjoining owners. The large sites appeal to plants that preserve an open, attractive appearance with low cost land for off-street truck loading and maneuvering space and parking.

*(3) Organized industrial districts.* The main appeal of land in the organized or planned industrial districts is that such land is under proprietary control. Proprietary control allows the land to be continually reserved for the exclusive use of selected industries. Ordinarily, industrial sites must be developed according to a land use plan that includes utilities and land use controls appropriate to the type of district.

The main sponsors of industrial districts are found among the railroads that develop sites with limited land use controls. Their motivation is freight traffic generation. Publicly owned districts encourage local employment by providing organized industrial districts. Their land use controls are less restrictive than the privately owned districts. Privately organized districts tend to be more selective, they have higher priced land, and they are found in the preferred locations.

Industrial sites in these districts are not adapted to every industry. Their sites are relatively high priced, but, the higher prices are offset by utility availability, superior locations and more services such as central display space, landscaping, and technical advice from industrial park operators. The sites are quite small, not suitable for larger plants. They appeal to industries that have a high degree of mutual attraction. They provide prestige locations that attract industries that maintain landscaping, construct attractive buildings, and maintain an open appearance. Most of the privately sponsored industrial districts favor distribution warehouses of the large corporate firms.

The inherent advantages of industrial parks explain their general appeal. First, the zoning and the environmental problems are resolved by the industrial park developer. He provides utilities and sites that have maximum utility. Second, they are located at strategic transportation points. Third, services supplied by the proprietor are helpful to small and medium sized firms that require space of high utility and an urban location with excellent transportation. Industrial depreciation is minimized in these areas since the buildings are relatively new and conform to modern industrial architecture.

*(4) Redeveloped land.* It is recognized that the older industrial districts of established cities lack utility. Land ownership is so fractionated that it is uneconomic to assemble land for industrial redevelopment. Consequently, industrial cities such as Detroit and St. Louis have redeveloped industrial land under urban renewal and model city programs. Such land is subject to certain restrictive land use controls. Land must typically be paid for in cash. Building plans must be approved and some of the sites tend to be odd-shaped, small, and uneconomic. These sites may be adversely affected by surrounding land uses.

The availability of relatively large sites in central areas, in part, compensates for these disadvantages. To the extent that unsightly, dilapidated buildings have been torn down, such space has added utility. The price of land zoned for exclusive industrial use is usually less than the price of undeveloped industrial land in the same area. Property depreciation tends to be retarded by the urban development plan that makes land available only for compatible and complementary industries. Financing buildings on these sites is generally less risky than financing of industrial buildings located in undeveloped rural areas or in older industrial areas.

## Site analysis

There is more to site analysis than a study of the property. In fact, the physical site itself may be the last item of review. To suggest a technique of weighing the mortgage security, consider the following outline that refers to regional, community and site location factors.

I. Regional factors
    A. Location in relation to markets
        1. Consumer
        2. Industrial

    B. Raw material sources

    C. Transportation costs and service

        1. Rail

        2. Air

        3. Highway access

        4. Water

    D. Fuel and power

        1. Availability

        2. Cost

    E. The labor supply

        1. Skilled

        2. Unskilled

        3. Professional

    F. Climate

 II. Community analysis

    A. State taxes

    B. Local taxes

    C. Legislation favorable to industry

        1. Industrial foundations

        2. Tax subsidies

        3. Site availability

        4. Labor laws

    D. Secondary site factors

        1. The type and number of industries

        2. The local availability of utilities

        3. Local transportation facilities

        4. Waste disposal facilities

        5. Local financial assistance

        6. The general attitude toward industry

III. Analyzing the site

    A. Size and shape

    B. Topography

    C. The availability and cost of utilities

        1. On-site

        2. Off-site

    D. Drainage and soil conditions

    E. Cost of land development

    F. The neighborhood

    G. Municipal services

    H. Local taxes

    I. Insurance expenses

    J. Industrial zoning

The list could be expanded for several pages. Individual circumstances and your knowledge of the local economy dictate the final elements to be considered. But certainly the items covering the three part analysis in the outline warrant at least a minimum review. *The regional analysis* is directed to the dominant industries in the region. Does the site in question appeal to market, labor, or raw material oriented industries—and to what extent? This is critical to industrial properties that have a national or regional market. Industries that have considerable freedom in site selection compare regions, not land areas.

*Community analysis* is significant to industries that locate branch plants within a region. This list shows that factors important to industrial operations are weighed more heavily; namely, the tax structure both state and local, and local legislation that affects daily operations. The utility and the availability of local industrial sites may be supported further by local revenue bonds. Note too that the *attitude towards industry* is listed prominently. This heading would include the amenities available to employees such as suitable housing, recreational facilities, educational advantages, and other factors associated with the community as a place to live and work.

The final point is *the site itself.* Most of these issues relate to physical characteristics, the size, the shape, the topography, drainage and soil conditions. Local experience will help judge the relative utility of the site for industrial use. The land, for example, must be level for sites using rail transportation. The cost of developing a level site is part of the land acquisition cost.

Another aspect relates to the influence of surrounding land on the demand for industrial property. Surrounding uses should be compatible and appropriate to the type of structure offered as mortgage security. The road access, degree of traffic congestion, and public transportation are issues qualifying the neighborhood. Finally, the industrial zoning and land use restrictions complete this list. Zoning codes listing prohibited industries and allowing nonindustrial uses in industrial districts are serious limitations. The importance of this issue justifies a more detailed explanation.

## Industrial zoning

Industrial zoning practices are undergoing considerable change. The requirements of industry and their attitude towards zoning restrictions varies markedly from past standards. Also, communities have become more enlightened by substituting environmental controls for the negative zoning of colonial times. The ability to use industrial property is affected by how local zoning practices have adapted to new concepts of industrial zoning.

To explain these issues the discussion turns first, to how present industrial zoning developed; second, to the effect of prohibited lists; and lastly, to progressively inclusive zoning. The more advanced zoning practices that overcome industrial zoning deficiencies are briefly noted.

The central problem of industrial zoning is caused by its early orientation—an orientation still influenced by the nuisance controls initiated by colonial governments. An ordinance of 1706 in Massachusetts prohibited the location of powder houses near dwellings. The concept of prohibiting the location of dangerous or noxious uses in residential areas extended to slaughter houses, houses for rendering tallow, for curing leather and so on.

Today this concept is observed in zoning ordinances that list *prohibited industries*. These local industrial zoning ordinances permit industries in certain districts with the exception of prohibited industries. Such lists limit the marketability of industrial real estate. Industries on the list are regarded as undesirable *per se*.

The objection to these lists is the assumption that the industry is guilty of incompatible operation. But, it is not the industry that should be penalized, only its undesirable operation. It would be quite acceptable to most localities to accept an industry provided that its operations were in harmony with surrounding land uses. This is accomplished by providing performance standards controlling industry.

*Performance standards* were introduced in professionally prepared zoning codes in the city of Chicago, Cook County, Illinois, and New York City, among many others. Performance standards substitute for the list of prohibited industries. Industries are accepted provided they meet performance standards as stated in the zoning ordinance. A list of items subject to control includes:

| | |
|---|---|
| Noise control | Toxic gases |
| Smoke emission | Sewage wastes |
| Odors | Electronic-magnetic interference |
| Heat | Radioactive emissions |
| Vibrations | Fire and explosive hazards |

For instance, an industry would be accepted if the noise generated did not exceed 53 decibels for sounds falling within 600-1200 cycles at the property line. (A decibel is the unit used to measure the level of sound volume.) Similar controls apply to other items on the list. For example, there are ways of measuring the emission of particulate matter found in smoke by the weight of foreign matter per cubic foot of air.

The second industrial zoning practice that affects property marketability relates to *progressively inclusive districts*. A zoning code following this zoning method normally starts with the R-1 district (or similar designation), which is reserved exclusively for residential purposes.

Succeeding districts typically provide for multiple family units of increasing density. In multiple family districts, which set aside land for apartment buildings, the progressively inclusive feature provides that uses of the preceding district are allowed, meaning single family dwellings. As the zoning code adds districts, the commercial and industrial districts, the same clause applies. The end result produces, for example, a retail zoning that allows uses of the preceding district, which authorizes apartment and dwelling use in a retail zone. If this same principle is followed for industrial districts, industry competes with nonindustrial land uses.

Coupled with the tendency to overzone for industrial purposes, buyers purchase industrially zoned land for nonindustrial purposes. Consequently, the district becomes neither a good commercial nor industrial district. It becomes a mixed district, often with poorly maintained, dilapidated, substandard buildings. Traffic congestion and incompatible land uses are plainly obvious in the older cities affected by this type of zoning. Industrial parks and redeveloped space in urban renewal and model city areas compensate for zoning limitations. Experienced lenders avoid industrial districts that follow undesirable zoning practices of the past.

# Industrial Building Analysis  what can the building be used for?

If the mortgage security is based primarily on real estate, there is considerable risk in financing a building adapted to only one industrial use (for example, a modern dairy). To explore this issue, it is important to recognize buildings classified by the type of plant layout.

## Industrial Buildings Classified by Plant Layout

First, industrial buildings are designated for *product layout*. The equipment is arranged according to a sequence of operations like an assembly line. The building layout reduces the problem of material handling. Processes will be organized around a single end product reducing space needed for material storage and plant traffic. The building is adapted to continuous flow production with raw materials entering at one point and the finished product emerging at another point. If the building is abandoned by the original occupant, the building usually requires extensive remodeling for reuse.

Second, industrial buildings are adapted to *process layout*. Space is organized to centralize various processes. For example, consider prefabricated metal production in which grinding operations are required for numerous products. A process layout would group grinding machines in one area. Welding, plating, finishing, machine shop, heat treating, cutting, sewing and threading are typical of industrial activities grouped according to processes for production of multiple products.

Rather than production of a single end product, these plants organize work according to job lots. A good example is apparel manufacturing. The plant provides for a functional division of processes. Process grouping provides for considerable flexibility in the placement of equipment. Changes in production will not involve extensive changes in equipment, location, and building design.

These buildings require special equipment to move products between process centers. More space is needed for storage. A building with the widest possible clear span and ceiling heights of at least 16 feet probably appeals to the largest number of industries.

## Single Story Buildings

For some purposes, multiple story buildings are adequate. In other cases the single story building is a necessity. For instance, the single story building will have a relatively high floor load bearing capacity. Noise and vibrations are less likely to be transmitted to other parts of the structure. Furthermore, the foundations and load bearing quality of the soil are less demanding. Foundations are less expensive. Besides these advantages, less space is lost for elevator shafts, stairwells and utility service ways.

Even the utility of the building is affected. Production layout for a process is generally more efficient in a single story structure. It is more easily expanded and adapted to a wider range of industrial operations.

Contrast these points with the multiple story building. The major advantage of such a building relates to the intensive use of available land area. In earlier generations the requirement to be near the railroad, and in central locations called for a high ratio of floor area to ground area. In some cities, this is still an advantage. Besides the multiple story building will generally have lower heating costs. The multiple story plant is adaptable to gravity flow, ramps, conveyors, and pipelines.

The record shows that multiple story buildings are adaptable to medium and light industry, say the hardware or garment industries. They are typical of industries producing multiple products and job lots. Frequently, the larger industrial buildings, such as the former Packard automobile plant in Detroit, Michigan, have been subdivided and adapted to multiple occupancy. Probably the location of multiple story buildings argues against their continued use. Traffic congestion, parking, the location of employees constitute their greatest limitations.

## Industrial Building Standards

Ideally, a loan on an industrial building will be placed on the building showing the maximum flexibility and greatest utility. This calls for a building with few columns and a clear span floor area. At the minimum, ceilings must be 16 feet high to accommodate pallet storage and overhead conveyors and cranes. Buildings with 10 or 12 foot ceilings have limited usefulness for light and medium industrial operations.

Moreover the building must be constructed with utility runs that are easily extended. A structure built on a modular plan, allowing the expansion of plumbing, power wiring, heating and air conditioning, is the ideal architectural form. A related issue is the tendency towards more employee service facilities such as lunch rooms, washrooms, and in the more developed industrial parks, recreational facilities.

# Judging Industrial Credit

Up to this point the analysis has dealt with the real estate security. The mortgage risks associated with industrial properties, many of which are highly specialized, requires more than the usual care in judging credit of the borrower. This is where the lender capitalizes on his technical industrial knowledge. His review of borrower credit starts with an analysis of the company and its standing in the industry. The next issue follows methods of judging credit from financial statements. Guidelines established by nationally known lenders are believed important to this type of analysis. Finally, mortgage terms are more controlling for mortgages secured by industrial real estate.

Robert Morris Agency ) standards for
D & B ) industry

## Company Standing in the Industry

The analysis of borrower credit starts by determining the competitive position of the loan applicant in the industry. In this respect, much depends on the type of product manufactured. Some products are more sensitive to the business cycle. It makes a considerable difference if the product manufactured is a consumer good or is a producer good sold only to other manufacturers. For example, sales of automated machinery to an automobile plant would be expected to show more cyclical variation than sales of breakfast foods. Considerable risk is also associated with firms producing defense goods.

To show how production has changed from year to year, some lenders require a detailed production history. Such a history will reveal the degree of plant modernization, the location of suppliers, the customer market, and the competitive advantage held in production. Prospects for continued sales also relate to the type of market: regional, national, or international. The competitive market in which the firm operates is related to the location of sales offices and the relative importance of the company in the industry and their credit policy to customers. In short, this information helps forecast the probability of continued sales that will insure solvency and repayment of the mortgage.

Related information covers the history of management including the background of company leaders and the effect of mergers, subsidiaries and the location of branch plants and their degree of modernization. Experienced lenders rely not only on written statements from the company but reports of Standard and Poor's, and Dun and Bradstreet reports.

In essence, the analysis of industrial property for mortgage purposes rests on its general marketability. In addition to the points covered here the lending officer establishes (1) the rate of industrial property absorbtion; (2) the degree of local government cooperation; (3) suitability of labor to local industry; and (4) the suitability of a location for a given industrial occupant.

In the first instance, the lender reviews industrial land use trends and projects the degree of speculative building, the possibility of new industrial prospects and the general economic climate for local industry. To assist in these judgments, commercial banks work closely with local government and state officials active in industrial promotion. A favorable industrial climate not indicated by past trends must be substantiated with affirmative action plans of local and state experts.

The degree of local government cooperation is evident from the willingness of local agencies to provide for water and sewerage facilities, and generally develop sites as a means of encouraging industrial development. Frequently, favorable zoning treatment and property tax abatement of various kinds serves as evidence of local support of local industry. To the extent that local cooperation is forthcoming, the lender faces less risk in underwriting the mortgage.

Similarly, some judgment must be made with respect to the suitability of local industry for the project in question. A high rate of employee absenteeism, or the inability to attract necessary skills at competitive wages are points in question. At the same time a review will be made of the proposed industry—it must not be too remote from the source of raw materials or its market for finished products since that would raise transportation and other acquisition costs.

## Evaluating Credit of the Borrower

Special care is taken in reviewing financial statements. Much weight is placed on historical analysis since financial ratios may change quite rapidly. Financial ratios are reviewed to determine a loan applicant's ability to service the mortgage. Ideally, balance sheets and profit-loss statements should cover a minimum of five years.

Balance sheet information should be reviewed to examine five leading ratios. A national lender might not consider an industrial loan unless balance sheet ratios meet the following minimum tests.

1. *Current assets* should be at least twice current liabilities.
2. The *net quick asset position* (current assets less inventories) must be more than sufficient to pay all current liabilities.
3. *Net fixed assets* should not exceed much more than 75 percent of the *net worth*.
4. Total debt including current liabilities and fixed liabilities should not exceed 100 percent of the net worth.
5. The total long-term debt should not exceed 50 percent of the net working capital (the difference between current assets and current liabilities).

To illustrate, consider a loan based on the following simplified balance sheet.

*Assets*

| | |
|---|---:|
| Cash | $ 200,000 |
| Accounts Receivable | 400,000 |
| Loans to Officers | 200,000 |
| Inventory | 800,000 |
| Total Current Assets | $1,600,000 |
| Equipment and Machinery | 900,000 |
| Total Assets | $2,500,000 |

*Liabilities and Capital*

| | |
|---|---:|
| Accounts Payable | $1,000,000 |
| Notes Payable | 100,000 |
| Total Current Liabilities | $1,100,000 |
| Long-Term Notes | 800,000 |
| Capital Stock | 600,000 |
| Total Liabilities and Stock | $2,500,000 |

According to the criteria suggested here, a loan would be turned down for the following reasons.

1. The ratio of current assets to current liabilities: $1,600,000/$1,100,000 = 1.45$. Current assets are less than twice the current liabilities.
2. Net quick asset position: total current assets, $1,600,000, are sufficient to pay total current liabilities, $1,100,000.
3. Net fixed assets are more than 75 percent of the net worth: $900,000/$600,000 = 150$ percent.

4. Long term debt exceeds 100 percent of the net worth: $800,000/$600,000 = 133 percent.
5. Long term debt exceeds 50 percent of the net working capital ($800,000/$1,600,000-$1,100,000) = 160 percent.

Profit and loss statements supplement the analysis of balance sheets. A review of these statements shows the profit history. To give the greatest security, annual sales should show an upward trend. If a new mortgage loan is proposed, profits should be adequate to cover all annual obligations, including the proposed loan. It is also important to know the record of dividends paid, salaries of key officials and profit before and after depreciation. In the latter case, if the company has used accelerated depreciation, the profit history may show an irregular pattern.

Provided these circumstances are favorable, loans on industrial property are frequently accompanied by special agreements made a part of the promissory note. A list of the more common restrictions includes:

1. Net working capital must be maintained at a fixed given amount.
2. Loans or advances to officers and directors are limited or prohibited.
3. Dividends or disbursements to officers are prohibited if the net effect is to reduce net working capital below a minimum figure.
4. Future borrowing is restricted to reasonable amounts.
5. The company's right to sell assets is limited during the life of the loan.

Besides these restrictions the lender would ordinarily require annual financial statements. If there is an outstanding debt on equipment or working capital, the mortgage lender may ask that these loans be subordinated to the first mortgage. Promissory notes may also prohibit the industrial company from mortgaging other property without permission of the first mortgage lender. Life insurance policies on the company director and provisions against merger without lender approval may be part of the mortgage agreement.

## Sale Leaseback Financing   Taxing Scheme

If funds are available to purchase real estate, financing may be arranged by sale of a plant to an investor who leases the property back to the seller. The leaseback has certain financial advantages for the buyer. The sale leaseback gives the buyer the opportunity to purchase an investment with income provided by a tenant of known financial strength. Furthermore, the purchase price and rent are interrelated.

The amount of rent and purchase price may be arranged to the mutual advantage of both parties. The buyer in particular can negotiate for the rate of return he requires on his purchase investment. An income tax advantage accrues to the buyer in the form of depreciation which provides a substantial income tax deduction and contributes to cash flow. Cash flow is defined here as the amount of income received after payment of income taxes and mortgage interest. There are instances in which the buyer arranges a first mortgage, which in effect is repaid out of rent proceeds.

Depending on individual income tax status and capital requirements, the sale leaseback may be equally advantageous to the seller. For one thing, the seller continues to use the property and yet he secures cash from the sale. Though he must pay rent on previously owned property, the sale leaseback provides funds from 100 percent of the value of property. This contrasts to a mortgage that covers only a partial interest. Under a long-term lease, use of the property is provided in much the same manner as the use would be provided under fee ownership. In addition, the rent payment is deductible as a business expense.

The relative advantages of a sale leaseback are highly dependent on the income tax status of both parties. The need for capital funds is also a controlling element. It should be noted further that the leased fee interest of the owner who has leased property, and the leasehold interest, the interest of the tenant, may be mortgaged and sold much as the unencumbered fee title. On balance the decision to negotiate a sale leaseback depends on financial and income tax aspects and not on the question of property control. Particularly for industrial properties that are difficult to finance under a mortgage, a sale leaseback is a popular means of financing large scale industrial properties.

Seller – business expense in rental payment
raises instant capital

buyer – taxes & interest deduction
picking up yield on investment
depreciation

lender must look to lessee for his credit to service
the mortgage

# Chapter 11

# Financing
# Agricultural Property

Commercial banks play a leading role in financing farm real estate. Not only is this an expanding market, but, trends in agricultural finance favor farms as long-term security. To explain this point it is relevant to study the market for agricultural loans. In this type of analysis, trends in agricultural production, marketing and processing techniques as well as land value trends, and the role of banks in agricultural real estate deserve separate comment. Next it seems appropriate to cover appraisal techniques unique to judging the loan security. Additional comment on the analysis of special purpose farms completes the discussion.

## The Market for Agricultural Mortgages

Certain economic trends favor farm real estate as mortgage security. Agricultural economists predict a growing demand for farm real estate loans. In meeting this demand, commercial banks will probably constitute a growing source of supply for long-term funds. In part, these predictions are supported by the changing market in farm mortgages, rising farm land values, and the financial demands of modern farming.

## The Market for Farm Real Estate Loans

Technological changes have created a favorable market for farm real estate credit. A recent study revealed that farmers produce 20 percent more on 6 percent fewer acres than they did ten years previously. Farm output per man hour increased 82 percent in ten years. The data further show that farms are becoming larger, more complex, and more efficient. Measured from 1975, farm mortgages outstanding increased from $18.8 billion ten years ago to $46.8 billion at the end of second quarter 1975—a 148.9 percent increase. The volume of long-term real estate credit will continue to grow primarily because—

1. Capital will continue to be substituted for labor
2. Increased operating inputs require more capital in herbicides, pesticides and other custom purchased services (crop dusting) which substitute for machinery purchases
3. Higher operating expenses are expected to continue, including the cost of credit
4. The structure of agriculture will continue to change: more credit will be demanded since larger farms require more credit than smaller farms
5. Farmers are becoming more business minded and long-term debt is accepted as a necessary part of farm operation.

### The demand for farm mortgages

The demand for farm mortgages arises from three needs; (1) to finance farm real estate transfers, (2) to refinance existing debt, and (3) to finance capital outlays, especially farm improvements. The total volume of real estate farm credit outstanding is estimated to increase to $63 billion by 1980. Adding other agricultural credit needs raises the total credit needs of agriculture to $140 billion by 1980. Commercial banks are expected to supply approximately 23 percent of the total agricultural credit by 1980.

Looking at total farm mortgage debt currently outstanding, $46.8 billion, commercial banks account for over $6 billion. From 1970 to the end of the second quarter of 1975, the volume of farm mortgage debt handled by commercial banks increased 40 percent. According to the available data, about 30 percent of farm mortgages are used to purchase land, another 50 percent of farm mortgages refinance existing loans, and the balance of farm mortgages are used for capital outlays and other purposes.

These mortgages are secured by farms classified into four main groups: (1) The large corporate farms which are professionally managed using the latest equipment and techniques. These farms may be expected to increase their long-term debt. (2) The next group are the modern commercial farms, proprietarily owned and operated. (3) Add to this list the part-time farms (which are increasing in number) and (4) the small marginal farms (which are decreasing).

## *The supply of farm mortgage credit*

Farm real estate credit differs from other real estate loans in at least two important respects: First, a considerable volume of farm real estate is seller financed. That is, sellers accept purchase money mortgages or instalment sales contracts as substitutes for cash. In some instances the purchase money mortgage will constitute a second lien subordinate to a first mortgage granted from institutional sources.

The second main characteristic associated with farm mortgages relates to participation of government, primarily, by the Farmers Home Administration. The Farmers Home Administration, operating under the Department of Agriculture, supplements commercial lenders. They administer direct loans, revolving funds for agriculture and administer a loan guarantee program similar to the Federal Housing Administration. In contrast, the Federal Land Bank System is an organization of Federal Land Bank associations that grant first mortgage loans to farmers.

In addition, the *Farm Credit Act of 1971* allowed federal intermediate credit banks to serve as a secondary source of funds. For the present purpose, their importance lies in their authority to make loans to commercial banks and to discount agricultural paper held by commercial banks. In this way commercial banks are encouraged to supply farm mortgage credit. Since the combined prospective growth of farm debt is 9.4 percent annually, it is relevant to review the main sources of farm real estate mortgages. Historically, farmers have satisfied their long-term capital requirements from the following four main sources: 1.) *Sellers of farms.* The amount of credit available from sellers in the form of small land contracts or purchase money mortgages depends on preferences of sellers. For instance, sellers may gain a tax advantage in taking part of the selling price in the form of a land contract. As a result interest rates on land contracts are generally lower than the prevailing interest rate on first mortgages. This is particularly the case if the instalment purchase agreement provides for a downpayment of less than 30 percent and interest rates of more than 4 percent. In these circumstances, capital gains enjoyed by the seller may be distributed over the life of the instalment contract. With a continued rise in land values, this source of credit may be expected to increase.

2.) *Insurance companies.* Insurance companies tend to be heavy investors in long-term securities with relatively high yields. Since insurance

*[handwritten margin note: (institutional lenders) credit bank purchase paper from bank secured by agricultural]*

companies operate under state laws, they have considerable flexibility in shifting loanable funds by geographic regions and by type of investment. The degree to which insurance companies participate in farm mortgages depends on trends in their cash flow which relate to policy premiums, loans, and the repayment rate of existing loans and investments. Historically insurance companies have preferred relatively large farm mortgages using mortgage bankers or commercial banks to assist in loan acquisitions. But, some companies do place farm loans directly.

More significantly, the relative return on farm mortgages must be competitive with other investments. In this respect, the degree to which insurance companies supply long-term mortgage credit depends on the degree to which the return on farm mortgages equals or exceeds the rates of return on non-farm investments.

③ *Commercial banks*. Commercial banks are attracted to farm mortgages because they have a long-run interest in promoting loans that stimulate local economic growth. To the extent that time deposits continue to grow relative to demand deposits, banks will have a greater supply of credit available for farm mortgages. The participation of commercial banks with federal and intermediate credit banks acts as a further incentive to invest in long-term farm mortgages. To be sure, the primary interest of a bank is to serve the *total* capital and credit needs of the community. Consequently in farming communities the primary thrust is directed to the short and intermediate credit needs of the community. To this extent commercial banks, though not underwriting farm mortgages directly, provide assistance in the placement of farm mortgages. goverment programs

④ *The farm credit system*. The farm credit system dominates long-term farm lending. This system includes federal land banks, the production credit associations and the Farmers Home Administration. For example, the Federal Land Bank, organized into 12 national districts, offers a variable interest rate mortgage. As a result, their interest rates tend to be relatively high during tight money periods. With the larger commercial banks, these agencies share the ability to secure loanable funds from national money markets. Mortgage money from these sources depends on national monetary conditions. In this sense these lenders are able to meet temporary or long-term variations in farm lending independently of other institutional and private lenders. To some extent the degree of capital available for farm mortgages depends on expectations of future land values, which to date have favored farms as loan security.

## Farm Land Value Trends

Historically, farm land has served as a hedge against inflation. As the purchasing value of the dollar declines, farm land values have generally increased. For example, surveys by the Department of Agriculture have shown that the average farm land value per acre from 1967 to 1975 has increased among the states from a minimum of 155 percent to a maximum of 350 percent.

The national index of average farm land values, based on 1967 prices, increased by 230 percent as of November, 1975. The index of farm land values by states is summarized in Table 11.1.

In part, the increase in farm land values has been attributed to the effect of expanding urban areas in farm communities. Certainly part of the increase is explained by the conversion of former agricultural land to urban development. Other authorities have attributed the rise in land values to technological advances in agriculture. Further, as prices of agricultural products increase, land values tend to increase. That is, farmers tend to bid up the price of land in the expectation of earning higher net incomes per acre.

## Farm Loan Policy

To understand the underwriting of farm mortgages, it is considered important to review past practices and how they bear on current loan policy. The main issues deal with the definition of value, the evidence that supports a value opinion and the loan to value ratio. It is suggested here that present requirements of the lender and borrower have revised much of the earlier concepts dealing with farm loans. Economic, environmental, monetary conditions, and circumstances surrounding farm mortgage credit have changed significantly from procedures developed before World War II.

### The Historical Definition of Value

In the past farm mortgage lenders were inclined to think in terms of normal value, which is believed to vary markedly from market value or even recent farm land sales. As late as 1965 the Federal Land Bank System defined agricultural value as "the amount a typical purchaser would, under usual conditions, be willing to pay and be justified in paying for the property for customary agricultural uses, including farm home advantages with the expectation of receiving normal net earnings from the farm and other dependable sources."

Observers have traced the concept of normal agricultural values to 1930 practices of the Farm Credit Administration and The Farm Security Administration. The definition was to avoid dangerously high loan to value ratios during periods of high land prices and unusually low loan to value ratios during periods of depressed prices. The definition

## Table 11.1
### Farm Real Estate Value Indexes of Average Value of Land and Buildings Per Acre, by States: 1950 to 1975*
### (1967 = 100)

| State | Index 1950 | Index 1960 | Index 1970 | Index 1975 |
|---|---|---|---|---|
| Northeast: Maine | 51 | 79 | 128 | 265 |
| New Hampshire | 47 | 66 | 149 | 265 |
| Vermont | 52 | 70 | 155 | 265 |
| Massachusetts | 49 | 72 | 126 | 265 |
| Rhode Island | 43 | 67 | 132 | 265 |
| Connecticut | 43 | 68 | 134 | 265 |
| Middle Atlantic: New York | 52 | 73 | 123 | 294 |
| New Jersey | 30 | 58 | 144 | 350 |
| Pennsylvania | 39 | 70 | 145 | 338 |
| Eastern North Central: Ohio | 40 | 73 | 115 | 228 |
| Indiana | 38 | 69 | 104 | 227 |
| Illinois | 42 | 71 | 107 | 233 |
| Michigan | 41 | 72 | 113 | 194 |
| Wisconsin | 53 | 76 | 124 | 251 |
| Western North Central: Minnesota | 47 | 80 | 118 | 266 |
| Iowa | 49 | 73 | 114 | 267 |
| Missouri | 38 | 63 | 124 | 218 |
| North Dakota | 40 | 69 | 120 | 290 |
| South Dakota | 49 | 74 | 112 | 229 |
| Nebraska | 46 | 69 | 115 | 242 |
| Kansas | 47 | 72 | 107 | 224 |
| South Atlantic: Delaware | 30 | 63 | 116 | 266 |
| Maryland | 29 | 61 | 138 | 258 |
| Virginia | 38 | 67 | 121 | 285 |
| West Virginia | 43 | 66 | 137 | 355 |
| North Carolina | 42 | 69 | 113 | 229 |
| South Carolina | 39 | 68 | 124 | 286 |
| Georgia | 26 | 55 | 138 | 302 |
| Florida | 28 | 74 | 121 | 233 |
| Eastern South Central: Kentucky | 44 | 71 | 110 | 220 |
| Tennessee | 43 | 66 | 123 | 251 |
| Alabama | 31 | 57 | 121 | 251 |
| Mississippi | 29 | 53 | 125 | 222 |
| Western South Central: Arkansas | 30 | 54 | 129 | 196 |
| Louisiana | 32 | 66 | 116 | 195 |
| Oklahoma | 36 | 61 | 115 | 224 |
| Texas | 36 | 67 | 119 | 205 |
| Mountain: Montana | 35 | 71 | 124 | 260 |
| Idaho | 45 | 76 | 120 | 260 |
| Wyoming | 37 | 62 | 116 | 241 |
| Colorado | 46 | 69 | 105 | 235 |
| New Mexico | 44 | 62 | 120 | 204 |
| Arizona | 29 | 56 | 127 | 217 |
| Utah | 52 | 80 | 137 | 249 |
| Nevada | 40 | 67 | 155 | 306 |
| Pacific: Washington | 45 | 73 | 124 | 197 |
| Oregon | 34 | 52 | 137 | 233 |
| California | 36 | 72 | 110 | 155 |

*As of November 1975.

Source: U. S. Bureau of the Census, *Statistical Abstract of the United States: 1975.* (96th edition.) Washington, D. C., 1975, p. 617; and *Farm Real Estate Market Developments,* Economic Research Service, U. S. Department of Agriculture, Supplement No. 1 to CD-80, February, 1976, p. 3.

allowed lenders to be more liberal in their loans during periods of depressed prices and more restrictive during periods of high land prices.

After the 1930s the growing disparity between the normalized concept of value and market value became more obvious. In place of the cyclical swings in farm land values preceding the 1930 depression, farm land prices have continued a steady rise in value. In assuming some degree of cyclical price variation, appraisers were instructed to use an assumed level of yields and prices regarded as normal—the average prices and costs prevailing between the 1910 and 1914 average—even 10, 12, 15 year moving averages were adopted for appraisal purposes.

A similar view is illustrated by appraisers who continued to use basic value, which is defined as: "Worth of a rural property derived from earnings under a typical operation, and from location and home use features as viewed from the actual, and not previously or properly expressed." Under this definition value is believed more enduring than price, showing less fluctuation over time. While earnings weigh heavily in applying this definition, assumed earnings were from typical or customary operations. An appropriate adjustment was made to account for the location and home use features of the farm in question.

As farm land values have continued to increase, lenders have been more willing to be guided by market value. Market value is defined as the most probable sales price. Given a reasonable time for sale under usual marketing and financial terms, the appraiser estimates value according to the most likely price to be realized under local market conditions. The underwriting officer, knowing the probable sale price in the event of foreclosure, then may judge the loan application according to buyer requirements and elements of risk and yield. Preferred practice is to start with the market value and then adjust the loan to value ratio and mortgage terms according to mortgage security, earning capacity of the farm and portfolio needs. This raises the issue of the evidence supporting the estimate of value.

## Determinants of Farm Land Value

It should be noted that appraisals for farm loan purposes have changed from practices prevailing before World War II. In the 1920s while farm land values were rising, many institutions granted farm mortgages in the belief that farm land prices would continue to increase. This led to a heavy dependence on land prices as a means of judging farm values.

The difference today lies in the shift from land values to the earning capacity of the farm. Like conventional income property, lenders judge farms according to their earning potential. In the case of ranches and pasture, the cattle carrying capacity of the land, and water availability relate to the earning capacity. Farms specializing in dry land farming or irrigated row crops are judged in the same way.

In shifting to the income technique, lenders must explain the paradox of relatively low rates of return on farm operation, which have been known to experience a 3 to 4 percent rate of return on investment, while other investments and mortgages earn upwards of 8 to 10 percent. However, care must be taken in interpreting the rate of return on farm capital. There is the problem of relating the return to farm assets judged on the purchase price less depreciation or current market value. Most industries base the rate of return on original cost, not current value. Relating the rate of return to the current market value of farm assets tends to lower the rate of return.

Probably the real reason for the acceptance of a low rate of return on farm assets results from opportunities for capital gain. If farmers anticipate rising land values and prices, they tend to bid up the price of farm assets, including land, to the point that their yield on investment gives below market rates of return. Therefore, individuals invest in farm properties not only for their current return but for their potential capital gain.

Loan to value ratios have followed historical precedents and are usually based at 65 percent of the appraised value. There seems to be no logical reason why this policy is followed, since a higher loan to value ratio would seem to be justified, given favorable investment prospects, earning capacity and competent management. The critical issue is the ability of the farm operator to service his debt. It is equally critical for the loan officer to evaluate the accounting procedures that relate to the funds available for debt service; namely, the method of estimating depreciation for income tax purposes on farm machinery, breeding stock and buildings.

## Appraisal for Farm Mortgages

Taken by itself the valuation of agricultural land for mortgage purposes would justify a separate textbook. While it is not feasible to cover the entire topic, it is considered important to cover the appraisal process, and the treatment of agricultural land prices and the income technique of appraisal as applied to agricultural properties. This approach is advised since the farm mortgage rests on the analysis of a farm operation, the real estate pledged as security, and the credit of the borrower. A review of the cash flow requirements of a farm operation illustrates this point.

Exhibit 11.1 shows the cash flow of a typical proprietary farm. Probably the most complicating factor is the fact that the farm is operated both as a household unit with all of its cash requirements and as a business operation with all the risks inherent in operating a business for profit.

### Exhibit 11.1

### Cash Flow Diagram of a Farm Operation

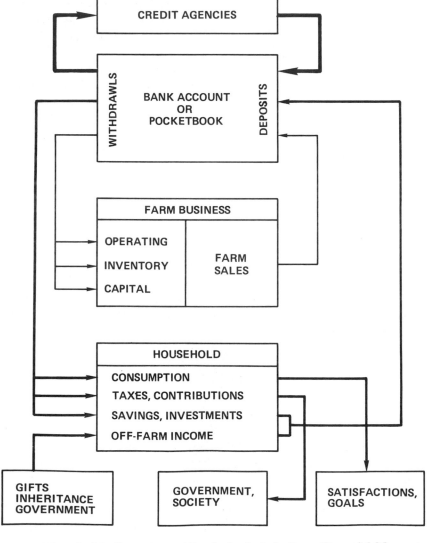

Source: Allan G. Mueller, "Flow-of-Funds Analysis in Farm Financial Management," *Journal of Farm Economics,* Vol. 48, (August 1966) , p. 663.

Note that the credit agencies interact with the cash flow for both the business operation and the household. In the case of a long-term mortgage, funds would be invested in land and buildings which in turn would create income available to service the loan and the household. The management of funds must meet the seasonal demands and cash flow requirements that change as a result of cost or price changes. Mortgage credit is part of the planning for longer run adjustments that may be coordinated with short-term credit. In considering the farm in this light, considerable emphasis is placed on earning capacity of the farm.

## The Appraisal Process

Professional appraisers holding recognized appraisal designations from organizations such as The American Society of Farm Managers and Rural Appraisers follow a fairly formal appraisal process. Exhibit 11.2 outlines the topics generally covered in a farm appraisal. While the outline presumes a narrative-appraisal report, form-type appraisals may be adapted so that the same information is reported in summary form.

The first part of the appraisal report covers descriptive material on the property appraised. Starting with the economic factors of the region and county, the appraiser proceeds to an analysis of the neighborhood. Of particular importance in this part of the appraisal is an analysis of the location. The location is judged with respect to access roads, and driving time to community and marketing facilities important to the farm operation. In cotton farming the distance to the cotton gin, or in row crop production, the distance to agricultural processing centers, is closely associated with value.

Since the appraisal will cover anticipated productivity, substantial weight is placed on soil analysis. Such analysis should include a soils map showing acreages by different types of soil and the identification of yields normally expected from classified soils. The descriptive material on farm buildings completes the preliminary analysis important to undertaking the three approaches to value. *govt programs available*

## The Income Approach *Assume maximum productivity and deduct for crop damage, land not tillable,*

At first glance, the complications of the income approach for agricultural property seem virtually insurmountable. Crop prices fluctuate, among other things, as a result of variations in international weather. Farm income in some circumstances is largely dependent on government programs and changing support prices. Yet decisions are made with respect to the purchase and sale of agricultural land and operating farms. The mortgage underwriter (and the appraiser) are in the

## Exhibit 11.2
## Essential Factors to be Considered, Documented, and Included in Rural Appraisal Reports.

TITLE PAGE
1. Name
2. Appraiser
3. Date

TABLE OF CONTENTS

LETTER OF TRANSMITTAL
1. Date
2. Salutation
3. Type of value
4. Identify property
5. Date of value estimate
6. Value estimate
7. Statement that report contains ___ pages and ___ exhibits
8. Signature

PURPOSE OF THE APPRAISAL

SUMMARY OF SALIENT FACTS AND CONCLUSIONS

FULL LEGAL DESCRIPTION

DESCRIPTION AND INTERPRETATION OF PERTINENT ECONOMIC FACTORS
1. Region
2. County

NEIGHBORHOOD ANALYSIS

SITE ANALYSIS
1. Description of the site
2. Highest and best use
3. Utilities available
4. Zoning
5. Restrictions

SOILS ANALYSIS
1. Classification
2. Description
3. Capabilities

IMPROVEMENT ANALYSIS
1. Structural and construction details
2. Age and size of buildings
3. General conditions
4. Estimate of remaining useful life
5. Estimate of value

EARNINGS APPROACH
1. Typical crops
2. Typical acreage
3. Typical yields
4. Share to the land
5. Landlord's gross return
6. Landlord's typical ownership expense
7. Typical net income attributable to the property
8. Selection of the capitalization rate
9. Value indicated by the earnings approach

MARKET DATA APPROACH
1. Presentation of market data on comparable properties
2. Analysis of market data
3. Relation of market data to subject property
4. Value indicated by market data approach

COST APPROACH
1. Estimate of cost of building new
2. Estimate of accrued depreciation
   a. Physical deterioration (justification)
   b. Functional obsolescence (justification)
   c. Economic obsolescence (justification)
3. Value of the improvements to the land
4. Addition of land value
5. Value indicated by cost approach

CORRELATION OF VALUES

FINAL ESTIMATE OF VALUE

CONTINGENT AND LIMITING CONDITIONS

APPRAISER'S CERTIFICATE

QUALIFICATIONS OF THE APPRAISER

ADDENDA—Maps, pictures, statistical and factual data, charts, zoning data, local ordinances or regulations, and other pertinent information not included in the body of report but necessary or desirable for documentation.

Source: *Professional Rural Appraisal Manual,* fourth ed. (Denver, Colorado: American Society of Farm Managers and Rural Appraisers, 1975), pp. 40-41.

position of interpreting the most current market behavior, however uncertain.

To resolve these issues, typical farm operations must be assumed. In the case of dry land farming typical and prudent crop rotations must be considered. Yields usually experienced on soils considering the soil profile, surface soil, the slope, and the condition of the soil with respect to drainage, alkali content, nutrient level and erosion, have a bearing on the stabilized typical yield assumed as a basis of projected gross income. In this part of the report, there is no substitute for verification of yields from known properties. If available, a five year statement of yields and income will help in projecting gross income.

The cost of operation is probably even more subjective. If crop share or net cash rents are available, these data, reduced to a per acre value, reveal the net yield to the property owner. If these are unavailable, typical costs of operation should be reviewed with local authorities and published cost studies.

In selecting the capitalization rates to convert net income to value, the appraiser must guard against using standard capitalization rates that may have been used in the past—and without suitable documentation. For some crops, such as apples, this is a critical point. Apple production in the Yakima Valley of Washington State varies according to frost damage and general market conditions. A record of earnings and prices for several preceding years may be secured from the cooperative packing company. By comparing sales of productive orchards on an acreage basis with their known yields, capitalization rates may be readily estimated. In other words, given the productive potential of an orchard, it is presumed that buyers bid for land and trees at some price giving them a typical market rate of return.

This technique relates farm net income to farm land prices and illustrates the market comparison method of deriving capitalization rates. The appraiser adopting this system is in the comfortable position of reporting market behavior and not what the farm *should be* earning at an assumed rate of return on invested capital. Experience has shown that rates of return up to 25 percent on orchards vary downward to few percentage points on dry land farming or ranches. If market value is the objective, reliance on market behavior gives the most accurate appraisal.

To apply this technique, use several sales examples to compute capitalization rates. Sale prices may vary, among other things, according to the bargaining power of the buyer and seller, the time of sale, the productivity of the land, and amenity or national income. Thus, capitalization rates, a function of sales prices and net incomes, will show a corresponding variation. Consequently, several repeated observations of derived capitalization rates will usually permit selection of a rate singularly appropriate to the property under valuation.

The derivation of capitalization rates illustrated below is from nine sales of dry farm lands in the state of Washington. Net income is calculated from a typical crop rotation and reported yields and crop share rents. Details of each sale are omitted for the purpose of this illustration.

| Sales Price | Net Income | Rate of Return |
|---|---|---|
| $34,600 | $2,670 | 7.7% |
| 36,000 | 3,020 | 8.4 |
| 35,000 | 3,300 | 9.4 |
| 45,700 | 4,360 | 9.6 |
| 32,800 | 3,540 | 10.8 Median |
| 35,000 | 3,820 | 10.9 |
| 35,100 | 3,860 | 11.0 |
| 25,500 | 2,930 | 11.5 |
| 22,000 | 3,550 | 16.2 |

The sales of property above, ranging in size from 100 acres to 160 acres, reveal capitalization rates extending from 7.7 percent to 16.2 percent. The latter rate was derived from property sold by an absentee owner, resulting in the unusually high capitalization rate of 16.2 percent. From these nine examples, the appraiser may conclude that a capitalization rate of 10 percent or 11 percent prevails in that area. The appraiser's familiarity with the property under appraisal and with the nine examples above would dictate his final choice of a capitalization rate.

## Comparable Sales Approach

Farm land sales confirm the cliché that no two properties are alike. Because of the lack of homogeneity among farms, considerable skill is required to reason from a given sale observation to market value of the property appraised. In this respect, farm appraising differs from other types of appraisal in that each sale must be judged according to the productivity of the soil and the value contribution from land improvements, i.e., fences, irrigation systems, and buildings.

To illustrate, refer to Exhibit 11.3, showing the presentation of a vacant land sale. In this illustration, the 80 acres sold at an average price of $210 per acre. But the property in question included 64 acres of more productive land which had an estimated value of $299 per acre. The remaining 16 acres were divided between alkali crop land of lower productivity and four acres in unproductive roads and drainage areas.

### Exhibit 11.3

### Comparable Sale One

| | | |
|---|---|---|
| Grantor-Grantee | : | John Jones to James R. Thompson |
| Date of Sale | : | June 30, 19_____. Warranty deed. |
| Recorded | : | Book 237, Page 17, Okanogan County. |
| Legal Description | : | S 1/2, SE 1/4, Section 23, T. 2 N, R. 3, E.W.M., 80 acres |
| Verified | : | Mr. James R. Thompson |
| Sales Price | | |
|    Total | : | $16,800. |
|    Per Unit Prices | : | 64 acres of dry farm land, @ $229 ...... $14,656 |
| | | 12 acres of alkali cropland, @ $179...... 2,148 |
| | | 4 acres of roads and creek drain ...... no value |
| | | 80 acres @ $210 (overall price) ........ $16,800 |
| | | (rounded) |
| Remarks | : | This sale is five miles southeast of the subject property in the same type of neighborhood. The Alderwood loam soil of this tract averages 45 bushels of wheat per acre. The tract under valuation, a Umatilla sandy loam area, produces typically 40 bushels of wheat per acre. The alkali area seriously restricts the yield on the 12 acre portion. In other respects the sale is generally comparable to the 80 acre parcel under valuation. |

In this manner, the appraiser may relate the $229 per acre value of dry land farm to the property in question that includes the same soil type. Calculating the value of different types of land in this way makes comparison to unique property more rational. However, experience and the interpretation of other sales proving the $229 per acre value is assumed in this example.

The other idea behind the presentation of Exhibit 11.3 is to present sales data with sufficient detail to permit intelligent comparison with the property under valuation. In this technique the inspection of the property sold is equally important to inspection of the property appraised. Topography, soil characteristics, water availability, land improvement, access and location are among the items deserving attention. These major value determining factors require direct comparison between comparable sales and the property in question.

To relate the main differences between the property sold and the property appraised, especially with respect to productivity, appraisers have "adjusted" the observed sale price as if the property sold is equivalent to the property appraised. For instance, it is implied that if a sale property is equal to the property under valuation with regard to a given feature such as location, the sale price would be "X" amount and therefore the market value is "X" amount. In this instance, it is assumed that the difference between the property sold and the property appraised (e.g., the major difference could be location) is a given dollar value. Thus, if the sale price was increased or decreased by the dollar assigned to the major difference, the market value may be more accurately determined.

Such a sale adjustment may be illustrated by assuming that land, which sold for $250 an acre, has an inferior location relative to the property appraised. The appraiser may assign a value of $25 per acre to compensate for the influence of location. Thus, the sale as adjusted for location, would indicate a market value of $275 per acre for the subject property. The same result may be accomplished by judging the location in percentage terms. For example, the location of the subject property may be considered 10 percent superior relative to location of the sale tract. Hence, the sale, again, indicates a market value of $275 per acre ($250 plus $25).

The same analysis may be extended to other sales and to other value-determining factors. Topography, soil productivity, quality of construction, or the time of sale are other features which are sometimes used to "adjust" the sale price. To repeat the same example, it may be found that the subject property is 20 percent superior to the sale tract, suggesting a market value of $300 per acre ($250 × 1.20). Or conversely, if the topography and soil of the subject tract has a value of only 80 percent of the property sold then the market indication is $200 ($250 × .80).

It will be noted that adjustment could be made also in absolute terms, i.e., $50 per acre and $87.50 per acre, in contrast to percentage allowances. The market value indicated by "adjustments" appears quite precise, certain, and definite whether expressed in absolute dollar amounts or percentage terms.

Several advantages for the adjustment of sales are claimed. A comparison of the property sold is related directly to the property under review. It is argued that subjective judgments are reduced to an objective basis for comparison. Moreover, properties may be compared in relation to specific features which bear directly on market value. Those using the method contend that the adjustments are approximate only and to this extent may contribute to market value accuracy. Further, the method identifies those items which have the greatest influence on market value.

An alternative method of analyzing sales is to summarize sales used in the appraisal report showing the proportion of land in irrigation and in different land productivity classes. Table 11.2 shows the percent of land in classes 1 and 2, the most productive land, and the percent in land class 5, the least productive. While these data are not weighed as a sales adjustment in the former example, they provide a method of comparing sales to the property appraised.

## Table 11.2
## A Summary of Comparable Sales

| Sale | Sale Price | Price Per Acre | Total Acreage | Irrigated Land | | Land Classes by Percent of Total Acreage | | | |
|------|-----------|----------------|---------------|----------------|------------|-----|-----|-----|-----|
| | | | | Total Acres | Percent of Total | 1,2 | 3 | 4 | 5 |
| One ...... | $35,000 | $291.70 | 120.00 | 30.0 | 25 | 7 | 7 | 11 | 75 |
| Two ..... | 40,000 | 593.30 | 67.42 | 64.7 | 96 | 54 | 0 | 42 | 4 |
| Three .... | 75,000 | 375.00 | 200.00 | 140.0 | 70 | 25 | 15 | 30 | 30 |
| Four ..... | 53,710 | 335.70 | 160.00 | 56.0 | 35 | 12 | 5 | 18 | 65 |
| Five ..... | 45,000 | 281.30 | 160.00 | 75.0 | 47 | 10 | 7 | 30 | 53 |
| Six ...... | 40,000 | 500.00 | 80.00 | 39.0 | 48 | 24 | 25 | 0 | 51 |
| Seven .... | 80,000 | 500.00 | 160.00 | 90.0 | 56 | 11 | 11 | 34 | 44 |
| Eight ..... | 65,000 | 488.00 | 133.19 | 62.6 | 47 | 26 | 5 | 16 | 53 |

In short, sales are listed in summary form to focus attention on the most important value elements of each item. For instance, Table 11.2 shows that Sale One sold for $291.70 per acre on an overall basis. The total acreage, irrigated acreage, the proportion of irrigated land and the acreage by land classes, can be easily compared with the property under appraisal. If the sale property is comparable, especially with respect to irrigated land and land classes, a market value approximating $290 per acre would seem to follow from this example. A greater proportion of similar irrigated land, all other things equal, would suggest a higher estimate of market value. If the property under valuation has a greater productive capacity, Sale One will probably indicate a lower limit of value judged in the light of other sales evidence.

Attention is invited to Sale Seven, exchanged for $80,000 or for $500 per acre, which has a total irrigated acreage equal to 56 percent of the 160 acres. If the subject property has a smaller irrigated land proportion, Sale Seven would indicate a maximum price per acre which can reasonably apply against the subject property.

Thus, by relating the subject property to specific comparisons, given in summary form after individual identification of each sale, the market analysis constitutes a logical, well reasoned statement which leads to a single conclusion—the market value.

## Evaluating Farm Buildings

Generally speaking, building cost is a poor guide to estimate farm building values. An appraisal for loan purposes depends heavily on the market value in the sense of the most probable sales price and the earning capacity of the farm. Accordingly, lending officers base their analysis on the fact that (1) farmers do not construct farm buildings to add to the value of their property, and (2) farm buildings are constructed to increase farm operating efficiency. The cost approach to value, while relevant in establishing income tax depreciation, is less appropriate in establishing market value since building cost seldom adds an equal amount to market value.

In determining this relationship, the true test turns on the question: If the building were destroyed, would it be reconstructed in exactly the same way? If the answer is no, then market value is less than reproduction cost.  *what does it add to productivity and efficiency?*

Placing a value on the building requires a study to determine if a building is related to the farm operation with respect to the livestock or crops being raised. Given the specific farm operation, the appraiser must consider if the building is over-built, overly expensive or inadequate in any way. In other words, how does the building contribute to farm operation? Or, to put it differently, would a typical buyer pay more for the farm with existing buildings; or if the buildings were nonexistent, how much less would the farm be worth?

To answer these and related questions, the farm loan appraisal must include an inventory of farm buildings and other improvements. The building inventory should be based on the following:

> Capacity and use of each building
> Building measurements
> Type of construction
> Present condition of building
> Building obsolescence
> Physical deterioration of property
> Building equipment
> Functional utility of the building.

If the farm includes an irrigation system, either a ditch or a sprinkler system, the same detailed description should be a part of the appraisal report. Water sources, with all the detail of quality of water and adequacy of supply, especially during critical growing periods, deserve special attention. These and other issues guard against the tendency to equate building cost with building value.

## Judging the Mortgage Security

Sufficient data have been presented to indicate the key elements in evaluating farm property for loan purposes. Though the main points may have been covered, it should be emphasized that farm properties are highly specialized. While loans on irrigated cotton land in Arizona or grazing lands of Montana may be fairly standardized, the broad range of farm operations calls for considerable detailed analysis, impossible to cover here. To insure that information necessary for decisions is at hand, some authorities recommend a checklist showing the minimum information that should be covered in each appraisal report.

Such a checklist is shown in Exhibit 11.4. The checklist shows the descriptive material relating to the property, namely, the location, soil types, maps and aerial photographs and assessed values. For the most

## Exhibit 11.4

### Rural Appraisal Checklist

Following is a checklist of items to be covered before properly inspection, during inspection, and before writing the final report:

> Name of client and address
> Occupants, if not owner-occupied
> Type of farm
> Location and distance from major cities and towns
> Legal description
> Farm map and aerial photos
> Soil map and soil types
> Location of schools
> Location of churches
> Location of shopping areas
> Location of roads
> Location of railroads
> Location of streams
> Location of ditches
> Assessed value for the last full year
> Taxes past five years
> Zoning and/or ordinances
> Government crop allotments
> Rights-of-way, easements, leases
> Utilities available
> Production records
> Cleared land acreage
> Woodland acreage
> Other acreage
> Fences
> Road and stream frontages
> Climatic information
> Rainfall
> Storms
> Temperature extremes
> Markets
> Measurements and descriptions of buildings
> Irrigation systems
> Wells and springs
> Sewage disposal systems
> Tile drains
> Sand, gravel, and mineral deposits

Source: *Professional Rural Appraisal Manual, op. cit.,* p. 40.

part, the balance of the material relates to the potential earning capacity of the farm. Production records over the preceding five years are probably recommended.

Note that the list includes acreage classified by land use type, building detail, and the water system. To be sure this list could be expanded for more specialized farms. The important point is to check that relevant material has not been omitted that would bear on the projection of income on the farm offered as loan security. Some lenders who process a relatively large volume of farm loans use a form appraisal that "standardizes" the type of appraisal information required; such a form is shown in Exhibit 11.5.

In further explanation, it should be noted that farm property, appraised according to the market, frequently constitutes a security superior to single purpose commercial property. Special note must also be taken on the review of farm operator efficiency. While two farms may show similar physical features and potential capacity, the skill of the farm manager—his knowledge, motivation and industry—may render one loan more than adequately secured while a loan on a similar property may be rejected. As corporation agriculture becomes more complex and as the bank undergoes increased pressure for nonfarm loans, considerable attention will be paid to management evaluation. This, in itself, requires technical knowledge and a searching inquiry by the farm loan officer.

# Exhibit 11.5

# A Farm Appraisal Report

## ON-SITE VISIT REPORT
*(abbreviated version)*

Name _____

Address _____

_____

Reason for Visit _____

_____

_____

Visitor's Name _____

Visitor's Affiliation _____

_____

The following items should be considered during the initial on-site visit (and possibly in future visits) to an applicant's agricultural business. Record brief and concise notations on this comment sheet.

COMMENTS

**A. LOCATION** (description; distance to trade center; availability of markets for products; availability and quality of community services, including churches and schools; availability of police and fire fighting services; kind of roads and amount of travel; quality of neighboring agricultural businesses; other comments)

**B. LAND** (total acreage operated: types, amount owned, approximate current market value, amount rented; mortgages and other liens against the land: acreage, ownership, current market value, total amount of mortgage or lien, balance outstanding, source of information; irrigation and drainage; size and shape of fields; convenience to buildings; obstacles in fields)*

**C. BUILDING AND IMPROVEMENTS, SUCH AS FENCES, IRRIGATION OR DRAINAGE SYSTEM** (description; adequacy; general arrangement; condition and appearance; other comments)

# Exhibit 11.5 Continued

COMMENTS

**D. LIVESTOCK** (breeds, numbers, and ages; quality and condition; feed on hand; production records; other comments)

_____
_____
_____

**E. MACHINERY AND EQUIPMENT** (adequacy for operation; general conditions; storage; other comments)

_____
_____
_____

**F. AGRICULTURALIST'S FAMILY** (description; competences)

_____
_____
_____

**G. AGRICULTURAL PRACTICES** (number of hired help relative to size of enterprise; competence of hired help; use of labor saving devices; hedging practices; crop rotation; contour plowing; use of insecticides and herbicides; emergency procedures against frost, drought, and other adverse weather conditions; conservation policies; breeding practices; use of veterinary and preventive medicine; irrigation contracts; credit standing with major suppliers; compliance with government regulations)

_____
_____
_____
_____
_____
_____

**H. MANAGEMENT CHARACTERISTICS** (specific and definite goals and objectives; ability to analyze accurately the difference between what is and what ought to be within the framework of his goals; good judgment; initiative and imagination necessary to acquire new knowledge of farming methods and production techniques; ambition, enthusiasm, and perseverence; managerial ability)

_____
_____
_____
_____

**I. CREDIT CHARACTERISTICS** (comprehends the responsibility and risk assumed in using credit; ability to handle large amounts of borrowed money in a productive way; credit reputation of honesty, dependability, and integrity)

_____
_____
_____

**J. LITIGATIONS PENDING**

_____
_____

Chapter 12

# Land Development
# Loans

In earlier times, land owners had virtually an unrestricted right to dispose of their property and to devote the property for their own
purposes without much government interference. Today, while the institution of private property is still strongly held, property owners must
observe a wide range of land use controls administered by federal, state
and local officials. In addition to relatively new public restrictions, the
financing techniques common to vacant land development stand apart
from financing of dwellings and income-producing property.

In large measure, land developers are like manufacturers. That is,
they are in the business of manufacturing land for urban use. To demonstrate the unique problems associated with financing land development, it is appropriate to review: (1) land use regulations; (2) characteristics of the land market; (3) subdivision development; and (4)
financing techniques.

## Land Use Regulations

Land use controls are an exercise of the police power: the right of government to regulate property for the public interest, convenience, ne-

245

cessity, safety, and morals. Typically, <u>no compensation is paid the owner for giving up rights under laws</u>, regulations and ordinances coming under the police power of the state and its administrative agencies. The many controls imposed by local governments, including building codes, housing codes, zoning regulations, the master plan and subdivision regulations, are locally administered as delegated to municipalities by the state legislature, by city charters or by the state constitutions.

More recently the federal government has enacted specific regulations to protect unwary purchasers in the case of interstate land sales or to improve the environment. The states, in turn, are increasingly active in providing for environmental controls and, at the same time, the states regulate the sale of land in the interest of preventing fraud, misrepresentation, and deceit. A brief review of these separate levels of administration shows their major differences and emphasis.

## Federal Land Use Controls

While an explanation of laws controlling land use might cover several chapters, certain relatively new laws deserve emphasis. Probably, it is more helpful to cover federal controls affecting the environment and then turn to regulations covering the sale and advertisement of land sold on an interstate basis.

### *National Environmental Policies Act of 1969*

In the National Environmental Policies Act Congress defined a national environmental policy. As it now stands, it is a federal responsibility to improve and coordinate plans, functions, programs, and sources so that the nation may—

1. fulfill the responsibilities of each generation as trustee of the environment for succeeding generations;
2. assure for all Americans safe, healthful, productive, aesthetically and culturally pleasing surroundings;
3. attain the widest range of beneficial uses of the environment without degradation, risk to health or safety, or other undesirable and unintended consequences;
4. preserve important historic, cultural, and natural aspects of our national heritage, and maintain, wherever possible, an environment which supports diversity and variety of individual choice;
5. achieve a balance between population and resource use which will permit high standards of living and a wide sharing of life's amenities; and
6. enhance the quality of renewable resources and approach the maximum attainable recycling of depletable resources.

The act goes on to explain that Congress recognizes that each person should enjoy a healthful environment and that each person has a responsibility to contribute to the preservation and enhancement of the environment.

As this applies to land development, the federal government judges new land developments according to how they alter the environment including the air, rain, estuarine and fresh water, and terrestrial environment including forests, dry land, wet land, range, urban and suburban land.

### The Coastal Zone Management Act of 1972

Real estate projects falling within a coastal zone must conform to ecological standards of the 1972 Coastal Zone Management Act. Coastal zone areas include water frontage on lakes, streams, rivers and oceans. Congress has stated that a coastal zone is rich in a variety of natural, commercial, recreational, industrial, and aesthetic resources of potential value to the welfare of the nation. In addition to the ecological imbalance, Congress has observed that ill-planned development threatens special natural and scenic characteristics of coastal zones. In the view of Congress, present state and local institutions for planning and regulating water uses in these areas are inadequate. Accordingly the act encourages the states to exercise more authority over land and waters of the coastal zone.

The main elements of the act authorize the Secretary of Commerce to make grants equal to two-thirds of the cost of preparing a land management program that applies to coastal land and waters. Congress has given the Secretary additional authority to pay up to two-thirds of the cost of administering a state land management program providing the plan meets acceptable standards. The direction that land use controls will take under this legislation is suggested by the following elements of the management program.

1. Identification of the boundaries of the coastal zone.
2. The definition of permissible land and water uses within the coastal zone.
3. An inventory and designation of areas particularly concerned within the coastal zone.
4. Identification of means by which the state proposes to exert control over land and water uses.
5. Development guidelines on priority of uses in particular areas.
6. Description of the organizational structure proposed to implement the management program.

Thus, land affecting the ecological balance of lakes, rivers, streams, and ocean waterfront will be subject to the land management plans developed under the Coastal Zone Management Act.

## Noise Control Act of 1972

United States policy now includes the promotion of an environment for all Americans free from noise that jeopardizes their health and welfare. In this legislation, the major sources of noise are identified as arising from transportation vehicles and equipment, machinery, appliances and other products in commerce.

Under the new policy, the Administrator of the Environmental Protection Agency must develop and publish criteria to control noise. The administrator shall publish proposed regulations controlling noise from construction equipment, transportation equipment, motors and engines, and electrical or electronic equipment. To the extent that noise arises from airports, railroad operations and motor carriers, these laws would have direct applicability to certain real estate developments. Manufacturing and transportation companies creating noise would fall under these regulations.

## Clean Air Act Amendments of 1970

The Clean Air Act Amendments provide for grants to pollution control agencies up to two-thirds of their cost to plan, develop, establish or improve control of air pollution. Real estate developments affecting the quality of air, primarily manufacturing firms, must conform to rules and regulations provided by this act.

## The Interstate Land Sales Full Disclosure Act

*to place before purchaser such info so that fraud could not be perpet[...]*

Developers proposing to sell subdivided lots over state boundaries must observe provisions of this Land Sales Disclosure Act. The legislation is designed to discourage fraud, misrepresentation, and deceit in the sale of subdivision land. The full disclosure provisions assume that if a purchaser has adequate information on property he is purchasing, no fraud is committed. At the present time the act covers subdivisions divided into 50 or more lots of less than five acres each offered for sale or lease as part of a promotional plan. It is now unlawful for a developer or agent to use any means of transportation or communication in interstate commerce to sell or lease any lots unless he conforms to the act. Exceptions include:

1. Sales under a contract obligating the seller to construct buildings within two years

*" contracts to give deed" is usually form in resort prop.*
*That means give purchaser deed once price is fully paid (seller finances sa[...]*
*But seller may not have prop. once you pay off. Or sells same lot 3 times.*

2. Real estate sold under court order
3. The sale of mortgages or deeds of trust
4. Securities issued by a real estate investment trust
5. The sale of real estate owned by government or its administrative agencies
6. Cemetery lots
7. Sales to a person for purposes of constructing buildings
8. Sales of real estate which are free of all encumbrances if the purchaser has inspected the lots which he proposes to purchase
9. Lots of five acres or more.

Subdivision lots coming under the act may not be sold unless a *Statement Of Record* has been registered with the Secretary of Housing and Urban Development, and a copy of the *Property Report* has been given to the purchaser in advance of the contract or agreement of sale. Failure to issue the proper report to the purchaser is grounds for considering the contract of sale voidable at the option of the purchaser. The all-encompassing scope of the act is shown by the following requirements for the statement of record:

1. The name and address of each person having an interest in the lots of the subdivision    owner
2. The legal description of the total area included in the subdivision and a statement of the topography, including a map showing block dimensions and streets
3. A statement of the condition of title to the land
4. A statement of the present condition of access to the subdivision, availability of sewage disposal facilities, also the location of the subdivision with respect to nearby municipalities, the nature of improvements to be installed and the schedule for completion
5. If there is a blanket encumbrance, a statement of the consequences for an individual purchaser of a failure to fulfill obligations of the encumbrance
6. Copies of articles of incorporation, instruments by which the trust is declared or created, copies of articles of partnership, and related papers showing ownership
7. Copies of the deed establishing title to the subdivision
8. Copies of all forms of conveyances to be used in selling lots
9. Copies of instruments creating easements or other restrictions
10. Certified financial statements as required by the Secretary
11. A statement of terms, conditions, prices and rents.

**Exhibit 12.1**

**Statement of Record Property Report**

PROPERTY REPORT

NOTICE AND DISCLAIMER BY OFFICE OF
INTERSTATE LAND SALES REGISTRATION
U.S. DEPARTMENT OF HOUSING AND URBAN DEVELOPMENT

The Interstate Land Sales Full Disclosure Act specifically prohibits any representation to the effect that the Federal Government has in any way passed upon the merits of, or given approval to, this subdivision, or passed upon the value of the property.

It is unlawful for anyone to make, or cause to be made to any prospective purchaser, any representation contrary to the foregoing or any representations which differ from the statements in this property report. If any such representations are made, please notify the Office of Interstate Land Sales Registration at the following address:

Office of Interstate Land Sales Registration
HUD Building, 451 Seventh Street, S.W.
Washington, D.C. 20410

Inspect the property and read all documents. Seek professional advice. Unless you received this properly prepared prior to the time you enter into a contract, you may void the contract by notice to the seller.

Unless you acknowledge in writing on a waiver of purchaser's revocation rights form that you have read and understood the property report and that you have personally inspected the lot prior to signing your contract, you may revoke your contract within 48 hours from the signing of your contract if you received the property report less than 48 hours prior to signing the contract.

1. NAME(S) OF DEVELOPER: Crocker Enterprises, Inc.

   ADDRESS: 14 West 5th Street, Minot, North Dakota

2. NAME OF SUBDIVISION: Thunderbird City

   LOCATION: Bottineau County, STATE OF North Dakota

   (a) EFFECTIVE DATE OF PROPERTY REPORT:

---

IMPORTANT READ CAREFULLY

Name of Subdivision:

By signing this receipt you acknowledge that you have received a copy of the property report prepared pursuant to the Rules and Regulations of the Office of Interstate Land Sales Registration, U.S. Department of Housing and Urban Development.

     Received by.....................................................
     Street Address.................................................
     Date...........................................................
     City.................................State.......................
     Zip...................

Notwithstanding your signature by which you acknowledged that your received the Property Report you still have other important rights under the Interstate Land Sales Full Disclosure Act.

Upon receipt of the statement of record, the property report relating to lots in the subdivision is issued stating information the Secretary believes important to a purchaser. The act specifies that the report should not be used for promotional purposes nor may the seller advertise or represent that the Secretary approves or recommends the subdivision. Exhibit 12.1 shows the first page of HUD's *sample* Property Report.

The enforcement is provided by allowing the purchaser to bring suit to recover his purchase price, the cost of improvements and reasonable court costs. Moreover, the Secretary has the right, upon proper showing, to issue a permit or temporary injunction or restraining order to enjoin such acts or practices. The act provides for the power to subpoena witnesses, books and papers and for fines of not more than $5,000 or imprisonment of up to five years or both.

Because the rationale of the act turns on full disclosure of facts, the property report tends to be fairly comprehensive. For instance the developer is required to list unusual conditions relating to the location of the subdivision. A location near an airport or possible air pollution by local plants or the frequency of floods will be noted if they are relevant to the property for sale. Considerable detail relates to the availability of water, electricity, telephone service and sewage disposal.

A detailed list of municipal services to the subdivision is covered in the property report. Even the potential marketability of the property will be noted. For example the property report may state that "the future value of land is very uncertain; do not count on appreciation." Or, further, "you may be required to pay the full amount of the obligation to a banker third party to whom the developer assigns your contract or note, even though the developer may have failed to fulfill promises he has made."

## State Administered Land Use Controls

*Tennessee does not have such an act !*

Some 25 states have laws pertaining to preparation of general plans and laws controlling the environmental effects of new real estate developments. In many respects these laws parallel the trend in federal legislation. In addition to these regulations, many states have enacted subdivision controls directed to protect the public from misrepresentation, deceit and fraud for intra-state transfers. Most of these laws follow the general practices and rules administered by the Department of Housing and Urban Development with respect to interstate transfers. The state laws have an added enforcement feature with the power to revoke or suspend real estate broker and salesmen licenses.

State laws generally operate by requiring a written notice of a proposed subdivision which must be given to a state agency. This notice must be given before subdivided land may be sold. The state review of the proposed subdivision may call for the following:

Name and address of the title owner

Name and address of the subdivision

Legal description of acreage in the subdivision map

Statement of title including encumbrances and unpaid taxes

Proposed sale terms and conditions

Statement covering the provision for sewage disposal and public utilities

Evidence of conformity with local regulations.

With this information the state agency makes an investigation and usually issues a public report. This report must be delivered to the respective purchaser on a form approved by the state agency. To guard against false and misleading advertising, subdividers may be asked to furnish copies of advertising material, brochures, radio transcripts and other promotional material. From the standpoint of subdivision financing, usually the supervising agency will require appropriate arrangements for release of liens and a completion bond to insure completion of improvements free of liens. The deed conveyance instruments must be adequate to protect purchasers.

For example subdivision land usually is pledged as security for a development loan. This means that each lot will be subject to a lien covering all the property. Since it is difficult to obtain an unconditional release of individual lots free of the blanket encumbrance, the owner-subdivider cannot sell lots unless he complies with requirements of state regulations.

It is not unusual for state law to permit lot sales subject to a blanket mortgage only if the developer agrees to impound sufficient money to protect the interest of the purchaser, or the owner places title to the subdivision in trust under an agreement providing for release of each lot from the blanket encumbrance or, alternately, the subdivider furnishes a bond in an amount and form approved by the state. Terms of the bond provide for the return of monies paid by the purchaser if proper release from the blanket encumbrance is not provided.

## Local Regulations

In some states every municipality must prepare a master or general plan. This plan guides community growth and suggests broad land use areas for maximum development. As a rule the general plan includes a study of economic, social, and physical features of the community. The general plan allocates land use to preserve neighborhoods, open space, and to promote the economic base. These plans are adopted only after extensive study and public hearings.

Other land use controls tend to implement the goals of the community as expressed in the master plan. For instance, the zoning ordinance will district land according to the master plan. Appropriate areas for residential, commercial and industrial, and public facilities will be allocated in the zoning ordinance. The building code, the housing code, the health and sanitation code are other local provisions that guide and control real estate developments.

Of special interest to land developers are local subdivision regulations. These regulations, locally administered and conceived, are not meant to protect the purchaser, but are intended to implement the master plan. Accordingly, the subdivision regulations cover the physical and environmental effects of new subdivisions.

Communities administering subdivision regulations require approval of the appropriate local office before lots may be recorded and sold. Usually land divided into five or more lots comes under the local subdivision regulation. Agricultural land that does not involve a new street is ordinarily exempt from subdivision regulations.

Generally speaking proposed subdivisions must be approved by the local planning and zoning agency. Their job is to insure that the proposed subdivision conforms with the zoning code and other regulations affecting the sale and development of lots. The layout of roads, public spaces, and lots must conform to existing and planned streets.

In addition to the county engineer, the fire and police departments, local school boards, the parks and recreation department may also pass on the proposed subdivision. In other instances the subdivider must seek approval of transportation and transit officials; and, the property tax assessor must review the subdivision for compliance with the county record system.

Clearly the financing of new land developments is a lost exercise unless the requirements of federal, state and local agencies are met. And the trend is fairly clear: Developers will face added delays and higher costs of compliance. Some authorities have noted the following five restrictions that will probably become increasingly evident:

1. Large scale developments will require federal or state agency approval.
2. Land use densities will be controlled to restrict population growth where it is deemed harmful to the environment.
3. It is increasingly evident that private land will be subject to added controls. Such controls may be exercised by a federal, state, and local agency or a combination of these groups.

4. Waterfront areas will be subject to more intensive land use restrictions. The coastal zones, rivers and lakes will have special restrictions applying to buildings and sewage disposal systems.
5. Public facilities, including public highways, bridges, buildings and other installations, will be placed according to the effect they have on the environment.

As the cost of compliance increases and as potential subdivision land is withdrawn from the market, more weight will be placed on the market analysis of new subdivisions—the topic of the next section.

## The Market for Developed Land

The risks arising from land development stem from (1) the heavy vacant land cost, (2) the large sums required for streets and utilities, (3) the lag between project conception and the time in which sales may be executed. While other investments may be equally large, money invested in land development is returned only over a relatively long period. Profits may not be realized until a substantial portion of the land is sold.

Moreover, feasibility analysis on a subdivision often rests on shaky grounds. Indeed there are techniques to project the potential demand —and these will be noted shortly. But the demand equation is only part of the problem because the price and the volume of sales depends on the supply of competing land. Yet, there is virtually no ideal or satisfactory way of measuring the future supply of residential land.

Optimistic attitudes by developers may lead to new projects which, individually, would be highly marketable, but if ten developers reach the same conclusion and proceed with their individual projects, the supply may soon outrun even the most optimistic projections of demand. In this regard developers should check with the local planning office to see what other projects are in process. Yet while the change of supply may not be forecast with reasonable certainty, estimates of demand may be viewed from observed trends affecting the real estate market. Accurate estimates of the demand for land tends to minimize at least part of the risk.

### The Demand for Land

More than any single factor, population largely governs the demand for residential, commercial, and industrial space. Certainly there are many other factors associated with the changing demand for space. Since population tends to correlate with growing and declining communities, population series are usually included in feasibility studies.

The <u>absolute population growth,</u> significant as it is, <u>tends to be less</u> <u>important than relative changes in population.</u> First, the investigator must identify the direction of past trends. Second, he must compare relative population growth between geographic areas. Suppose, for example, that the state population growth over the last ten years shows a 10 percent increase. By comparing population growth for a selected county over the same period, it may be concluded that the community in question is showing a relative decline in population compared to state growth. This conclusion would follow if the population over the last ten years grew by only 3 percent, say, compared to a state average population growth of 10 percent.

For a given project, <u>characteristics of the population may be equally</u> <u>significant.</u> Characteristics of population refer to the age group, the educational level, the ethnic makeup, and the size of family. Other important population trends relate to shifting personal incomes, skills and sources of employment.

These relative population figures help to predict the potential for single family dwellings, condominiums, multiple family units and their probable location requirements, expected price and the land absorption rate. Turning to three broad land use types, related data show how population statistics help to predict the potential demand for land.

## Residential land

The demand for residential space tends to be concentrated in mobile homes, condominiums and cooperatives, the rental occupancy market, and owner occupancy, primarily, in single-family, detached dwellings. For financing purposes, it is essential that the trend in the demand for residential space be determined from empirical data.

The more cautious lenders review building permit data over past years with special emphasis on building permit records in more recent months. Permit data usually show the number of building permits for single family dwellings and the number of building permits for multiple family dwellings showing the number of apartment units in each project. Generally these data are classified by city and county distributions and provide an up-to-date indication of changes in the current housing supply. Though a dwelling permit does not necessarily follow with actual construction (construction is postponed or deferred indefinitely), <u>permit data provide the best source of current data.</u>

<u>The number of mortgages and deeds recorded gives a current indica-</u> <u>tion of increasing or decreasing trends in demand.</u> Prudence recommends that land development projects be undertaken only after a certificates of occupancy

careful review of population, building permit data, and deed and mort-gages recordings gathered on a local and current basis. In these studies, changes over time reveal growing or declining markets.

## Commercial land

Most communities allocate too much land for commercial use. Land owners mistakenly believe that commercial zoning enhances real estate values; in reality, land assumes "commercial" value according to its utility for commercial purposes, the amount of land demanded, and the supply of suitable commercial space.

Studies have shown that there is a limit to the amount of commer-cial space that can be absorbed in the community. To be sure, this ratio varies according to the local economic base, but for a major land development project relating to commercial property, some estimate of the potential demand for commercial space seems warranted. For shop-ping centers the analysis will be quite detailed. For other projects such as planned unit developments, commercial land use relates to access, competing facilities and the local buying power of the projected population.

## Industrial land

Industrial land may be divided into (1) industrial acreage, (2) sites in planned industrial districts, (3) centrally located land, and (4) land in redevelopment or urban renewal projects. If the project is an in-dustrial park, a substantial investment will be required for utilities adapted to industrial occupants. The complicating factor is the rela-tively low land rate absorption for industrial property. For this reason, developers of industrial parks recommend financing of the utility and road system in phases. In a 500 acre industrial park, caution dictates that only part of the project be improved for current use, say 100 acres or so. As the 100 acres are sold, phase II calls for extension of utilities to the next 100 acres.

Forecasting industrial land absorption rates for smaller communities is quite hazardous. Buyers of industrial land have numerous options to satisfy their locational requirements. Even industries oriented to a spe-cific market area may locate among competing industrial parks, freeway locations, and redeveloped land. Their space requirements are not quite as confined as they are for commercial or residential property. Some industries may even select with indifference among various cities or states since their products are highly valuable and light in weight allowing economical shipping to widely scattered markets. Again, some estimate should be made on the expected time required to market industrial land before project approval.

## Subdivision Development

Producers supply goods to satisfy consumer demands. So too, must the subdivider produce residential space to meet local demand. On this point, the developer wants to guard against developing a subdivision of $30,000 lots to meet a demand that exists for only $10,000 lots. Because of the immediate investment required to develop a subdivision and because receipts from the sale of subdivided lots are stretched over several years, considerable attention is paid to judging the site potential. Providing the site seems adapted to local demand for residential land, the next step requires a pro forma income and cost estimate which is then converted to a projected cash flow over the marketing period. A few selected examples illustrates how this problem is approached before more specific financing techniques are explained.

**Exhibit 12.2**

**Rating a Subdivision Site**

| *Site Desirability Features* | *Reject* | *1* | *2* | *3* | *4* | *5* | *Rating* |
|---|---|---|---|---|---|---|---|
| Protection Against Inharmonious Land Uses | | 4 | 8 | 12 | 16 | 20 | |
| Physical and Social Attractiveness | | 4 | 8 | 12 | 16 | 20 | |
| Adequacy of Civic, Social and Commercial centers | | 4 | 8 | 12 | 16 | 20 | |
| Adequacy of Transportation | | 4 | 8 | 12 | 16 | 20 | |
| Sufficiency of Utilities and Services | | 2 | 4 | 6 | 8 | 10 | |
| Level of Taxes and Special Assessments | | 2 | 4 | 6 | 8 | 10 | |
| RATING OF SITE DESIRABILITY | | | | | | | |
| Relative Marketability | | 16 | 12 | 8 | 4 | 0 | |
| RATING OF LOCATION | Rating of Site Desirability minus Adjustment for Relative Marketability | | | | | | |

## Site Suitability

The complex factors important to successful subdivisions recommend the use of a check sheet or rating grid to help evaluate residential sites. See Exhibit 12.2. While such a grid tends to be highly subjective, it focuses attention on the main advantages and deficiencies of a given location. The grid rating in this example, ranging from 0 to 100 percent, provides a means of comparing alternative sites. Note that the form heavily weighs amenities of residential space: protection against inharmonious land uses, relative attractiveness of the site, adequacy of commercial, social and governmental centers and, finally, access or the adequacy of transportation. Utilities and property taxes carry, individually, only half the weight shown for the first four items.

A more detailed checklist is shown in Exhibit 12.3. While this checklist requires judgments on good, average, or poor for the listed items, it does not have a numerical rating system. Reliance is placed on judgment of the evaluator to determine the suitability of the site with respect to minimum requirements listed in Exhibit 12.3. Financing land developments of this type calls for an evaluation of the site, listing in detail the minimum features that agree with buyer preferences.

### Estimating the Feasibility of Land Developments

Land development costs tend to be unique to each project. Unlike building construction, there are few features that are common to subdivisions. They vary according to the vacant land costs, extension of utilities to the project, and street and utility installations. The latter costs vary according to the topography and soil conditions. Probably the best rule of thumb is to make sure that all projected costs are included in the feasibility study. Such a list would include costs grouped under the following headings, preferably shown on a *total cost* and a *per lot* basis:

| | |
|---|---|
| Vacant land cost | Sidewalks |
| Improvement costs | Street paving |
|   Sanitary sewers | Other development costs |
|     On-site |   Interest (2 years) |
|     Off-site |   Property taxes (2 years) |
|   Water mains |   Engineering and supervision |
|     On-site |   Repair and replacements |
|     Off-site |   Developer overhead |
|   Storm sewers |   Total development costs |
|     On-site | Selling expenses |
|     Off-site | Total costs |
|   Curbs | Average sales price |
| | Estimated profit |

**Exhibit 12.3**

**A Checklist for Judging Site Suitability**

| Site Characteristics | Good | Average | Poor | None |
|---|---|---|---|---|
| Convenience<br>  Schools<br>  Shopping<br>  Church<br><br>  Work<br>  Public transportation<br>  Parks | | | | |
| Utilities<br>  Gas<br>  Electricity<br>  Water | | | | |
|   Sanitary sewer<br>  Storm sewer<br>  Garbage pickup | | | | |
|   Snow removal<br>  Paved streets<br>  Traffic volume<br>  Freeways | | | | |
| Neighborhood<br>  Well-maintained neighbor-<br>    hoods<br>  Residential zoning<br>  Industrial encroachment | | | | |
|   Noise—industrial, traffic,<br>    airplanes<br>  Wind dust, air pollution<br>  Special hazards—floods<br>    plain, tornado or<br>    hurricane belt | | | | |
|   Topography<br>  View<br>  Off-street parking | | | | |
|   Recreational facilities<br>  Membership in special swim,<br>    tennis, golf or recreational<br>    clubs | | | | |

Note that interest, either foregone on money invested in land or the actual interest cost if the land is financed, is listed as an expense. Provision is also made for property taxes levied against the property while it is under development. The two years shown in this example may be extended over the estimated term. An allowance is listed for developer overhead to cover management and administrative expenses and for selling expense before the estimated profit per lot is entered.

It would be a mistake to consider a 100 lot subdivision with an average lot price of $5,000 as worth $500,000. Subdivisions are like other deferred income property such as timber or the extractive industries. A subdivision requires an initial outlay and projection of sale receipts over some sales period. Because income is deferred, it must be discounted to present value to determine project feasibility.

To illustrate, consider the purchase of 100 acres of land for $500,000. Assume the land may be subdivided into 300 lots with an average value of $10,000 per lot. The projection must be made over the period necessary to market all 300 lots. Such a schedule based on annual cash flows is shown in Table 12.1. In practice this schedule may be more detailed showing monthly expenditures and receipts.

**Table 12.1**

**Annual Cash Flow Schedule of a Proposed Subdivision Development**

| End of Year | 1 | 2 | 3 | 4 | 5 | Total |
|---|---|---|---|---|---|---|
| Number of Lots Sold | 0 | 50 | 75 | 75 | 100 | 300 |
| Vacant Land 100 acres | ($500,000) | | | | | ($500,000) |
| Development Costs | ($150,000) | ($100,000) | | | | ($250,000) |
| Property Taxes | ($5,500) | ($5,500) | ($5,500) | ($10,000) | ($15,000) | ($41,500) |
| Lot Sales Income | | $500,000 | $750,000 | $750,000 | $1,000,000 | $3,000,000 |
| Net income | ($655,500) | $394,500 | $744,500 | $740,000 | $ 985,000 | $2,208,500 |

It is presumed that no lot sales will be available for sale until the second year. At the end of the first year the cost outlay includes the land cost, property taxes and development costs of $150,000. The expenditures are equal to a negative cash flow of $655,500. At the end of the second year development costs, property taxes and lot sales provide an estimated net income of $394,500. In subsequent years projected lot sales provide sufficient income to offset property tax expenditures and other out-of-pocket costs. Over the five-year term, sales total $3 million producing a total income of $2,208,500.

Recall that income from subdivision sales represents deferred income. Table 12.2 shows how these incomes and expenses are discounted to produce the present worth of the subdivision development. At the end of the first year, $655,000 has been spent. Using a 9.0 percent discount (which could be higher depending on the current capitalization and interest rate), this expenditure has a present worth of $600,897. The present worth of one factor .9174 means that $1 postponed for one year, discounted at 9.0 percent has a present worth of $.9174. This calculation results from the formula for the present worth of one: 1/ (1 + .09) or $1.00/1.09. The net incomes shown in Table 12.1 are discounted by the appropriate present worth of one factor for each of the five years. Though in the fifth year a net income of $985,000 is anticipated, this sum, because it is postponed for five years, has a present worth of $640,151. The projected net income for each year capitalized in this way reveals that the subdivision has a present worth of $1,470,424. This is equal to a profit of approximately $4,868 per lot.

**Table 12.2**
**The Valuation of a Proposed Subdivision**

| End of Year | Net Income Projection | Present Worth of One (9 Percent) | Present Worth |
|---|---|---|---|
| 1 | ($655,000) | .9174 | ($600,897) |
| 2 | 394,500 | .8417 | 332,051 |
| 3 | 744,500 | .7722 | 574,903 |
| 4 | 740,000 | .7084 | 524,216 |
| 5 | 985,000 | .6499 | 640,151 |
| Present Worth of the Developed Subdivision | | | $1,470,424 |

# Land Financing Techniques

Lenders are reluctant to finance unimproved land—and for good reason: prices of vacant, unimproved land are subject to much speculation, conjecture, and uncertainty. A default on a loan based on land value may remain an unproductive loan in contrast to other improved real estate that has a proven use. To minimize risk of loss for this type of security, lenders have adopted rules that guide the placement of loans secured by vacant land.

## Reducing Risks in Land Development Loans

*First,* because the value of land is subject to unpredictable fluctuation in contrast to income properties, most knowledgeable lenders reduce risks by limiting loans on vacant land to 50 percent of the current estimated market value. In the event of foreclosure and probably in the face of a declining market, the lender has greater prospects of recovering principal if the loan is based on a realistic market value and on a 50 percent loan to value ratio.

*Secondly,* for development of a subdivision, some lenders limit the loan to 75 percent of the appraised value of the completed subdivision. It is also recommended that the maximum loan not exceed the cost of development. This latter qualification prevents land developers from securing the maximum loan based on the appraised value on lots which may remain unsold. Thus, without this proviso developers could pocket the excess of the appraised value over the cost of development even though the expected sales were unrealized. By limiting loans to the cost of development, the lender has greater prospects of recovering principal if the subdivision is unsuccessful.

*Thirdly,* institutional loans for land development tend typically to be short-term, say three, or four years. The lender is then protected from the possibility of default on a loan secured by fairly non-liquid assets that have little basis of recovery. A relatively short-term loan secured by vacant land is a less risky proposition than a longer-term commitment based on unimproved land.

*Fourthly,* because of the uncertainty of land sales after development, lenders may base the credit primarily on the credit of the borrower—not the value of the pledged real estate. In the case of the corporation, this would mean that a review of assets of the corporation, their credit rating and development history would be a prerequisite to loan approval. If a developer is an individual or partnership, personal assets of the individual, his reputation, character, and competency in real estate would be part of the credit review. Thus, in the event of default the lender is secured not only by value of real estate but primarily by the personal assets of the borrower.

*Fifthly,* lenders are advised to base the loan on a careful review of a competent feasibility and marketability report. By comparing the projected sales with evidence of competing subdivisions and a marketability study based upon local market conditions, the lender has a means of rejecting a subdivision of $20,000 lots for a market that would absorb only $10,000 lots. The projection of costs and sales based on evidence of the market would seem to be one of the first prerequisites to loan approval.

*Sixthly,* lenders encourage developers to improve land in development stages and phases. This is particularly advised where the cost of land improvements and utility installation is considerably more than the value of the land. In the event of an unsuccessful subdivision, both the lender and developer have limited their risk to only a portion of the land potentially available for subdivision. Such an arrangement tends to minimize the required capital for land development and, consequently, minimizes the degree of risk.

## Financing Plans

Though financing plans may assume many different forms, probably most plans could be classified in four categories—though financing details may vary widely: the land contract, purchase money mortgage, option to purchase, and the conventional first mortgage. A separate discussion of each of these plans shows how they vary.

*Land contracts*  don't see here much

The land contract is a device to finance a subdivision at the expense of the seller. It is more widely used if the land under contract is undergoing a change in use, for example, from farm use to subdivision use; and if subdivision lots may be sold within three or four years. problem is it takes more than land to develop. Must have hard $$

Suppose, for example, the seller has 80 acres of farm land worth $500 per acre. If the property is adapted to subdivision purposes, a developer-builder may offer the seller $5,000 per acre, paying $5,000 down and agreeing to pay the balance as lots are sold. Ordinarily, the land contract would provide for the release of a subdivided lot from the contract with the developer-builder paying a flat amount per lot, say $1,000, until the contract is fulfilled. Under these circumstances the seller, while assuming some risk, is induced to sell under these terms because of the substantial capital gains: $500 per acre for farm use compared to $5,000 per acre for residential use. The builder, on his part, finances vacant land with a minimum of equity capital. Providing the seller agrees to release each subdivided lot from the contract, granting title to the house and lot buyer, the purchaser of the dwelling acquires title free and clear of the land contract.

Usually the contract will be arranged in anticipation of an approved development and construction loan to finance the subdivision and dwellings. The construction loan, in turn, will be approved in anticipation of a long-term commitment by permanent lenders.

The key to successful financing under these land contract arrangements lies in the feasibility of the subdivision. A poorly designed subdivision, a subdivision with over-priced lots, or the lack of permanent financing may endanger the financial capability of the developer-builder. In part, his solvency is protected by the land contract that requires interest only payments while the property is under development. The land is paid for by the ultimate purchaser of the house and lot.

There are certain other dangers arising from contractual relations of the buyer and seller. Since the seller retains title, liens placed against the title may prevent the seller from granting free and clear title at the time the contract is fulfilled. However, the seller also assumes a certain risk in enforcing the terms of the contract if the builder is unsuccessful in disposing of subdivided lots. Under a favorable market, land contracts provide a popular way of financing land potentially adapted to development.

## Purchase money mortgages

The purchase money mortgage serves as a substitute for cash. That is, the selling landowner would normally agree to a nominal downpayment and accept a purchase money mortgage for the balance of the purchase price. (Since in most states the purchase money mortgage does not include a promissory note, the seller is secured only by the value of the real estate pledged.) The difference between this arrangement and the land contract lies in the transfer of title. In accepting an equity payment and a purchase money mortgage, the seller transfers title to the buyer. In other respects, the purchase money mortgage is similar to the land contract: the purchase money mortgage includes a release clause that grants title to the developed lot buyer free of the purchase money mortgage. Both plans represent the purchase of land using credit advanced by the selling landowner. Similar to the land contract, the plan would preferably include a construction loan, and arrangement for permanent financing is usually part of the financing plan.

*[handwritten margin notes: wrong! Again $$ hard to find when 1st mort is on prop. & bank has to take a second mortgage]*

## Option to purchase *[handwritten: not financing technique]*

An option is a right to purchase real property within a specified time on stated terms in return for a price. With respect to land development, the option allows the developer to commit land to his project without committing equity funds. For example, 40 acres may be acquired for immediate subdivision while another 40 or more acres could be committed to the same project under an option granted by the same seller. In essence, the option binds the seller for a specified time but does not bind the buyer while the option is effective. In this sense the option is a unilateral contract; if it is exercised, the option leads to a bilateral contract for a sale and purchase. Usually, when the option is executed it must be in writing and is accompanied by a contract for sale to be completed when the option is exercised.

It should be noted that the seller under an option does not sell the land under any interest. By the same token, the person holding the option has no legal obligation to purchase the property described. But under the option contract, the seller gives up his right to sell to others during the time covered by the option. At the same time the option gives the buyer time to develop adjoining property allowing him to commit additional land covered by the option as development progress recommends. In short, the land developer may postpone his decision to commit other land to the project until questions of financing and feasibility are resolved. The practice is recommended since the price of the option is usually less than the sale price and, if exercised, the consideration paid for the option is normally applied to the agreed purchase price.

*First mortgage financing* or conventional — what we are most concerned with.

While not as common as other forms of financing, some institutions require security of the mortgage and a promissory note for land developments. These plans are similar to other financing plans under the contract and purchase money mortgage. But in this instance the lender has the added security of a promissory note—the personal obligation of the owner-developer to repay the loan.

The innovation that might be mentioned for first mortgage financing —and this also applies to non-subdivision development—relates to the subordination clause. Suppose, for instance, that the land is purchased under a first mortgage and a nominal down payment. If the land seller agrees to subordinate his interest to a subsequent loan, the developer in effect pledges the security of the land and the building for additional loans for construction. While the seller assumes a junior or secondary lien position, favorable feasibility prospects and opportunities for capital gain may warrant the added risk. Sellers may be induced to enter such an arrangement also if the mortgage interest rate is comparable to the relatively high risk assumed.

## Subdivision Development: *A Case Study*

To show the complexity of land development, a 28.1 acre subdivision of 47 lots illustrates the detail required for land development. The cost of preparing the land for sale is summarized in Table 12.3. Note that the development cost of $185,543 is considerably in excess of the land cost of $140,500. At the time this report was prepared, the subdivision was completed with ten lots sold at the end of 18 months.

Sales projected over a 30 month period totalled $484,000. After development costs of $366,000, the estimated profit was $118,000. These figures are summarized in Table 12.4.

The project was financed with a loan of $355,000 with an interest charge of 4½ percent above the prime interest rate. It should be noted that the cost-price relationships in this subdivision follow from the relatively low density land use plan. The 28.1 acres were subdivided with an average of 1.67 lots per acre. With the costs shown in Table 12.3, this amounted to an average estimated sale price of $10,298. Note that this figure is more than double the vacant land cost. The cost of development, therefore, is partly related to the number of lots per acre, the relation between front footage and depth of each lot and the physical cost of land preparation.

Because of the large capital outlay necessary before lots are offered for sale, considerable risk is attached to land development financing. This case demonstrates the dependence the lender has on credit of the borrower, the subdivision feasibility and marketability study and the real estate market at the time of subdivision completion.

## Table 12.3
## Land Subdivision Costs

Legal and Closing Costs

| | | |
|---|---:|---:|
| Interest, 18 Months | $36,582 | |
| Title Charges | 675 | |
| Recording Fees | 12 | |
| Loan Service Charge to Lender | 3,350 | |
| Title Binder | 641 | |
| Total Closing Costs | | $ 41,260 |

Engineering Costs

| | | |
|---|---:|---:|
| 47 Lots, @ $175/lot | $ 8,225 | |
| Aerial Topographic Map | 1,200 | |
| Retention: Sedimentation | 600 | |
| Sewer Staking, 3760 LF @ 30¢/LF | 1,128 | |
| Boundary Survey | 523 | |
| Total Engineering Costs | | $11,676 |

Clearing and Grading Costs

| | | |
|---|---:|---:|
| 2,328 Linear Feet of Street @ $3.25/ft. | $ 7,566 | |
| 2,566 Linear Feet of Shoulder @ $2.00/ft. | 5,132 | |
| Engineering | 500 | |
| Total Clearing & Grading Costs | | $ 13,198 |

Storm Sewers

| | | |
|---|---:|---:|
| 224′ of 18″ Storm Drain @ $5.70/ft. | $ 1,391 | |
| 516′ of 24″ Storm Drain @ $7.10/ft. | 3,663 | |
| 76′ of Catch Basin @ $38.00/ft. | 2,888 | |
| 6 — 24″ Headwalls @ $170 | 1,020 | |
| 2 — 18″ Headwalls @ $142 | 284 | |
| 515′ of Clearing @ $1.00/ft. | 515 | |
| 1 Catch Basin @ $764 | 764 | |
| Total Storm Sewer Cost | | $ 10,525 |

## Table 12.3 *Continued.*

Sanitary Sewers
  Linear Feet of
  Sewer Depth

| | | | |
|---|---|---|---|
| 0-8' | 1,772 feet 8" @ $ 3.85................ | | $ 6,822 |
| 8-10' | 1,052 feet 8" @ $ 4.25................ | | 4,471 |
| 10-12' | 704 feet 8" @ $ 4,90................ | | 3,450 |
| 12-14' | 37 feet 8" @ $ 6.40................ | | 237 |
| 14-16' | 42 feet 8" @ $ 9.80................ | | 411 |
| 16-18' | 20 feet 8" @ $13.50................ | | 499 |
| 18-20' | 20 feet 8" @ $20.00................ | | 400 |
| | 998 feet 6" @ $ 3.10................ | | 3,094 |

Other Sanitary Sewer Costs

| | |
|---|---|
| 45 Wyes: Bends @ $25.00 each ..................... | $ 1,125 |
| 239' of Manholes @ $38.00/ft. ..................... | 9,082 |
| 24 Rings: Covers @ $75.00 each .................. | 1,800 |
| 1 Outside Drop .................................. | 500 |
| 32' Cast Iron Pipe @ $10.00/ft. ..................... | 320 |
| 2,095' Clearing @ $1.00/ft. ..................... | 2,095 |
| 3 Retention Ponds ............................... | 3,675 |

| | |
|---|---|
| Total Cost of Sanitary Sewer ....................... | $ 37,981 |

Water Mains

| | Labor | Material | |
|---|---|---|---|
| 1010 feet 8" AC Class 200 @ | $1.25 | $2.06 ...... | $ 3,343 |
| 72 feet 8" Cast Iron @ | $1.25 | $3.25 ...... | 324 |
| 1520 feet 6" AC Class 200 @ | $1.10 | $1.46 ...... | 3,891 |
| 216 feet 6" Cast Iron @ | $1.10 | $2.29 ...... | 732 |
| 670 feet 2½" PVC @ | $1.00 | $ .33 ...... | 891 |
| Not Itemized ........................................ | | | 7,582 |

| | |
|---|---|
| Total Cost of Water Main Installation ................ | $ 16,763 |

Streets

| | |
|---|---|
| Curbing, 7,127 linear feet, 10 catch basins ............. | $16,819 |
| Paving, 10,492 square yards of asphalt ................. | 34,085 |
| Miscellaneous ...................................... | 3,236 |

| | |
|---|---|
| Total Street Costs ............................... | 54,140 |
| Total Development Costs ........................ | $185,543 |
| Vacant Land Cost, 28.1 acres, @ $5,000/Ac. ............. | 140,500 |
| Land and Development Costs ........................... | $326,043 |

## Table 12.4

### Sales Projection, 28.1 Acre Subdivision (47 Lots)

| | |
|---|---|
| 10 Lots sold 1st 18 months @ $10,000 ................ | $100,000 |
| 10 Lots sold next 6 months @ $10,000 ................ | $100,000 |
| 23 Lots sold next 6 months @ $12,000 ................ | $276,000 |
| 4 Lots unbuildable or club facilities @ $2,000 ......... | $ 8,000 |

| | |
|---|---|
| Total Sales Projection, 47 Lots ........................ | $484,000 |
| Less Development Costs, 1st 18 months ................. | $326,043 |
| Less Additional Carrying Charges, next 12 months ....... | 39,957 |
| Total Cost ...................................... | —366,000 |
| Total Profit ...................................... | $118,000 |

Chapter 13

# Shopping Center Mortgages

*Disadvantages*
1. *vacancies*
2. *heavy taxes*
3. *replacement of obsolete equipment*

Leading authorities regard the professionally developed shopping center as a superior investment. The rent schedule compensates for inflation and shopping center investments create cash flow. As this chapter suggests, the economics of shopping centers favor their continued growth. To deal adequately with this type of mortgage security, the vocabulary associated with mortgages on shopping centers is explained throughout the chapter.

It will be demonstrated that for this type of property, mortgage lenders reduce risk by detailed financial analysis. In most respects, the criteria applied to shopping centers rest on objective income and expense data not always available for single family dwellings or industrial properties. Before dealing with these financial aspects, a general section on the nature of shopping centers is presented. This is followed by a discussion of the elements of mortgage security. A discussion of shopping center leases completes the chapter.

## The Nature of Shopping Centers
Probably the most common classification of a shopping center depends on the market area served: the region, the community, or the neighbor-

hood. For some purposes it is more useful to emphasize the design of shopping centers which varies within shopping center types. It will be found that shopping center expenses and operation vary considerably between classifications, especially with respect to the enclosed, air conditioned shopping mall.

## Types of Shopping Centers

Technically a shopping center is defined by the Urban Land Institute as—

> A group of commercial establishments planned, developed, owned, and managed as a unit related in location, size, and type of shops to the trade area to which the unit serves; it provides on-site parking in definite relationship to the type and sizes of the stores.

The Urban Land Institute emphasizes differences in the tenant mix between the three main types of shopping centers. From this point of view, neither the land area, nor the square foot area of the building determines the type of center. To pursue this point centers are judged according to three groups: the regional, the community, and the neighborhood center.

### Regional centers

The regional center conforms to this classification if it is dominated by a full line department store of at least 100,000 square feet of gross leasable area. Gross leasable area is the floor area designed for tenant occupancy including basements, mezzanines, and multiple stories. The area is measured from the center line of joint partitions and outside wall exteriors. To put it differently, for all shopping centers the area in which tenants pay rent represents the gross leasable area.

The more prominent regional centers have more than one department store tenant. As a rule regional centers will generally have 400,000 square feet of gross leasable area, though in some instances a regional center may have a gross leasable area of as much as 1,000,000 square feet. Tenants tend to concentrate in general merchandise, apparel, furniture, and household furnishings. The most common tenants according to a survey of 109 regional centers by the Urban Land Institute include the following shown in the order of their occurrence:

1. Ladies Wear
2. Menswear
3. Family Shoe
4. Ladies Specialty
5. Cards & Gifts
6. Ladies Shoe
7. Jewelry
8. Medical & Dental
9. Candy, Nuts
10. Restaurant

269

While subject to exception, regional shopping centers typically require a 35 acre to 100 acre site. The leading tenant is associated with 15 to 100 retail establishments supported by a primary market population of 200,000.

## ✓ *The community center*

The community center is a less ambitious development. It is organized around a junior department store or variety store serving as the leading tenant with a supermarket, apparel, hardware, and appliance stores. Community centers fall between neighborhood and regional centers and display characteristics of both types. The leading junior department store will have approximately 25,000 square feet with 15 to 35 other compatible stores. Site requirements typically range from 5 acres to 40 acres. A minimum trade area of about 100,000 people supports a community center. Most community centers have between 122,000 to 204,000 square feet of gross leasable area with 150,000 square feet being fairly typical. The ten most frequently found tenants in community shopping centers are listed in order of their appearance:

1. Ladies Wear
2. Supermarket
3. Beauty Shop
4. Family Shoe
5. Medical & Dental
6. Drug Store
7. Barber Shop
8. Cleaners & Dryers
9. Menswear
10. Variety Store

## ✓*Neighborhood centers*

Stores in neighborhood centers specialize in <u>convenience</u> goods: primarily foods, drugs, and sundries. Personal services are popular, for example, laundry and dry cleaning, barber shops, and shoe repairing. The supermarket is the leading attraction of the neighborhood center. The gross leasable area generally lies between 36,000 square feet and 70,000 square feet. The required land area varies from 4 acres to 20 acres. Most of these centers will have from 10 to 15 smaller stores in service businesses. The smaller neighborhood center generally requires a population of 17,000 to 35,000.

Tenants most often found in neighborhood centers are arranged in order of their popularity:

1. Supermarket
2. Beauty Shop
3. Barber Shop
4. Drug Store
5. Laundry & Cleaner
6. Ladies Wear
7. Medical & Dental
8. Restaurant
9. Variety Store
10. Coin Laundry

It will be observed that tenants vary between the three shopping center classifications. Though the listing of tenants reveals their significance in terms of number of stores, it should not be implied that tenant importance rests solely on the frequency of their occurrence. The leading tenants dominate each type of center. They are primarily responsible for attracting customers to the center. Typically they are stores that occupy the larger gross leasable area. Moreover, the rent per square foot varies considerably among tenants listed. Therefore, the list of tenants emphasizes the difference in tenant mix and not their relative financial importance.

*Shopping centers classified by design*

Exhibit 13.1 illustrates classification based on the most common types of architecture. Of prime importance is the exposure of the shopping center to pedestrian and vehicle traffic. The mixture of pedestrian traffic, customer parking, employee parking, garbage collection, and service vehicles require careful planning. The placement of the leading tenants is another critical issue. Common observation of shopping centers in each category shows that leading tenants in a neighborhood center, say a drug store and supermarket, are separated. The specialty stores and service establishments are placed between the leading tenants. This gives each small tenant maximum exposure to shopping center patrons. The same principle generally will be observed in other types of centers.

## Shopping Center Operations

Reported statistics on shopping center operations are always suspect. Experience of the older shopping centers with contract rents below current economic rent may be expected to vary substantially from new shopping centers. Operating expenses vary according to the age of the structure and its location. Utility charges for shopping centers maintaining air conditioned enclosed malls in Florida vary from operating expenses of centers in Minnesota or Michigan. Real estate taxes, the largest single shopping center expense, shows much variation between and among the states and localities. Some shopping centers are in high income dominant areas, others are in declining areas or have been built in anticipation of increasing population and buying power. Even their land and building costs show wide differences. It is understandable then that average operating experience—meaning gross income and operating expenses—may be used as guides to interpret local experience. Certainly large deviations of estimates of local expenses and gross incomes from published sources should be explained on rational grounds.

## Exhibit 13.1

### Shopping Center Floor Plans Showing Key Tenant Locations

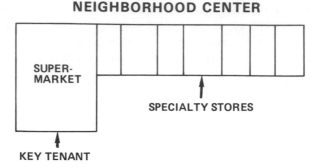

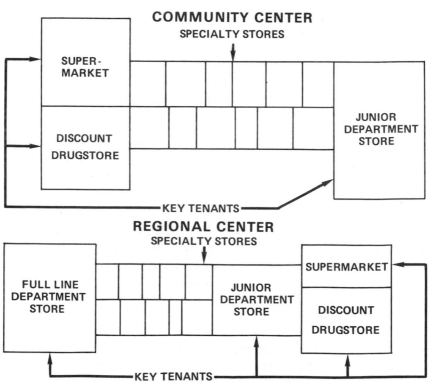

With these qualifications operating ratios of shopping centers are shown in Table 13.1. The income includes gross rent receipts, common charges and miscellaneous income. The common area charges refer to levies for promotion, parking lot expenses, lighting outside areas, janitorial and other maintenance charges for maintaining public areas. Normally these expenses are shared by tenants by some per unit pro rata basis among the tenants. While the individual differences in shopping center operation may be expected, Table 13.1 reveals a surprising uniformity in the relative proportion of operating expenses. Note that real estate taxes, nationally, constitute 12.0 percent to 13.3 percent of total receipts. While real estate taxes show much variation between individual centers, it is probably safe to say that real estate taxes are universally the largest single expense. This is followed by administrative, management expenses, and public area maintenance. Utilities, advertising, and insurance make up the balance of shopping center expenses.

**Table 13.1**
**Median Operating Ratios of Regional, Community and Neighborhood Centers**
*(in percent)*

| *Operating Item* | *Regional* (109 Cases) | *Community* (120 Cases) | *Neighborhood* (124 Cases) |
|---|---|---|---|
| **Gross Income** | | | |
| Rent Area | 88.1 | 96.1 | 95.5 |
| Common Charges | 7.5 | 3.2 | 3.6 |
| Other | 4.8 | 3.0 | 2.5 |
| Total Receipts | 100.0 | 100.0 | 100.0 |
| **Operating Expenses** | | | |
| Building Maintenance | 1.6 | 2.2 | 2.3 |
| Public Area Maintenance | 6.3 | 4.6 | 4.2 |
| Utilities | 3.7 | 1.7 | 1.7 |
| Advertising | 1.5 | 1.3 | 1.0 |
| Real Estate Taxes | 12.0 | 12.1 | 13.3 |
| Insurance | 1.2 | 2.0 | 2.0 |
| Administrative | 5.2 | 5.5 | 5.4 |
| Total Expenses | 34.8 | 34.0 | 30.0 |
| Operating Balance | 65.2 | 66.0 | 70.0 |

Source: Urban Land Institute.
Note: Totals may not add to 100 because median values are shown for each item.

The data indicate that shopping centers show an operating balance ranging from 65 to 70 percent. Compared to the appraisal format, some allowance should be made for vacancy expenses and a reserve for replacement for short-lived equipment and fixtures.

To analyze a given shopping center, it is more appropriate to compare expenses on the basis of per square foot of gross leasable area. Data are available that show these expenses for each individual shopping center on a square foot basis and classified by age of center and geographic location. Because such data tend to be historical, they are not reproduced here. Detailed surveys of shopping centers operations are published by the Urban Land Institute—probably the best source of statistical data on shopping centers available.

Special attention should be directed to the rental structure common to shopping centers. It is customary to provide for a minimum rent supplemented by a stated percent of gross sales. The leading tenants, including the department stores, variety stores, supermarkets, and drug stores of national chains, bargain and usually receive the lowest possible minimum rent. Frequently, the minimum rent is less than the prevailing rate of return on invested land and building capital. But without the leading tenants, most lenders are reluctant to grant construction loans or long-term financing on a shopping center. The project is too speculative without the support of leading tenants.

Given the required leading tenants, shopping center developers then negotiate for rents from specialty stores and local stores which typically have a higher markup and lower turnover. While current figures are always dated in a textbook, consider rental differences (per square foot) between high sales volume, low markup stores compared to low sales volume, high markup stores. For example, sales per square foot of gross leasable area for supermarkets in neighborhood shopping centers have recently ranged from *$93.87* to *$149.85*. The median middle range of rent per gross leasable area has been reported to fall between *$1.34* to *$2.00* per square foot. High sales volume and low markup of leading tenants produce relatively low square foot rents. Music and record stores, in contrast, show sales per square foot of gross leasable area from *$26.67 to $45.47*. Their median rents extend from *$5.00* to *$6.00* per square foot of gross leasable area. As a rule, the leading tenants pay less rent per square foot than specialty tenants.

There is also a substantial difference in percentage rents paid on gross sales. A survey by the National Institute of Real Estate Brokers indicated that percentage rents for supermarkets are typically 1.0 percent to 1.5 percent of gross sales. Liquor stores typically pay from 4 percent to 6 percent of gross sales. Other retailers such as jewelry stores pay similar high percentage rents: 6 percent to 8 percent of sales; hosiery and lingerie, 6 to 9 percent; gift shops, 6 to 11 percent; dry cleaning and laundry, 5 to 8 percent.

## Downtown Retail Stores

The financing issues associated with downtown property are significantly different than the problems of financing a shopping center development. The common complaint of downtowns includes the lack of parking, poor street lighting and high property taxes. To be sure these issues are significant and bear importantly on opportunities for development, but the inherent weaknesses of downtowns stand in marked contrast to shopping centers.

Probably the most crucial problem relates to fractionated ownership of relatively small land parcels. Remember that the downtowns were platted during the pre-automobile era. Lots were relatively small, and they were subdivided for purchase and improvement by a single occupant. Today retailing requires larger frontages and more floor space. Yet it is uneconomical to assemble enough land for an integrated shopping complex in most downtowns. There are too many property owners who hold out for exorbitant prices; with exceptions (the downtown mall, for example), land uses follow a highly mixed pattern. Tenants often have little mutual attraction and their buildings show little integrated planning and harmony.

Add to this other deficiencies such as inadequate parking, often poorly located and of questionable quality. The final result offers a poor alternative to the shopping center. The population shifts to the suburbs and the abandonment of the downtown to low income groups argue against the continuation of downtown for comparison shopping. If property taxes remain at a relatively high level, investors then have a disincentive to rehabilitate the downtown. A related point concerns the financial aspects of downtown investment. Typically, the land value will be relatively high in proportion to the total investment. In a shopping center, the converse is true. Here land represents a smaller proportion of the shopping center value, giving the investor greater after tax cash flow because of building depreciation.

More significant is the change in downtown functions from a retailing center to office, hotel, convention, government and entertainment center, as illustrated by Atlanta, Georgia. The discussion on shopping center management illustrates how these points differ in a shopping center operation.

## Judging Mortgage Security

*Income Analysis is most impt. ★*
*as w/ all income-producing real estate:*
*multi-fam.*
*commercial*

Shopping center analysis is unusually complex. The expert in this field requires knowledge of shopping center architecture and planning. The economics of retailing, forecasting techniques, and mortgage finance are part of the typical analysis. For the present purpose attention is invited to the minimum data required by the mortgage lender. By concentrating on a select group of criteria, you avoid committing funds on poorly recommended projects.

For instance, a review of poorly placed mortgages on shopping centers shows that even a minimum familiarity with shopping centers would help avoid bad loans. A neighborhood shopping center near Macon, Georgia, has operated at a loss, primarily because of poor planning—the ceiling of the main store building is limited to ten feet. Major tenants require higher ceilings for advertising, display and lighting fixtures. The cost of poor planning, as the above example illustrates, can be fairly substantial.

It is suggested that errors of this type will be minimized by a review of four items: (1) retail sales forecasting, (2) an analysis of site characteristics, (3) shopping center management, and (4) tenant selection. While the loan officer ordinarily does not undertake these detailed studies, a review of the data will help the loan officer to judge the competence of feasibility studies.

## ⓘ Retail Sales Forecasts

The first objective is to forecast the probable volume of sales in the proposed shopping center. If an existing center is under review, past sales will guide the financing decision. To forecast sales some determination must be made over the market area that accounts for 80 percent of the gross sales.

The market area served by a given shopping center is not subject to precise measure. Also it is not the distance from a shopping center that determines patronage, but the time of travel. It has been found that a neighborhood shopping center may be profitable even though it is located across the street from a regional center. This apparent paradox is caused by the differing tenant mix; the neighborhood center specializes in convenience goods and services while tenants of the regional center offer comparison shopping. As a general rule, shopping center experts have observed the following trends:

| Center | Distance of Market Area *think in terms of time* |
|---|---|
| Neighborhood | 1.5 miles |
| Community | 3 to 5 miles |
| Regional | 8 miles or more depending on travel time |

For the regional center a 20 mile distance represents a common limit, though the market area depends on the type of highway travel to the site. Again depending on the population density, the drawing power between regional centers may extend from five to ten miles.

With the market area defined, the next issue is to determine population and its projection over the next ten years. Next the personal income is calculated for the area in question. With a given income, the purchasing power may be projected for the main retail expenditures proposed for the center. From these data the total retail expenditure pattern for the market area may be calculated.

The next issue is to estimate the potential sales of the center in question. In this respect sales to be gained beyond the normal trade area, vary by type of center. For a neighborhood center, probably not more than two to five percent of the total business will be gained outside the immediate trade area. A large regional shopping center may expect as much as 20 percent of their sales to be gained from outside the primary trade area. Reliance must be placed on experience, the analysis for access, and an estimate of how well the proposed shopping center will compete with other retail centers.

For instance, the projection will consider the existing population, zoning restrictions, geographic barriers that restrict the development of new residential areas, and public improvements such as industrial parks, public parks, cemeteries, airports and other uses incompatible with residential expansion.

## ② Site Characteristics

Site analysis is fairly critical to shopping center evaluation. First, the location: Access to and from the center must have sufficient traffic load carrying capacity to avoid future congestion. For regional centers, access must be from main traffic routes with convenient routes to limited access highways. Visual exposure must be superior.

In the case of community centers, they are preferably located at major intersections. Because the trade does not require high speed travel, this type of center does not need ready access to a freeway. Demands of the neighborhood center are less restrictive. Access must be from collector street intersections avoiding local neighborhood streets.

Other physical characteristics cover the topography, which must be level or gently sloping. A proposed site must be in one piece undivided by public streets or easements. Like industrial and apartment house sites, utilities must be adequate, the soil must have proper load bearing capacity and zoning should conform to the planned shopping center.

Parking must conform to the normal parking requirement of 5.5 parking spaces per 1,000 square feet of gross leasable area. Though this standard may not serve peak loads during the Christmas shopping season, it is more economical to provide parking for an average demand, not a peak demand. The parking plan must separate customers from truck movement. The site layout must eliminate poor store location and distribute stores between leading tenants. Foot traffic must be separated from vehicular traffic. Landscaping, lighting, store fronts, and the like must not impose on customers or competing stores.

## ③ Shopping Center Management  *experience, controls (tenant selection & under lease)*

Experienced lenders are reluctant to finance a center that is not under competent management. So much depends on past experience, perform-

277

ance and familiarity with shopping centers. Given favorable economic and financial arrangements, the shopping center succeeds or fails according to management quality. For this type of property, success is more than a matter of site selection, construction, mortgage loan negotiation, and tenant solicitation. In the final analysis, the object is to create a desirable image for the center as a whole. Each tenant should benefit from center popularity and from the mutual attraction of other compatible tenants. To carry out these goals, certain management techniques stand out from other types of property.

## Tenant restrictions

One of the crucial management problems concerns the many restrictions imposed on tenants. While restrictive in the conventional sense, such management controls lead to the highest possible level of gross sales. For instance, tenants will be subject to sign control. Other architectural controls lead to an integrated shopping center that adds to the attractiveness of the area. Street lighting, advertising sign design, landscaping and the architecture are planned so that each tenant benefits from attractive surroundings.

Similar management controls are directed to the main issue: to maximize the shopping potential. Hours of operation are arranged so that each tenant creates traffic for the neighboring tenant. It would be unwise to have stores occupying strategic positions that are not open during hours of normal operation—including night-time operations. Consequently management may require that tenants observe night-time and other stated hours of operation including days of operation.

Related practices cover the type of goods offered for sale. For example, the supermarket with the lowest possible percentage rent, typically 1 percent of gross sales, usually would not be encouraged to sell garden equipment in competition with a hardware store that pays a percentage rent of 6 or 8 percent of gross sales. In short, the developer prefers that tenants subject to low percentage rent not compete with specialty stores that have higher mark-up, lower turnover and higher percentage rents. Some of these problems are resolved by the merchant association.

## The merchant association

The merchant association is unique to shopping centers. It substitutes for chambers of commerce that promote downtown retail sales. The task of the merchant association is to merchandise the center, to create the shopping center as an institution and to work toward the best possible image. Their many promotional schemes help develop the center as a community attraction.

Financing of the merchant association is ordinarily allocated on the square foot area occupied by each tenant. In some instances, association charges are levied on a per front foot basis or as a percentage of the rent paid. The Urban Land Institute recommends that each tenant share association expenses according to a stated percentage of sales volume. The voting power in the merchant association follows the same general format. Some centers govern the association by allowing one vote per store or by allocating votes on the basis of the square foot space occupied. Management may reserve and exercise 25 percent of all voting rights.

As part of the merchant association operation, promotional plans will be directed to institutional types of advertising. Through the association, member tenants receive monthly sales reports on each tenant so that they may compare their own operation with neighboring tenants. In this way, each tenant is aware of his relative sales volume. The association helps work toward uniform store hours and days of operation. Throughout the year the association also sponsors numerous promotional activities.

④ Tenant Selection

It is difficult to overestimate the dominant role of the key tenants. The ability to secure a key tenant depends on the strength of the location, the policy of key tenants in locating branch stores and the competition of existing centers. Usually, key tenants investigate locations and are not governed by developer promotional campaigns. Given the commitment of key tenants, smaller tenants will be attracted largely by the prestige and estimated pedestrian traffic created by the major tenants. Local tenants may not be attracted to the center unless the center has at least one national chain store.

The arrangement of tenant types follows fairly rigid rules. For the smaller center, service stores tend to be grouped together. With the qualification that each shopping center will provide for a major tenant, other typical tenants compatible with shopping center operation fall within the following groups (These are not necessarily all inclusive.):

*Shopping Center Tenants*

| | |
|---|---|
| Food specialty | Perfume |
| Department | Tobacco |
| Variety | Camera |
| Apparel | Hobby shops |
| Furniture & home furnishings | Sporting goods |
| Hardware | Auto accessories |
| Drugs | Key shop |

279

Eating and drinking

Other stores

  Gifts

  Art supplies

  Music

  Jewelry

  Liquor

  Leather

  Import

Garden shop

Services

Financial institutions

Medical Offices

Recreation

  Theater

  Auditorium

  Bowling alleys

The list includes not only retail stores but service stores offering personal services, such as beauty shops, barber shops, radio stores, shoe repair and similar services.

Here lies the main difference between a shopping center and the downtown. With proprietary control, the shopping center operator groups compatible tenants. It is unlikely that an attorney's office will be located next to a ladies apparel store. The attorney creates little pedestrian traffic. A ladies or family shoe store would be more compatible. Note that poor traffic generators tend to be sited at more distant locations: theatres, office space and banks. Stores offering compatible goods group together to maximize pedestrian traffic. In the downtown this principle is seldom observed.

## Financing Methods

*[handwritten: Real Estate Taxes go on whether rented up or not. Must have reserves for replacement expenses]*

Shopping center financing may vary significantly from conventional, first mortgage financing. At the outset interim financing and long-term permanent loans are unlikely without provision of a key tenant lease. By the same token letters of commitment are withheld unless legal fees, architectural fees and land controls are arranged. Financing a center requires land acquisition, the presentation of the loan proposal and special financing techniques common to shopping centers.

### Land Acquisition

Developers may acquire potential shopping center sites under a deferred purchase plan in anticipation of a sale and leaseback of the whole property. The alternative is a ground lease in which the owner subordinates the lease to a first mortgage. This is especially attractive if the owner defers payment of the ground rent until the shopping center earns income. This plan is accompanied by participation of the landowner in shopping center income. Some lenders may finance a leasehold interest with an unsubordinated ground lease with ground rent starting on the effective date of the lease.

Not Done Much↓

A more common arrangement relies on a land contract with the owner subordinating his interest to a first mortgage. This is a typical device to reduce capital required for land. The more conventional procedure requires the outright purchase of the land in anticipation of a first mortgage on the completed project.

## Construction Costs

A loan application would include the sponsor's construction cost breakdown. The project cost of a shopping center at the very minimum would stratify cost by the following categories.

> Cost of buildings (total square feet)
> Utilities and site improvements
> Paving
> Architect and engineering fees
> General contractor overhead and profit
> Re-zoning and sewer expenses
> Land costs

If the appraised value of the land varies from the sponsor's cost this would be footnoted in the report. For example, the land may have been acquired ten years prior to the loan application. Original cost would probably not equal the current appraised value.

At the same time, the loan application would include the appraiser's estimate of cost. The latter cost would be taken from costs of recently constructed properties of like kind and design. In other instances, the cost of construction would be based on interviews with local contractors to gain insight on prevailing costs. These data may be supplemented by cost manuals prepared by commercial appraisal firms.

Details on costs would normally be included in the appraisal report substantiating the current estimate of the replacement cost. For appraisal purposes, costs would be shown separately for the building, site costs (namely, paving, lighting, striping and concrete bumpers), concrete drives and loading docks, concrete walks, and canopies. In addition, the interim financing interest cost, property taxes during construction, and leasing expenses, if any, would be a part of the appraised cost estimate.

## Presentation of the Loan Proposal

While the financing plan assumes many forms, the loan application is accompanied by a detailed proposal review. Exhibit 13.2 represents a typical checklist covering a proposed shopping center or the financing of an existing center. In most cases the loan proposal includes an economic survey which serves as the basis for a pro forma profit and loss

Base tenant gives you 15-20% of cash flow necessary to service debt + draws other tenants.

statement and rent schedule of a proposed center. If it is an existing center, data on market area characteristics supplement profit and loss statements. The loan proposal includes a diagram of the site with the layout plan showing the location of key tenants, parking areas and access routes.

## Exhibit 13.2

## A Shopping Center Checklist

1. Market area characteristics.
   a. Population.
   b. Buying power.
   c. Economic base of the area.
2. Location of competing shopping areas.
3. Site characteristics.
   a. Land.
   b. Access routes.
   c. Traffic patterns and counts.
   d. Shopping center layout.
      (1) Site plan.
      (2) Gross leasable area.
      (3) Parking plan and ratio.
      (4) Tenant location.
      (5) Amenities of the center.
   e. Tenant information.
      (1) Tenant composition: key tenants.
      (2) Tenant credit rating.
      (3) Sales per square foot.
   f. Lease data.
      (1) Minimum rent by tenants.
      (2) Percentage rents for prior years.
      (3) Lease termination dates (options).
      (4) Tenant charges paid.
      (5) Taxes, insurance and operating expense escalation clauses.
4. Profit and loss statements for preceding five years.
5. Pro forma profit and loss statements and a rent schedule.
6. Income and expense date by gross leasable area.
   a. Utilities.
   b. Maintenance.
   c. Repairs.
   d. Management expense.
   e. Lease commission.
   f. Ground rental.
   g. Merchants association.
   h. Insurance (net).
   i. Real estate taxes (net).
   j. Miscellaneous.
7. Developer or management experience and financial responsibility.
8. A copy of the standard lease form and copies of all leases in effect.

Particular attention is placed on tenant information: especially the tenant composition, tenant credit ratings, and the expected sales per square foot—or for an existing center, a historical record of actual sales per square foot.

Lease data are equally important. A copy of the lease form with leases for the key tenants showing financial arrangements are described in some detail. The lease termination dates are significant in that leases should not end in the same year. Leases to tenants should be of sufficient length, 5, 10 or 15 years to ensure the stability of shopping center operation. To reduce variation in rental income, it is better to spread termination dates over different years. The tax and insurance escalation clauses, heating, ventilation and air conditioning charges of enclosed malls, details of the merchant association and other charges make up part of the loan proposal. Either profit and loss statements of preceding years or pro forma profit and loss statements, accompanied by a current rent schedule serve as the basis for the final financial plan. The developer's past experience and financial rsponsibility analysis completes this part of the mortgage proposal.

## Financing Techniques

*owner would like to have net - net - net (net) leases. Leasee pays taxes, ins., maintenance*

Turning first to first mortgage financing, the amount of the loan will *The more variables* be based on the estimated market value derived from the capitalization *you remove* of the net income. For new centers, a conservative approach would *from own-* eliminate maximum payout on the loan according to the amount of *er, better* property leased. For instance, the first mortgage would initially be limited to 80 percent of the amount of approved loan until 90 percent of *off you* the space was leased. Some shopping center lenders stipulate further that *are as* the total amount of the mortgage cannot exceed the actual cost of land *lender.* and buildings. As customary in other income properties, lenders may require a fixed interest rate and a share of gross rents or a share of percentage rents. Some developers have offered a 15 percent ownership share in the developing corporation as part of the financing package.

To illustrate, shopping center financial data are reproduced in Tables 13.2 and 13.3. The material relates to an existing center financed for repurchase to an institutional lender. It will be noted that Table 13.2 lists the gross leasable area by tenants. The original lease term and the options are identified in each case. The minimum and the overage rent are shown for the current year. Since the center is five years old some of the tenants have exceeded the minimum square foot rental provided by the percentage leases. As customary in most centers, the tenants pay common area charges and repairs to the common areas. In this case the tenants agree to pay the annual increase in the property taxes over the base year and escalating insurance charges. In the last

Table 13.2

# Shopping Center Financial Data as of June 30, 19___.

| Tenant | Gross Leasable Area | Lease Term | Minimum Rent Per Year | Overage Rent | Owner Costs Paid by Tenant | | Annual Expected Gross Rent |
|---|---|---|---|---|---|---|---|
| T. G. & Y. | 7,720 | '63-'75 + 2 5-yr. options | $ 9,000 | $ 3,013 | * | $ 250 | $ 12,265 |
| Dillon | 11,800 | '61-'77 + 1 3-yr. option | 9,200 | 11,275 | * Rprs. Tax Ins. | 300 700 5,650 600 | 28,175 |
| Lucille's Fashions | 2,500 | '65-'77 + 2 5-yr. options | 7,500 | — | * | 100 | 7,600 |
| Beneficial Finance | 1,500 | '69-'74 | 4,500 | — | * Rprs. | 100 100 | 4,700 |
| Norton Rexall | 4,000 + bsmt. 1,700 | '65-'77 + 2 5-yr. options | 7,500 | 1,490 | * Rprs. | 200 300 | 9,490 |
| Tempo Store | 30,000 | '64-'84 + 2 5-yr. options | 35,100 | — | * | 600 | 35,700 |
| Cinderella Dry Cleaning | 2,100 | '65-'75 | 5,100 | — | * Rprs. | 100 100 | 5,300 |
| King's Food Host | 4,210 | '68-'86 + 1 5-yr. option | 17,880 | — | * Rprs. Tax | 150 300 2,130 | 20,460 |
| Pizza Pit | 1,500 | '68-'78 + 1 5-yr. option | 7,620 | — | * Rprs. Ins. | 100 250 200 | 8,170 |
| Fred Oil Company | 2,600 | '68-'78 + 2 5-yr. options | $ 9,600 | — | * | 100 | $ 9,700 |
| Mr. Steak | 3,160 | '68-'83 + 2 5-yr. options | 16,500 | — | * Rprs. Ins. Tax | 200 250 400 1,790 | 19,140 |
| Mellers Photo | 80 | '71-'81 (terminable) | 1,800 | — | * Rprs. Ins. | 50 100 50 | 2,000 |
| Stevenson Clothing | 1,820 | '68-'73 + 4 5-yr. options | 4,800 | — | * Rprs. | 100 200 | 5,100 |
| Casa Tialoc | 1,070 | '70-'75 + 1 3-yr. options | 3,600 | — | * Rprs. | 100 200 | 3,900 |
| Liquor Store | 430 | '68-'71 + 2 5-yr. options | 2,400 | — | * Rprs. | 100 100 | 2,600 |
| Reed Beauty Shop | 890 | '69-'74 + 1 5-yr. option | 3,330 | — | * Rprs. | 100 120 | 3,550 |
| Perryman Yarn Shop | 430 | '71-'73 + 1 5-yr. option | 1,800 | — | * | 100 | 1,900 |
| Peoples S&L Association | 430 | '70-'72 + 2 2-yr. options | 2,400 | — | * | 100 | 2,500 |
| Beckley Barber Shop | 540 | '69-'74 + 1 5-yr. option | $ 1,500 | — | * | 100 | $ 1,600 |
| Drummer Boy | 1,800 | '69-'89 + 1 10-yr. option | 12,360 | — | Rprs. Tax Ins. | 100 1,230 150 | 13,840 |
| 1st State Bank | 6,400 + bsmt. 6,400 | '70-'80 + 5 5-yr. options | 32,880 | — | * Rprs. | 300 600 | 33,780 |
| Taco House | 950 | '70-'84 + 1 5-yr. option | 6,300 | — | Ins. Tax. | 150 1,000 | 7,450 |
| Canterbury Court | 10,000 | '70-'85 + 2 5-yr. options | 21,600 | — | * Rprs. Tax. Ins. | 350 500 2,800 1,050 | 26,300 |
| Total | $102,330 | | | | | | $240,500 |

* Pro rata share of parking lot utility costs and parking lot maintenance.

## Table 13.3

### Shopping Center Income Statement

Gross income

| | | |
|---|---|---|
| Base rents | | $ 424,300 |
| Overage rents | | 16,200 |
| Adjusted gross income | | 440,500 |
| Less vacancy allowance, 5% | | −26,493 |
| | | $ 414,007 |
| Management | $ 4,100 | |
| Real Estate Taxes | 52,000 | |
| Insurance | 13,400 | |
| Administrative Expenses | 4,000 | |
| Repairs and Maintenance | 3,200 | |
| Automobile and Miscellaneous | 4,160 | |
| Reserves for Replacement | 8,500 | |
| Total expenses | | −89,360 |
| Net income to land and improvements | | $ 324,647 |

Income to land:

Land value of developed 22 acres
($45,000 per acre) $990,000 × 10%

| | |
|---|---|
| = Income to developed land | −99,000 |
| Net income attributable to improvements | $ 225,647 |
| $225,647 ÷ 11.5% | 1,962,148 |
| Add land value | 990,000 |
| Total Value | $2,952,148 |
| Or Say | $3,000,000 |

column the annual expected gross rent applies to the succeeding year. This final figure serves as the net income for appraisal purposes. This financial statement is accompanied by actual statements from preceding years.

Table 13.3 capitalizes the net income as derived from Table 13.2. The land value is entered on a cost basis. In most respects, the capitalization agrees with capitalization of net income procedures. A variation of the capitalization process for shopping centers would require the capitalization of overage rent at a higher capitalization rate than the rate applied to the minimum rent. Appraisers following this method contend that the risks of earning overage rent justifies the relatively higher capitalization rate. The competition from other centers, the uncertainty of local employment with a consequent lowering of gross sales warrant this treatment. With the assumption of the capitalization rate and net income shown in Table 13.3, the estimated market value from capitalization of net income is $3,000,000.

The capitalized value, as shown in Table 13.3, constitutes market value for the maximum possible loan. The actual loan to value ratio, however, may be much lower: it depends on the financial responsibility of the developer, his experience in operating like centers and the local economic base. Prospects for competition from other developing areas may warrant a mortgage loan less than the maximum legal loan to value ratio. The shopping center checklist of Exhibit 13.2, with all of its associated data, would help determine the final mortgage loan. For the case at hand, equity participation was provided to the lender with an option to purchase shares in the developing corporation.

## Shopping Center Leases

While shopping center leases share common elements of typical leases, they have special features not found in other developments. A good lease on a shopping center protects the owner's income from unforeseen expenses. This is not to minimize other features of the lease that control tenant operations. These issues have already been noted. Instead, attention is drawn to financial covenants that relate directly to mortgage security.

Take, for instance, a new shopping center. The best plan, as followed by successful developers, recommends construction of building shells, complete in their exterior finishing but reserving the final floor, wall, ceiling, lighting, wiring, and plumbing installation to the tenant. If each store space were to be finished before each lease was executed, most tenants would probably have to reconstruct interiors to conform to their special requirements. The preferred practice provides for a stated square foot minimum rent with a cost allowance per square foot for interior completion. This system gives tenants flexibility in designing space according to their preferences and it fixes owner capital costs.

A related issue covers the provision for real property taxes. If a new center is under development, the owner faces the risk of increasing real estate taxes over the lease term. (Recall that property taxes are the largest single operating expense of a shopping center.) If property taxes tend to increase each year—by reason of increased assessments or higher tax levies—the net income available for mortgage servicing might be endangered. The lease agreement may call for owner payments of a fixed property tax per square foot with the tenant assuming the balance of property taxes prorated for his leased space. Alternatively, the owner and tenant may agree to a real estate property tax base during the first year of operation. In this case, tenants agree to pay their pro rata share of property taxes over the base year payment.

However arranged, the tax escalation clause protects the owner's ability to repay the loan by eliminating an open-ended property tax liability. Tax escalation clauses of this type shift the risk of increased property taxes to the tenant who, in turn, is expected to shift higher property taxes to the customer.

Continued inflation in building costs tends to increase fire insurance premiums. A similar insurance premium escalation clause provides that increased fire insurance premiums over the base year (the first year of the lease) will be paid by tenants. Similar stops relating to trash removal, music piped through the mall and tenant spaces, heating, electricity, and air conditioning costs are increasingly being subjected to escalator clauses.

Prospects for mortgage repayment are improved by lease terms that shift higher costs of operation to the tenant. In shopping center leases that may extend to twenty years, it is reasoned that tenants may transfer the burden of higher operating costs in the form of higher prices in sympathy with general price movements. The owner of leased property has less flexibility to recover increased costs of operation. In a sense these lease provisions define the owner's fiscal obligation over the lease and option terms.

Rent can be based on flat rate, percentage of sales or combo. (base against a %) Combo gives lender base on which to judge pro forma.

---

# Chapter 14

# Mortgage
# Credit
# Analysis

---

It will be recalled that a mortgage loan is secured by the pledge of real estate and the personal promise of the borrower. On the former, the value of the real estate secures the principal; on the latter, the credit of the borrower secures the principal. Opinion is divided on which security should be given the greatest weight in underwriting the mortgage. Some lenders hold that the credit status and financial ability of the borrower may change unpredictably and that the best security for the loan lies in the real estate and not in the varying credit status of the borrower.

The alternative position is expressed by lenders who claim that real estate values are subject to considerable variation. The risk assumed in changing real estate values recommends, according to this view, heavy reliance on the financial status of the borrower. Advocates of this position believe the mortgage payment is made by individuals with satisfactory credit. If this latter view is taken, more weight will be given to credit analysis; less weight will be given to property values.

Probably there is no single answer satisfactory to all lenders. In some cases the risk associated with a particular property will call for a lower loan to value ratio or an unusually stronger credit rating. Conversely, a weak financial position could be overcome by varying mortgage terms according to the risk or by a well secured real estate security. In this chapter attention is especially directed to the financial analysis of the borrower. Because the analysis varies by type of property, the first portion of the chapter reviews credit analysis for single family dwelling loans separately from the credit analysis of income property.

Before covering credit analysis, it seems appropriate to review the new *Real Estate Settlement Procedures Act of 1974* as revised by the *Real Estate Settlement Procedures Act Amendments of 1975*. The burden of complying with this law lies with the mortgage lender who is required to furnish the proposed borrower certain information as part of the loan application. For this reason it seems convenient to detail these new requirements before covering techniques of credit analysis.

## Real Estate Settlement Procedures

The *Real Estate Settlement Procedures Act of 1974* (RESPA) was originally enacted—

> to further the national housing goal of encouraging homeownership by regulating certain lending practices and closing and settlement procedures in federally related mortgage transactions to the end that unnecessary costs and difficulties of purchasing housing are minimized, and for other purposes.

The 1974 act was amended by the *Real Estate Settlement Procedures Act Amendments of 1975*. Under this legislation mortgage lenders must follow several procedures which are itemized below. Detailed administrative requirements are provided by Regulation X issued by the Secretary of Housing and Urban Development.

*RESPA's purpose: uniform closing system, advance disclosure of settlement costs, eliminate kickbacks.*

### The Basic Requirements of RESPA

While it is not feasible to cover all details of the act, it is deemed relevant to list the main points that apply to mortgage administration. As a practical matter language of the act encompasses almost every mortgage loan involved in the purchase or transfer of one to four-family residential property. More specifically the act covers "federally related mortgage loans" which are defined as loans (1) secured by residential property designed for the occupancy of from one-to-four families and (2) made by a federally regulated or insured lender or insured, guaranteed or assisted by HUD, VA, or other federal agencies or intended to be sold by the originating lender to FNMA, FHLMC, GNMA or a financial institution from which it is to be purchased by the FHLMC.

1. *Distribution of Settlement Costs Booklet.* After June 30, 1976, this information booklet prepared or approved by HUD must be given or

mailed to the loan applicant *within three business days* of the time of the written loan application. The settlement booklet provides, in clear and concise language, an explanation of (a) each settlement cost; (b) the standard real estate settlement form; (c) escrow accounts; (d) the choices available to buyers in selecting persons to perform services incident to settlement; and (e) the unfair practices and unreasonable or unnecessary charges to be avoided by the prospective buyer.

**2.** *Advance Disclosure of Settlement Costs.* Lenders must give borrowers—at the time of loan application—a good faith estimate of the amount or range of settlement charges. Preprinted forms in the information booklet may be used for this purpose.

**3.** *Uniform Settlement Statement.* Both the buyer and seller must be given a prescribed form which the borrower has the right to inspect during the business day prior to settlement. This statement lists settlement charges including real estate commissions, lenders' fees, escrow reserve amounts, and title charges normal to closing a real estate transaction. See Exhibit 14.1.

The form includes charges separately contracted for by the buyer and seller (i.e., appraisal fees, termite inspection). Items paid directly by the buyer may be crossed out on the seller's statement; items paid directly by the seller may be crossed out on the buyer's statement. Further, on the day before settlement, the borrower has the right to inspect the settlement statements.

**4.** *Prohibition Against Kickback Fees.* Section 8 of the act prohibits payments of a fee, kickback, or thing of value which is merely incident to the real estate settlement. That is, payments or receipts, split fees or percentages of any charge made or received other than for services actually performed are clearly prohibited. The definition includes referral fees and unearned fees. The act is intended to prohibit payment of a portion of an attorney's fee to another attorney, lender or real estate agent for the referral of prospective clients, but does not prohibit payments pursuant to cooperative arrangements between real estate agents or brokers. Agreements between brokers to share commissions are permitted.

**5.** *Prohibition Against Seller's Selection of Title Company.* No seller may require, directly or indirectly, as a condition of selling the property, that title insurance must be purchased by the buyer from any particular title company. A seller who violates this provision is liable to the buyer in an amount equal to three times all charges made for the title insurance.

**6.** *Limitation on Escrow Deposits.* Generally the amount of escrow the lender may require at settlement and monthly charges thereafter for taxes, insurance and related items is limited.

# Exhibit 14.1
## Disclosure Settlement Statement

FORM APPROVED
OMB NO. 63-R-1501

HUD-1 REV. 5/76

| A. | | | B. | TYPE OF LOAN | |
|---|---|---|---|---|---|
| | | | 1. ☐ FHA  2. ☐ FmHA  3. ☐ CONV. UNINS. | | |
| U. S. DEPARTMENT OF HOUSING AND URBAN DEVELOPMENT | | | 4. ☐ VA  5. ☐ CONV. INS. | | |
| | | | 6. FILE NUMBER: | | 7. LOAN NUMBER: |
| **SETTLEMENT STATEMENT** | | | 8. MORTGAGE INSURANCE CASE NUMBER: | | |

C. *NOTE:  This form is furnished to give you a statement of actual settlement costs.  Amounts paid to and by the settlement agent are shown.  Items marked "(p.o.c.)" were paid outside the closing; they are shown here for informational purposes and are not included in the totals.*

| D. NAME OF BORROWER: | E. NAME OF SELLER: | F. NAME OF LENDER: |
|---|---|---|
| | | |

| G. PROPERTY LOCATION: | H. SETTLEMENT AGENT: | I. SETTLEMENT DATE: |
|---|---|---|
| | PLACE OF SETTLEMENT: | |

| J. | SUMMARY OF BORROWER'S TRANSACTION | | K. | SUMMARY OF SELLER'S TRANSACTION | |
|---|---|---|---|---|---|
| **100. GROSS AMOUNT DUE FROM BORROWER:** | | | **400. GROSS AMOUNT DUE TO SELLER:** | | |
| 101. Contract sales price | | | 401. Contract sales price | | |
| 102. Personal property | | | 402. Personal property | | |
| 103. Settlement charges to borrower *(line 1400)* | | | 403. | | |
| 104. | | | 404. | | |
| 105. | | | 405. | | |
| *Adjustments for items paid by seller in advance* | | | *Adjustments for items paid by seller in advance* | | |
| 106. City/town taxes        to | | | 406. City/town taxes        to | | |
| 107. County taxes        to | | | 407. County taxes        to | | |
| 108. Assessments        to | | | 408. Assessments        to | | |
| 109. | | | 409. | | |
| 110. | | | 410. | | |
| 111. | | | 411. | | |
| 112. | | | 412. | | |
| **120. GROSS AMOUNT DUE FROM BORROWER** | | | **420. GROSS AMOUNT DUE TO SELLER** | | |
| **200. AMOUNTS PAID BY OR IN BEHALF OF BORROWER:** | | | **500. REDUCTIONS IN AMOUNT DUE TO SELLER:** | | |
| 201. Deposit or earnest money | | | 501. Excess deposit *(see instructions)* | | |
| 202. Principal amount of new loan(s) | | | 502. Settlement charges to seller *(line 1400)* | | |
| 203. Existing loan(s) taken subject to | | | 503. Existing loan(s) taken subject to | | |
| 204. | | | 504. Payoff of first mortgage loan | | |
| 205. | | | 505. Payoff of second mortgage loan | | |
| 206. | | | 506. | | |
| 207. | | | 507. | | |
| 208. | | | 508. | | |
| 209. | | | 509. | | |
| *Adjustments for items unpaid by seller* | | | *Adjustments for items unpaid by seller* | | |
| 210. City/town taxes        to | | | 510. City/town taxes        to | | |
| 211. County taxes        to | | | 511. County taxes        to | | |
| 212. Assessments        to | | | 512. Assessments        to | | |
| 213. | | | 513. | | |
| 214. | | | 514. | | |
| 215. | | | 515. | | |
| 216. | | | 516. | | |
| 217. | | | 517. | | |
| 218. | | | 518. | | |
| 219. | | | 519. | | |
| **220. TOTAL PAID BY/FOR BORROWER** | | | **520. TOTAL REDUCTION AMOUNT DUE SELLER** | | |
| **300. CASH AT SETTLEMENT FROM/TO BORROWER** | | | **600. CASH AT SETTLEMENT TO/FROM SELLER** | | |
| 301. Gross amount due from borrower *(line 120)* | | | 601. Gross amount due to seller *(line 420)* | | |
| 302. Less amounts paid by/for borrower *(line 220)* | ( | ) | 602. Less reductions in amount due seller *(line 520)* | ( | ) |
| 303. CASH (☐ FROM) (☐ TO) BORROWER | | | 603. CASH (☐ TO) (☐ FROM) SELLER | | |

# Exhibit 14.1 *continued.*

| L.             SETTLEMENT CHARGES | PAID FROM BORROWER'S FUNDS AT SETTLEMENT | PAID FROM SELLER'S FUNDS AT SETTLEMENT |
|---|---|---|
| **700.** TOTAL SALES/BROKER'S COMMISSION based on price $       @    % = | | |
| *Division of Commission (line 700) as follows:* | | |
| 701. $      to | | |
| 702. $      to | | |
| 703. Commission paid at Settlement | | |
| 704. | | |
| **800.** ITEMS PAYABLE IN CONNECTION WITH LOAN | | |
| 801. Loan Origination Fee    % | | |
| 802. Loan Discount    % | | |
| 803. Appraisal Fee    to | | |
| 804. Credit Report    to | | |
| 805. Lender's Inspection Fee | | |
| 806. Mortgage Insurance Application Fee to | | |
| 807. Assumption Fee | | |
| 808. | | |
| 809. | | |
| 810. | | |
| 811. | | |
| **900.** ITEMS REQUIRED BY LENDER TO BE PAID IN ADVANCE | | |
| 901. Interest from    to    @ $    /day | | |
| 902. Mortgage Insurance Premium for    months to | | |
| 903. Hazard Insurance Premium for    years to | | |
| 904.    years to | | |
| 905. | | |
| **1000.** RESERVES DEPOSITED WITH LENDER | | |
| 1001. Hazard insurance    months @ $    per month | | |
| 1002. Mortgage insurance    months @ $    per month | | |
| 1003. City property taxes    months @ $    per month | | |
| 1004. County property taxes    months @ $    per month | | |
| 1005. Annual assessments    months @ $    per month | | |
| 1006.    months @ $    per month | | |
| 1007.    months @ $    per month | | |
| 1008.    months @ $    per month | | |
| **1100.** TITLE CHARGES | | |
| 1101. Settlement or closing fee    to | | |
| 1102. Abstract or title search    to | | |
| 1103. Title examination    to | | |
| 1104. Title insurance binder    to | | |
| 1105. Document preparation    to | | |
| 1106. Notary fees    to | | |
| 1107. Attorney's fees    to | | |
| *(includes above items numbers;*    ) | | |
| 1108. Title insurance    to | | |
| *(includes above items numbers;*    ) | | |
| 1109. Lender's coverage    $ | | |
| 1110. Owner's coverage    $ | | |
| 1111. | | |
| 1112. | | |
| 1113. | | |
| **1200.** GOVERNMENT RECORDING AND TRANSFER CHARGES | | |
| 1201. Recording fees: Deed $    ; Mortgage $    ; Releases $ | | |
| 1202. City/county tax/stamps: Deed $    ; Mortgage $ | | |
| 1203. State tax/stamps: Deed $    ; Mortgage $ | | |
| 1204. | | |
| 1205. | | |
| **1300.** ADDITIONAL SETTLEMENT CHARGES | | |
| 1301. Survey    to | | |
| 1302. Pest inspection    to | | |
| 1303. | | |
| 1304. | | |
| 1305. | | |
| **1400.** TOTAL SETTLEMENT CHARGES *(enter on lines 103, Section J and 502, Section K)* | | |

HUD-1 REV. 5/76

Exhibit 14.2

## Exhibit 14.2
## Residential Loan Application Form

**RESIDENTIAL LOAN APPLICATION**

| MORTGAGE APPLIED FOR | Type | Amount | Interest Rate | No. of Months | Monthly Payment Principal & Interest | Escrow/Impounds (to be collected monthly) |
|---|---|---|---|---|---|---|
| | ☐Conv. ☐FHA ☐VA | $ | % | | $ | ☐Taxes ☐Hazard Ins. ☐MI ☐ |

Prepayment Option

**SUBJECT PROPERTY**

| Property Street Address | | City | | County | | State | Zip | No. Units |
|---|---|---|---|---|---|---|---|---|

| Legal Description (Attach description if necessary) | Year Built | Property is: ☐ Fee ☐ Leasehold ☐Condo ☐PUD ☐DeMinimis PUD |
|---|---|---|

Purpose of Loan: ☐ Purchase ☐ Construction-Perm. ☐ Construction ☐ Refinance ☐ Other (Explain)

| Complete this line if Construction-Perm. or Construction Loan | Lot Value Data | Original Cost | Present Value (a) | Cost of Imps. (b) | Total (a+b) | ENTER TOTAL AS PURCHASE PRICE IN DETAILS OF PURCHASE |
|---|---|---|---|---|---|---|
| Year Acquired | | $ | $ | $ | $ | |

| Complete this line if a Refinance Loan | Purpose of Refinance | Describe Improvement [ ] made [ ] to be made |
|---|---|---|
| Year Acquired | Original Cost | Amt. Existing Liens | | Cost: $ |
| | $ | $ | | |

| Title Will Vest in What Names? | How Will Title Be Held? (Tenancy) |
|---|---|

| Note Will Be Signed By? | Source of Down Payment and Settlement Charges? |
|---|---|

| **BORROWER** | | | | | **CO-BORROWER*** | | | |
|---|---|---|---|---|---|---|---|---|
| Name | | Age | Sex** | School Yrs | Name | | Age | Sex** School Yrs |
| Present Address | No. Years | ☐ Own | ☐ Rent | | Present Address | No. Years | ☐ Own | ☐ Rent |
| Street | | | | | Street | | | |
| City/State/Zip | | | | | City/State/Zip | | | |

Former address if less than 2 years at present address

| Street | | | | | Street | | | |
|---|---|---|---|---|---|---|---|---|
| City/State/Zip | | | | | City/State/Zip | | | |
| Years at former address | | ☐ Own | ☐ Rent | | Years at former address | | ☐ Own | ☐ Rent |

| Marital Status | ☐Married Yrs. ☐Unmarried ☐Separated | (Check One)** ☐ American Indian ☐ Negro/Black ☐ Oriental ☐ Spanish American ☐ Other Minority ☐ White (Non-minority) | Marital Status | ☐Married Yrs. ☐Unmarried ☐Separated | (Check One)** ☐ American Indian ☐ Negro/Black ☐ Oriental ☐ Spanish American ☐ Other Minority ☐ White (Non-minority) |
|---|---|---|---|---|---|

Dependents other than Co-Borrower / Dependents other than listed by Borrower

| Number | Ages | | Number | Ages | |
|---|---|---|---|---|---|

| Name and Address of Employer | Years employed in this line of work or profession? _____ years Years on this job _____ ☐Self Employed*** | Name and Address of Employer | Years employed in this line of work or profession? _____ years Years on this job _____ ☐Self Employed*** |
|---|---|---|---|

| Position/Title | Type of Business | Position/Title | Type of Business |
|---|---|---|---|

| **GROSS MONTHLY INCOME** | | | | **MONTHLY HOUSING EXPENSE** | | | **DETAILS OF PURCHASE** | |
|---|---|---|---|---|---|---|---|---|
| Item | Borrower | Co-Borrower | Total | | PREVIOUS | PROPOSED | | |
| Base Income | $ | $ | $ | Rent | | | a. Purchase Price | $ |
| Overtime | | | | First Mortgage (P&I) | | $ | b. Total Closing Costs | |
| Bonuses | | | | Other Financing (P&I) | | | c. Pre Paid Escrows | |
| Commissions | | | | Hazard Insurance | | | d. Total (a + b + c) | $ |
| Dividends/Interest | | | | Taxes (Real Estate) | | | e. Amt. This Mortgage | ( ) |
| Net Rental Income | | | | Assessments | | | f. Other Financing | ( ) |
| Other (SEE SCHEDULE BELOW) | | | | Mortgage Insurance | | | g. Present Equity in Lot | ( ) |
| | | | | Homeowner Assn. Dues | | | h. Amt. of Deposit | ( ) |
| | | | | Total Monthly Pmt | $ | $ | i. Closing costs paid by Seller | ( ) |
| | | | | Utilities | | | j. Cash required for closing | $ |
| Total | $ | $ | $ | Total | $ | $ | | |

**DESCRIBE OTHER INCOME**

B—Borrower C—Co-Borrower  NOTE: ALIMONY/CHILD SUPPORT PAYMENTS NEED NOT BE LISTED UNLESS THEIR CONSIDERATION IS DESIRED

| | Monthly Amt. |
|---|---|
| | $ |

**IF EMPLOYED IN CURRENT POSITION FOR LESS THAN TWO YEARS COMPLETE THE FOLLOWING**

| B/C | Previous Employer/School | City/State | Type of Business | Position/Title | Dates From/To | Monthly Salary |
|---|---|---|---|---|---|---|
| | | | | | | $ |

**QUESTIONS APPLY TO BOTH BORROWERS**

If Yes, explain on attached sheet

| | Borrower Yes or No | Co-Borrower Yes or No | | Borrower Yes or No | Co-Borrower Yes or No |
|---|---|---|---|---|---|
| Have you any outstanding judgments, ever taken bankruptcy, had property foreclosed upon, or given deed in lieu thereof? | | | Do you have health and accident insurance? | | |
| Co-Maker or endorser on any notes? | | | Do you have major medical coverage? | | |
| Defendant/Participant in a Law Suit? | | | Do you intend to occupy property? | | |
| Obligated for child support/alimony payments? | | | Will this property be your primary residence? | | |
| Any portion of the down payment borrowed? | | | Have you previously owned a home? | | |
| | | | Value of previously owned home | $ | $ |

*Complete this section and all other co-borrower questions about spouse if the spouse will be jointly obligated with the borrower on the loan or if the borrower is relying on the spouse's income or on community property in obtaining the loan.
**This information is requested only for statistical purposes in accordance with the intent of fair housing law. Furnishing this information is voluntary, but borrowers are urged to do so. No lending decision will be made on the basis of this information or on whether or not it is furnished.
***FHLMC requires self employed to furnish signed copies of one or more most recent Federal Tax Returns or audited Profit and Loss Statements. FNMA requires business credit report, signed Federal income Tax returns for last two years, and, if available, audited P/L plus balance sheet for same period.

FHLMC 65 Rev. 3/76                                                         FNMA 1003 Rev. 3/76

# Exhibit 14.2 *continued.*

This Statement and any applicable supporting schedules may be completed jointly by both married and unmarried co-borrowers if their assets and liabilities are sufficiently joined so that the Statement can be meaningfully and fairly presented on a combined basis; otherwise separate Statements and Schedules are required (FHLMC 65A/FNMA 1003A). If the co-borrower section was completed about spouse, complete this statement and supporting schedules about spouse also.

☐ Completed Jointly ☐ Not Completed Jointly

| ASSETS | | | LIABILITIES AND PLEDGED ASSETS | | |
|---|---|---|---|---|---|
| Description | | Cash or Market Value | Owed To (Name, Address and Account Number) | Mo. Pmt. and Mos. left to pay | Unpaid Balance |
| Cash Toward Purchase held by | | | Indicate by (*) which will be satisfied upon sale or upon refinancing of subject property. | | |
| | | | Installment Debt (include "revolving" charge accounts) | $ Pmt./Mos. / | $ |
| Checking and Savings Accounts (Indicate names of Institutions/Acct. Nos.) | | | | / | |
| | | | | / | |
| | | | | / | |
| Stocks and Bonds (No./description) | | | | / | |
| | | | | / | |
| Life Insurance Net Cash Value *Face Amount ($* | | | Automobile Loan | | |
| SUBTOTAL LIQUID ASSETS | | | | | |
| Real Estate Owned (*Enter Total Market Value from Real Estate Schedule*) | | | Real Estate Loans (Itemize and Identify Lender) | / | |
| Vested Interest in Retirement Fund | | | | | |
| Net Worth of Business Owned (ATTACH FINANCIAL STATEMENT) | | | | | |
| Auto (Make and Year) | | | Other Debt Including Stock Pledges (Itemize) | | |
| | | | | / | |
| Furniture and Personal Property | | | Alimony and Child Support Payments | | |
| Other Assets (Itemize) | | | | / | |
| | | | TOTAL MONTHLY PAYMENTS | $ | |
| TOTAL ASSETS | A. $ | | NET WORTH (A.−B.) $ | TOTAL LIABILITIES | B. $ |

## SCHEDULE OF REAL ESTATE OWNED (If Additional Properties Owned Attach Separate Schedule)

| Address of Property (Indicate S if Sold, PS if Pending Sale or R if Rental being held for income) | Type of Property | Present Market Value | Amount of Mortgages & Liens | Gross Rental Income | Mortgage Payments | Taxes, Ins. Maintenance and Misc. | Net Rental Income |
|---|---|---|---|---|---|---|---|
| | | | | | | | |
| | | | | | | | |
| | | | | | | | |
| TOTALS → | | | | | | | |

## LIST PREVIOUS CREDIT REFERENCES

| B—Borrower   C—Co-Borrower | Owed To (Name and Address) | Account Number | Purpose | Highest Balance | Date Paid |
|---|---|---|---|---|---|
| | | | | $ | |
| | | | | | |
| | | | | | |

AGREEMENT: The undersigned hereby applies for the loan described herein to be secured by a first mortgage or trust deed on the property described herein and represents that no part of said premises will be used for any purpose forbidden by law or restriction and that all statements made in this application are true and made for the purpose of obtaining the loan. Verification may be obtained from any source named herein. The original or a copy of this application will be retained by the lender even if the loan is not granted.

I fully understand that it is a federal crime punishable by fine or imprisonment or both to knowingly make any false statements concerning any of the above facts, as applicable under the provisions of Title 18, United States Code, Section 1014.

Signature (Borrower) _____ Date _____ Signature (Co-Borrower) _____ Date _____

Home Phone _____ Business Phone _____ Home Phone _____ Business Phone _____

The Federal Equal Credit Opportunity Act prohibits creditors from discriminating against credit applicants on the basis of sex or marital status. The Federal Agency which administers compliance with this law concerning this _____ is _____
(type of lender)        (regulatory agency and address)

Additionally the Federal Fair Housing Act also prohibits discrimination on the basis of race, color, religion, sex or national origin.

## FOR LENDER'S USE ONLY

(FNMA REQUIREMENT ONLY) This application was taken by _____ , a full time employee of
                                                  Interviewer

_____ , in a face to face interview with the prospective borrower.
(Name of Lender)

## Impact on Lenders

As this act is administered, most lenders ask the buyer, seller, and real estate agent to supply information the lender needs under RESPA to prepare the advance disclosure statement at the time of loan application. Ideally, the lender would be advised to make the advance disclosure at the time of loan application. Since the time of compliance is tied to the loan application and the actual commitment, considerable care must be taken in identifying these dates.

# Credit Analysis for Single Family Dwelling Loans

Underwriters of single family dwellings face two central questions relating, first, to the ability of the borrower to make the proposed mortgage payments and, secondly, to his or her willingness to satisfy long-term credit obligations. This two part analysis starts with the loan application.

## The Loan Application

Some mortgage lenders prefer a preliminary application form. This one-page source of information gives details of the price and main characteristics of the dwelling and a summary of the borrower's financial status, income, and terms of the proposed loan. The advantage of the preliminary form lies in the screening out of loan applicants who are poorly qualified for the requested loan. Probably there are circumstances where this approach helps in counseling the unqualified borrower and it saves considerable effort and time if the loan has little chance of approval.

For those cases in which the loan application is completed by an attorney, a real estate broker, or loan originator in the office, probably considerable screening has taken place before the applicant prepares a formal loan application. In this event a more detailed form is completed serving as the foundation for this analysis of borrower credit. Exhibit 14.2 illustrates the more complete form of a loan application.

Note that the form summarizes the details of the property offered for security including any outstanding liens or mortgages. Sufficient personal detail is given to guide the analysis. Personal data include a statement of income and assets of the borrower. Credit data reveal outstanding obligations, terms of repayments and other financial data. This form serves as the basis for mortgage credit analysis and is supplemented by other verifying documents.

Certain precautionary steps must be followed if the application is submitted by a new borrower. The prospect should be told that the application includes information for the analysis of the loan transaction, that such information helps determine if a borrower can be expected to make the anticipated mortgage payments and that careful analysis of the application prevents borrowers from assuming obligations that are impossible to satisfy. If the borrower is approached in this way, he or she probably gives more accurate information and reduces subsequent investigative expenses.

## The Equal Credit Opportunity Act

*ECOA*

Effective October 20, 1975, the Equal Credit Opportunity Act amended the Consumer Credit Protection Act (Public Law 90-321) by adding a new section which provided—

> It shall be unlawful for any creditor to discriminate against any applicant on the basis of sex or marital status with respect to any aspect of a credit transaction. (Section 701)

In the words of the act, congressional policy was based on the following statement:

> The Congress finds that there is a need to insure that the various financial institutions and other firms engaged in the extensions of credit exercise their responsibility to make credit available with fairness, impartiality, and without discrimination on the basis of sex or marital status. . . .

It is the purpose of the act to require that financial institutions and other firms engaged in the extension of credit make credit equally available to all credit worthy customers without regard to sex or marital status. The Equal Credit Opportunity Act amendments of 1976 add race, color, religion, national origin, and age to the categories of prohibited discrimination.

With respect to judging mortgage credit certain regulations issued by the Federal Reserve Board as Regulation B deserve comment. The main points that affect mortgage processing include:

1. *Credit scoring on the basis of marital status.* The Regulation forbids the use of sex or marital status in credit scoring systems.
2. *Reasons for denying credit.* Upon the request of an applicant, creditors are required to provide the reasons for terminating or denying credit. and where info obtained.
3. *Childbearing.* Creditors may not inquire into birth control practices or into childbearing capabilities or intentions, or assume, from her age, that an applicant or an applicant's spouse may drop out of the labor force due to childbearing and thus have an interruption of income.

4. *Income.* A creditor may not discount part-time income but may examine the probable continuity of the applicant's job. A creditor may ask and consider whether and to what extent an applicant's income is affected by obligations to make alimony, child support or maintenance payments. Further, a creditor may ask to what extent an applicant is relying on alimony or child support or maintenance payments to repay the debt being incurred. *But the applicant must first be informed that no such disclosure is necessary if the applicant does not rely on such income to obtain the credit.* Where an applicant chooses to rely on alimony, a creditor shall consider such payments as income to the extent the payments are likely to be made consistently. [Emphasis supplied]

5. *Recordkeeping.* Creditors must keep applications and related materials, including any written charges submitted by the applicant alleging discrimination for 15 months following the date the creditor gives the applicant notice of action. For all accounts established on or after November 1, 1976, the creditor must identify for consumer reporting agencies or others to whom the creditor furnishes information those accounts that both spouses may use or for which they are both liable, so that the credit history can be utilized in the name of each spouse. No later than February 1, 1977, the creditor is required to inform holders of accounts existing prior to November 1, 1976, of a similar right to have credit history reported in both names.

Enforcement of the act is provided by the right of the aggrieved applicant to file suit against creditors for actual and punitive damages up to $10,000, the right to bring a class action lawsuit on behalf of a group of aggrieved applicants, or by the action of federal agencies.

For the purposes of this act, discrimination on the basis of sex or marital status is viewed as treating "an applicant less favorably than other applicants on the basis of sex or marital status." In fact, Regulation B requires that loan officers give mortgage applicants the following notice:

The Federal Equal Credit Opportunity Act prohibits creditors from discriminating against credit applicants on the basis of sex or marital status. The Federal agency which administers compliance with this law concerning this (insert appropriate description—bank, store, etc.) is (name and address of the appropriate agency).

Both the spouses are entitled to the credit history of the account where both are contractually liable for the account or are allowed to use it.

Special consumer compliance team of Fed Reserve is auditing banks for enforcement

Additionally, applicants are entitled to a statement of the reasons for denial or termination of credit, at the applicant's request.

While much of the interpretation of the new act will rest with legal counsel, the regulation provides that for an applicant seeking credit, who relies on the credit worthiness of the non-applicant spouse, the lender may request and consider any information that might be considered about the spouse. Further, lenders may require the signature of both husband and wife where state law requires both signatures to pass clear title, to create liens or waive potential rights to property or to assign earnings. In passing on a mortgage application, therefore, loan officers must work closely with legal counsel to insure that Regulation B is followed in passing on mortgage credit.

## Analyzing Borrower Ability to Pay

The three main elements of this analysis relate to the *anticipated income, a review of assets and liabilities* and the *estimated housing expenses,* including the proposed mortgage payments. With favorable relationships in the three items, approval of borrower credit largely depends on the willingness of the borrower to satisfy debts.

### Anticipated income

The key issue in evaluating borrower income relates to the amount of income that can be reliably expected over the early years of the loan and its relative stability. While it is most difficult to make predictions over the life of the loan, it is critically important to make sure that the amount of income during the initial life of the mortgage is sufficient to pay the borrower's anticipated lending cost and mortgage service in addition to other debts.

*(1) Current Income.* Consequently, mortgage lenders redefine annual personal income for mortgage purposes in terms of *effective income*: Effective income refers to that income which is reasonably certain less nonrecurring income earned on an infrequent basis. According to HUD, effective income "is the estimated amount of the mortgagor's earning capacity that is likely to prevail, . . . over the first five years of the [mortgage] term." (Mortgage Credit Analysis Handbook, 4155.1, Washington, D.C.: HUD, July, 1972 as amended, p. 1-29.)

Examples of income that normally would not be included in the effective income would be Christmas bonuses, overtime pay, and possibly nonrepetitive income of short duration such as royalties, profits, commissions, extra dividends and the like. Normally the borrower would report income from all sources including income which is likely to be nonrecurring. The mortgage loan officer must recalculate income to eliminate incomes of a temporary nature.

In measuring the financial capacity of the borrower, some lenders are guided by the *net effective income* which HUD defines as effective income less the estimated Federal Income Tax. The estimate is made by reference to IRS tables showing Federal Income Tax withholding rates applicable to monthly income. It would seem equally valid to consider monthly income after deducting state income taxes and social security payments. With these deductions the lender may compute the borrower's actual monthly "take-home" pay with his total obligations.

In calculating effective income, remember that the law requires income from an employed spouse to be included in the borrower's income for mortgage credit purposes. Since the estimation of effective income tends to be very subjective, it is good practice to require the borrower to submit an income statement (even federal personal income tax statements) over the preceding five years. Income from bonuses or profits then may be judged with respect to the past experience of income that could be expected in the future. The next issue is to judge the relative stability of income.

*(2) Stability of Income.* Though subject to certain exceptions, stable incomes typically are found among middle income groups such as junior management, borrowers practicing the professions, namely, lawyers, accountants, architects, white collar trades and skilled workers, government employees and utility personnel. At the other extreme are professional groups subject to highly varying incomes—musicians, entertainers, salesmen, actors, and writers. Because of the likelihood of income interruption among certain income groups, the standard procedure is to ask for a record of past income to establish some reasonable average of expected income.

In this regard, verification of employment is a valuable information source. Employment verification shows how long the person has been employed, and usually verification includes comments on prospects for promotion or higher salaries in the immediate future. Most loan applications call for a history of employment that indicates a degree of stability. Frequent job changes may call for a cautious reexamination of borrower qualifications. Exhibit 14.3 illustrates an employment verification used for this purpose.

## Assets and liabilities

The first question to resolve concerns cash assets sufficient to meet the down payment and closing costs. After this question is resolved, it is relevant to determine if the borrower has reserves that would substitute for income loss in times of family emergencies. Since the asset position depends on savings and checking accounts, it is customary to verify deposits. A typical deposit verification form is illustrated in Exhibit 14.4.

# Exhibit 14.3
# Employment Verification Form

Previous Editions Obsolete

FHA FORM NO. 2004-G Rev. 5/75
VA FORM NO. 26-8497 Rev. 5/75

VETERANS ADMINISTRATION
and
U. S. DEPARTMENT OF HOUSING AND URBAN DEVELOPMENT
FEDERAL HOUSING ADMINISTRATION

FORM APPROVED
OMB NO. 63-R1288

## REQUEST FOR VERIFICATION OF EMPLOYMENT

INSTRUCTIONS: Lender – Complete Items 1 through 6. Have applicant complete Items 7 and 8. Forward the completed form directly to the employer named in Item 1.
Employer – Complete Items 9A through 15 and return form directly to lender named in Item 2.

### PART I    REQUEST

| 1. TO: (Name and Address of Employer): | 2. FROM: (Name and Address of Lender): |
|---|---|

| 3. Signature of Lender: | 4. Title of Lender: | 5. Date: | 6. HUD-FHA or VA Number: |
|---|---|---|---|

I certify that this verification has been sent directly to the employer and has not passed through the hands of the applicant or any other interested party.

I have applied for a mortgage loan and stated that I am employed by you. My signature below authorizes verification of this information.

| 7. Name and Address of Applicant: | 8. Employee's Identification Number: _____ |
|---|---|
| | Signature of applicant |

### PART II    VERIFICATION

| 9 A. Is applicant now employed by you? ☐ Yes ☐ No | 10A. Position or Job Title: | 11. TO BE COMPLETED BY MILITARY PERSONNEL ONLY. |
|---|---|---|

9B. Present Base Pay is $ _____

This amount is paid:
☐ Annually ☐ Hourly
☐ Monthly ☐ Other (Specify)
☐ Weekly

Pay Grade:

10B. Length of Applicant's employment:

| | | |
|---|---|---|
| Base Pay | $ | |
| Rations | $ | |

9C. EARNINGS LAST 12 MONTHS

Amount $

Basic Earnings $

Normal Hours worked per Week:

Overtime Earnings $ _____
☐ Regular
☐ Temporary

Other Income $ _____
☐ Regular
☐ Temporary

10C. Probability of continued employment:

10D. Date Applicant left:

10E. Reason for leaving:

| | |
|---|---|
| Flight or Hazard | $ |
| Clothing | $ |
| Quarters | $ |
| Pro-Pay | $ |
| Overseas or Combat | $ |

12. REMARKS:

| 13. Signature of Employer: | 14. Title of Employer: | 15. Date: |
|---|---|---|

**RETURN DIRECTLY TO LENDER**

☆ G. P. O. 1976 — 641-224 / 633. REGION NO. 4

## Exhibit 14.4
## Deposit Verification Form

**Federal National Mortgage Association**

# REQUEST FOR VERIFICATION OF DEPOSIT

*INSTRUCTIONS:* LENDER - Complete Items 1 thru 8. Have applicant(s) complete Item 9. Forward directly to depository named in Item 1.
DEPOSITORY - Please complete Items 10 thru 15 and return DIRECTLY to lender named in Item 2.

### PART I - REQUEST

| 1. TO (Name and address of depository) | 2. FROM (Name and address of lender) |
|---|---|

| 3. SIGNATURE OF LENDER | 4. TITLE | 5. DATE | 6. LENDER'S NUMBER (Optional) |
|---|---|---|---|

7. INFORMATION TO BE VERIFIED

| TYPE OF ACCOUNT | ACCOUNT IN NAME OF | ACCOUNT NUMBER | BALANCE |
|---|---|---|---|
| | | | $ |
| | | | $ |
| | | | $ |
| | | | $ |

TO DEPOSITORY. I have applied for a mortgage loan and stated in my financial statement that the balance on deposit with you is as shown above. You are authorized to verify this information and to supply the lender identified above with the information requested in Items 10 thru 12. Your response is solely a matter of courtesy for which no responsibility is attached to your institution or any of your officers.

| 8. NAME AND ADDRESS OF APPLICANT(s) | 9. SIGNATURE OF APPLICANT(s) |
|---|---|

## TO BE COMPLETED BY DEPOSITORY

### PART II - VERIFICATION OF DEPOSITORY

10. DEPOSIT ACCOUNTS OF APPLICANT(s)

| TYPE OF ACCOUNT | ACCOUNT NUMBER | CURRENT BALANCE | AVERAGE BALANCE FOR PREVIOUS TWO MONTHS | DATE OPENED |
|---|---|---|---|---|
| | | $ | $ | |
| | | $ | $ | |
| | | $ | $ | |
| | | $ | $ | |

11. LOANS OUTSTANDING TO APPLICANT(s)

| LOAN NUMBER | DATE OF LOAN | ORIGINAL AMOUNT | CURRENT BALANCE | INSTALLMENTS (Monthly/Quarterly) | SECURED BY | NUMBER OF LATE PAYMENTS |
|---|---|---|---|---|---|---|
| | | $ | $ | $ per | | |
| | | $ | $ | $ per | | |
| | | $ | $ | $ per | | |

12. ADDITIONAL INFORMATION WHICH MAY BE OF ASSISTANCE IN DETERMINATION OF CREDIT WORTHINESS:
(Please include information on loans paid-in-full as in Item 11 above)

Subject to the requirements of the Fair Credit Reporting Act, the information provided in Items 10 thru 12 is furnished to you in strict confidence in response to your request. The accuracy of such information is not guaranteed.

| 13. SIGNATURE OF DEPOSITORY | 14. TITLE | 15. DATE |
|---|---|---|

This form is to be transmitted directly to the lender and is not to be transmitted through the applicant or any other party.

FNMA Form 1006
*Rev. Dec. 75*

★ ★ ★ ★ THIS FORM MUST BE REPRODUCED BY LENDER ★ ★ ★ ★

In determining liabilities, the loan application will identify instalment debt or other recurring obligations of the borrower. By citing the remaining balance of monthly payments it may be determined if the income is sufficient to pay total obligations and family expenses, considering the proposed loan.

In considering net worth, care must be taken to guard against the over valuation of real estate, especially vacant land, and other assets such as household furniture and personal property. Moreover, these are typically nonliquid assets, and if they are over valued, they may give a false indication of the borrower's ability to pay in times of income decline.

## Willingness to pay

Probably the most important document indicating a willingness to pay is a credit report. Credit reporting agencies include information on employment, past credit deficiencies, and any judgments that may have been filed against the potential borrower. A credit report must be supplemented by other related information.

The interviewer must evaluate the motivation of the borrower in applying for the loan. In the case of a mortgage on a single family dwelling, family and social relationships are critical items for review.

To a large degree a borrower with a substantial down payment demonstrates a higher motivation to continue payments than a borrower who negotiates for nominal down payments and monthly payments of little more than monthly rent. Occasionally it will be found that the applicant is seeking a loan for personal reasons not associated with home ownership, i.e., to meet personal expenses, business expenses, or for nonrelated housing purposes. Failure of the borrower to establish a savings account or to support insurance programs suggests a low motivation. If these indications are associated with bankruptcy, judgment suits and other legal actions, there would be logical reasons to question the loan.

Where the lender's decision to turn down an applicant's request for credit is based in any way on information received from a credit reporting agency, the Fair Credit Reporting Act requires the lender to supply the applicant with the name and address of the agency making the report. Where the unfavorable information came from a source other than a credit reporting agency, the lender must inform the applicant of his right to make a written request as to the nature of this information. Subsequent disclosure of the nature of the information to the applicant upon such written request is required.

## Housing expenses

It is a cardinal rule that borrowers are unlikely to change their consumption patterns over the short run. Spending habits are slow to change and when they do change it is usually only after a painful adjustment. For this reason, a review of past housing expenses in the light of the new mortgage and an associated new house purchase deserves careful scrutiny. An estimate of housing expenses including mortgage payments, insurance, property taxes on a monthly pro rata basis, and utility expenses provides the mortgage officer with data to compare with the stabilized, effective income. The loan must conform to these two rules: (1) Housing expenses should not increase dramatically over past experience, and (2) housing expenses should compare favorably with effective income. For this purpose monthly housing expenses would include:

1. Mortgage principal
2. Mortgage insurance premium (FHA or PMI)
3. Service charges, if any
4. Hazard insurance
5. Taxes and special assessment payments
6. Maintenance and repair expenses
7. Heating and other utility charges
8. Homeowner Association assessments (cooperatives, condominiums, planned unit developments).

In this respect, lenders have been inclined to say that the mortgage payment should not be more than 25 percent of income. Generally speaking low and moderate income families tend to pay a higher proportion of income to housing, while upper income groups show a declining proportion of housing expenses. Between these extremes are the middle income groups who conform pretty closely to the 25 percent rule. Recent evidence suggests that under a conservative lending policy this ratio is being lowered.

Price increases in food and energy have caused consumers to allocate more of their budget to nonhousing expenses. For example, records of the Bureau of Labor Statistics indicate that from 1962 to 1967 a family of four would allocate about 20 percent of its annual gross income to food, 25 percent to housing and 19 percent to taxes. Continuing trends suggest that the proportion to housing will drop to 23 percent of average gross annual income.

Consider the average monthly mortgage payment required in 1965: A $107 payment for a new single family dwelling which sold for $22,900 with an average loan of $16,923 and a conventional mortgage of 5.74 percent interest at 24.8 years.

By 1974 these figures had increased to a $240 per month payment for a new home purchase of $39,700 with a loan of $29,700 on a conventional mortgage 8.86 percent interest for 26.2 years. These data suggest most strongly that the underwriting rule of allowing mortgage payments to rise to 25 percent of annual gross income probably must be adjusted downward.

Another general guideline has been developed by FHA to determine the adequacy of net effective income: For loans on single family dwellings, net effective income is considered adequate if *total monthly housing expenses* (mortgage payments, insurance, taxes, repairs and utilities) are not more than *35 percent* of net effective income (net effective income is defined as effective income less Federal Income Taxes).

Still another FHA guide to determining the adequacy of income relates *total obligations* of the borrower to net effective income. Total obligations include monthly housing expenses and other recurring charges such as state income taxes, retirement deductions, life insurance premiums, and loan payments. As a general rule, FHA considers effective income as adequate for a specific mortgage if the borrower's total obligations do not exceed *50 percent* of net effective income (Mortgage Credit Analysis Handbook, *op. cit.*).

To be sure these rules must be taken *cum grano salis*—with a grain of salt. A young professional with excellent prospects for rising income would probably represent a good mortgage risk though his or her financial ratios were marginal at best. By the same token, a person with substantial assets with only a minimum income relative to the requested loan would probably be rated more highly than a borrower with a higher income of less stability and with a lower asset position. Weighing the importance of these items calls for experienced judgment and a case by case analysis of each borrower.

## The HUD Rating System

It will be recognized that the evaluation of mortgage credit risks is highly subjective. To focus attention on the elements deemed important to credit analysis and to make this process more objective HUD employs a rating system to judge mortgage credit. As shown in Exhibit 14.5 the evaluation of mortgage risks depends on six factors.

Each of the factors used to evaluate mortgagor risks are rated "acceptable" or "rejected." The mortgage is not approved if one of the six factors are rated as rejected. In judging *credit characteristics of the mortgagor* HUD includes—Character; Credit history; Family life and relationship, Attitude toward obligations; and Ability to manage affairs.

When judging the first item, it is assumed that past performance serves as the most reliable guide in forecasting the borrower's probability of meeting mortgage payments. Similarly, a harmonious domestic relationship minimizes the chance of foreclosure. Likewise the attitude toward obligations (determined from other lenders), and a record of prompt payment of personal obligations contributes to an acceptable rating.

### Exhibit 14.5
### Evaluation of Mortgagor Risk Report

| *Mortgagor Features* | *Rating* |
|---|---|
| 1. Credit Characteristics of Mortgagor | _____ |
| 2. Motivating Interest in Ownership of the Property | _____ |
| 3. Importance of Monetary Interest to Mortgagor | _____ |
| 4. Adequacy of Available Assets for Transaction | _____ |
| 5. Stability of Effective Income | _____ |
| 6. Adequacy of Effective Income for Total Obligations | _____ |
| Mortgagor Rating | _____ |

Source: *Mortgage Credit Analysis Handbook 4155.1*. Washington, D.C.: Departpartment of Housing and Urban Development, July, 1972 as amended, p. 2–3.

The second item, *motivating interest in ownership,* relates to those conditions which would tend to make a borrower want to continue owning the property even with a nominal monetary interest. Typically, motivating interest tends to be high for housing suitable to the family. According to HUD, a home that is designed, located and constructed to serve family needs indicates a strong motivation.

The importance of the *monetary interest of the borrower* is judged in relation to the amount of cash that the borrower has invested in the property. In some instances work to be performed or materials furnished by the borrower before closing the loan substitutes for a cash investment. The idea here is that the borrower who has invested a substantial portion of his net worth in the property will strive hard to protect his investment—at least compared to a borrower whose investment is limited only to a small portion of his net worth.

In judging the fourth item—*adequacy of available assets*—the mortgage analyst determines if the available assets are sufficient to close the loan transaction. By adhering to this rule, the borrower will hold the property free and clear of all liens after the mortgage has been approved and recorded. If the borrower is an operative-builder assets for the transaction include the net working capital (current assets less current liabilities). Rejecting borrowers who do not conform to this requirement eliminates irregular financing that may endanger the borrower's ability to meet first mortgage payments. In rating the fifth item, the *stability of effective income*, the lender considers all sources of income available to the borrower. Each source of income, however, is analyzed to determine whether it has the required stability for mortgage approval. Similarly, the last item, *adequacy of effective income for total obligations*, allows the lender to make certain that the loan proposed is within the ability of the borrower to satisfy mortgage payments. To help in this analysis HUD studies—

1. The mortgagor's past paying record
2. Evidence of previous saving, if any, out of income
3. Changes that have recently occurred in the amount of other obligations of the mortgagor
4. Changes that have recently occurred in the mortgagor's effective income
5. The effect of any increase or decrease in housing expenses on the amount of effective income remaining for other obligations and living expenses of the family.

As a rule the mortgage payments according to HUD regulations should not be more than the estimated monthly rental to property proposed for the loan.

Besides these points, there is a relation between the mortgage term and the remaining economic life of the building. Risk tends to decrease as the ratio of mortgage term to remaining economic life of the building is progressively less. In judging mortgage risks lenders generally agree that (1) loans for short terms are subject to less risk than loans for long terms, (2) shortening the term of a loan reduces risks by reducing the possibility of a decline in value that exceeds the rate of loan amortization, and (3) shortening the term of the loan may increase total monthly payments to the point that they increase the mortgage credit risk. In the latter case the gain in equity resulting from reducing the loan term may be offset by the loss of the borrower's ability to meet monthly payments.

These items are summarized on FHA Form 2900-2 shown in Exhibit 14.6. Note that in Section 18 the mortgage rating is summarized on the basis of the six factors considered by FHA. This form also reports other information considered by FHA, namely, assets, liabilities, employment, monthly income, settlement requirements, future monthly payments, and previous monthly housing expenses and fixed charges.

## The Mortgage Pattern

Up to this point analysis of the residential loan has concentrated on borrower credit. Before making the loan commitment, the borrower's

# Exhibit 14.6
# FHA Credit Analysis Form

Form Approved
OMB No 63—R1062

| U.S. DEPARTMENT OF HOUSING AND URBAN DEVELOPMENT<br>FEDERAL HOUSING ADMINISTRATION | 2. FHA Case No.<br>▲ |
|---|---|

**1. SPECIAL PROCESSING ▲**

1. ☐ Veteran    2. ☐ Assistance Payment    4. ☐ _____

### CREDIT ANALYSIS PAGE
**MORTGAGE TO BE INSURED UNDER**
☐ SEC. 203(b) ☐ SEC. _____

**3**

5.

**3. PROPERTY ADDRESS**

**4. MORTGAGORS:**

| | Soc. | | Sex ▲ ___ |
|---|---|---|---|
| Mtgor. | Sec. No. | | Age ▲ ___ |
| Co-Mtgor. | Soc Sec. No. | | Sex ▲ ___<br>Age ▲ ___ |

Address _____

| Married ▲ | Yrs. | No. of Dependents ▲ | | Ages ▲ |
|---|---|---|---|---|
| Co-Mortgagor(s) | | | Sex ▲ | Age(s) ▲ |

▲ *(Check One)*

1 ☐ White *(Non-Minority)*   3 ☐ American Indian   5 ☐ Spanish American

2 ☐ Negro/Black   4 ☐ Oriental   6 ☐ Other Minority

| 6.<br>MORTGAGE<br>APPLIED FOR ➡ | Mortgage Amount<br>$ | Interest Rate<br>% | No. of Months | Monthly Payment<br>Principal & Interest<br>$ |
|---|---|---|---|---|

**7. PURPOSE OF LOAN:** ▲   ☐ Finance Constr. on Own Land   ☐ Finance Purchase   ☐ Refinance Exist. Loan   ☐ Finance Impr. to Exist. Prop.   ☐ Other

**MORTGAGOR WILL BE:**   ☐ Occupant   ☐ Landlord   ☐ Builder   ☐ Escrow Commit. Mortgagor

| 8. ASSETS | |
|---|---|
| Cash accounts _____ | $ _____ |
| Marketable securities _____ | _____ |
| Other (explain) _____ | _____ |
| **OTHER ASSETS** (A) TOTAL ▲ | $ _____ |
| Cash deposit on purchase . . . . . . . . . . | _____ |
| Other (explain) _____ | _____ |
| _____ | _____ |
| _____ | _____ |
| (B) TOTAL | $ _____ |

| 9. LIABILITIES | Monthly Payt. | Unpd. Bal. |
|---|---|---|
| Automobile . . . . . . . . . . . . . . . . . . . . | $ ___ | $ ___ |
| Debts, other Real Estate . . . . . . . . . . . | ___ | ___ |
| Life Insurance Loans . . . . . . . . . . . . . | ___ | ___ |
| Notes payable . . . . . . . . . . . . . . . . . | ___ | ___ |
| Credit Union . . . . . . . . . . . . . . . | ___ | ___ |
| Retail accounts . . . . . . . . . . . . . . | ___ | ___ |
| _____ | ___ | ___ |
| _____ | ___ | ___ |
| _____ | ___ | ___ |
| TOTAL | $ | ▲ $ |

| 10. EMPLOYMENT | |
|---|---|
| Mortgagor's occupation _____ | |
| Employer's name & address _____ | |
| _____ years employed ___ | |
| Co-Mtgor. occupation _____ | |
| Employer's name & address _____ | |
| _____ years employed ___ | |

| 11. MONTHLY INCOME | |
|---|---|
| **EFFECTIVE INCOME** | **MONTHLY INCOME** |
| ▲ $ _____ . . . . . . Mortgagor's base pay . . . . ▲ $ _____ | |
| . . . . . . . . Other Earnings . . . . . . . . _____ | |
| ▲ _____ . . . . . Co-Mortgagor's base pay . . . ▲ _____ | |
| . . . . . . . . Other Earnings . . . . . . . . _____ | |
| . . . . . . Income, other Real Estate . . . . . _____ | |
| . . . . . . . . . . . . . Other . . . . . . _____ | |
| ▲ _____ . . . . . . . . . . TOTAL . . . . . . . . ▲ $ _____ | |
| . . . . . Less Federal Income . . . . . . . | |
| ▲ $ ___ NET EFFECTIVE INCOME | |

| 12. SETTLEMENT REQUIREMENTS | | |
|---|---|---|
| (a) Existing debt (Refinancing only) . . . . . $ ___ | $ ___ |
| (b) Sale price (Realty only) . . . . . . . . . . . ___ | ▲ ___ |
| (c) Repairs & Improvements . . . . . . . . . . . ___ | |
| (d) Closing Costs . . . . . . . . . . . . . . . . . ___ | ▲ ___ |
| (e) TOTAL (a+b+c+d) Acquisition cost ___ | ▲ ___ |
| (f) Mortgage amount . . . . . . . . . . . . . . ___ | |
| (g) Mortgagor's required investment(e-f) . . . ___ | |
| (h) Prepayable expenses . . . . . . . . . . . . . ___ | ___ |
| (i) Non-realty & other items . . . . . . . . . . . ___ | ___ |
| (j) TOTAL REQUIREMENTS (g+h+i) ___ | ___ |
| (k) Amt.pd. ☐ cash ☐ Other (explain) . . ___ | ___ |
| (l) Amt. to be pd. ☐ cash ☐ Other (explain) ___ | |
| (m) Tot. assets available for closing (B) (A) $ ___ | $ ___ |

| 13. FUTURE MONTHLY PAYMENTS | | |
|---|---|---|
| (a) Principal & Interest . . . . . . . . . . . . $ ___ | $ ___ |
| (b) FHA Mortgage Insurance Premium . . . . ___ | |
| (c) Ground rent (Leasehold only) . . . . . . . ___ | |
| (d) TOTAL DEBT SERVICE (a+b+c) . . . . ___ | |
| (e) Hazard Insurance . . . . . . . . . . . . . ___ | |
| (f) Taxes, special assessments . . . . . . . . ___ | ▲ ___ |
| (g) TOTAL MTG. PAYT. (d+e+f) . . . . . . ___ | ▲ ___ |
| (h) Maintenance & Common Expense . . . . . ___ | ▲ ___ |
| (i) Heat & utilities . . . . . . . . . . . . . . . ___ | |
| (j) TOTAL HSG. EXPENSE (g+h+i) . . . . . ___ | ▲ ___ |
| (k) Other recurring charges (explain) . . . . . ___ | |
| (l) TOTAL FIXED PAYT. (i+k) . . . . . . . $ ___ | ▲ $ ___ |

| 14. PREVIOUS MONTHLY HOUSING EXPENSE | |
|---|---|
| Mortgage payment or rent . . . . . . . . . . . . . . . . . . . . . . $ ___ |
| Hazard Insurance . . . . . . . . . . . . . . . . . . . . . . . . . ___ |
| Taxes, special assessments . . . . . . . . . . . . . . . . . . . ___ |
| Maintenance . . . . . . . . . . . . . . . . . . . . . . . . . . . . ___ |
| Heat & Utilities . . . . . . . . . . . . . . . . . . . . . . . . . . . ___ |
| Other (explain) . . . . . . . . . . . . . . . . . . . . . . . . . . . ___ |
| TOTAL ▲ $ ___ |

| 15. PREVIOUS MONTHLY FIXED CHARGES | |
|---|---|
| Federal, State & Local income taxes . . . . . . . . . . . . . . . $ ___ |
| Prem. for $ _____ Life Insurance . . . . . . . . . . . ___ |
| Social Security & Retirement Payments . . . . . . . . . . . . . ___ |
| Installment account payments . . . . . . . . . . . . . . . . . . . ___ |
| Operating Expenses, other Real Estate . . . . . . . . . . . . . ___ |
| Other (explain) . . . . . . . . . . . . . . . . . . . . . . . . . . . ___ |
| TOTAL $ ___ |

| 16. Do you own other Real Estate ☐ Yes ☐ No | Is it to be sold ☐ Yes ☐ No | FHA mortgage ☐ Yes ☐ No | Sales Price $ ___ | Orig-Mtg. Amt. $ ___ |
|---|---|---|---|---|
| Unpaid Bal. $ ___ | Address ___ | | | Lender ___ |

**17. RATIOS:** Loan to Value ___ % : Term to Remain. Econ. Life ___ % : Total Payt. to Rental Value ___ % : Debt Serv. to Rent Inc. ___ %

**18. MORTGAGOR RATING** ___

Credit Characteristics _____   Motivating Interest in Ownership _____   Importance of Monetary Interest _____

Adequacy of Available Assets _____   Stability of Effective Income _____   Adequacy of Effective Income _____

Remarks:

☐ Head of Household

Ratio of net effective income to:

Housing Expense _____ %

Total Fixed Payment _____ %

| Examiner: | Reviewer | Date: | 19 |
|---|---|---|---|

credit is judged in relation to the real estate pledged as security. With these two factors in mind, the lender considers terms of the mortgage. The relation between (1) borrower credit, (2), the real estate pledged as security and (3) the mortgage is known as the mortgage pattern. By rating these three elements, it is held that the degree of overall mortgage insurance risk may be calculated. For instance, if either the borrower and his credit, or the real estate are marginal, then mortgage terms may be adjusted to satisfy safety of principal.

Exhibit 14.7 indicates that the three elements of real estate credit are highly interrelated. A given loan may be unsatisfactory with a 90 percent loan but subject to approval with a 50 percent loan to value ratio. Or it may be possible to extend credit to a borrower with interest only payments for five years with amortization at the end of the period. This would accommodate the borrower with limited income during the early years of the mortgage with a high expectation of higher income as the mortgage matures. In short, the mortgage lender is not faced with a yes or no proposition; he may select the mortgage pattern that fits individual circumstances.

**Exhibit 14.7**
**Elements of Real Estate Credit**

```
BORROWER CREDIT                          REAL ESTATE

EFFECTIVE INCOME                         MARKET VALUE
ASSETS                                   LOCATION
CREDIT                                   BEST USE


                  MORTGAGE

                  MATURITY
                  LOAN TO VALUE RATIO
                  INTEREST RATE
```

## Mortgage Credit Analysis for Income Properties

Mortgage credit analysis for income properties is considerably more complex. The required documentation includes much data unique to mortgages on income property; the loan application shows greater flexibility in mortgage terms; credit of the borrower, especially for new projects, is more critical; and some projects are judged in terms of their cash flow.

These points are suggested by the documentation normally included for loan approval. The following list is taken from an application on two apartment projects, one of five buildings containing 252 apartments and another loan on three adjoining buildings containing 198 units.

1. Transmittal letter.
2. Summary of loan request.
3. Loan applications: Sunset Downs 1; Sunset Downs 2.
4. Historical information on borrower.
5. Summary financial statements of the first partner.
6. Summary financial statements of the second partner.
7. Statement of equity source.
8. Plot plan of the proposed development: Sunset Downs 1, Sunset Downs 2.
9. Appraisal data
   a. Appraiser's certificate of value.
   b. Summary of appraisal data.
   c. Supplementary property data.

To indicate the complexities encountered in income property analysis, some of the unique aspects of the loan application, borrower credit and cash flow analysis, deserve special comment.

## The Loan Application

There is no special format for the loan application. In outlining the requested loan terms, considerable variation will be encountered. For example, in a proposed loan for an apartment house project, the loan was approved on the basis of the *requested application* for $3,430,000 at an interest rate of 8½ percent for 30 years with the lender retaining the right to reset the terms of the loan during the first six months of the fifteenth year so that the loan would be amortized at the end of the twenty-fifth year.

In still another loan application, the borrower applied for a $750,000 loan or an amount equal to 75 percent of the appraised value, whichever is less, subject to an occupancy requirement:

> Closing of the loan in the amount of $750,000 shall be subject to a rental achievement of 80 percent of the gross rental area of not less than $4.00 per annum per square foot. In the event that said occupancy requirement is not met by the disbursement date, the amount of disbursement shall be $625,000. A six month period from date of closing will be allowed to satisfy the occupancy requirement and receive the additional $125,000 funding.

In the mortgage loan application the borrower may apply for restrictions on prepayment penalties, i.e., during the first ten years a partial repayment of no more than ten percent of the original amount of the loan may be made in any loan year, noncumulative. The loan can be paid in full during the eleventh year by paying an amount equal to 103 percent of the remaining balance which charges are to reduce by 1½ percent each year thereafter till the sixteenth year; no penalties are applied after the sixteenth year.

## Financial Analysis of the Borrower

For the larger income projects, it is frequently the case that the borrower is a corporation of substantial means in which real estate is incidental to other business. At the opposite extreme are the corporations who develop real estate as their sole activity. If a corporation is involved, a balance sheet and profit and loss statement over the preceding five years is necessary.

### Exhibit 14.8
### A Financial Statement of a Mortgage Applicant

*Statement of Net Worth as of June 30, 19—*

**Assets**

| | | | |
|---|---|---|---|
| *Current Assets* | | | |
| Cash | $ 34,193 | | |
| Accounts Receivable | 28,465 | | |
| Notes Receivable, Unsecured | 131,000 | | $ 193,658 |
| *Investments* | | | |
| 200 sh. General Motors | 8,400 | | |
| 100 sh. Detroit Edison | 4,400 | $ 12,800 | |
| Golf Acres Land | 1,500,000 | | |
| Francis Building, ½ interest | 175,000 | | |
| 208 S. Mackinaw | 650,000 | | |
| 360 acres Jackson County | 360,000 | | |
| 200 acres for Subdivision | 2,000,000 | 4,685,000 | 4,697,800 |
| *Other* | | | |
| Home | 42,000 | | |
| Car, 1970 Cadillac | 6,250 | | 48,250 |
| | | | $4,939,708 |

**Liabilities**

| | | | |
|---|---|---|---|
| *Current Liabilities* | | | |
| Accounts Payable | $ 16,128 | | |
| Notes Payable, Bank | 135,000 | | 151,128 |
| *Mortgages Payable* | | | |
| 208 S. Mackinaw | 330,000 | | 330,000 |
| Net Worth | | | $4,458,580 |
| | | | $4,939,708 |

In the case of an individual (such as a builder), balance sheet analysis is more complex. The problem is illustrated by the balance sheet taken from a builder applying for a $6,000,000 loan to construct a shopping center of 400,000 square feet of gross leasable area. The statement was prepared by a Certified Public Accountant. See Exhibit 14.8. Unaudited or uncertified statements should be avoided.

Note that the value of real estate is greater than the total net worth of $4.458 million. Without appraising the assets shown as real estate, it is not clear that in the event of a mortgage default, personal assets of the borrower would be available to protect the principal. During a recession and in the face of delinquent payments, the borrower's assets may be as illiquid as the mortgage principal. Hence, the main problem is to make sure that assets are sufficiently liquid to insure continuation of mortgage payments.

Moreover, in the case of corporate borrowers, lenders look more favorably toward businesses that show an increasing net worth over past years or stable or rising profits. Extreme variation in net worth or profits of declining trends may require the lender to disapprove the loan or require additional collateral.

The importance of judging a financial statement is indicated by regulations of the Department of Housing and Urban Development governing the interpretation of financial statements of sponsors of apartment projects. In reviewing current assets, defined as the total amount of cash and other assets convertible into cash during the normal course of business operations, certain items must be omitted for mortgage credit purposes. To qualify for FHA insurance on these properties, four rules have been adopted in listing current assets:

1.  Do not include in current assets any amounts paid on account of land to be used for the project under consideration.
2.  Do not include cost of other land owned, or properties, unless the sponsor has a recognized cash equity in the land and/or properties which are readily marketable properties intended for the sales market.
3.  In evaluating current assets, including stocks and bonds, it is important to ascertain that they are carried on the balance sheet in accordance with accepted accounting principles, i.e., cost or market price, whichever is the lower.
4.  The inclusion of anticipated profits in working capital is not in accord with sound analytical procedure. (*Mortgage Credit Analysis for Project Mortgage Insurance, Section 207*, 4470.1. Wahington, D.C.: Department of Housing and Urban Development, October, 1974, pp. 2-13.)

When judging current liabilities, which are obligations payable in approximately one year, HUD includes any liabilities for land or other contract payments included as liens on the land for the proposed project. HUD includes as current liabilities amounts due officers, employees or stockholders of the project sponsor.

## Cash Flow Analysis

An evaluation of the investor applying for the loan does not constitute the main security for an income property loan. Nor is it likely that the appraisal report giving the current market value estimate is satisfactory, by itself, in judging the real estate security. For income properties, lenders are more inclined to look to the net income as a source of mortgage and principal payment. In reviewing the net income potential certain precautionary steps are usually taken.

If the mortgage application is accompanied by an appraisal undertaken by an independent appraiser, prudence suggests that rental data be verified in the field. If the project is an existing operation, present rents are easily reviewed. Some correlation should be made, moreover, between the current rents and the current *market* rents.

By the same token expenses of operation must bear a reasonable relationship to actual experiences of like properties. For certain income properties such as office buildings, apartments, and shopping centers, national organizations undertake annual income and expense surveys which are readily available.

Another way of verifying data is to reduce elements of the loan to a per unit basis, especially for multiple family or transient housing, such as motels and hotels. Depending on the type of construction, the maximum loan will usually fall within known limits on a per unit apartment basis, per room basis, or square foot. By judging the loan in this way another check is made on the appropriateness of the capitalization rate used in the valuation process.

Cash flow, as used by mortgage lenders, refers to the amount of net income after mortgage interest and principal payments. Because net income is viewed as the main source of mortgage payments, it is critically important to determine if the net income will be more than enough to satisfy debt service. Some lenders are reluctant to grant mortgages on income properties if the mortgage payments are more than 80 percent of the estimated net income. Alternatively, if vacancies are expected to extend over several months, it is relevant to determine if cash reserves are sufficient to carry the property, even up to two or three years and still meet prescribed mortgage payments.

Assuming a normal occupancy rate, lenders frequently weigh the loan feasibility by comparing the first mortgage as a multiple of gross possible income. In apartment house financing, some lenders in the Southeast limit first mortgages to not more than five times the gross possible income.

Furthermore, considerable importance is attached to the mortgage constant—the annual mortgage payment expressed as a percent of the original loan. This figure is derived by multiplying the monthly mortgage payment by 12. Or expressed directly in percentage, the monthly instalment of one, under a given mortgage, times 12.

The rate of return on property investment normally must be above the mortgage constant for loans of high loan to value ratios. These points will be reviewed in greater detail in the chapter on estimating real estate yields.

To illustrate further, consider the cost and income valuation for a proposed new medical office building. The loan summary below shows the economic value, by components, reduced to the price per square foot of rentable area (R.A.). Note that real estate taxes and operating expenses, though detailed in the appraisal report, are shown here as a stabilized percent of gross income.

PHYSICAL VALUE:

| | | |
|---|---|---:|
| Land @ $125 per Fr.Ft. or $2.22/Sq.Ft. | | $ 40,000 |
| Building @ $21.77/Sq.Ft. | | 177,582 |
| Site Improvements—Paving, Landscaping, etc. | | 6,620 |
| Other—Fees, Miscellaneous, Interim Financing Fees, | | |
| Miscellaneous Fees | | 40,465 |
| | | $264,667 |
| Total Physical Value— | Say | $265,000 |

ECONOMIC VALUE:

| | | |
|---|---|---|
| Gross Income (see attached | | |
| breakdown | $48,939 | $6.00/Sq.Ft.R.A. |
| Less 5% Vacancy | 2,447 | |
| Stabilized Income | $46,492 | $5.70/Sq.Ft.R.A. |
| Real Estate Taxes (see attached | | |
| breakdown) | 7,429 | $ .91/Sq.Ft.R.A. 16% Sta. Inc. |
| Operating Expenses (see attached | | |
| breakdown) | 11,175 | $1.37/Sq.Ft.R.A. 24% Sta. Inc. |
| Total Expenses | $18,604 | $2.28/Sq.Ft.R.A. |
| Net Income | $27,888 | $3.42/Sq.Ft.R.A. |

Net Income Before Depreciation Capitalized @ 9.5% = $295,000

This method of presentation allows the mortgage committee to make a ready comparison of income data with other known properties or published surveys. While the mortgage loan submission includes other documentation, the data on income properties must be reduced to summary form to allow professional analysis.

In still another income loan on a medical-dental facility, data were shown on a per square foot basis with the break even point calculated and with a calculation of the equity return.

Loan to Value
  With Excess Land
    330,000 ÷ 440,000                                          75%
  With Excess Land
    330,000 ÷ 365,000                                          90%

Loan Per Square Foot
    330,000 ÷ 13,380 sq.ft.                                    $24.66
  Net Rental Area
    330,000 ÷ 12,250 sq. ft.                                   $26.93

Breakeven Point
  Expenses                $22,950.00
  Mortgage Pmt.            35,310.00
  Participation             1,347.50
  Annual Breakeven         59,607.50

  Percent of Occupancy                                         88%
  Breakeven Per Square Foot (Annual)                           $4.45 + per sq. ft.

Equity Return
  Appraised Value         $440,000     N.I.B.C.R.     $41,056.25
  Loan Amount              330,000     Debt Service    35,310.00
  Equity                  $110,000                    $ 5,746.25

                        Yield = 5.22%
Net Income to Debt Service                             1.16×

By reducing these data to ratios and break even points, the feasibility of the loan may be more easily indicated.

It is fairly clear that judging mortgage credit for income properties is considerably more complex. A typical loan submission as shown by application for a shopping center loan included the following elements:

1. Loan summary
2. City data
3. Neighborhood data
4. Description of improvements
5. Site data
6. Land comparables
7. Cost approach
8. Income approach
9. Mortgage loan ratios
10. Final summary and correlation of values
11. Sponsor's financial responsibility
12. Lease
13. Loan agreement
14. Definitions and limiting conditions
15. Qualifications and experience
16. Building plans

These illustrations suggest the technical aspects of judging mortgage credit for income properties. While the borrower's credit is significant, much depends on the feasibility of the project itself; its net income, its income tax advantages, its yield on equity and the various ratios that are common to a mortgage on income properties. Chapter 18, dealing with investment yields, reviews these points in greater detail.

# Chapter 15

# Construction Loan
# Administration

The construction loan provides interim financing for the construction of a new structure. Typically the loan is a term loan over a relatively short period which is paid out in instalments as the building construction progresses. In most respects, the construction mortgage assumes characteristics of a commercial loan. The security is highly dependent on the character, credit, and the ability of the contractor-borrower. Since some mortgage lenders are prohibited by statute or inhibited by policy from making loans on vacant or uncompleted buildings, certain institutions, such as commercial banks, have developed specialized procedures to process construction loans.

## Construction Loan Requirements

Construction loan administration demands specialized talent in loan administration. Though the loan security places heavy emphasis on the financial ability of the builder-borrower, good practice insures that no moneys are advanced unless the construction in progress has a value greater than the outstanding loan.

The main difference between a construction loan and other mortgage loans is the requirement of in-depth knowledge of construction materials, construction methods and estimation. Even though the assistance of architects, subcontractors, building officials and others play an important role, the final responsibility rests with the loan officer who must evaluate the proposed construction—not only the initial plans and specifications but the contractor's conformity with building plans and specifications during construction.

In addition, considerable importance is attached to the appraiser's analysis of the proposed building. Probably he will give the greatest weight to the reproduction cost and the land value, primarily because the mortgaged property has no operating experience. In the case of income property, the project will be valued from a projection of annual gross income and net operating expenses.

Above all, construction loans have characteristics normal to other mortgages; they require considerable expertise in contract administration. Here all elements of enforceable contracts are common to the construction loan. Successful completion of a construction loan calls for documentation before the loan is approved, preparation of a construction loan agreement, and careful observance of the contract law during the loan pay-out period and preceding the time of final settlement. While some of these functions may be delegated to nonstaff members working for a fee, most of these operations are undertaken by commercial banks that specialize in construction loans. Their activities concentrate around the construction loan application, documentation before loan approval, the construction loan agreement, and residential construction loans.

## Construction Loan Application

In many respects the construction loan illustrates characteristics of conventional long-term mortgages. The difference lies in the additional features unique to the construction loan because of the nature of the real estate security and the unusually high dependence on contractual arrangements. Typically, construction loan arrangements involve a borrower (who could be a developer of a shopping center or an individual who builds a new house on his own lot) who contracts with a builder for construction of the proposed building. The construction loan serves as interim financing to pay the contractor pending negotiation of the permanent loan. The construction loan application then includes information on both the borrower and contractor.

A fairly common arrangement is illustrated in Exhibit 15.1. (1) Here the borrower or developer prepares plans and arranges for construction with a contractor under a construction contract. The borrow-

**Exhibit 15.1**

**Diagram of a Construction Loan**

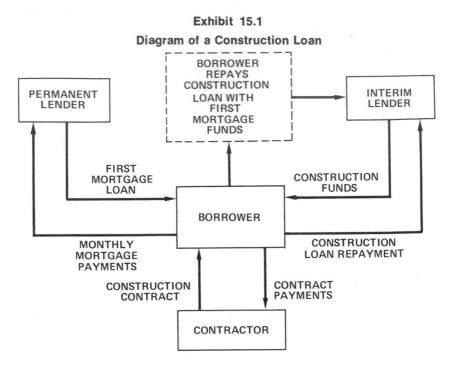

er's equity may be his investment in land or the borrower places a sum or equity on deposit with the construction lender. (2) With the construction contract in hand, the borrower then turns to the interim construction lender, who upon approval, will (3) execute a construction loan agreement. Construction funds are made available as construction proceeds. (4) Preceding this step a permanent lender may have executed a take-out commitment to the interim construction lender based upon the borrower's loan application for a permanent loan. As construction is completed, (5) the permanent lender accepts the first mortgage from the borrower and advances funds to the borrower (6) who in turn transfers first mortgage funds to satisfy the outstanding construction loan.

## Construction Loan Details

If a construction loan assumes the form illustrated in Exhibit 15.1, the construction lender will require fairly complete information on the borrower, the contractor, the site and the proposed building. A real estate appraisal indicates the feasibility of the project, which if satisfactory will be reviewed in the light of the disbursement request and the validity of the take-out commitment.

Both the borrower and contractor are subject to a credit examination typical of a mortgage application. Of prime importance is the legal form that each party assumes: a partnership, a corporation, a joint venture and the like. The authority of each party to contract and the assets of the legal entity entering into the enterprise require special review. Balance sheets for preceding years and profit and loss statements for business entities preferably over the last five years, together with credit reports and business references provide supplementary credit information. If the legal entity is a corporation with few assets, the sponsors may act as guarantors which will require a personal financial statement from both parties.

## Borrower Data

In the case of the borrower, particular attention is given to past development experience. If the project covers multiple family projects or a shopping center, the lender should review past performance. Most lenders avoid financing major projects initiated by borrowers who have had limited or no major development experience. Providing the borrower's past experience is considered adequate, the next question relates to the amount of equity invested and its source. If equity capital has been borrowed then the borrower has no personal capital invested. Normally the greater the equity the more incentive the borrower has in working toward a successful project.

## Contractor Data

With respect to the contractor, a recitation of past construction experience of a similar nature is generally required. Some lenders require a record of construction presently under contract and the stage of completion. A checklist of contractor data would cover at the minimum the following items:

> Legal entity of the contractor organization
> Balance sheet statement of preceding years (audited)
> Profit and Loss statements of preceding years (audited)
> Business experience
> Work in progress; Percent completed to date
> Credit references
> Credit report
> Financial statement of guarantors (if required).

Providing both the borrower and the contractor meet the minimum acceptable criteria, the construction lender reviews the property, the site and the proposed building improvements.

## Site Data

It is the lender's responsibility to insure that funds are not spent on a site inappropriate for the proposed construction. The construction loan application, therefore, will include a legal description and a current site survey showing encumbrances, easements, rights of way and other title restrictions. A location map with access routes clearly indicated represent other required data. For some properties a topographic survey will help evaluate the site plan, layout, and drainage facilities. On occasion a soil survey proves useful to indicate the load bearing quality of the soil; i.e., an industrial plant must have soil of noncompressible solids, the soil must be adequate to support foundations proposed and it must have desirable drainage properties. The conformity of the plans with building codes, zoning ordinances, and environmental controls should be reviewed as part of the site data analysis.

## Analysis of Building Improvements

Not only must the proposed improvement be economically feasible, but the structure must be adapted to the site and location. Moreover, a detailed review of the construction cost is an essential part of the construction loan review. To accomplish these ends the construction loan application should include architectural plans and building specifications, including a site layout plan.

For the review of construction costs, some lenders hire a nonstaff member to make an engineering review of local building costs for the proposed construction. Usually the contractor will be asked to submit a list of subcontractors with bids or subcontracts. For a commercial project, shopping center, apartment house or other rental property, a list of units or square feet of leasable or rentable area with the proposed rents and prices should be part of the loan application. Such information enables the appraiser to compare the income appraisal with the anticipated cost of construction.

## Other Requirements

The proposed time schedule with cash disbursement requirements will be included by the contractor as part of the application. A feasibility study of the property will be undertaken by a fee appraiser or a qualified staff member and sometimes both. The lender will examine the take-out commitment for reservations or other restrictions that may restrict satisfaction of the construction loan.

## Construction Loan Documentation

It is worthwhile to review documentation before issuing the construction loan commitment and agreement. Some of the items below are common to a standard mortgage loan application.

1. A title policy
2. A survey by a registered surveyor
3. Site and building plan
4. Fire and casualty insurance policies *general liability*
   *builder's risk (insures imp. as*
5. Building permits *placed on prop.)*
6. Zoning approval *hazard (fire & extended coverag.*
7. Legally enforceable contracts and subcontracts or binding bids
8. Documents authorizing corporate authority to contract for the borrower and contractor
9. Letter of commitment from a permanent lender
10. Verification of building costs and estimates
11. Appraisal analysis of feasibility.

With these documents in hand the lender is in a clear position to evaluate the construction loan agreement.

Furthermore, when administering an approved construction loan these documents will be used for reference. For example, during construction the building placement will be physically inspected to see that building set back requirements have been met. Many other items such as contract observance, zoning ordinance, and similar items will be verified against these original documents.

If the project covers income property, the documentation helps determine the feasibility of the project in the light of the local market, local operating costs, and the demand for new facilities. Given a local demand and a satisfactory review of these items, the next step is to negotiate the construction loan agreement.

## Construction Loan Agreement

In addition to the mortgage in the conventional long-term loan, the construction loan agreement is probably the most significant contract controlling the construction loan. Duties of the contractor and responsibilities of the lender are set forth in detail. Certain elements of the construction loan agreement cover general administration of the loan.

First, the amount and the anticipated term of the loan will be noted with provisions to pay interest and principal. Practices vary from interest charges paid monthly on the total balance until principal is repaid, to the practice of levying interest only on the amount disbursed. In this portion of the agreement, the loan will be identified as a first lien with an agreement that the borrower assumes the agreed upon service charge or loan fees and other costs of preparing the loan. Usually the agreement will refer to the permanent investor's take out commitment and list the contractor with the disbursement plan. The loan will specify that the improvement proposed will be in substantial conformance to the exhibited plans and specifications.

Depending on the record of the contractor, a performance bond or completion bond may be specified. It is within the prerogatives of the lender to require performance bonds for subcontractors, especially if they are small, independent firms. Other elements of the construction loan agreement will warrant that the borrower has marketable title and the capacity to contract. Typically, funds will not be advanced unless the contractor statement is filed stating that all subcontractors have been paid in the amount due with signed lien waivers. Lien waivers waive the right of material suppliers and laborers to file liens against the borrower's property for nonpayment.

The lender will be given the right to inspect for compliance with the contract as well as the right to verify all contracts. The lender reserves the right to assign the contract but prohibits an assignment by the borrower.

A considerable portion of the contract defines default of the construction loan agreement. The default could be (1) disapproval of construction by the lender for the contractor's failure to correct within a reasonable period, (2) unreasonable delay in construction progress, or (3) bankruptcy and insolvency by the contractor.

Disbursement procedures specify the total amount of the loan and the itemization of payments requested under the disbursement plan. Such items include title expenses, architect's fees, interest payments, insurance premiums and construction funds. In some instances, lenders require a construction inspection signed by an architect or a designated inspector before disbursements are executed. The contract specifies conditions under which the final disbursement will be made; namely, full waivers from all subcontractors and suppliers, a letter of final acceptance of construction from the borrower and the final inspection and approval by the architect or the permanent lender.

## Closing the Construction Loan

Assuming that the construction loan agreement is accepted and assuming that required documentation meets lender approval, the next step is to execute all the required documents. The lender will insure that the building contract between the borrower and the builder is signed and executed with all the necessary subcontracts or bids. If the take-out agreement meets lender approval, then the contract loan agreement is signed. The surveyor will be asked to execute a pre-construction affidavit which is a sworn statement from the contractor that no work has been started nor material been delivered to the site which would serve as a basis for a lien that would have priority over the construction mortgage. At this time it is presumed that the borrower's down payment or equity is collected by the lender for disbursement before lender construction money is advanced.

With insurance ordered or in effect, the next step is to record mortgage papers and the contract. No funds will be advanced until an on-site inspection reveals that no work has been started nor materials delivered to the site prior to recording of the construction mortgage. Provided these steps are in order the lender gives written notice to the owner and the contractor to begin construction.

It should be added that the lender's review of the construction contract should conform to standard contract law. In addition a legal review should disclose that the contract shows a definite dollar value of services to be performed with stated terms and conditions of payment and a time limitation for completion of the building. Penalty clauses for nonperformance will agree with customary penalties for the type of construction in question.

There is one final point. During the preliminary review the construction lender should make sure that the available construction funds, including the construction loan and the borrower's equity, are sufficient to complete the project. For this reason considerable care is taken in reviewing builder costs given in the plans and specifications submitted.

This requirement cannot be over-emphasized. The final loan security is a completed building constructed according to approved plans and specifications. A shortage of funds before completion may develop into a series of judgments from unpaid subcontractors and create a problem of disposing of an incomplete building, foreclosure, and other litigation. Providing legal and financial prerequisites are in order, the necessary loan agreement is executed and the lender directs his energies to contract administration.

## Contract Administration

Given the construction loan agreement, the next task requires a continual monitoring of construction. In fact it is common for the construction loan agreement to provide for a hold-back of money due, typically 10 per cent of the amount of the contract, which is disbursed only after certification by the borrower and architect that the work has been completed. In states that give laborers and suppliers statutory liens for nonpayment, the hold-back provides a reserve for this contingency.

The payout schedule shown in Exhibit 15.2 illustrates a schedule based on four payments less the agreed upon hold-back. The construction lender must institute inspections at these points and compare actual construction with plans and specifications. Here a particular knowledge of construction is required. For instance, there have been occasions when contractors have used green, uncured lumber for wood frame construction in violation of the building contract. On other occasions contractors have substituted, say, hemlock roof rafters for Douglas fir or have cut costs with improper framing and nailing. For example, some plumbing contractors have been known to sever bearing supports when installing water pipes.

For this reason the construction lender is dependent on a knowledgeable inspector or architect's certificate of compliance with construction contract. As a rule disbursement of the construction loan according to a schedule comparable to Exhibit 15.2 is made only after the physical inspection and approval by the architect or other appointed expert. Some lenders use pay out forms that include waivers of mechanics' and materialmen's liens against the property. Such a form is shown in Exhibit 15.3.

*10% retainage is common. Retainage is important to making sure project is completed at a satisfactory level, material & mechanic men's are paid.*

**Exhibit 15.2**
**Payout Schedule for a Single Family Dwelling**

| Item | Payout Schedule |
|------|-----------------|
| Foundation and rough grading<br>First floor joists<br>Framing complete with subfloors<br>Exterior wall and roof sheathing, chimney | 25% |
| Roughed in plumbing, heating and air conditioning ducts, electrical wiring<br>Exterior wall and roof finish, windows and doors<br>Dry wall interior | 25% |
| Basement floor and heating plant<br>Interior finish, except flooring | 25% |
| All finish flooring, finished cabinets<br>Ready for Occupancy (less hold-back) | 25% |

During construction, the construction loan officer insures that the construction loan is not in default in any manner. Default may occur if the contractor fails to comply with terms in the construction loan agreement. Noncompliance by subcontractors or failure to acquire the required insurance during construction, or violations of the local build-

# Exhibit 15.3

# Direct Construction Cost Breakdown and Request for Partial Payment

Direct Construction Cost Breakdown & Request For Partial Payment

TO: _____     REQUISITION NO. _____

OWNER/BORROWER _____     DATE _____

LOCATION _____     LOAN AMOUNT _____

PROJECT NAME _____

In accordance with provisions of the building loan agreement dated _____ , this requisition is submitted for the

amount of $ _____ due for work performed for the period _____

to _____ and as itemized below by trades or contract breakdown.

## SUMMARY OF COST DATA

1. Total Amount of Original Contract          _____

2. Contractor's Cash Fee                      _____

3. Total Contract Amount Including Fee         _____

4. Total Approved Change Orders to-Date
   (As Per Attached Schedule)                  _____

5. Total Amount Approved Change Orders
   & Contract To Date                          _____

6. Total Projected Change Orders (Pending
   But Not Approved)                           _____

7. Total Projected Direct Construction Cost (5 & 6)   _____

8. Total Paid To Date Including This Request    _____

We hereby certify that 1.) any and all documents supporting this requisition are genuine; 2.) that the amounts shown above are complete and accurate; and 3.) the total amount "Balance to Complete" is the total sum of the amounts now due and hereafter to become due to aforesaid contractor or sub-contractors and there are no agreements obligating Borrower to make any payments other than those set forth. The undersigned further warrants and represents that he will not authorize, directly or indirectly, the doing of any work or furnishing of any materials upon said premises for any cause whatsoever which will be an expense or claim in addition to the amounts set forth above without the written consent of the Lender.

Borrower _____

The undersigned hereby certifies that it has received $ _____ payments in full for all previous requisitions and that all material and labor evidence by said requisitions have been paid for by the General Contractor.

General Contractor

_____

03 0177 (1−75)

# Exhibit 15.3 *Continued.*

Trade Breakdown

| | A | B | C | D | E | F | G |
|---|---|---|---|---|---|---|---|
| Item No. | Description of Work | Contract Amount | % Comp. leted to Date | Amount Completed To Date | Amount Previously Completed | Amount This Request | Balance To Complete |
| 1. | | | | | | | |
| 2. | | | | | | | |
| 3. | | | | | | | |
| 4. | | | | | | | |
| 5. | | | | | | | |
| 6. | | | | | | | |
| 7. | | | | | | | |
| 8. | | | | | | | |
| 9. | | | | | | | |
| 10. | | | | | | | |
| 11. | | | | | | | |
| 12. | | | | | | | |
| 13. | | | | | | | |
| 14. | | | | | | | |
| 15. | | | | | | | |
| 16. | | | | | | | |
| 17. | | | | | | | |
| 18. | | | | | | | |
| 19. | | | | | | | |
| 20. | | | | | | | |
| 21. | | | | | | | |
| 22. | | | | | | | |
| 23. | | | | | | | |
| 24. | | | | | | | |
| 25. | | | | | | | |
| 26. | | | | | | | |
| 27. | | | | | | | |
| 28. | | | | | | | |
| 29. | | | | | | | |
| 30. | | | | | | | |
| 31. | | | | | | | |
| 32. | | | | | | | |
| 33. | | | | | | | |
| 34. | | | | | | | |
| 35. | | | | | | | |
| 36. | | | | | | | |
| 37. | | | | | | | |
| 38. | | | | | | | |
| 39. | | | | | | | |
| 40. | | | | | | | |
| 41. | | | | | | | |
| 42. | | | | | | | |
| 43. | | | | | | | |
| 44. | | | | | | | |
| 45. | | | | | | | |
| 46. | | | | | | | |
| 47. | | | | | | | |
| 48. | | | | | | | |
| 49. | | | | | | | |
| 50. | | | | | | | |
| 51. | | | | | | | |
| 52. | | | | | | | |
| 53. | | | | | | | |
| 54. | | | | | | | |
| 55. | | | | | | | |
| 56. | | | | | | | |
| 57. | | | | | | | |
| 58. | | | | | | | |
| 59. | | | | | | | |
| 60. | | | | | | | |
| | Totals | | | | | | |

1. Total Amount Completed To Date (Original Contract Cost Column D)    _____

2. Amount Due To Date (From Change Order Schedule)    _____

3. Sub-Total    _____

4. Less Retainage    _____

5. Net Amount Due To Date (3 minus 4)    _____

6. Less Previous Amount Paid    _____

7. Amount This Request for Direct Construction (5 minus 6)    _____

ing code or other violations of the construction loan agreement may provide grounds for giving notice of noncompliance and placing the loan in default.

In other instances the permanent lender, especially for commercial projects of some consequence, will require approval by the permanent lender. Failure to correct deficiencies within a reasonable period constitutes grounds for default. In still other cases financial difficulties of the contractor may cause unreasonable delays in construction progress. If the delay is clearly in violation of the contract, the construction lender has the option of declaring the loan in default. Likewise bankruptcy, insolvency, assignment for benefit of creditors, or the assignment of an interest by the borrower may jeopardize loan security and again give the interim lender the option of claiming default.

## Mechanics' Lien

Both the borrower and the construction lender are vulnerable to liens of laborers, subcontractors, and suppliers furnishing materials for construction. For this reason it is believed helpful to review general procedures followed in coping with this threat to construction loan security. Local attorneys should be consulted for variations in state law. Familiarity with the general philosophy of lien laws illustrates the importance of following state law to minimize the possibility of a mechanics' lien. At the outset it may be noted that the right to file a mechanics' lien is a carry over from the time when craftsmen working on clothing, shoes, and other personal property kept the object until paid for the work performed.

Such physical possession is impossible in real estate. The law substitutes the right to file a lien against real estate on which the worker has contributed work or materials. Such persons, within certain limitations, may look to the real estate for payment of their services.

Though the construction lender or the borrower may have made payments as agreed, it is generally held that a person is entitled to a mechanics' lien if he has improved the real estate at the request or *consent* of the legal owner. Thus, a lender or borrower with no knowledge of nonpayment of services or materials by the contractor or subcontractors may have a continuing liability for the payment to third parties (subcontractors) because of the implied consent to the work or purchase. Generally the amount of the lien may not be more than the value of services or materials and may attach to the owner's interest at the time of filing the lien or to any interest of the owner which is subsequently acquired.

In fact some states follow the rule that a subcontractor who has not been paid by contractor can file a lien against the owner-borrower independent of the amount owed to the contractor. Thus, if the subcontractors are not paid, the borrower-owner may be forced to pay for services twice—once to the contractor and once to the unpaid subcontractor—to avoid a judgment lien.

Of particular importance to the construction lender is the time at which the lien becomes effective and its priority over other liens such as a construction mortgage. In certain states a mechanic's lien is effective when the worker begins work on the real estate. In these circumstances a construction mortgage recorded before the time the work began has priority over a mechanic' lien. In still other states the lien begins as soon as any construction starts. Therefore, a plumber who performs work starting 60 days after ground preparation would have a lien dating back to time when construction first started.

A selected few states commence the date of the lien when the work was ordered. In at least one other state a lien attaches when it is filed which may be any time during construction or within four months of completion of construction. With so many common variations, it is fairly clear that legal advice is an important aspect of construction loan administration.

Certain other points are relevant to the issue of a mechanics' lien. An owner or the construction loan officer may secure waivers from contractors, subcontractors, laborers and suppliers before work starts or at the very least before pay outs. It is generally true that signing of a waiver by a contractor does not deprive subcontractors and laborers, who have not signed the waiver, of the right to file a lien. If it is suspected that suppliers, laborers and others have not been paid, they must file a waiver separately to avoid creation of a lien. Depending on the individual state, the right to file a lien terminates if no action is taken before the lien period expires. Another important point relates to the priority of the claims. A mechanics' lien usually has priority over earlier claims that have not been recorded. Similarly a mechanics' lien is generally subordinate to documents recorded before the mechanics' lien is filed. Because of the importance of the recording requirement, comment on recording practices among the various states seems advised.

## Establishing Priority of Claims by Recording

Recording statutes may be traced to English common law that gave priority to the person who first acquired the property. That is, if "A" deeded to "B" and later "A" died and his heirs not knowing of the transfer, deeded the same property to "C", "B" would win: he was the first to acquire an interest. To correct for such inequities, recording statutes developed among the several states that have certain common features:

1. The instrument to be recorded such as the mortgage must be acknowledged before a public official.
2. The entire instrument is recorded, and is not merely a memorandum.
3. Legal priority against subsequent parties is established by the act of recording.
4. The instrument recorded, i.e., a mortgage or deed, is valid between parties to the instrument without the recording.

As a general rule the act of recording changes the common law ruling of priorities. In the former example, transfers from the heirs of "A" to "C" had no effect because the heirs of "A" had no interest in the property transferred.

As first provided by the *Massachusetts Bay Colony Act of 1640,* priority was given to the party who first recorded the instrument with the local recorder. These are called the "race" statutes: the first to win the race to the recording office wins priority; in other words, the first in time is the first in right. Suppose for example that "A" transfers to "B" under the following circumstances:

"A" ————————————————→ "B"; "B" records in January
"A" (heirs) ————————————————→ "C"; "C" records in June
Result: "B" wins

In this case, "B" prevails since he recorded in January. If however he failed to record, in some circumstances, "C" would prevail over "B" since he won the race. The final result depends on state statutes.

In this respect the state statutes may be divided into three categories. Purely *race* type statutes are found only in Louisiana and North Carolina. However, certain other states apply the race concept to mortgages only. Some 25 states are known as *notice* statute states. The notice statute corrects for the possibility of fraud in the case of a subsequent purchaser who knew that there was a prior unrecorded transfer and who then acquired title by subsequently obtaining a deed and recording it first. The notice statute corrects for this deficiency. These statutes provide that a second purchaser will prevail against the prior purchaser who did not record, so long as the subsequent purchaser has no notice of the prior purchase, even if he never records his second purchase. Thus, with the notice statute, parties filing a lien such as a mortgage or deed and having no other notice, can assume that if no other transfer is recorded, there are no prior claims.

About half of the states administer *race-notice* statutes. In states where these statutes apply, subsequent purchasers without notice will always win, where the prior purchaser has not recorded and the subsequent purchaser records first. The rule here requires that (1) a subsequent party must have no knowledge of other liens and (2) he must also record his title or lien first. The states following this rule are listed below.

| | | |
|---|---|---|
| Alaska | Minnesota | Oregon |
| California | Mississippi | Pennsylvania |
| District of Columbia | Montana | South Carolina |
| Georgia | Nebraska | South Dakota |
| Hawaii | Nevada | Utah |
| Idaho | New Jersey | Washington |
| Indiana | New York | Wisconsin |
| Maryland | North Dakota | Wyoming |
| Michigan | | |

These comments help explain the importance of steps in construction loan approval. (*1*) Consider again the inspection of property *before* a construction loan is approved. This usually prevents the possible priority of a mechanics' or materialmen's lien that may have priority because materials were delivered or work was commenced before recording of the construction loan. (*2*) The importance of securing waivers from suppliers or others who have performed services is indicated by the right to file liens against the real estate, harming innocent parties such as the borrower or construction lender. (*3*) While the act of recording generally established priority against subsequent parties, it is equally clear that in certain states the recording must be without notice of prior claims to be effective. A final interpretation of these matters should be part of the legal review of construction loan administration.

## Residential Construction Loans

To be sure, the material on construction loans presented here applies to construction loans on residential property. Yet, for single family dwellings additional comments are believed in order. Banks which are actively engaged in financing construction loans on dwellings occasionally face clients with inadequate capital reserves, with an overly optimistic development program and limited management abilities. Accordingly, experience has shown that special precautions must be taken in financing individual houses on scattered lots—similar problems are encountered in subdivision tracts. Some of the main precautions to be observed are considered for these two groups.

Problems w/ Residential Development

### Scattered Lot Development

Most of the rules listed here have been drawn from construction loan experience with the relatively small builder who specializes in custom construction. The activity of such builders ranges from speculative building, for the low and moderate income buyer, to the custom built luxury dwelling constructed under architectural supervision. The additional points to be observed for these loans may be summarized in a few selected points.

*rotection* *1. Builder Reputation.* Considerable risks are assumed in granting con-
*Bank* struction loans to contractors without a past record of achievement. On this issue it is helpful to secure trade references and to review projects completed by the loan applicant. It is relatively easy to verify the reputation and standing of contractors from former clients. To proceed without considering the reputation of the contractor constitutes poor construction loan policy.

*2. Guarantors.* It is more than likely that construction loans will be granted to individually owned corporations with few assets. The same comment applies to general and limited partnerships. Before approval of the construction loan, which will be assumed by the contractor's entity, lenders require that the owner-principals personally guarantee completion and payment of all liabilities and bills. This step protects the lender from trying to collect from a debtor who has limited or no net worth.

*3. No Split Borrowings.* Some contractors may be operating with more than one construction loan from different lenders. Further, the lender must insure that proceeds from the loan are not used to finance construction of properties not covered by the loan. There is a tendency to over extend working capital over the short run in anticipation of optimistic sales projections. Compelling builders not to split borrowings without written consent avoids this possibility.

*4. Restrictions on Land Investment.* Operating builders buy land in advance of actual need. If this policy absorbs working capital, insufficient funds may remain to complete the proposed structure. To guard against this eventuality, lenders prohibit borrowers and principals from investing in land or building lots without the expressed approval of the lending bank.

*5. Acceptable Lots.* In scattered lot developments, special attention must be given utility availability. The site should be improved and adapted to single family dwelling use. If septic tanks are required, the soil should be tested for compliance with sanitary and health codes. Water, natural gas, fire protection, police protection, special assessments, and access are among the items reviewed since scattered lots are not always in well planned subdivisions.

*6. Adequate Available Funds.* It is unlikely that the estimated cost of construction will be equal to the amount of the final approved loan. If plan revisions of the borrower lead to cost increases or if the cost estimate has been inordinately low, there is the possibility that the builder will be unable to fulfill the construction contract. If the loan is placed with a low volume builder, such a cost overrun may jeopardize loan repayment. A careful review of financial resources and the cost estimate, protects the construction lender from the possibility of loan default from this cause.

7. _Loan Limitations_. Among the standard rules governing construction loans is the requirement that the loan should be made only on dwellings that may be sold within a reasonable time. In addition the owner must have sufficient assets to carry the property until the market absorbs completed houses. Careful planning in this respect protects the builder and lender alike from over extending the supply of houses in the face of a limited demand. As part of the appraisal process, the staff appraiser should indicate the potential demand for the number of units under construction. In no event should one builder be authorized loans beyond the anticipated demand over a reasonable time.

8. _No Residential Encroachment_. The greatest degree of loan security is provided by the structure that conforms to other dwellings in the neighborhood. For scattered lots, in particular, adjoining buildings, adjacent land use and neighborhood trends are more than usually important. To put it differently, a proposed structure must be saleable, it must be well located in regard to design and value, it must conform with the neighborhood and it must not suffer from encroachment by depreciated property, incompatible land uses, or other factors detrimental to residential use.

9. _Changes in Plans_. Most construction loan agreements provide that both the owner and contractor must seek permission in writing from the construction lender before "extras" are approved. Deviations from the plan that would increase cost would normally require an additional advance from the owner and possibly requests for additional funds from the lender. The record shows that changes and additions during construction constitute a major source of loss in construction loans. It should be clearly understood that under no circumstances should verbal orders be accepted for work not covered by plans and specifications. In short, the lender must be notified of proposals to change plans and specifications.

10. _Performance Bonds_. Performance bonds are rarely used for single family construction. For other types of construction, unless waived, performance bonds from an approved surety company should be requested of the contractor. The lending bank should be listed as a co-beneficiary and in most states the bond may be recorded. Conditions of the bond must be explicitly followed as determined by field inspections.

The foregoing points demonstrate most clearly that construction loans on scattered lots require a review not found in more specialized

*Construction Loan Administration*

construction loans. Construction lenders are faced with certain other unique problems in financing single family dwelling construction in recorded subdivisions.

## Subdivision Construction Loans

The management ability of the operator-builder is the critical element in construction financing of subdivisions. For developers new to the bank, a detailed investigation of the administrative ability and management organization introduces new aspects to construction financing. FHA and VA personnel, Dun and Bradstreet reports, credit reports and the volume and quality of past subdivision developments are among the matters to investigate. The home builder's operation must encompass construction activity, financing, and merchandising operations. For in the final analysis subdivision development is a business of manufacturing subdivision lots and dwellings.

It is not always true that the bank supplying construction funds will make the permanent loan to the home buyer. Yet the bank is dependent on permanent financing to satisfy construction loan payments. It is vitally important to review arrangements the builder proposes to finance dwelling sales.

Banks financing subdivision developments prefer that the builder establish his commercial checking accounts with the lending bank. In a sense this provides the bank with a flow of information on the use of borrowed funds and the working capital of the builder. For in this case the construction loan will include financing of the vacant land, cost of building, overhead, financing and carrying charges, take-out commitment fees, insurance, and possibly property taxes. Moreover, cash flow may be restricted by the time required to merchandise the houses while paying fixed costs which continue until each dwelling is sold. Some builders prefer to arrange subcontracts and the purchase of materials with an agreement that payments due will be from construction loan payments. This protects the builder from obligations to pay subcontractors or suppliers until the construction loan payments are made.

Suspected weaknesses in the financial condition of the operative-builder may require a contract bond or a performance bond. A legal opinion should be obtained to the effect that the bond gives the bank the necessary protection. Payments should not be provided that are not in compliance with the bond.

An additional responsibility on the part of the construction lender deals with cotracts for land leveling, street work, and off-site utilities. Again, the bank should be the co-beneficiary of a contract bond or performance bond which meets the approval of the bank's legal counsel. In marginal cases the bank is advised to continue checking into the trade for indications that payments may be lagging. Note also that the bonding requirement enforced by the city or county has no relation to the construction loan. The public bond insures only that the street is constructed according to the subdivision plan and local regulations.

In the event the builder proposes FHA and VA financing, no pay outs should be made unless the required FHA and VA inspections are made. Exceptions noted by the FHA, the VA, or the bank should be remedied immediately according to plans and specifications. The payment schedule listed in the performance bond should control payments to the operative-builder with no exceptions.

# Chapter 16

# Mortgage Collection Policies

Next to problems associated with mortgage origination, probably mortgage collection policies are the most critical aspect of mortgage servicing. Effective control over delinquencies leads to fewer defaults, a lower number of foreclosures, and more significantly, lower mortgage servicing costs.

The problem is even more serious in view of the rising foreclosure rate. The annual survey of the Federal Home Loan Bank Board indicates that the number of foreclosures has increased in absolute numbers and in percentage of mortgage loans outstanding. For example, total mortgages foreclosed in 1963 numbered 95,856 mortgages. In 1973, this total increased to 135,820 representing 0.405 percent of mortgaged structures.

A more recent report prepared by the Mortgage Bankers Association of America for the end of the first quarter, 1976, shows that *4.31 percent* of all mortgages outstanding on one-to four-family dwellings were 30 days or more past due. Some .68 percent of these mortgages were under foreclosure or 90 days or more delinquent. The same report showed a much higher rate of delinquency for FHA and VA loans. FHA loans 30 days or more delinquent represented 5.02 percent of all

FHA mortgage loans outstanding. For the same time period, VA loans had a 30 day or more delinquency rate of 4.04 percent; the comparable figure for conventional loans revealed a delinquency rate of some 2.64 percent.[1]

To lower these costs of mortgage administration, it seems worthwhile to identify the causes of mortgage delinquency. A discussion of accepted techniques to prevent delinquencies, and in the event delinquencies have occurred, specific collection procedures are recommended for different types of delinquencies. Reporting forms, special collection procedures, and practices required by government agencies complete the chapter.

At the outset a distinction should be made between administrative functions: mortgage collections and mortgage foreclosures. Collection procedures emphasize prevention and curing of delinquencies. The collection team must organize a system of workable techniques and good follow-up procedures. A continuous review of delinquent accounts is part of the supervisory tasks of the collection department. In contrast, foreclosure depends upon those activities terminating the loan in compliance with statutes, the mortgage agreement and lender policies that govern the foreclosure of insured and guaranteed mortgages.

## Main Reasons for Delinquencies

To guide collection policies it is convenient to classify delinquent borrowers into three categories: the indifferent borrower, personal emergencies, and the deliberate delinquent. Methods of curing the delinquent loan vary considerably among the three types of delinquencies. While each case is judged on its own merits, there are recognized methods of dealing with delinquent borrowers ranging from "customary collection procedures" to the more specialized techniques adapted to the problem loan.

### The Indifferent Borrower

A loan is classified as delinquent if not paid on the due date. For purposes of mortgage servicing, a loan due on the 1st of the month is one day delinquent if it is not paid by the second of the same month. Some borrowers are occasionally delinquent because of their "forgetfulness" in making timely payments. This type of delinquency is probably the easiest to cure and can be prevented by following proven collection procedures. However, collection personnel should be forewarned that

---

1. *National Delinquency Survey*, Economics and Research Department, Mortgage Bankers Association of America, as of March 31, 1976.

the so-called forgetfulness could be intentional, which may progress to habitual and deliberate delinquencies.

Then there is the borrower who is occasionally delinquent because he fails to provide payment before going on a lengthy trip. To be sure, such an eventuality could occur through forgetfulness or oversight, especially if the trip is undertaken for urgent business reasons or family emergencies. A careful analysis of this type of delinquency and appropriate preventive measures prevents the recurrence of this type of delinquency. Advance arrangements may be made for mortgage payments if prolonged and unavoidable trips are necessary.

Probably the more serious is the borrower who at first is only occasionally delinquent but who progresses to a habitual delinquent. Frequently this situation develops because the borrower has not been properly informed at the time of closing. The borrower who is making his first mortgage loan may not be aware of the urgency of timely payments. Unless the closing agent impresses upon the new borrower the importance of prompt payments, the new borrower stands a good chance of being a repetitively delinquent borrower.

## ② Personal Emergencies

Considerable tact, analysis and know-how are required for those categories that may lean to temporary nonpayment which may extend over several weeks to those cases that appear unresolvable. Investigation of each of these problem loans dictates the remedies recommended for curing the default. The representative list of delinquencies falling in this category would include:

| | |
|---|---|
| Family sickness | Too many family debts |
| Unemployment | Property in process of sale |
| Reduction of income because of change of jobs | Divorce or separation |
| | Poor personal spending habits |
| Seasonal loss of income | Delinquencies unknown to spouse |
| Short-term strikes | |

Special attention must be paid to delinquencies arising from personal emergencies. Personal inquiry and counseling is advised in these cases. Some of the recommended personal inquiries warrant brief mention.

*Family Sickness.* It is the responsibility of the collection office to determine the extent of disability, insurance and other assistance available to the borrower and, above all, to be aware of the possibility of exaggeration. The extent to which these procedures are instituted depends on the borrower's past credit record. Patience and understanding is certainly advised in these cases.

*Unemployment.* Delinquent payments stemming from unemployment, change of jobs, the seasonal loss of income and the like require special investigation. The extent to which a collection policy may be successful depends on the nature of the unemployment: (1) When did the employment end? (2) Is it temporary? (3) What other sources of income, including unemployment compensation and savings are available to satisfy family debts? Usually foreclosure proceedings are not recommended unless it is definitely clear that other sources of income will not be forthcoming. It is also a question of whether the unemployment was voluntary or involuntary. In the case of voluntary unemployment, a change of jobs may increase the borrower's ability to service the mortgage.

*Short-Term Strikes.* Again it must be determined what resources a borrower may turn to in the event of a short-term strike. The lender should expect payments from family reserves, union resources, or from part time or temporary employment. Much depends on the expected duration of the strike.

*Family Debts.* Policies vary according to whether the over extension of family credit is a chronic condition or is a temporary oversight. If the delinquency is a first time occurrence, the borrower should be given an opportunity to correct the deficiency. Usually most borrowers will give family shelter priority over other obligations.

*Divorce or Separation.* Here the representative must interview both spouses. Even a third party interview is advised with a minister, a counselor, a friend or relative who may indicate whether reconciliation seems probable. In the end, the collection staff must know who is responsible for the mortgage, and what arrangements will be made for correcting the present delinquency. Usually, marital difficulties call for a personal adjustment which may be remedied without instituting foreclosure procedures.

*Poor Personal Spending Habits.* Usually delinquencies call for firmness on the part of the lender. The problem arises with families who have no experience in budgeting or who have an inclination to spend compulsively. In either case, family budgeting, counseling and strict enforcement are clearly advised.

*Delinquencies Unknown to Spouse.* One or the other party responsible for mortgage payments may divert funds to personal use. Gambling, drinking, personal debts are such examples. Occasionally an oversight or poor planning on the part of the person responsible for family bills results in a loan delinquency. A solution calls for an interview with both parties. In some circumstances, a visit to both parties in their home may be the best solution. Whatever action is taken, the delinquency should not be allowed to be repeated on these grounds. Early action usually protects the lender from repeated delinquencies from this cause.

## ③ The Deliberate Delinquent

This classification refers to the chronic delinquent who has the ability to pay but who for personal reasons does not meet his financial responsibilities. This is an expensive customer for a lender since these persons are not inclined to cooperate nor do they have an interest in making regular payments on time. Their usual response is that they will meet their obligations when they are ready to make payment.

It should be noted that each borrower appears first as a temporary delinquent; only later does he become a chronic delinquent. The critical problem is to discover reasons for the delinquency and then to act on accepted collection procedures starting with an initial person-to-person contact, follow-up techniques, and possibly initiating a foreclosure. Between these steps it may be necessary to reevaluate causes of delinquency and to formulate new collection procedures.

### Temporary Unemployment

The Emergency Homeowners' Relief Act of 1975 provided temporary relief to delinquent borrowers subject to temporary unemployment or loss of income. Though the law was originally effective for only one year the possibility of extension or similar legislation and the philosophy behind the act deserves additional explanation.

The purpose of the act was to prevent widespread mortgage defaults and the distress-sale of homes resulting from the temporary loss of employment and income. The Secretary of Housing and Urban Development was authorized to make repayable emergency mortgage relief payments on behalf of distressed home owners. Such payments would be allowed if it was determined that such action was necessary to avoid foreclosure and that there was a *reasonable prospect* that the homeowner would be able to make adjustments necessary for full resumption of mortgage payments.

Assistance under the act is available provided:

1. The lender has informed the borrower of the intent to foreclose.
2. The lender and borrower indicate to the Secretary of Housing and Urban Development in writing that the borrower is in need of mortgage relief.
3. Mortgage payments have been delinquent for at least three months.
4. The borrower has incurred a substantial reduction of income as the result of unemployment or adverse economic conditions.

5. There is a reasonable prospect that the borrower will be able to fully resume mortgage payments.
6. The mortgaged property is the principal residence of the borrower.

The mortgage relief fund payments could be used to pay principal, interest, taxes, hazard insurance and mortgage insurance premiums to a maximum of $250 per month. The relief payments are repayable by the home owner upon such terms and conditions as the Secretary of Housing and Urban Development deems appropriate. Lenders faced with foreclosure by homeowners coming under the act are encouraged to exercise forbearance where such temporary relief may be available and effective.

The Federal Deposit Insurance Corporation, October 24, 1975, urged each "insured bank to review their requirements and the objectives of this act, together with the long-term prospects for repayment by delinquent borrowers before instituting foreclosure action." The Federal Deposit Insurance Corporation agreed to refrain from adversely classifying residential mortgage loans which would be covered by the act "so long as the safety and soundness of the institution is not thereby jeopardized."

While only temporary as originally enacted, the act is based on prudent collection policy prospects for repayment. At the same time the act gives relief to the lender who encourages the borrower to take advantage of temporary mortgage relief assistance.

## Prevention of Delinquencies

Before discussing measures to resolve delinquencies, preventive measures cannot be overemphasized. Frequently, delinquent borrowers may be traced to absence of preventive steps that minimize delinquencies. Such preventive measures are adopted as an important procedural step in mortgage administration. It will be noted also that preventive measures are often outside of the collection department—they call for cooperative efforts from different departments of the more highly organized mortgage servicing operation.

### ⓘ Preparing the Borrower

Experience has shown that personal indoctrination of the borrower at the inception of the loan reduces delinquencies from many causes. Preparation should start at the closing and continue through the early life of the loan. Unfortunately, the organization of the mortgage department does not always lend itself to the recommended procedures. Steps noted here, however, may be adapted to a collection system, however managed and operated.

*The closing interview*

Closings are often undertaken by an attorney, a real estate broker or an escrow agent. These parties have no continued interest in providing for current mortgage payments. Yet, the ideal place to minimize loan delinquencies is at the time of closing when emphasis could personally be placed on the fact that payments are due on the dates stipulated.

To stress this point, some lenders provide an information booklet at closing which explains the importance of prompt payment. During the closing interview, the information booklet gives the closing agent an opportunity to go over the appropriate section describing the importance of prompt payment. At the least, persons responsible for closing should be briefed on the need to stress the importance of making monthly payments on or before the required date.

*Letter communications*

Exhibit 16.1 illustrates the initial letter the borrower might receive after the date of closing. Note that the letter is written in a conversational style, stressing again the due date and the importance of meeting the payments on the time and date specified.

For those loans in which a new borrower assumes an existing mortgage, an indoctrination letter might be sent. Some lenders combine this letter with the welcome letter. Again, such a letter should stress the significance of the mortgage booklet, if it is enclosed. Or, some lenders enclose a copy of the promissory note with due date underlined, explaining that the note is enclosed for reference only.

Though phasing out because of electronic data processing, some lenders still use payment books, pre-addressed envelopes, or combinations of coupon computer cards and passbooks. If these forms are sent, the lender again has an opportunity to communicate the due date and the importance of returning the monthly payment on time.

## ② The Initial Payment Period

Over the initial months, the collection department should monitor new loans, and if the payment is not made within five days of the due date, a courteous telephone call or a friendly reminder should be sent. While these monitoring activities may increase the cost of administration, they inform the borrower that the company expects prompt payments. For a borrower undertaking his first mortgage, this step is doubly important.

Other similar devices help establish a rapport with the borrower. For example, returning monthly payments for nominal deficiencies or a clerical error is preferred to making escrow adjustments for shortages

## Exhibit 16.1

## Initial Payment Letter

Mr. & Mrs. David Smith
1213 West Ave.
Kilcummin, VA 12345

Re: Account Number 12345

Dear Mr. & Mrs. Smith:

We welcome you as a mortgage client and offer you the services of our Loan Administration Department.

We suggest that you completely review your Deed of Trust, which sets forth all of the pertinent information regarding your mortgage obligation. If you have any questions regarding these obligations, please call this office at 123-4567.

In accordance with the terms of your Deed of Trust, please note that your mortgage payments are due on the first of each month as shown below and will be applied in the following manner.

| | | |
|---|---|---|
| First Payment due on | : | January 1, 19xx |
| Real Estate Taxes | | $ 44.61 |
| Hazard Insurance | | 9.92 |
| Mortgage Insurance | | |
| Life Insurance | | |
| Total Escrow | | $ 54.53 |
| Interest & Principal | | 251.84 |
| Total Monthly Payment | | $306.37 |

Late Charge Applicable after:  the 15th of every month.
Late Charge                                  $ 12.25

Enclosed is an amortization schedule which indicates the breakdown of interest and principal for each month. Additional principal payments may be made only if received prior to the 10th of the month and in the amounts shown on the schedule.

Your escrow account will be analyzed periodically to determine whether sufficien funds are in the account to meet future payments for taxes and insurance. You will be advised of this analysis and any required adjustments in your monthly payment. Should you make any change in your hazard insurance coverage, please notify this office at once. Additionally, if you receive tax or insurance bills, please be sure to forward them to this office.

For your convenience in making your payments, a supply of coupons and return envelopes are enclosed. To insure proper credit, please enclose one coupon with each payment and make your check payable to the National Bank of Kilcummin. Should you find yourself without payment coupons, please forward to us your check noting your account number and advise us that you are out of coupons.

If we can be of assistance in any way, please do not hesitate to call on us. We look forward to serving you.

Very truly yours,


Loan Administration Department

Encl:  2

or overlooking the mistake. Such techniques show that the company is operated efficiently. Some lenders sell mortgage insurance, household insurance, and other related coverages which are collected along with the regular monthly mortgage payment. Reports indicate that these measures help reduce delinquencies.

## Other Administrative Measures

Up to this point corrective measures have been suggested that anticipate or correct for known delinquencies. Other lenders have had considerable success with congratulatory letters. A letter prepared on this note which is sent annually with escrow information on interest and principal payments, provides excellent opportunities to send this type of communication. Chances are the borrower who receives this type letter will make an extra effort to meet payments in succeeding months.

Suppose, however, the case covers a borrower who was once delinquent but who is now current in his payments. A letter of congratulations to the borrower who brought his payments to a current status creates good will and would surely help guard against further delinquency.

In other instances, collection procedures could be designed to help minimize the possibility of delinquencies. For example, if a property sale is in process, collection should be encouraged to the closing date. Care must be taken to prevent the borrower from postponing payments until the final closing date, which may extend over several weeks or months. If preliminary statements of the unpaid balance are given prior to the date of closing, some borrowers might postpone further mortgage payments pending the sale. Meanwhile, the lender is burdened with a delinquent loan which is not remedied until the closing date.

## Recommended Collection Procedures

Opinion is partly divided on specific procedures to follow in collecting delinquent payments. Much depends on circumstances of the delinquency, the personality of the collecting officer, the attitude of the borrower and the type of mortgaged property. Agreement is fairly common though on a broad set of rules that have proven effective. The specific illustrations offered here are merely suggestive of methods that may be adapted to a specific collection office. In fact, persons responsible for collection procedures are advised to continually monitor collection procedures and test new ideas that others have found useful. Collection tends to vary between rountine collections and special collection techniques used for the problem loan.

## Routine Procedures

Most companies send reminder notices of a delinquency if the payment has not been received usually after the fifth day or at the most fifteen days. The purpose of the reminder is to indicate that the company knows the payment has not been made and that the account is observed daily. The reminder should be worded to imply that the borrower has merely overlooked his payment, it is implied further that the borrower intends to make the payment as soon as possible. Most first reminder notices do not include the amount of the payment. Usually lenders include the due date with accompanying language that the payment was expected at that time. Exhibit 16.2 illustrates a reminder notice that has served well for at least one lender.

### Exhibit 16.2

### Reminder Notice

---

### FRIENDLY REMINDER

#### Your Mortgage loan payment

*on*

*which was due* ...........................................

*has not, according to our records, reached us.*

    *We assume that this was an oversight on your part, and we ask that you let us have your remittance by return mail.*

                    *Mortgage Loan Department*
                    *National Trust Company*
                    *Any, State 12345*

TO:

---

At this point a careful record should be kept of delinquent notices, interviews, telephone calls and other steps taken to collect the loan giving dates and the type of communication used to effect payment. This record is not only required by offices such as the VA, but a log of collection steps taken helps in arriving at the correct decision with respect to a possible foreclosure.

An alternative to the reminder notices is the self-addressed envelope which presumably encourages the borrower to enclose the payment by early mail. While this is a reminder, others have observed that self-addressed envelopes train the borrower to wait for receipt of the envelope before making payment. Instead of educating the borrower to make timely payments the envelope may condition the borrower to continue the delinquent payment habit. Moreover, envelopes are more costly than reminder notices.

Another approach is illustrated by the reminder notice that a late charge will be assessed unless the payment is received within the grace period. If this is the first offense, the letter may state that the late charge will be waived if the payment is received within a stated time. The late charge is a device for payments due after 15 days from the due date. Some authorities recommend that if payments are received without a late charge a follow-up card should be sent to the borrower waiving the late charge on the occasion of the first late payment. This procedure is justified on grounds that the borrower may have forgotten the late charge requirement and that the waivers will not be repeated in the future.

A borrower repeating delinquency after 15 days of the due date is normally assessed a late charge. Experience recommends that late payments without the late charge should be returned for the inclusion of the late charge. In short, a late charge is collected from borrowers who have been informed of the late charge policy.

Borrowers who are consistently delinquent and who pay numerous late charges, may be given a letter stating that they could have saved "x" number of dollars in the past year if their payments had been paid on or before the due date. In some cases this will change paying habits of borrowers who are confronted with the total amount of late charges.

*Telephone interviews*

Some offices initiate reminder letters and late charge letters during the first 30 days of the loan delinquency.

At this point a personal telephone call may also be advised. If the phone call is made within the 30 days, the collection officer should not be satisfied merely with the response that payment will be in the mail on the next day. Instead the telephone interviewer should seek answers to questions that are both informative and remedial. Suggested questions attempt to elicit responses on four points: (1) Why was the payment not made on the due date? (2) When will the payment be made? (3) Will payments be made within the due date in future months? (4) If the loan is considerably delinquent what will be the source of funds?

Cooperation from phone calls depends largely on the way the interview is conducted. No threatening tones, courteously worded phrases and no hostility must be practiced. The interviewer must create a favorable impression while not apologizing for the call. The borrower must understand that the call is made because the payments are due on an agreed date, the borrower agreed to the payment schedule, and the payment was not made.

Indeed, the first task of a telephone interviewer is to determine the reason for the delinquency. The borrower's attitude must be sensed: Is he cooperative in times of crises or is he disregarding his obligation and ignoring suggestions for help? A record of calls and the classification of the delinquency is equally important to reminder letters and notices of default.

In determining the cause of delinquency the interviewer must not be satisfied with simple generalizations. Detail all facts. For instance, excessive debts may be given as an explanation of the mortgage delinquency. A more thorough investigation is needed by securing answers to a specific set of questions:

> Who does the borrower owe?
> For what purposes were the debts incurred?
> What are the remaining balances?
> What are the monthly payments?
> Which payments are delinquent?
> What is the amount of outstanding delinquency?
> What is the borrower's monthly take-home pay?
> Is the family income sufficient to pay all debts and support the family?
> Can existing debts be refinanced?

Other similar queries are common to other excuses, i.e., sickness, unemployment, and the like. Indeed the success of trained telephone interviewers has led some lenders to regard telephone interviews as the primary collection procedure.

The argument is based on the view that reminder letters, form letters, and threats are largely ignored by the habitual late payer; that the only effective method is to establish personal contact by telephone. Probably successful telephone response depends on the skill and training of the interviewer. Among the more important interview techniques are the following requirements:

> Plan the call in advance
> Avoid arguments
> Find out all relevant facts
> Avoid irrelevant discussion; remember the purpose of the call
> Avoid threats
> Use strict follow-up procedures.

Telephone interviewers must follow professional rules of interviewing. It is quite clear that telephone interviews casually performed by the inexperienced could increase delinquencies and raise foreclosure rates.

*Personal conferences*

A loan which is delinquent beyond 30 days requires a personal interview. Lenders are divided on the question of whether the interview should be in the office or in the home of the delinquent borrower. Probably the final choice depends on circumstances of the delinquency, the length of time the loan has been carried and the attitude of the borrower. Both techniques must follow standard procedures.

*(1) Office of the Lender.* Loans facing the possibility of foreclosure—according to some collection officers—are best handled by an office interview. Person-to-person contact can be established and, with the loan file in hand, the interviewer may personally work out the best method of reinstating mortgage payments. If this approach is taken, lenders agree that both husband and wife should be present. In this way the interviewer may secure more information for analysis and diagnosis of the delinquent problem. With both parties at the interview an arrangement may be negotiated which both husband and wife sign and agree to observe in the future.

The interview should be directed to one of the following:

(1) An arrangement that provides for current payments plus an amount which will bring the loan up to date within the borrower's budget.

(2) A grant of authority to charge the borrower's personal checking account for mortgage payments if the borrower has a relatively small delinquency.

(3) For income property, an assignment of rents until the deficiency is remedied.

(4) Immediate payment of the delinquency.

Because the borrower may not continue with the reinstatement plan, a record should be kept of the interview and later action taken by the borrower in response to the collection officer's recommendation. After the interview, a classification should be made of the borrower giving reasons for the delinquency and recommendations for follow-up procedures.

*(2) Home Interviews.* At some point probably most experienced collection officers recommend a home interview—preferably in the presence of both husband and wife. The person selected for the interview is not advised to act as a collector; he is there to gain information, to gain cooperation and to make recommendations acceptable to both parties.

347

Questions on loan payment are answered by requesting the borrower to call the collection office. This latter step is suggested by lenders who guard against the borrower's belief that payments may be ignored until the field man calls again. Lenders with this experience do not recommend collections in the field. The contrasting view is that collections should be made whenever possible. The prevailing view recommends against accepting payments in the field.

It is the responsibility of the field representative to obtain all details concerning the delinquency. At the same time the present condition of the property should be reviewed—a review which may affect the decision to foreclose. Property subject to neglect adds to the possibility of foreclosure. Moreover, if the property is in good condition, it is more likely that the borrower will work out a plan of reinstatement. Clearly, it is unwise to recommend foreclosure without inspecting the property and counseling with the borrower in his or her own home.

## Follow-Up Records

Good payment habits require accurate collection records. Accurate records are required for strict follow-up procedures. For example, if the borrower agrees to make past delinquent payment by a certain date, he should be personally called if the payment is not received at the agreed time. A card file should be kept current to record all contacts with the borrower, written and oral, and other comments such as attitude of the borrower, condition of the property, and other circumstances that relate to the probability of payment. Any irregularities observed in payment habits of the borrower such as checks returned for insufficient funds or chronic delinquent records should be recorded for later remedial action. Even if the borrower calls to say that he is unable to make a payment, this fact should be noted since it illustrates a favorable attitude toward fulfilling payment obligations. A record of delinquencies also enables the staff to file proper notices required for FHA or VA loans.

## Special Collection Procedures

Under this heading fall unusual methods that have met with varying degrees of success. They attempt to shock the buyer out of an attitude of complacence into an attitude of cooperation. Circumstances in which these procedures will be used vary widely. The final objective is to place the loan on a current basis and avoid foreclosure.

Consider for example a mortgage payment on a dwelling over two payments delinquent. In these circumstances lenders have reported considerable success in sending a staff appraiser to appraise the property. It is hoped that the borrower will act to correct the payment deficiency

# Exhibit 16.3

# Home Mortgage Default Notice

Form Approved
OMB No. 63 R-1066

U.S. DEPARTMENT OF HOUSING AND URBAN DEVELOPMENT
HOUSING MANAGEMENT
SINGLE FAMILY DEFAULT MONITORING SYSTEM
(INITIAL CASE DATA REPORT)

HUD-92068A
(1-76)

Page _____ of _____ pages

CARD NO. [ 1 ] (1)

MORTGAGEE-HUD-ID-NUMBER (2-6)

MORTGAGEE SUBCODE (7-9)    NAME ADDRESS CHANGE ☐

CARD NO. [ 2 ] (1)    DUPLICATE (2-9)    WHEN KEY-PUNCHING

NAME OF MORTGAGEE (10-39)

ADDRESS (40-69)

CITY (10-24)    STATE (25,26)    ZIP CODE (27-31)

NAME OF CONTACT

PERIOD ENDING DATE

TELEPHONE (Include Area Code)

| | | CASE 1 | | | | CASE 2 | | | | CASE 3 | | | | CASE 4 | | |
|---|---|---|---|---|---|---|---|---|---|---|---|---|---|---|---|---|---|
| (Key Punch only) CARD NO. [3] DUPLICATE FROM CARD 2. | 1/2-9 | | | | | | | | | | | | | | | | |
| (A) MORTGAGE LOAN NUMBER | 22-33 | | | | | | | | | | | | | | | | |
| (B) FHA CASE NUMBER | 10-21 | | | | | | | | | | | | | | | | |
| (C) TRANSACTION INDICATOR | 34 | | | | | | | | | | | | | | | | |
| SERVICING ACQUIRED | | 7 | | | | 7 | | | | 7 | | | | 7 | | | |
| (D) DATE OF OLDEST UNPAID INSTALLMENT | 35-38 | | | | | | | | | | | | | | | | |
| (E) COLLECTION EFFORTS | 39 | 1 | | | | 1 | | | | 1 | | | | 1 | | | |
| SPECIAL FORBEARANCE - CURRENT | | | 2 | | | | 2 | | | | 2 | | | | 2 | | |
| INFORMAL FORBEARANCE | | | | 3 | | | | 3 | | | | 3 | | | | 3 | |
| SPECIAL FORBEARANCE - DELINQUENT | | | | | 4 | | | | 4 | | | | 4 | | | | 4 |
| NO COLLECTION PROGRAM | | | | | | | | | | | | | | | | | |
| (F) COUNSELING STATUS | 40 | | | | | | | | | | | | | | | | |
| BEING COUNSELED | | 1 | | | | 1 | | | | 1 | | | | 1 | | | |
| RECOMMENDED | | | 2 | | | | 2 | | | | 2 | | | | 2 | | |
| NOT RECOMMENDED | | | | 3 | | | | 3 | | | | 3 | | | | 3 | |
| UNKNOWN | | | | | 4 | | | | 4 | | | | 4 | | | | 4 |
| (G) OCCUPANCY STATUS | 41 | | | | | | | | | | | | | | | | |
| BORROWER | | 1 | | | | 1 | | | | 1 | | | | 1 | | | |
| TENANT | | | 2 | | | | 2 | | | | 2 | | | | 2 | | |
| VACANT | | | | 3 | | | | 3 | | | | 3 | | | | 3 | |
| ADVERSE | | | | | 4 | | | | 4 | | | | 4 | | | | 4 |
| UNKNOWN | | | | | | 5 | | | | 5 | | | | 5 | | | | 5 |
| (H) TERMINATION EFFORTS | 42 | | | | | | | | | | | | | | | | |
| ASSIGNMENT IN PROCESS (NOT HUD 9828) | | 1 | | | | 1 | | | | 1 | | | | 1 | | | |
| DEED IN LIEU STARTED | | | 2 | | | | 2 | | | | 2 | | | | 2 | | |
| FORECLOSURE STARTED | | | | 3 | | | | 3 | | | | 3 | | | | 3 | |
| ASSIGNMENT COMPLETED (NOT HUD 9828) | | | | | 4 | | | | 4 | | | | 4 | | | | 4 |
| DEED IN LIEU COMPLETED | | | | | | 5 | | | | 5 | | | | 5 | | | | 5 |
| FORECLOSURE COMPLETED | | | | | | | 6 | | | | 6 | | | | 6 | | | | 6 |
| (I) ESTIMATED DATE OF CONVEYANCE | 43-48 | | | | | | | | | | | | | | | | |
| (J) MORTGAGOR NAME | 49-79 | | | | | | | | | | | | | | | | |
| (Key-Punch only) CARD NO. [4] DUPLICATE FROM CARD 3. | 1/2-21 | | | | | | | | | | | | | | | | |
| (K) PROPERTY STREET NO. | 22-28 | | | | | | | | | | | | | | | | |
| (L) PROPERTY STREET | 29-53 | | | | | | | | | | | | | | | | |
| (M) PROPERTY CITY | 54-68 | | | | | | | | | | | | | | | | |
| (N) PROPERTY STATE | 69,70 | | | | | | | | | | | | | | | | |
| (O) PROPERTY ZIP | 71-75 | | | | | | | | | | | | | | | | |

Replaces FHA Form 2068 which is obsolete.

349

**Exhibit 16.3** *continued*

**Home Mortgage Default Notice**

INSTRUCTIONS FOR COMPLETING FORM HUD 92068A, INITIAL CASE DATA REPORT

This form must be completed for all HUD insured mortgages for which the loan is 90 or more days delinquent as of the date of the report (i.e., when the mortgagee's January installment has not been paid by March 31, he must report the case in the report for the period ending March 31). Information on HUD Section 312 loans serviced through FNMA is to be excluded. Subsequent reports on a case shall be made on the turnaround report, Form HUD 92068B, Status of Single Family Mortgages in Default, supplied to the mortgagee by HUD for monthly update on previously reported cases.

Form HUD 92068A shall be submitted by the holding mortgagee or its servicer but not by both, no later than five (5) working days after the end of each month to:

HLS-SFDMS Control Room
Department of Housing and Urban Development
Washington, D.C. 20410

When the mortgagee is also submitting Form HUD 92068B and Form HUD 92068C, they should be mailed in one package.

Form HUD 92068A has been designed for manual or automated reporting to HUD. Thus, the form is arranged to facilitate an 80 character punch card record. HUD has prescribed automated record formats for accepting a variety of computer generated or computer compatible report responses from and to mortgagees. Mortgagees who wish to utilize such mechanisms for reporting may do so initially. Subsequently, mortgagees may, at their option, change from automated report responses to manual or from manual reports. However, if a mortgagee plans to change his reporting medium, after the initial report cycle, he is requested to inform HUD-SFDMS Control Room at the above address.

The required mortgage information, and up to four default cases, can be posted on a single page. Where more than four cases are being reported, additional pages shall be used. Once the mortgagee has provided complete identification information to HUD (HUD-ID-Number, Name, Address, etc.) in subsequent reporting periods, will require only posting of the ID-Number, the mortgagee name, the period ending date, and the appropriate page control information.

If the mortgagee wishes to have default cases sequenced in a special order to facilitate preparation of these forms, the three-digit Subcode may be used. This Subcode will enable the mortgagee to subdivide the reported cases into managed sizes based upon the assignment of delinquent loans to units of the mortgagee's organization. When the Subcode is utilized, additional pages must be used for each different Subcode. In this case the Subcode as well as the Mortgagee-HUD-ID-Number must be posted on every page.

There are special words and/or symbols that may not be used in entering information since they are reserved for the Data Management System used by HUD to process and manage the case data. As a general rule, alpha characters that should be used are A through Z, 0 through 9, the dash or hyphen, and the plus sign. Do not use any of the following words or symbols.

AND
AT
BY
OAS
OR
+        Commercial AT Sign
*        Asterisk
?        Question Mark
:        Colon
( )      Parenthesis

Alternates for some of the words (AND, AT, END) are as follows:

- Alternate for "AND" and "AT" is a "+". An example would be "SMITH AND JONES" with "AT SPRING STREETS" replaced by "SMITH + JONES" or "14th + SPRING STREETS".

- Alternate for "END" using the example "WEST END ASSOCIATION" would be "WEST-END ASSOCIATION" or "WESTEND ASSOCIATION".

DETAIL INSTRUCTIONS

Period Ending Date - Enter "as of" date of this report. This should be the last day of the reporting month (e.g., March 31, 1976, May 31, 1976, etc.).

Mortgagee-HUD-ID-Number - Enter the first five digits of the number assigned by HUD to the mortgagee at the time of its approval. A mortgagee must report all delinquency data under a single HUD-ID-Number. This same number shall also be used on the Form HUD 92068C, Distribution of Insured Mortgages Serviced and Delinquent by HUD Area Insuring Office Jurisdiction.

Mortgagee Subcode (optional use) - Enter Subcode if desired for the mortgagee's internal reporting purposes. Separate pages must be used for each different Subcode. Subcodes may have unique address.

Mortgagee Name, Address, Etc. - Enter the name of the submitting mortgagee and the desired mailing address for future mailing purposes. The federal standard two letter State code abbreviation should be used. When additional pages are used with the same Mortgagee-HUD-ID-Number (or Subcode) the mortgagee's name should be on every page but the address need not be posted on subsequent pages.

Name/Address Change - This box is to be marked only when the mortgagee wishes to notify HUD of a new name/number and or mailing address. Enter the new name and/or address on the appropriate adjacent spaces.

Name of Contact and Telephone Number - Enter the name and telephone number of a person to whom questions may be referred regarding the SFDMS reporting.

Case Data Items

(A) Mortgagee Loan Number - Enter the mortgagee loan number by which the mortgagee identifies the case. This number cannot exceed a combination of 12 alpha or numeric characters, including separating hyphens, etc.

(B) FHA Case Number - Enter the appropriate FHA case number as it appears on your records.

(C) Transaction Indicator - Circle the number 7 if the mortgagee is reporting a case where servicing has been newly acquired and the case meets criteria for reporting as an initial report. The Collection Efforts area as follows.

(D) Date of Oldest Unpaid Installment - Enter the date (month, year) of the oldest scheduled unpaid installment due under the mortgage (e.g., February 1976 as 02/76).

(E) Collection Efforts - Circle the appropriate number (1-4) which best describes the collection effort that exists as of the reporting date. If any termination effort is currently in effect, do not circle any of the numbers in this item. The Collection Efforts area as follows.

1. Special Forbearance - Current occurs when the mortgagor is still delinquent under the mortgage but is complying with terms of a special written forbearance agreement.

2. Informal Forbearance occurs when the mortgagor is still delinquent under the mortgage but there is an existing informal agreement.

3. Special Forbearance - Delinquent occurs when the mortgagor has not kept the terms of the special written forbearance agreement.

4. No Collection Program occurs when there is no repayment plan worked out with the mortgagor to cure delinquency.

(F) Counseling Status - Circle the appropriate number (1-4) that best describes the mortgagee's recommendation for, or the existence of, counseling by a HUD-approved counseling agency. Cases recommended for counseling by the mortgagee shall be forwarded for counseling when-ever these facilities are available. If a termination effort is currently in effect, do not circle any of the numbers in this item Counseling Status includes the following:

1. Being Counseled occurs when the mortgagor is being counseled by a HUD-approved agency or organization other than the mortgagee.

2. Recommended occurs when the mortgagee recommends the mortgagor for counseling by a HUD-approved agency or organization.

3. Not Recommended occurs when the mortgagee does not recommend counseling for the mortgagor.

4. Unknown occurs when the mortgagee has no knowledge of whether the mortgagor identifying, is, or should be, counseled by a HUD-approved agency or organization.

(G) Occupancy Status - Circle the appropriate number (1-5) which indicates the mortgagee's knowledge of the occupancy status of the property. If a property is of multiple units, and is occupied in part by the borrower, circle number 1. If not "borrower-occupied," select number 2-5, but in no case should more than one number be circled to indicate occupancy status. One number must always be circled in this item. Occupancy Status includes the following:

1. Borrower occurs when the property is occupied by the mortgagor.

2. Tenant occurs when the property is occupied by a renter.

3. Vacant occurs when the property is known to be vacant.

4. Adverse occurs when the property is occupied by an adverse occupant or squatter.

5. Unknown occurs when the mortgagee has not made inspection at time of report or is unable to determine status at present time.

(H) Termination Efforts - Circle the appropriate number (1-6) which describes any termination effort in effect at the end of the reporting period. If more than one termination effort is in effect, circle only the Collection Efforts of that started most recently. The Termination Efforts are as follows:

1. Assignment in Process (not HUD 9828) occurs when the mortgagee has requested, in writing, the assignment of the mortgage to the local HUD Area Insuring Office Director.

2. Assignment Completed (not HUD 9828) occurs after the HUD Area/Insuring Office Director accepts, in writing, the assignment and forwards the filed Form 2777, Application for Insurance Benefits and General Assignment.

3. Deed-in-lieu Started occurs when the mortgagor(s) has signed the appropriate legal documents transferring ownership.

4. Foreclosure Started occurs when the mortgagee has forwarded the necessary legal documents to the foreclosure attorney for that action. Include in this category foreclosure starts under the HUD 9828 procedure.

5. Deed-in-lieu Completed occurs when the mortgagee has filed FHA Form 1025, Property Transfer and Application for Insurance Benefits.

6. Foreclosure Completed occurs at the completion of the forced sale of the mortgaged property at public auction either by a court or some other prescribed method.

(I) Estimated Date of Conveyance - For cases on which foreclosure or deed-in-lieu has been completed, and reported as such in the current month, the estimated date (month, day, year) the property will be conveyed to HUD must be entered in the appropriate space (e.g., November 12, 1976 entered as 11/12/76). The mortgagee should estimate this date, giving consideration to redemption periods, etc. that would postpone conveyance to some future time.

(J) Mortgagor Name - Enter the name currently shown on the mortgagee's records for the owner(s) of the property as it would appear on a mailing address.

(K-0) Property Address - Enter the number, street name, city, state and zip code of the property securing the loan. The Federal standard two letter state code abbreviation should be used.

GPO 1975 O - 594-343

or will at the very least contact the collection office. At the same time the field representative may inspect the property for its present condition and review the borrower's attitude towards the property. If foreclosure is inevitable, this information will be required.

Other lenders have reported success with telegrams—especially recommended for borrowers who are difficult to reach by telephone. Since a telegram is not strictly a private communication, care must be taken in not publicly exposing the borrower to a lack of privacy or character assassination. Careful wording of the telegram will be required to avoid litigation. Special delivery or letters by certified mail serve a similar purpose.

These steps are recommended to delinquent buyers who respond only to harsh treatment and usually this technique would be used after others have failed. In this case, legal advice may be required to avoid a lawsuit by the borrower who may accuse the lender of harassment.

In other instances collection letters by attorneys have proven helpful. If the letter is accompanied by an attorney's charge, it carries with it the possibility of court proceedings and may cause the borrower to remedy the delinquency. Collection authorities recommend this step only after others have failed; attorneys are poor substitutes for routine collection procedures. Ordinarily, the lender anticipates immediate foreclosure if this approach is applied.

Similarly, the threat of foreclosure or acceleration is another last resort. It should only be used if the person making the threat is willing to take the promised action. To threaten and not carry out a promised threat is universally regarded as poor collection policy.

## FHA and VA Requirements

FHA and VA loans require notice of default. For loans that are delinquent by three instalments, FHA requires written notice of default. Exhibit 16.3 illustrates the required FHA default notice. In the case of property abandonment or possible vandalism, the reporting date may be earlier. Copies of this report go to the FHA field office, the lender, and a copy to the borrower at the lender's option.

The Veterans Administration requires Notice of Default (Form 26-6850) and a Notice of Intention to Foreclose (Form 26-6851). The Notice of Default for loans 60 days delinquent must be filed with the local VA office within 45 days, providing a 105 day maximum delinquency period before notice must be filed. In the case of potential property damage, the report may be filed earlier.

Since the VA sends a representative to interview the borrower, early reporting is usually advised. Because the VA makes a determined effort to seek borrower cooperation, some lenders instruct collection departments to file a Notice of Default within 75 days of first delinquency 'rather than the maximum of 105 days. After the delinquency has reached three months, the Notice of Intention to Foreclose is another required filing. This notice, which should be sent by registered mail, must be sent not less than 30 days before starting foreclosure. Exhibits 16.4 and 16.5 illustrate how these two forms are completed.

Note that the Notice of Default requires a brief summary of reasons for the default and the steps that were taken to remedy the delinquency. The same type of summary is called for in the Notice of Intention to Foreclose. The requirement of default notice procedure must be rigidly observed. For example, the initial report to the FHA should state: Foreclosure is imminent: a deed in lieu of foreclosure is being considered: or five payments or less have not been made. FHA requires additional reports if the notice states that five or less payments have not been made, or if one of the eight following events occurs:

1. The account is reinstated
2. A forbearance agreement, approved by FHA, has been put into effect
3. Foreclosure action has started
4. A foreclosure has been completed
5. A deed in lieu of foreclosure has been granted by the borrower
6. The mortgage has been assigned to FHA in exchange for debentures
7. A report must be submitted immediately and every 60 days until the default is corrected
8. If six monthly payments are delinquent.

Some collection offices send the borrower a copy of the Notice of Default or Notice of Intention to Foreclose. A description of attempted collection efforts with the listing of contacts, notices and letters, sometimes is effective in making borrowers correct the delinquency.

## Recommending Foreclosure

One point that deserves mention is the application for forbearance. For example, a change in the facts such as a lower income, may recommend approval for the forbearance as stated on the application. Approval depends on the questions—does the borrower have a favorable attitude toward meeting payments, and, is there a strong possibility of placing the account on a current basis? A history of regular payments, though several months behind, are indicative of favorable attitudes. Exhibit 16.6 illustrates an application which has been helpful in analyzing these prospects.

# Exhibit 16.4

# VA FORM 26–6850 Notice of Default

Form Approved
OMB No. 76-R0130

**VETERANS ADMINISTRATION**

## NOTICE OF DEFAULT

(Chapter 37, Title 38, U.S.C.) (Submit Original Only)

| DATE OF THIS NOTICE | VA LOAN NUMBER | HOLDER'S LOAN NUMBER |
|---|---|---|
| | | |

**PART I – HOLDER'S NOTICE** (Submit both Parts I and II)

TO (Complete Regional Office/Center Address)

Veterans Administration
Loan Guaranty Division

HOLDER'S NAME, ADDRESS AND PHONE NUMBER

SERVICING AGENT'S NAME, ADDRESS AND PHONE NUMBER (Complete only if different from holder shown above)

PURPOSE OF LOAN (Check)

☐ HOME   ☐ FARM   ☐ BUSINESS
☐ HOME CONDOMINIUM   ☐ HOME REFINANCING   ☐ MOBILE HOME

### DESCRIPTION OF DELINQUENT LOAN

| 1. NAME AND ADDRESS OF ORIGINAL OBLIGOR(S) | 2. NAME AND ADDRESS OF PRESENT OWNER(S) | 3. LOCATION OF PROPERTY |
|---|---|---|
| | | |

| 4A. DATE OF FIRST UNCURED DEFAULT | 5. AMOUNT OF EACH INSTALLMENT | | 6. OTHER DEFAULT (Specify, i.e., real estate taxes, insurance, special assessments, etc.) |
|---|---|---|---|
| | PRINCIPAL AND INTEREST | $ | |
| 4B. INSTALLMENT PERIOD (Specify) | TAX AND INSURANCE | | |
| | OTHER | | |
| | TOTAL | $ | |

| 7. INSTALLMENT PAYMENTS NOT MADE | | | | | | | | | 8. AMOUNT OF DEFAULT | |
|---|---|---|---|---|---|---|---|---|---|---|
| √ | MONTH | YEAR | √ | MONTH | YEAR | √ | MONTH | YEAR | PRINCIPAL | $ |
| | JAN | | | MAY | | | SEP | | INTEREST | |
| | FEB | | | JUN | | | OCT | | TAX AND INSURANCE | |
| | MAR | | | JUL | | | NOV | | TOTAL | $ |
| | APR | | | AUG | | | DEC | | 9A. OUTSTANDING LOAN BALANCE AS OF (Date) | 9B. AMOUNT $ |

### HOLDER'S LOAN SERVICING

10. CONTACT WITH OBLIGOR MADE (Check)
☐ BY LETTER OR WIRE   ☐ IN PERSON   ☐ BY TELEPHONE

11. LOAN HAS BEEN EXTENDED? (Check)   ☐ YES   ☐ NO

12. DATE OF EXTENSION (Month, day, year)

13. IS PROPERTY VACANT?   ☐ YES   ☐ NO

14. IS PROPERTY OCCUPIED BY   ☐ ORIGINAL BORROWER   ☐ TRANSFEREE   ☐ TENANT   ☐ OTHER (Specify)

15. REASON FOR DEFAULT (Check (√) appropriate reason, or specify other reason in space provided.)

| DEATH OF OBLIGOR | EXTENSIVE OBLIGATIONS | OBLIGOR ENTERED MILITARY SERVICE |
|---|---|---|
| ILLNESS OF OBLIGOR | IMPROPER REGARD FOR OBLIGATIONS | |
| MARITAL DIFFICULTIES | UNSATISFACTORY PROPERTY OR EQUIP. | |
| CURTAILMENT OF INCOME | POOR MANAGEMENT | |

16. FURTHER INDULGENCE IS WARRANTED   ☐ YES   ☐ NO   REMARKS:

17A. GROUND RENT PAYABLE (Site Rental) IF ANY   $

17B. AMOUNT PAST DUE, IF ANY   $

18. SUMMARY OF LOAN SERVICING FOLLOWING DEFAULT (Include results of personal contacts and names and addresses of other obligors not shown in items 1 and 2, and status of employment and name and address of employer) (Continue on reverse if necessary.)

### OBLIGOR'S MILITARY STATUS

19. OBLIGOR IS NOT ON ACTIVE DUTY OR HAS RECEIVED NOTICE TO REPORT THEREFOR IN 90 DAYS?   ☐ YES   ☐ NO

20. DATE IF ENTRANCE ON MILITARY DUTY

21. MILITARY RANK

22. BRANCH OF SERVICE   ☐ ARMY   ☐ NAVY   ☐ AIR FORCE   ☐ MARINE CORPS   ☐ COAST GUARD   ☐ U.S. PUBLIC HEALTH

23. MAILING ADDRESS

| 24. NAME AND TITLE OF AUTHORIZED OFFICIAL (Print or type)   ☐ HOLDER   ☐ SERVICING AGENT | 25. SIGNATURE OF AUTHORIZED OFFICIAL |
|---|---|
| | |

VA FORM 26-6850, NOV 1971

---

*COMPLETE, DETACH, AND RETURN TO HOLDER*

**PART II – VA ACKNOWLEDGEMENT**

| HOLDER'S LOAN NUMBER | VA LOAN NUMBER   L | DATE OF THIS RECEIPT |
|---|---|---|
| | | |

THIS WILL ACKNOWLEDGE RECEIPT OF YOUR LOAN DEFAULT NOTICE, DATED ___ LOAN NUMBER ABOVE, MADE TO (Obligor's name)

| NAME AND TITLE OF AUTHORIZED OFFICIAL | SIGNATURE OF AUTHORIZED OFFICIAL |
|---|---|
| | |

| HOLDER OR SERVICING AGENT'S NAME AND ADDRESS | FROM (Complete Regional Office/Center address)   Veterans Administration   Loan Guaranty Division |
|---|---|
| | |

VA FORM NOV 1971 **26-6850**

# Exhibit 16.5

# VA FORM 26–6851 Notice of Intention to Foreclose

Form Approved
OMB No. 76-R0131

| VETERANS ADMINISTRATION<br>**NOTICE OF INTENTION TO FORECLOSE**<br>*(Submit original only by Certified Mail)* | DATE OF THIS NOTICE | VA LOAN NUMBER | HOLDER'S LOAN NUMBER |
|---|---|---|---|

## PART I – HOLDER'S NOTICE

| TO *(Complete Regional Office/Center address)*<br>Veterans Administration<br>Loan Guaranty Division | 1b. HOLDER'S NAME, ADDRESS AND PHONE NUMBER |
|---|---|
| | 1c. SERVICING AGENT'S NAME, ADDRESS AND PHONE NUMBER *(Complete only if different from holder shown in 1b above)* |
| 1a. NAME OF PROPERTY OWNER | |

| 2. ORIGINAL VETERAN BORROWER *(Name and present or last known address if different from Item 1a)* | 3A. LOCATION OF PROPERTY | 3B. PURPOSE OF LOAN *(Check)*<br>☐ HOME ☐ HOME *(Refinancing)*<br>☐ HOME *(Condominium)* ☐ BUSINESS<br>☐ FARM ☐ MOBILE HOME |
|---|---|---|

| 4. DATE OF FIRST UNCURED DEFAULT | 5. POSSIBILITIES OF CURING DEFAULT HAVE BEEN EXHAUSTED?<br>☐ YES ☐ NO *(If "No", explain in Item 13)* | 6. WERE OTHER TRANSFEREES INVOLVED?<br>☐ YES ☐ NO *(If "Yes", complete as much as possible of Item 7)* |
|---|---|---|

### 7. OTHER TRANSFEREE DATA

| NAME<br>(A) | LAST KNOWN ADDRESS<br>(B) | NAME OF EMPLOYER<br>(C) | ADDRESS OF EMPLOYER *(If known)*<br>(D) |
|---|---|---|---|
| | | | |
| | | | |
| | | | |

### 8. REPOSSESSION AND/OR FORECLOSURE DATA / 9. UNPAID BALANCE OF LOAN, INCLUDING UNPAID ACCRUED INTEREST

| A. PROCEEDINGS WILL BE INSTITUTED ON OR AFTER *(Date)* | B. PROCEEDINGS UNDER EMERGENCY PROVISIONS OF VAR 4280 (E) OR 4317 (A) WERE INSTITUTED ON *(Date)* | C. ESTIMATED COST OF FORECLOSURE AND/OR REPOSSESSION<br>$ | 9. A. DATE | 9. B. AMOUNT<br>$ |
|---|---|---|---|---|

| 10. TOTAL AMOUNT OF DELINQUENCY | | 11. OTHER PRIOR LIENS *(If any)* | |
|---|---|---|---|
| A. PRINCIPAL | $ | A. SPECIAL ASSESSMENTS *(Include future installments)*<br>$ | B. PAST DUE GROUND RENTS<br>$ |
| B. INTEREST | | C. DELINQUENT TAXES<br>$ | D. OTHER *(Specify)*<br>$ |
| C. CHARGES *(Under VAR 4276 (A) or 4313 (A))* | | 12. VOLUNTARY CONVEYANCE DATA *(VAR 4283 (C) or (4320 (C))* | |
| D. TOTAL DELINQUENCY | $ | A. IS DEED IN LIEU OF FORECLOSURE OR VOLUNTARY CONVEYANCE OF THE SECURITY OBTAINABLE? *(If "Yes", fill in Item B)* ☐ YES ☐ NO | B. WOULD IT BE LEGALLY FEASIBLE TO ACCEPT SUCH CONVEYANCE? ☐ YES ☐ NO |

| 13. SUMMARY OF LOAN SERVICING SINCE NOTICE OF DEFAULT WAS GIVEN |
|---|
| |

### 14. OCCUPANCY DATA

| A. IS PROPERTY OCCUPIED?<br>☐ YES ☐ NO | B. OCCUPANT IS *(Check)*<br>☐ ORIGINAL BORROWER ☐ TRANSFEREE ☐ TENANT ☐ OTHER *(Specify)* | C. RENTAL RATE *(Month, year, etc.)*<br>$ PER |
|---|---|---|
| D, IF VACANT, KEYS TO PROPERTY MAY BE OBTAINED FROM: | E. NAME OF OCCUPANT *(If other than original borrower)* | |
| F. IF VACANT, HAVE STEPS BEEN TAKEN TO PROTECT PROPERTY?<br>☐ YES ☐ NO | G. DATE TO WHICH RENT IS PAID | H. DATE LEASE EXPIRES |

| 15. NAME AND TITLE OF AUTHORIZED OFFICIAL<br>☐ HOLDER<br>☐ SERVICING AGENT | 16. SIGNATURE OF AUTHORIZED OFFICIAL |
|---|---|

VA FORM 26-6851

---

*COMPLETE, DETACH AND RETURN TO HOLDER*

| **PART II**<br>VETERANS ADMINISTRATION ACKNOWLEDGMENT | 1. HOLDER'S LOAN NUMBER | 2. VA LOAN NUMBER<br>L |
|---|---|---|
| IMPORTANT – Be sure you comply with VAR 4282 or 4319 and send us copies of all procedural papers or copy of notice of sale. No sale should be held unless notice has been received from VA regarding the amount to be specified under VAR 4283(A) or 4320 (A). | | 3. DATE OF RECEIPT |
| 4. RECEIPT IS ACKNOWLEDGED OF *(Check one)*<br>☐ NOTICE OF INTENTION TO FORECLOSE<br>☐ NOTICE OF INTENTION TO REPOSSESS<br>☐ NOTICE UNDER VAR 4280 (E) OR 4317 (A) | 5. SIGNATURE AND TITLE OF LOAN GUARANTY OFFICIAL | |
| 6. HOLDER OR SERVICING AGENT'S NAME AND ADDRESS | 7. FROM *(Complete Regional Office/Center address)*<br>VETERANS ADMINISTRATION<br>LOAN GUARANTY DIVISION | |

VA FORM
NOV 1971 **26-6851**

# Exhibit 16.6

## An Application for Forbearance

FHA FORM NO. 371
Rev. 6/64

Project No.
Project Name
Project Location

### FORBEARANCE AND MODIFICATION AGREEMENT

*(For Insured Mortgages Pursuant to Sec. 220.753 and 220.765 of the Regulations)*

THIS AGREEMENT, made by and between
hereafter called Mortgagor, and
hereafter called Mortgagee, and

as Trustee(s), witnesseth:

1. WHEREAS, Mortgagor has executed its Note dated                          , 19        , for
\$                      , as secured by a Mortgage (Deed of Trust), hereafter called Mortgage, of even date, re-
corded in Book                , Page                , County of                , State of
to which Mortgage and the record thereof reference is made for the payment terms and all other covenants and
conditions therein contained, to the same extent as though herein at length set out and made a part of this
Agreement; and,

2. WHEREAS, Mortgagee is the owner and holder of said Note and Mortgage which Note and Mortgage are
in default.

NOW, THEREFORE, in consideration of the mutual promises herein, the parties hereto agree as follows:

A. The payment terms of the Note and Mortgage are modified as follows:
Interest at the rate of                          per centum per annum shall be payable monthly on the first
day of                          and on the first day of each month thereafter until the Note is paid. Regular
installments to principal now due or otherwise falling due under the terms of the Note and Mortgage during the
period of this Agreement are hereby deferred and shall not be due and payable until the first day of the first
month following the Final Forbearance Payment Date, hereafter described, or following the date to which the
Final Forbearance Payment Date is extended in writing.

B. Beginning with the first day of                          , hereafter referred to as Initial Forbearance Payment Date, and continuing on the first day of each succeeding month thereafter to and including the
first day of                          , hereafter referred to as Final Forbearance Payment Date, Mortgagor
agrees to pay to Mortgagee a Stipulated Payment consisting of the sum of accruals as provided in the Mortgage
for ground rents, water rates, taxes, assessments, hazard insurance premiums and mortgage insurance premiums,
plus \$                          .

C. In addition, on or before the tenth day of each month during the term of this Agreement, Mortgagor
agrees to pay to Mortgagee net income for the previous month as shown by a monthly accounting of receipts and
disbursements satisfactory to the Mortgagee. A copy of said accounting shall be furnished to the Commissioner.

As herein used, net income shall include all cash receipts from said property in excess of: (1) necessary and reasonable disbursements satisfactory to Mortgagee for operating expenses, exclusive of depreciation;
(2) the Stipulated Payment; (3) franchise and other taxes incident to the operation of the property, payment of
which is not provided for under the provisions of the Mortgage.

D. All sums received shall be applied to overdue monthly payments in the order in which they become
due under the Note and Mortgage (as herein modified with respect to principal). Any excess funds remaining
after such application shall be deposited by the Mortgagee in a special fund to be applied in accordance with
paragraph F.

E. Failure of Mortgagor to make any payments required by the terms of this Agreement within ten days
of the due date, or the breach by Mortgagor of any of the other covenants herein set forth or set forth in said
Mortgage, or failure to pay operating and maintenance expenses when due, shall constitute a default under this
Agreement and under the Mortgage and the entire principal sum and accrued interest and all other sums secured
by said Mortgage shall at once become due and payable, without notice at the option of Mortgagee.

So long as there is compliance with these terms, Mortgagee agrees to forbear from taking any action
with respect to any default in interest under the Mortgage and to forbear from claiming under its contract of insurance with the Federal Housing Commissioner.

F. The aggregate sum of regular installments to principal deferred herein and any delinquent interest
shall be due and payable in a lump sum on the first day of the first month following Final Forbearance Payment Date, or following the date to which Final Forbearance Date is extended in writing, and the Mortgagor
shall resume payments in accordance with the terms of the Note and Mortgage existing prior to the Agreement
(unless a Modification Agreement is entered into and approved by the Commissioner).

355

# Exhibit 16.6 *continued*

## An Application for Forebearance

NOTHING HEREIN CONTAINED shall in anywise impair the security now held for said indebtedness, it being the intent of the parties hereto that the terms and provisions of said Note and Mortgage shall continue in full force and effect except as modified hereby.

In the event this Agreement is executed on a date later than Initial Forbearance Payment Date, then all Stipulated Payments, all accountings hereby required, and all Net Income accrued to the date of execution, if not already paid, shall be immediately paid to Mortgagee.

This Agreement shall be effective only upon the approval of the Federal Housing Commissioner evidenced in the space provided below.

IN WITNESS WHEREOF, the Mortgagor has duly executed this instrument this          day of      , 19    .

ATTEST:

_____      By _____
*Secretary*                                   *President*

IN WITNESS WHEREOF, the Mortgagee has executed this instrument this        day of      , 19    .

ATTEST:

_____      By _____
*Secretary*                                   *President*

THE TRUSTEE has executed this instrument to acknowledge his (its) assent thereto and agrees to continue to act in such capacity under the terms as modified herein.

_____
*Trustee*

ATTEST:

_____      By _____

APPROVED:

FEDERAL HOUSING COMMISSIONER

By _____      Date: _____

FHA-Wash., D. C.

19426+-P Rev. 6/64

356

A seriously delinquent loan, over 90 days, with only a remote possibility of collection requires an analysis of the advisability of enforcing the acceleration clause or initiating foreclosure. Such an analysis calls for a complete review of the collection file, property inspection and reappraisal to establish the most probable sales price and the interpretation of personal interviews with the borrowers. The prediction of possible results of foreclosure action, its risks and its advisability, in terms of alternatives is necessary to the final decision. Foreclosure to a great extent depends on the following:

*Considerations in making foreclosure recommendation*

1. The remaining balance of a loan (including unpaid taxes, liens and insurance)
2. The current market value of the property to be realized at foreclosure sale
3. The mortgage terms, including interest, maturity, and the loan to value ratio
4. Special restraints imposed by statutory foreclosure laws; namely, equity of redemption and statutory equity of redemption
5. Legal costs of foreclosure
6. The cost of rehabilitating abandoned or vandalized property
7. Reimbursement by federal agencies in the case of insured or guaranteed loans.

With this information the borrower's record is reviewed in the light of his present financial position, attitude toward the outstanding debt, and his past payment record. A summary of these facts with a recommendation for foreclosure or other alternatives completes the collection agent's responsibility.

## Collection Management

The discussion has dealt with methods of resolving individual cases. Equally important is the collection system. The preferred system should enable the staff to quickly identify rising trends in delinquencies, to disclose the problem cases, and to make a periodic review of the effectiveness of collection procedures. Certain reports must be prepared for management to guide the development of an effective collection program.

### Monthly Reports

The collection department is usually responsible for listing delinquencies by 30 day, 60 day, 90 day or more categories showing the number of loans, the type of loan, and the dollar volume. The reports allow comparison with earlier reports on a month to month basis, allowing for seasonal changes and allowing a comparison with other national reports. A dangerous rise in delinquencies is quickly recognized which can be remedied by strengthening collection procedures.

## Individual Account Review

Problem delinquent borrowers usually in the 60 day and 90 day delinquent category, deserve a monthly summary review. Such reports should show the borrower's problem, and the effectiveness of steps taken to remedy the delinquency. Such a summary should be sufficiently factual to allow discussion by staff members. As a loan moves from the 60 day to the 90 day category, this review provides staff with the opportunities to introduce new collection procedures.

## Collection Efficiency

This portion of the review evaluates the cost and effectiveness of organizational collection procedures. Here the time and cost of preparing various notices of default, reminder letters, personal interviews, and telephone effectiveness may result in improved collection practices. The analysis identifies collection activity that leads to the highest quality of effectiveness. Ordinarily, as the number of delinquencies increase, collection procedures deteriorate. This is because more staff time is taken in processing new delinquencies at the expense of follow-up procedures of past delinquencies. In these circumstances, priorities must be established for resources devoted to collection. That is, a doubling of collection expenses may not necessarily double collection receipts. An acceptable balance must be established in which a given sum devoted to collection produces an acceptable financial result.

Quite often, measuring collection efficiency is another way of evaluating underwriting procedures. Simply stated, collection problems may be created by above market appraisals, inadequate credit evaluation, or optimistic projections of the loan production staff. On the other hand, rising delinquencies may point out shortcomings in follow-up procedures relating to repeat delinquents.

# Chapter 17

# Mortgage Portfolio Administration

Certain administrative problems encountered in working with mortgage portfolios require explanation. Among the leading problems important to mortgage administration are foreclosure procedures that govern rights of foreclosure on defaulted mortgages. In view of the costs of foreclosing, it seems advisable to explain the characteristics of mortgages that are closely associated with high probabilities of default. And since the mortgage portfolio must contribute to organizational objectives, the chapter includes a discussion of mortgage portfolio yields and their profitability.

## Foreclosure Procedures

Foreclosure procedures may be instituted if the borrower defaults according to terms of the mortgage. It is popularly believed that failure to pay principal and interest constitutes the sole reason for foreclosing on a mortgage. A review of mortgage covenants, however, indicates that the borrower must agree to certain other conditions while the mortgage is effective. The lender has the right to foreclose if these conditions are not met. That is, the borrower ordinarily has the duty to pay property taxes, special assessments, and maintain a fire insurance policy in effect. At the same time, he agrees not to commit undue waste.

To be sure, the lender hopes to avoid foreclosure. Indeed, the main effort of mortgage collection is directed to avoiding the possibility of foreclosure. In those instances in which foreclosure seems the only reasonable remedy, foreclosure procedures must rigidly follow state law.

It is true that states vary considerably in procedures controlling the right of foreclosure. The requirement of notice, the time of foreclosure and the period of redemption also vary between states. Generally, foreclosure must proceed under one of four main categories: (1) strict foreclosure, (2) foreclosure by action and sale, (3) foreclosure by entry and possession (or writ of entry), and (4) foreclosure by power of sale. Within each category, foreclosure procedures follow fairly uniform requirements.

*Types of Foreclosure*

① **Strict Foreclosure** *by act of court*

Strict foreclosure applies to Connecticut, Illinois and Vermont. Though permitted in other states, its use is usually limited to extinguishing redemption rights of subordinate mortgages or liens. Strict foreclosure is probably limited because a borrower whose equity exceeds the amount of the debt has no right to the additional sum which he would receive if foreclosure proceeded by a public sale. Under strict foreclosure, the borrower's rights to the property cease after a given date. Here the title vests with the lender when the court issues a decree, effectively terminating all rights of the mortgagor.

Because of the possible injustice against the borrower, some states confine strict foreclosure to mortgages in which the value of the security does not exceed the debt plus accrued interest and costs. In addition the lender may have to take the property in full satisfaction of the mortgage, waiving deficiency judgments. Title is conveyed by instituting a suit for a judicial decree to transfer title.

② **Foreclosure by Action and Sale** *by court (prove debt, prove mortgage) (court authorizes sale & issue title after sale)*

Though permitted in all states, foreclosure by action and sale is closely regulated by statute and by orders of the court. Because of certain legal requirements which must be observed, this method of foreclosure is usually more costly and takes longer to acquire clear title. However, it is the most common method of foreclosure. In general most states require a fairly standard procedure that includes a set of fairly common steps. The timing and details of execution, however, are unique to each state:

1. The lender institutes a suit for foreclosure in the local court of jurisdiction.
2. The case is tried, with the defendant or borrower submitting a defense against the court action. At the end of the court proceeding, a decree is entered.
3. The court determines the amount due on the mortgage and issues an order authorizing sale of the real estate subject to the defaulted mortgage.
4. The sale will be executed according to state law and reported to the court for confirmation. In some states if the property is sold for less than the mortgage principal, a deficiency judgment may be entered against the borrower. Conversely, if the price received at sale is greater than the mortgage principal, the surplus will be paid according to priorities established by state law. After all lien claimants are satisfied, the amount remaining is paid to the defaulting borrower.

In most states these procedures are subject to numerous qualifications. Statutory redemption periods restrict the right of the purchaser during the redemption period. Further, foreclosure sales are not final unless they are confirmed by the court. Moreover, the statutes require posting of notice of the sale. It may even require that the sale be published a certain number of days in a designated local newspaper. Usually the foreclosure sale may only be undertaken after a stated number of days after publication. In most jurisdictions the purchaser is entitled to a title free of defects and outstanding liens, though some courts transfer title subject to all outstanding liens.

③ **Foreclosure by Entry and Possession** by court *lender attains writ of possession which tells*

Possession by the lender may be taken under this procedure under *borrower* peaceable possession or by writ of entry—for example, in Massachu-*to get out.* setts, Maine, New Hampshire, and Rhode Island. If possession is taken *sale occurs* peaceably, according to state law, the lender must record a Certificate *w/out fur-ther judicial* of Entry, or the lender must publish the entry with details of posses-*action* sion and record an affidavit attesting to the publication.

Under the writ of entry the lender declares the borrower's default and secures a judgment granting the lender possession if the borrower does not satisfy the judgment within a given time. After the period of statutory redemption expires, title passes to the lender. Deficiency judgments may be obtained for that portion of the mortgage that is not satisfied by current estimates of the value of the real estate. That is, if the current value of the real estate is less than the outstanding mortgage, a judgment for the unsatisfied portion may be obtained.

④ Foreclosure by Power of Sale   Tennessee

*[handwritten margin note: borrower grants to lender right t͟ sell prop. w/out court interven͟ tion. Lender must give notice of public Sa͟ lender se͟ prop. at p͟ outcry]*

In the absence of a statute to the contrary, the lender may add a clause to the mortgage granting the lender power of sale in the event of default. Eighteen states permit the use of this clause, though statutes of other states require foreclosure by action and sale, effectively voiding the power of sale clauses. Lenders favor power of sale clauses since their use avoids court supervision. Like strict foreclosure, generally the mortgagee must give notice of the sale, which is followed by sale at public auction. Such notice typically cites the time and place of sale and states the facts of default. Failure to sell the property at the highest possible price may cause the court to set aside the sale. In these sales, especially if the sale is undertaken by a public official, the mortgagee ordinarily has the right to submit a bid, which is generally not less than the outstanding principal.

It should be mentioned that in the face of an impending foreclosure, the mortgagor may voluntarily transfer property to the mortgagee under a deed in lieu of foreclosure. With this device, the lender assumes all rights of the mortgagor, subject to outstanding liens and other obligations filed against the mortgaged property. Foreclosure under judicial decree, on the other hand, normally removes outstanding liens attached to the mortgaged property. Another disadvantage relates to the possibility of duress. If it is found that the lender has taken undue advantage of the mortgagor, the lender faces the possibility of a suit on the basis of mortgagee fraud. If there is no danger of this possibility, a deed in lieu of foreclosure saves time, attorney's fees, and other foreclosure costs.

Another point deserving qualification concerns deficiency judgments. In some states they are prohibited. Other states limit them. Where deficiency judgments prevail, the mortgagee, upon the borrower's default, may elect either to exercise his rights against the property, i.e., institute foreclosure, or attempt collection against the personal assets of the borrower. This action is advised if the value of the real estate is less than the outstanding mortgage and the borrower has substantial assets. Under favorable statutes, a deficiency judgment may be collected if the lender after foreclosure does not recover the full amount of the outstanding debt.

## Mortgage Risk Analysis

A crucial problem in administering mortgages is the prevention of mortgage default. In fact, under favorable mortgage terms, the borrower may find it more profitable to abandon the mortgage than to continue making payments. This situation frequently arises among owners who have small equity and who must move after relatively short periods of ownership. In such a case, the equity interest may not be sufficient to pay for costs of property transfer. This may occur even under favorable market conditions. If the market is unfavorable or if the mortgage is placed on property in a declining area, the borrower has an added incentive for abandoning the property and foregoing mortgage payments.

This point is illustrated in Table 17.1 showing the reduction in principal over selected years for a 9 percent, 30 year mortgage. The example further assumes a $30,000 sale and a 95 percent loan to value ratio. Under these conditions the monthly mortgage payment will be $229.32. For the first payment, the interest will amount to $213.75 while the remainder of $15.57 applies to principal reduction. With the relatively small payment on principal, the equity build-up at the end of the first year totals only $199.50. Hence the total equity including the original downpayment gives the owner an interest of $1,699.50.

### Table 17.1

### Percent of Mortgage Repaid at the End of Selected Years, 9%, 30 Year Term

| End of Year | Percent of Mortgage Repaid | Owner Equity 95% Loan [a] |
|---|---|---|
| Beginning of year | | $ 1,500.00 |
| 1 | .7 | 1,699.50 |
| 2 | 1.4 | 1,899.00 |
| 3 | 2.2 | 2,127.00 |
| 4 | 3.1 | 2,383.50 |
| 5 | 4.1 | 2,668.50 |
| 10 | 10.6 | 4,521.00 |
| 15 | 20.7 | 7,399.50 |
| 20 | 61.2 | 18,942.00 |
| 25 | 96.1 | 28,888.50 |
| 30 | 100.0 | 30,000.00 |

[a] A $30,000 purchase is assumed with an initial $1,500 equity and a $28,500 mortgage.

If the $30,000 property must be sold during the first year, the equity interest would be insufficient to pay for the typical 6 percent real estate commission and other legal costs associated with a property transfer. It will be noted that this circumstance prevails through the third year. After the fourth or fifth year the equity increases to the point that a favorable sale and loan assumption is more likely. If land and building costs have increased more rapidly than the property has depreciated, these circumstances are even more favorable for refinancing or continuation of the loan. However, if the market is unfavorable, an owner faced with an unavoidable change of residence may elect to rent or abandon the property.

These comments apply only against property that has been well maintained in a neighborhood showing stable or rising values. If the property has been unduly depreciated, poorly maintained, and subject to unusual wear and tear or if the neighborhood has declined or if the community is temporarily over supplied with housing, there is an even greater likelihood of a substantial number of mortgage defaults.

For these reasons, mortgage risk analysis assumes unusual importance. While mortgage default and foreclosures may not be entirely eliminated, they may be reduced to an acceptable point by reducing the number of mortgages known to have a high rate of default. It should be added that in qualifying mortgage risks, mortgage officers must not discriminate on the basis of national origin or race. This is required by the Fair Housing Act of 1968.

## Financial Causes of Mortgage Default and Delinquency

The possibility of foreclosure depends partly on factors associated with the mortgage security; namely, factors associated with financial aspects of the mortgage and the real estate subject to the mortgage. To reduce mortgage risk arising from the real estate, attention is directed to location, suitability of the property for which it is used, construction features, depreciation in all its forms, neighborhood trends and the local economy. While economic trends and local economies are not subject to much control, the financial aspects have been subject to much study and analysis since they are more directly controllable by the lender. The causes of mortgage delinquency and foreclosure from financial aspects are grouped under the financial factors related to the particular mortgage and the individual borrower.

*Financial causes of mortgage default*

It is customary to consider mortgages in default only if they have been delinquent for 90 days or more. Similarly, a delinquent mortgage is usually regarded as a mortgage in which payments are 15 or more days past due. The more common causes of delinquencies and foreclosure are listed under the following points. Broadly speaking, mortgage delinquencies and foreclosure rates increase with—

1. an increase in the loan to value ratio,
2. an increase in the housing expense to income ratio,
3. unfavorable borrower characteristics,
4. an increase in the term of the mortgage,
5. mortgages arranged with subordinate financing,
6. the decreasing age of the borrower,

7. a decrease in the borrower's occupational level,
8. a lower value property,
9. new mortgages relative to existing mortgages.

Studies by various agencies and financial organizations have consistently reported that the number of foreclosures increases as the loan to value ratio increases. Apparently the small downpayment fails to provide sufficient equity for the borrower to encourage continuation of mortgage payments in the face of a change of residence or decreased income. With a higher equity interest, the borrower has a greater inducement to protect his investment by securing other local employment or by disposing of the property through normal trade arrangements.

Studies by federal housing agencies have shown that the borrower with a relatively high housing expense to income ratio has a higher than average foreclosure rate. A study of FHA and VA loans for example indicated that 33 percent of FHA and 41 percent of VA loans that were foreclosed had housing expense to income ratios of 30 percent or more, i.e., the higher the housing expenses to income the greater the probability of foreclosure. Other studies have shown a similar trend for conventional loans. At the time, typical housing expense to income ratios for FHA and VA loans fell between 22 and 23 percent. These data suggest that borrowers with unusually high housing expenses (which includes utility costs, property taxes, insurance in addition to mortgage payments) may not have the resources, the willingness or ability to make mortgage payments with unusually high housing expenses.

Data from at least one study undertaken by the United States Savings and Loan League found a close correlation between certain borrower characteristics and mortgage risks. Delinquent payments were more than likely for borrowers with incomes derived from their own business, unskilled laborers and salesmen. Management executives, white collar workers and professionals were at the other extreme with the lowest rate of mortgage delinquency. Family disruption by death or divorce resulted in a higher than average rate of mortgage delinquency. Finally borrowers under 40 showed a trend toward higher delinquencies than borrowers over 40; borrowers with less than five years of job tenure were more risky than borrowers that held a job for more than five years.

Increasing the term of the mortgage, as numerous studies have shown, seems to increase mortgage delinquencies and foreclosures. In part, this relationship may arise from a common cause: the borrowers that seek the longest mortgage terms to reduce monthly payments may also be the marginal borrower with relatively low incomes, low equity and poor income stability. On the other hand as the mortgage term is extended, the equity build-up decreases to the point that, at least in the early years of the mortgage the equity may actually decrease. This result arises from physical depreciation of the structure or a decline in local real estate values. For whatever reason, the available statistics suggest that longer-term mortgages are more likely to be foreclosed than mortgages of shorter terms.

Conventional first mortgages may be granted with a third party accepting a second mortgage or junior lien. Again the second mortgage raises two questions. The first question deals with the low equity position of the borrower. If the need for secondary financing exists, the asset position of the borrower is low, his equity position is reduced. Such a borrower is in the same relative position as the borrower who negotiates the highest possible loan to value ratio.

The second issue concerns the additional monthly payments to satisfy the junior lien. In periods of income loss, job changes or other difficulties, a borrower facing two mortgage payments stands a good chance of falling in the delinquent or mortgage default category. While there may be exceptions to these generalizations, as a group, mortgages negotiated with subordinate financing have a higher probability of foreclosure than conventional first mortgage and equity payments.

Statistically speaking, the records show that young borrowers have higher foreclosure rates than borrowers, say, over 40. These relationships are not too surprising, since it may be anticipated that the younger borrower has less job seniority, changes jobs more frequently and has less income security. The borrower over 40, as a group, probably has greater family responsibilities and is more likely to be established in a chosen occupation with greater income security.

By the same token it may be anticipated that the lower the occupational level the greater the chance of foreclosure. The unskilled worker generally may be expected to have less income security than a skilled machinist or a school teacher. The higher the level of training, other things remaining equal, the less likely the borrower will be in default.

A lower purchase price and a decrease in the borrower's equity are probably related to the same cause. It would be reasonable to assume that lower purchase prices are highly correlated with lower incomes, smaller assets and lower occupational levels, all of which have been associated with relatively high foreclosure rates.

A mortgage in which payments have been made for a number of years, say 3 to 5 years, has a greater chance of avoiding foreclosure than a mortgage of less than one year. Observers have noticed that borrowers with a record of current payments over five years have established habits that are more likely to insure continued observance of mortgage payments. Moreover, a borrower with a record of paying for five years has probably increased the equity to the point that he would avoid foreclosure by sale, or by making payments from savings. As it has been suggested previously, the new mortgage is more likely to include borrowers with no established habits of repayment and with a relatively low equity. The combination results in mortgages that have a higher probability of foreclosure.

A study of FHA mortgages confirms many of these generalizations on foreclosure rates. With respect to the length of the mortgage, it was found that the least risk mortgage consisted of 20 year mortgages on new dwellings. The next least risky mortgage included mortgages recently endorsed for 20 years on existing homes, and 25 year mortgages on new dwellings.[1]

A group of properties showing the highest rate of foreclosure, as it might be suspected, dealt with 25 year mortgages on existing property and all 30 year mortgages. Numerically, default probabilities on 30 year mortgages were eight times greater than default experience on 20 year mortgages on new dwellings. In sum, the shorter the mortgage term, the greater rate of equity buildup, which in itself discourages default. Clearly, risks rise proportionately with the increase in the length of mortgage. The data also suggest that default rates on 25 and 20 year mortgages on existing dwellings are four times greater than on new dwellings financed under identical mortgage terms.

Studies of FHA loans have confirmed relative risks on mortgages with relatively high loan to value ratios. Substantial increases in default were related to fairly nominal increases in loan to value ratios. Default rates increased 16 percent when the loan to value ratio changed from 90 to 91 percent; they increased by 50 percent when the loan to value ratio on FHA loans increased from 96 to 97 percent.

The observation that younger borrowers tend to have higher foreclosure rates than older borrowers is also supported by the evidence. It is also true that family heads under 30 require generally higher loan to value financing and loans of longer maturities, both of which are associated with high default rates.

In contrast, the middle aged and older borrowers tend to make the largest downpayments and have mortgages with shorter maturities. This has led some observers to conclude that the financing characteristics of the mortgage are the determining factor in accounting for rising mortgage default. Age of the borrower is less significant since younger families tend to demand more low downpayment loans than older families. Similarly, families with lower income demand more favorable mortgage maturities and loan to value ratios than higher income families. This suggests that the terms of the mortgage are more directly related to mortgage default than borrower characteristics.

---

1. Consult George M. von Furstenberg, "Default Risk on FHA-Insured Home Mortgages As A Function of the Terms of Financing: A Quantitatine Analysis," *Journal of Finance,* June 6, 1969. pp. 459-478.

*Causes of mortgage delinquency*

A recent study of 370 mortgages revealed that approximately 25 percent average 14 days of delinquency a month. Such a delinquency rate
applied to a portfolio of $100,000,000 could account for an annual loss
of $100,000 or more. These losses are caused, for example, by payments
due on the first of the month which are not collected until the 15th of
the month, causing lenders to lose the use of the money for 15 days.
Like causes of mortgage foreclosure, these delinquencies, which may
eventually turn to foreclosures, are related to the following well defined characteristics:

> The ratio of property value to annual income
> The ratio of monthly mortgage payments to monthly income
> The percentage of purchase price provided as downpayment
> Stable annual income
> Number of satisfactory credit references
> Number of family members
> The ages of family members
> Previous marital experiences
> Stability of spouse's employment.

It is clear that some of these characteristics measure the effect of a
single item. For example, the ratio of property value to annual income
and the ratio of monthly mortgage payments to monthly income are
common to the borrower's income. Likewise it may be expected that
the number of family members increases with the age of family members. As a result of the statistical analysis of conventional loans, it was
concluded that mortgage delinquencies were predicted by the five main
characteristics listed below in the order of their importance.

> The loan payment to income ratio (net monthly)
> Unsatisfactory credit report
> Age differences between spouses
> Employment stability
> Age of wife.

The first two items agree with the common observations of other
studies. In the third category, it would seem that if the wife is as old
or older than the husband, better repayments result. Though this gen-
eralization may not hold true for all mortgage portfolios, it was significant in the study of 370 conventional loans in the St. Louis area. It
would be reasonable to expect that borrowers with a stable employment would have better repayment habits. An unexplained variable is
the age of the wife at the time of the loan. This study revealed that
the younger the wife, the more likely that favorable repayment habits
result. With the exception of the age of wife item, it would seem that

some of the financial aspects of a mortgage borrower constitute double counting. Such financial items as the income to loan ratio, the income to price ratio, the downpayment percentage, and the ratio of monthly payment to monthly income are measurements of essentially the same financial characteristics of a loan applicant.

## Property Characteristics Associated with Default

The probability of foreclosure rests not only on borrower characteristics and financial aspects of the mortgage, but on the property pledged as security. To be sure, loans that face the possibility of foreclosure depend on how current economic conditions affect different classes of borrowers. A layoff in military aircraft production may affect loans of a large group of borrowers dependent on a single large industry. Or even a region dependent on exports of a major product may affect skilled workers in contrast to professional workers. In other words, different conditions lead to a varied pattern of delinquencies and foreclosures when economic conditions change. While these variables may not be predicted, there are certain rules to guide mortgage lending and portfolio management that deal with property characteristics.

Large mortgage lenders maintain records so that they may *diversify* their mortgage portfolio with respect to geographic areas and types of properties mortgaged. A separate discussion of these two points shows how they lead to mortgage portfolio policy.

### Geographic diversification

With respect to a bank's lending area, it will be observed that the probability of foreclosure is least for properties located in the direction of growth. Neighborhoods are always in the process of change. As new neighborhoods are created families migrate from the older districts causing real estate values to increase in one area and decline relatively in others.

One investigator has recommended that neighborhoods showing the highest degree of mortgage risk may be identified by comparing the rate of change in substandard housing as shown by census information. The number of dilapidated, substandard housing is regarded as a good index indicating declining neighborhoods and relatively high mortgage risks. By projecting past rates of change, it is claimed that neighborhoods showing the highest and lowest risk may be identified.

While these techniques may not be universally applicable, they do suggest that the probability of foreclosure varies widely between neighborhoods of different characteristics. Accordingly, mortgage administrators maintain familiarity with neighborhoods to diversify the portfolio by favoring growth areas and limiting mortgages in declining areas. Some lenders, faced with mortgage applications from declining areas compensate for the higher risks of default by charging higher interest rates.

Since September 30, 1976, certain lenders have been required by the Home Mortgage Disclosure Act of 1975 to disclose mortgage loan data by census tract or ZIP code. The act affects lenders with over $10 million in assets that are located in a Standard Metropolitan Statistical Area, federally insured or regulated, and that originate insured or guaranteed loans, or loans intended to be sold to FNMA, GNMA, or FHLMC. The required reports on the geographic location of mortgages must also be made available to the public at the lender's home or branch office.

In the final analysis the lending officer will be guided by a continual review with real estate brokers, builders, appraisers, and others active in the real estate market. Information from these sources tends to be the most current source of information available since published statistics lag several months behind the market. Besides, statistics relevant to neighborhoods are generally unavailable because published statistical data are seldom classified by small neighborhoods. A portfolio diversified by neighborhoods and other geographic areas is probably highly recommended.

*Property types*

The degree of risk among property types varies over the business cycle. Within the lending locality, real estate markets may show diverse patterns when compared to national trends. At one time multiple family loans may be preferred; at other times, the market may be more favorable for loans on single family dwellings or selected commercial properties such as shopping centers, industrial buildings and the like.

A diversification program would probably include a higher proportion of loans on single family dwellings, diversified by new and existing buildings, by neighborhoods and by value groups. Again a frequent review of the market with members of the real estate industry on a local basis serves as the best guide of portfolio diversification.

Lending authorities should review the present demand for funds among these property types with a listing of loans in the portfolio showing the number of loans by property type, by value groups, by age, by floor area, by type of construction and by location. An undue concentration in the more risky loans would be readily indicated by a tabulation of this type.

## Analyzing Portfolio Yields

Income from a mortgage portfolio arises from origination fees, interest income, and profit from warehousing operations. Since most of the mortgage activity in commercial banks is in single family dwellings, mortgages on these properties are used as an illustration. The contribution of the mortgage portfolio to earnings is measured by discounting the expected earnings from the portfolio over the average investment term. To put it differently, a given portfolio will create monthly income over time which must be discounted to find the present value. In this way it is possible to determine if the yield on portfolios compares favorably with this yield on alternative investments. In addition the portfolio yield may be compared to the banks after tax cost of capital.

### Origination Fees

Banks charge the borrower a fee for processing the loan application. If the mortgage covers FHA properties, the origination fee will be limited to 1 percent of the mortgage balance. The net income from origination fees should be converted to a net contribution by deducting the cost attributed to the loan origination. An examination will disclose that costs are either fixed and independent of loan size, i.e., office overhead and salaried employees, or, costs vary with the size of the loan such as bonus payments to personnel who operate on a commission basis. Income from this source would be found by calculating—

Origination fees
*Less* the fixed costs of mortgage origination
*Less* costs that vary with loan size
_____
Net income from origination fees

Most observers report losses on single family loan originations. The outlay required to originate and process the loan before approval normally exceeds the origination fee paid by the borrower. These losses are expected to be recovered by net interest income and income from warehousing operations.

### Interest Income

Considering an inventory of mortgages, interest income is derived from the outstanding principal balance each month. Since this is a variable amount that changes monthly, the true value of the portfolio is determined by multiplying the monthly mortgage interest rate by the principal balance of the loan at the beginning of each month.

$$\frac{r\,(RB)}{(1+i)^1} + \frac{r\,(RB_2)}{(1+i)^2} + \ldots \frac{r\,(RBn)}{(1+i)^n}$$

—where r equals the mortgage interest rate and RB stands for the remaining balance of the mortgage at the end of each month. The discounted value of this income over the estimated life of the mortgage determines the present worth of income from each mortgage. The discount rate used to convert income to a present value should be equal to the average cost of capital. If this cost of capital *exceeds* the mortgage interest rate, the bank loses money while the loan is held in inventory. This will probably be the case for long-standing mortgages that have a low return relative to new mortgages.

The present value calculation above considers gross income only. To show the true networth of the inventory, the cost of servicing loans should be deducted from the expected income. If c is the estimated monthly cost of servicing a loan then the present value of the mortgage inventory would be equal to

$$\frac{r\text{-}c\,(RB_1)}{(1+i)^1} + \frac{r\text{-}c\,(RB_2)}{(1+i)^2} + \ldots \frac{r\text{-}c\,(RB_n)}{(1+i)^n}$$

An inflation factor could be introduced to record the expected increase in cost over the time of discount.

The last qualification relates to the probability of loan termination. It is unlikely that the mortgage will be held in inventory over its full maturity. Loan officers know that a certain proportion of mortgages will be terminated each month. For a single loan there is some probable life that would hold fairly true for the whole portfolio. For this purpose the discount period should equal the expected average life of mortgages held in the portfolio.

## Warehousing Operations

Suppose that the bank originates FHA mortgages that are subject to discount points paid by the seller. Assume also that the bank expects to sell the mortgage to FNMA or GNMA. If the discount points paid by the seller are greater than the discount points paid by FNMA, the bank earns a profit. In contrast if the discount points paid to the seller are less than the discount on resale, then the bank experiences a loss. Income from this source may be found by deducting the discount from the sale to FNMA from the discount received from the seller. Expected profits from this operation would be found by—

$$M \times (D_1 - D_2) = P$$

Profit is indicated by multiplying a mortgage with a face value of M by $D_1$, equal to the discount paid to the seller, and $D_2$, the discount received from FNMA. In that the profit would be postponed until the time of sale, the profit must be discounted to present value.

$$\frac{P}{(1 + i)\,n}$$

The discount rate is equal to the cost of capital; the period of discount, n, would be the expected number of months that the loan would be held in inventory before resale.

By subjecting loans to the present value calculation the potential profit of expanding a group of mortgages may be readily indicated. Loan personnel may calculate the relative merits of holding mortgages in inventory or selling mortgages in the secondary market. The profitability of different types of loans may be related to the cost of servicing loans of differing qualities. Alternatively, the discount points needed to break even on different types of loans given fixed commitments may be shown by these data. In short, the investment analysis of mortgage portfolios is another decision tool to evaluate the potential profitability of the mortgage operation.

## Mortgage Portfolio Policy

The proportion of assets placed in the mortgage portfolio must conform to statutory limitations. Given these restrictions, however, a bank will establish policies that guide the proportion of assets placed in long-term mortgages, short-term construction loans, and other types of mortgage investments. Mortgage investment policy will vary with the demand for commercial loans, and the availability of money, and the return earned on alternative investments. With a higher proportion of deposits, especially time deposits and certificates of deposits, banks will be more favorably disposed to invest larger amounts in mortgages. An established policy will undergo continual review as monetary conditions change.

It would be difficult to administer a current mortgage policy without statistical data on the mortgage portfolio. Some of the calculations suggested here can be applied to individual mortgages for the entire portfolio by using an in-house computer. Descriptive statistics on each loan would also give management an insight into the current status of the mortgage portfolio. Given a long-term policy objective, current policy may be revised as financial conditions change.

A written statement of policy serves as a broad guide in evaluating each mortgage application. A written statement also helps to delegate authority, to place responsibility and to execute the many details associated with mortgage administration. It is even more desirable to prepare a manual of procedure. Such a working manual describes the steps to be followed in processing a mortgage application and its administration. The manual should include an explanation of how to fill out typical mortgage forms. Manuals provide a standard procedure in guiding the mortgage staff in processing mortgages. It is particularly helpful in training new personnel; it serves as a record in reviewing operations of the department. Furthermore, in the case of banks, the manual serves as documentary evidence to auditors that legal procedures are being followed.

# Chapter 18

# Real Estate Investment Yields

When allocating funds to real estate considerable importance is attached to the method of calculating investment yields. The valuation procedure is adapted to methods of treating income for investment purposes. While it is not uncommon to approve mortgage loans on fairly simplistic capitalization methods, especially if the borrower's credit is satisfactory, the simpler methods of estimating yield may distort or conceal true investment results. The complications of new financing techniques and the income tax aspects of real estate investments have led the more sophisticated investor to rely on more realistic investment models. Such models usually use computers or calculators programmed to simulate proposed investments under different mortgage financing plans.

It is the purpose of this chapter to expose mortgage personnel to advanced methods of calculating real estate investment yields. For comparison purposes the more conventional rate of return investment models are presented first. Real estate investment yield calculated under mortgage equity techniques with their special set of assumptions are followed by variations of the cash flow analysis. The chapter concludes with methods of estimating return on mortgages. A concise treatment of the special concept of Internal Rate of Return has been included, as an appendix to this chapter, for the more sophisticated student.

To introduce methods of estimating yields on real estate, brief comment on investor motives helps to interpret the different methods of capitalization. Depending on investment objectives, investors vary the weight they attach to different characteristics of individual investments. It will be found that most investors attach importance to one or more of the following objectives for investing in real estate:

> Maintaining a high degree of liquidity
> (This item refers to the ability to convert assets to cash when needed, i.e., a savings deposit.)
> Maximizing current income
> (The investor in this category seeks the maximum current income.)
> Investment for future income
> (Some investors prefer to postpone income to future years.)
> Protecting investments from inflation
> Decreasing income tax liabilities
> (Individuals in high marginal income tax brackets prefer investments with income tax advantages.)
> Investing for capital gain purposes
> (Certain investors prefer to sacrifice current income for opportunities to earn future capital gains.)
> Protecting capital investments
> (Investors in this group, such as trust officers invest primarily to protect capital.)

Even a casual review of this list reveals that not all of the investment objectives are compatible. For instance, if liquidity is the prime objective, it is unlikely that a highly liquid investment would give much protection against inflation. Similarly, maximizing current income may lead to a highly risky investment.

Because of these differences, methods of calculating yields on real estate investments vary according to the particular investment objective. The method of calculating yield will be that which gives the best alternative in selecting the ideal investment. Hence, yield estimation gives the analyst data with which to make the best possible decision.

## Conventional Rate of Return Estimates

Historically investors have measured rate of return on invested capital much as interest is estimated on a mortgage. In this application only three main variables are relevant to the investment calculation—the gross income, the operating expenses, and the capitalization rate. Given these first two items, the value is calculated by the capitalization in perpetuity formula.

## Capitalization in Perpetuity

Accepting the premise of a stable income, market value is indicated by the capitalization in perpetuity. Suppose, for example, land has a current annual rental income of $10,000 per year. After examining the relative risks and returns on other like properties, you decide that an 8 percent return on invested capital would be fair and reasonable. Therefore, with a $10,000 annual income, the property would have an indicated value of $125,000 as indicated by the capitalization formula in perpetuity.

$$\text{Market Value} = I/R$$
$$= \$10,000/.08$$
$$= \$125,000$$

where I equals net income and R refers to the capitalization rate (or rate of return). The stabilized annual income is the income expected over a reasonable period. Thus, an unusually high annual income, because of temporary economic conditions or an income resulting from temporary depressed conditions, would not qualify as a "stabilized" income. An annual, stabilized net income, therefore, is an annual net income that may be reasonably expected in the light of current and anticipated economic conditions.

Under the conventional treatment of income from real estate, using this example, an investor would pay $125,000 for an income property that earned an annual stabilized income of $10,000 over an economic life and he would earn an 8 percent rate of return on his total investment. Presumably under this model, an investor would select an investment earning the highest rate of return. An investment returning $12,500 annually from a $125,000 investment, on its face, would be preferred to another investment earning $10,000.

To illustrate further, a loan application for an office building of 39,495 square feet of rentable space in Houston, Texas was valued in this exact manner. Quoting from the loan appraisal:

> ...As previously stated, I have arrived at an annual *stabilized net income* of $134,840 to land and improvements. The following is my opinion of the capitalized value of this income: [emphasis supplied]
>
> Net Annual Stabilized Income . . . . . . . . . . . . . . . . . .$    134,840
> Capitalization Rate Overall Rate, 10.00% . . . . . . . .   1,348,400
> Value Indicated by Income Approach . . . . . . . . . . .$  1,350,000

In other words, given a net annual stabilized net income of $134,840 over the economic life of the proposed building, the appraiser has estimated the value by the capitalization formula in perpetuity using a 10 percent rate of return. In this example, a stabilized annual income of

$134,840 is assumed to be from the land and building together. Consequently, the indicated value of $1,350,000 applies to land and building. While satisfactory for some purposes, this conventional treatment of the rate of return has serious limitations for more complex mortgage applications.

## Limitations of Rate of Return Calculations

It will be observed that the capitalization formula in perpetuity assumes that there is a relationship between a change in income and a change in value. Or, in the first example, that market value is equal to 12.5 times net income. The 12.5 figure, a multiplier, is found by dividing the capitalization rate into 1.0; thus, $1/.08 = 12.5$. Therefore,

$$\text{Market Value} = 12.5 \text{ (Net Income)}$$
$$= 12.5 \text{ ($10,000)}$$
$$= \$125,000$$

In this example, with an 8 percent capitalization rate, every $1.00 increase in net income increases market value by $12.50. In the office building example, the assumption is that with every increase in net income of $1.00, value increases by $10.00. Therefore, given the capitalization rate, value is determined by net income.

Yet, there are other more compelling deficiencies of this method of treating income from real estate. *First,* the implied assumption that the property will be held to the end of its economic life, say 40, 50 or more years depending on the quality of construction. On analysis this is an unrealistic assumption. The tax effects of real estate ownership penalize individuals who own depreciable income property over a relatively long period. To be sure corporate investors and certain institutions may hold property over many generations, but usually their motives do not conform to the typical investor. The concensus is that investors in real property are unlikely to maintain ownership over the economic life as the conventional rate of return capitalization assumes.

*Second,* it is implicitly assumed that property is held free and clear of debt; that the property is purchased for cash; and that financing plays no part in the investment decision. This again is subject to question. Real estate investors have an economic inducement to finance investment property purchases rather than pay cash. Indeed the available financing may control project feasibility. The project would be uneconomic under one financing plan and quite acceptable with more favorable mortgage terms. The rate of return calculations illustrated here do not account for the effect of financing terms on investment decisions.

*Third,* because of income tax laws, the record shows that investors consider the income tax aspects of real estate ownership: (1) the interest deductibility of mortgage interest, and (2) the depreciation allowance on buildings and capital gains treatment of a real estate sale. In fact, it may be demonstrated that the investment appeal of some properties arises primarily from these income tax advantages. Yet, the rate of return calculation makes no allowance for the investment advantages of interest deductibility of a mortgage and the deductibility of depreciation.

It will be noted further that the rate of return calculation makes no allowance for projections of capital gain or loss. However, inquiry and market experience reveal that investors buy and sell real estate not only for its current income return but for opportunities of future capital gains. There are other instances in which capital loss may be anticipated over the life of the investment, which becomes part of the investment decision, changing capitalization rates and property values. The rate of return method omits this step in the capitalization process.

*Fourth,* critics of the conventional capitalization method consider it unrealistic to "stabilize" income over the economic life of the building—40 or 50 years or more. There is no way to project with any accuracy future incomes over 50, 40, 30 or 20 years. Moreover, it is held that investors do not make these calculations, that they are more concerned with the projected income over the early years of ownership. Accordingly, some authorities believe it is more realistic to consider net income for only a relatively short term—for example, five or ten years, · and then assume the property will be sold at the end of the assumed investment period to realize capital gains. In sum, the rate of return calculation seems grossly inadequate for investment analysis under the present financial environment.

## Mortgage Equity Capitalization

With the almost universal financing of income property, close observers of the market have emphasized the annual rate of return earned on equity capital. The return on equity is the amount actually invested exclusive of financing. For instance, the example below indicates that the amount of income remaining after mortgage payments produces a relatively high return on equity.

| | |
|---|---|
| Property value | $100,000 |
| Mortgage | 90,000 |
| Equity capital | $ 10,000 |
| Net income *before* mortgage payments and net income taxes | $ 15,000 |
| Rate of return on equity   $15,000/$10,000 = 150% | |

379

While the investment earns a relatively high and unusual rate of return on the equity capital of $10,000, it is also true that the investor must meet mortgage payments from annual net income. A $90,000 mortgage earning a 9.5 percent interest rate over 25 years would require annual mortgage payments totaling $9,436 per year. The net income available *before* net income taxes and after mortgage payments would be

| | |
|---|---|
| Net income *before* mortgage payments and net income taxes ........................ | $15,000 |
| Less annual mortgage payments ........... | −9,436 |
| Net income *after* mortgage payments and before net income taxes ................ | $ 5,564 |

Hence, after considering mortgage payments, the income available to the investor is considerably reduced. Under mortgage equity capitalization, only the income after mortgage payments is capitalized to estimate value. In addition, mortgage equity capitalization considers the present worth of the property, assuming a sale at the end of the investment period.

As the result of his mortgage experience with the New York Life Insurance Company, Mr. L. W. Ellwood formulated a short method of valuing property by capitalizing the return to equity after mortgage payments. The other refinements of this procedure were believed more compatible with the market. At least some of the limitations to the rate of return method of calculating yield were eliminated by this approach to yield analysis. The following assumptions common to equity capitalization show the main differences between this method and the conventional capitalization process:

1. Mortgage equity capitalization relates the real estate return to the equity interest, not to the whole property.
2. This method assumes that the investor will hold the property for a relatively short period—5, 10, or 15 years.
3. The value of the investment is partly a function of anticipated capital gains or losses.
4. The return on equity capital is partly dependent on financing terms: the mortgage interest rate, the term of the mortgage and the loan to value ratio.

Proponents of mortgage equity capitalization consider these assumptions as representative of the market. It is held that investors buy and sell property in anticipation of capital gains over a relatively few years and anticipate a return on their equity investment. They typically finance property and they hold the property over the investment period that maximizes their return on equity. Further, short-term projections of income and expected capital gains or losses are believed more accurate than the "stabilized" income assumed over a 40 or 50 year property life which, according to this view, is quite unrealistic.

Therefore, to use this method additional variables must enter the capitalization process. In place of the annual gross income, net operating expenses and capitalization rate under the rate of return method, the value is a function of some seven items:

$V = f(M,i,n,y,d \text{ or } a,N,I)$

Where:

$M$ = mortgage loan-to-value ratio
$i$ = mortgage interest
$n$ = length of mortgage
$y$ = anticipated yield on equity
$d$ = anticipated depreciation
$a$ = anticipated appreciation
$N$ = investment projection period
$I$ = net annual income before depreciation or
amortization of mortgage

Thus, the price paid for income property depends, first, on the mortgage terms, including the loan-to-value ratio, the mortgage interest rate, and the length of the mortgage. Secondly, equity capitalization requires an estimate of the investor's required yield on equity and, thirdly, a forecast of the probable appreciation or depreciation over the investment period. Finally, a projected period for holding the investment must be selected. Then, given the net income, the resulting value will allow the anticipated yield, given the other variables of the equation.

To illustrate this method with an example, assume the following facts:

1. Loan-to-value ratio, 75 percent.
2. Interest rate, 7.5 percent.
3. 25-year loan.
4. Required yield on equity, 15 percent.
5. No anticipated depreciation or appreciation.
6. Investment period, ten years.
7. Net annual income, $20,000.

With these facts, mortgage equity capitalization with the value of the equity would be $51,804. See Table 18.1.

In other words, the net annual income is reduced by the annual amount to service the mortgage, $13,781.86, with the remaining income representing an annual return to equity of $6,218.14. The only relevant income to capitalize is that income remaining *after* annual mortgage payments, principal and interest.

In this example, since no appreciation or depreciation is anticipated, the property is assumed to sell for its present value, $207,217.27. However, this sum will not be realized until the date of sale, 10 years post-

## Table 18.1

### Mortgage Equity Capitalization

| | |
|---|---:|
| Net Annual Income . . . . . . . . . . . . . . . . . . . . . . . . . . . . . . . . . . . . . . | $ 20,000.00 |
| Less Mortgage Requirement .75 of $207,217 × .08867894 . . . . . . | −13,781.86 |
| Annual Amount of Equity . . . . . . . . . . . . . . . . . . . . . . . . . . . . . . . . . | $ 6,218.14 |
| Present Worth of Reversion | |
| Reversion, 10 years deferred . . . . . . . . . . . . . . . . . . . . . . . . . . . . | $207,217.27 |
| Less Mortgage Balance (1-P) | |
| (1 −.2028249 = .7971751 × $155,413 . . . . . . . . . . . . . . . . . . | −123,891.37 |
| Reversion to Equity . . . . . . . . . . . . . . . . . . . . . . . . . . . . . . . . . . . . . . | $ 83,325.90 |
| Present Worth of Equity | |
| 83,325.90 × (Present Worth of One, | |
| 10 years, 15%), 0.247184 . . . . . . . . . . . . . . . . . . . . . . . . . . . . . | $ 20,596.82 |
| Present Worth of Income | |
| $6,218.14 × (Present Worth of One per Annum, | |
| 10 years, 15%), 5.01876 . . . . . . . . . . . . . . . . . . . . . . . . . . . . . . | +31,207.40 |
| Equity Value . . . . . . . . . . . . . . . . . . . . . . . . . . . . . . . . . . . . . . . . . . . . | $ 51,804.22 |
| Add Mortgage . . . . . . . . . . . . . . . . . . . . . . . . . . . . . . . . . . . . . . . . . . | +155,412.95 |
| Capital Value* . . . . . . . . . . . . . . . . . . . . . . . . . . . . . . . . . . . . . . . . . . | $207,217.17 |

* Values were calculated by computer to 14 decimal places and therefore totals may not add due to rounding.

poned. At this time the unpaid, remaining balance of the mortgage is $123,891.37. After paying the remaining balance of the mortgage, the investor is left with $83,325.90. Since this sum will not be realized until ten years later, it must be converted to a present value—which is $20,596.82.

Adding the present worth of the income after mortgage payments, discounted over the ten years, gives the present worth ($31,207.40) of the annual income of $6,218.14. In other words, the right to an annual income of $6,218.14 for ten years, discounted at 15 percent, has a present worth of $31,207.40. Therefore, the property value is equal to (1) $51,804.22 ($31,207.40 + $20,596.82) and (2) the face value of the 75 percent mortgage, $155,412.95.

Note that the value of the equity consists of two parts: (1) the present worth of the reversion, i.e., the sale price less the remaining value of the mortgage, and (2) the present worth of annual net income after mortgage payments. Therefore, given a mortgage of $155,412.95, you would pay $51,804.22 for the equity. And in doing so, you would earn a 15 percent yield on your equity investment.

To explain further, part of the annual net income of $20,000 goes to service the annual mortgage payments of $13,781.86 and the remainder of $6,218.14 represents a return on the equity. Under the mortgage equity capitalization procedure, income is always divided as illustrated in Exhibit 18.1.

**Exhibit 18.1**

**Allocation of Net Income Under Mortgage Equity Capitalization**

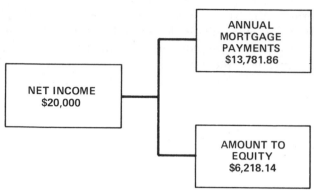

Recall that the market value is equal to the mortgage, $155,412.95, plus the present worth of the equity, $51,804. With a given mortgage, this is another way of saying that the present worth of the equity consists of two parts: (1) the present worth of the income, $31,207.40 as shown in Table 18.1 and (2) the present worth of the reversion, $20,596.82.

The reversion is defined as the projected sale price less the remaining balance of the mortgage. Because the reversionary value is realized only at the end of the projection period, this sum is discounted to its present worth. These relationships are demonstrated in Exhibit 18.2.

**Exhibit 18.2**

**The Allocation of Market Value Under Mortgage Equity Capitalization**

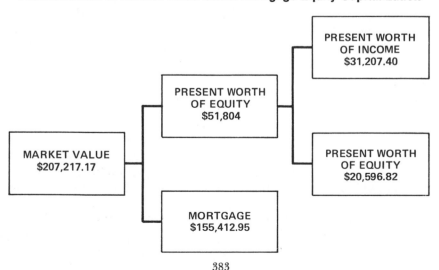

Capitalizing net income under the mortgage equity method is simplified by the use of the formula

$$r = Y - MC$$

Under this formula the basic capitalization rate (r) is equal to the required equity yield (Y) less the loan-to-value ratio (M) times the mortgage coefficient (C). The mortgage coefficient accounts for the repayment of principal over the investment period.

In the present case, the basic capitalization rate is equal to 9.65 percent.

$$r = .15 - (.75)(.0713106)$$
$$= .0965$$

The factor for C may be calculated by formula or given by tables, for a 25-year, 75 percent mortgage with a 9.5 percent interest rate.[1]

If the property is assumed to increase or decrease in value over the investment period, the capitalization would be equal to—

$$R = r + \text{depreciation} \quad 1/s_{\overline{n}|} \quad \text{or}$$

$$R = r - \text{appreciation} \quad 1/s_{\overline{n}|}$$

In other words, the capitalization rate is increased or decreased by the amount of capital gain or loss. For example, if the property is expected to depreciate by 20 percent over the next ten years, the basic capitalization rate is increased by .20 times the sinking fund factor at the expected yield rate. The sinking fund factor refers to an interest-bearing fund established to accumulate interest. In another sense, the sinking fund factor represents a deposit which earns cumulative interest that recovers a given sum. Sinking fund factors are illustrated in Table 18.2 for 50 periods and an interest rate of 9 percent.

Conversely, if the property is expected to appreciate by 20 percent, the capitalization rate is decreased by 20 percent of the sinking fund factor at the yield rate over the projection period. In the earlier example, with no appreciation or depreciation and a basic capitalization rate of 9.65 percent, the market value is equal to—

$$\text{Market Value} = \frac{d \text{ (net income)}}{r \text{ (capitalization rate)}}$$
$$= \frac{\$20,000}{.0965}$$
$$= \$207,217 \text{ (rounded)}$$

Under assumed mortgages, projection periods and capitalization rates, tables that give the basic capitalization rate, sinking fund factors, and mortgage coefficients for varying mortgage terms are available.

---

1. See *Ellwood Tables*, Part II (Chicago: American Institute of Real Estate Appraisers, 1970), p. 208.

**Table 18.2**

| PERIODS | AMOUNT OF ONE | AMOUNT OF ONE PER PERIOD | SINKING FUND | PRESENT WORTH OF ONE | PRESENT WORTH OF ONE PER PERIOD | PARTIAL PAYMENT |
|---|---|---|---|---|---|---|
| 1 | 1.0900 | 1.0000 | 1.0000000000 | .9174311927 | .9174311927 | 1.0000000000 |
| 2 | 1.1881 | 2.0900 | .4784688995 | .8416799933 | 1.7591111859 | .5684688995 |
| 3 | 1.2950 | 3.2781 | .3050547573 | .7721834801 | 2.5312946660 | .3950547573 |
| 4 | 1.4116 | 4.5731 | .2186686621 | .7084252111 | 3.2397198771 | .3086686621 |
| 5 | 1.5386 | 5.9847 | .1670924570 | .6499313863 | 3.8896512634 | .2570924570 |
| 6 | 1.6771 | 7.5233 | .1329197833 | .5962673269 | 4.4859185902 | .2229197833 |
| 7 | 1.8280 | 9.2004 | .1086905168 | .5470342448 | 5.0329528351 | .1986905168 |
| 8 | 1.9926 | 11.0285 | .0906743778 | .5018662797 | 5.5348191147 | .1806743778 |
| 9 | 2.1719 | 13.0210 | .0767988021 | .4604277795 | 5.9952468943 | .1667988021 |
| 10 | 2.3674 | 15.1929 | .0658200899 | .4224108069 | 6.4176577012 | .1558200899 |
| 11 | 2.5804 | 17.5603 | .0569466567 | .3875328504 | 6.8051905515 | .1469466567 |
| 12 | 2.8127 | 20.1407 | .0496506585 | .3555347251 | 7.1607252766 | .1396506585 |
| 13 | 3.0658 | 22.9534 | .0435665597 | .3261786469 | 7.4869039235 | .1335665597 |
| 14 | 3.3417 | 26.0192 | .0384331730 | .2992464650 | 7.7861503885 | .1284331730 |
| 15 | 3.6425 | 29.3609 | .0340588827 | .2745380413 | 8.0606884299 | .1240588827 |
| 16 | 3.9703 | 33.0034 | .0302990097 | .2518697627 | 8.3125581925 | .1202990097 |
| 17 | 4.3276 | 36.9737 | .0270462485 | .2310731768 | 8.5436313693 | .1170462485 |
| 18 | 4.7171 | 41.3013 | .0242122907 | .2119937402 | 8.7556251094 | .1142122907 |
| 19 | 5.1417 | 46.0185 | .0217304107 | .1944896699 | 8.9501147793 | .1117304107 |
| 20 | 5.6044 | 51.1601 | .0195464750 | .1784308898 | 9.1285456691 | .1095464750 |
| 21 | 6.1088 | 56.7645 | .0176166348 | .1636980640 | 9.2922437331 | .1076166348 |
| 22 | 6.6586 | 62.8733 | .0159049930 | .1501817101 | 9.4424254432 | .1059049930 |
| 23 | 7.2579 | 69.5319 | .0143818800 | .1377813854 | 9.5802068286 | .1043818800 |
| 24 | 7.9111 | 76.7898 | .0130225607 | .1264049408 | 9.7066117694 | .1030225607 |
| 25 | 8.6231 | 84.7009 | .0118062505 | .1159678354 | 9.8225796049 | .1018062505 |
| 26 | 9.3992 | 93.3240 | .0107153599 | .1063925097 | 9.9289721146 | .1007153599 |
| 27 | 10.2451 | 102.7231 | .0097349054 | .0976073070 | 10.0265799217 | .0997349054 |
| 28 | 11.1671 | 112.9682 | .0088520473 | .0895484468 | 10.1161283685 | .0988520473 |
| 29 | 12.1722 | 124.1354 | .0080557226 | .0821545384 | 10.1982829069 | .0980557226 |
| 30 | 13.2677 | 136.3075 | .0073363514 | .0753711361 | 10.2736540430 | .0973363514 |
| 31 | 14.4618 | 149.5752 | .0066855995 | .0691478313 | 10.3428018743 | .0966855995 |
| 32 | 15.7633 | 164.0370 | .0060961861 | .0634383773 | 10.4062402517 | .0960961861 |
| 33 | 17.1820 | 179.8003 | .0055617255 | .0582005462 | 10.4644405979 | .0955617255 |
| 34 | 18.7284 | 196.9823 | .0050765971 | .0533948130 | 10.5178354109 | .0950765971 |
| 35 | 20.4140 | 215.7108 | .0046358375 | .0489860670 | 10.5668214779 | .0946358375 |
| 36 | 22.2512 | 236.1247 | .0042350500 | .0449613459 | 10.6117628237 | .0942350500 |
| 37 | 24.2538 | 258.3759 | .0038703293 | .0412305925 | 10.6529934163 | .0938703293 |
| 38 | 26.4367 | 282.6298 | .0035381975 | .0378262317 | 10.6908196480 | .0935381975 |
| 39 | 28.8160 | 309.0665 | .0032355500 | .0347029648 | 10.7255226128 | .0932355500 |
| 40 | 31.4094 | 337.8824 | .0029596092 | .0318375824 | 10.7573601952 | .0929596092 |
| 41 | 34.2363 | 369.2919 | .0027078853 | .0292087912 | 10.7865689865 | .0927078853 |
| 42 | 37.3175 | 403.5281 | .0024781420 | .0267970562 | 10.8133660426 | .0924781420 |
| 43 | 40.6761 | 440.8457 | .0022683675 | .0245844552 | 10.8379504978 | .0922683675 |
| 44 | 44.3370 | 481.5218 | .0020767493 | .0225545461 | 10.8605050439 | .0920767493 |
| 45 | 48.3273 | 525.8587 | .0019016514 | .0206922441 | 10.8811972880 | .0919016514 |
| 46 | 52.6767 | 574.1860 | .0017415959 | .0189837102 | 10.9001809981 | .0917415959 |
| 47 | 57.4176 | 626.8628 | .0015952455 | .0174162479 | 10.9175972460 | .0915952455 |
| 48 | 62.5852 | 684.2804 | .0014613892 | .0159782090 | 10.9335754550 | .0914613892 |
| 49 | 68.2179 | 746.8656 | .0013389289 | .0146589074 | 10.9482343624 | .0913389289 |
| 50 | 74.3575 | 815.0836 | .0012268681 | .0134485389 | 10.9616829013 | .0912268681 |

Source: William M. Shenkel, *Capitalization Tables For Investment Purposes,* Department of Real Estate and Urban Development (Athens: University of Georgia, 1972), p. 72.

Note: This table illustrates the six capitalization factors. Each factor refers to $1.00 or a fraction. In the first column, the amount of one shows that the compound amount of $1.00 is $1.09 at the end of the first year. The amount of one per period shows the accumulation of $1.00 payments which are compounded at nine percent each year. The sinking fund factor shows the annual deposit, which earns nine percent annual interest, that accumulates to $1.00. The present worth of one shows the discounted value of a future sum. The present worth of one per period indicates the present worth of a future income, discounted at nine percent. The last column, the partial payment, indicates the instalment necessary to amortize a loan at nine percent interest.

Consult published financial tables for more comprehensive capitalization factors.

Computer programs are also readily available to compute these values directly.

While the mortgage equity capitalization overcomes deficiencies of the rate of return capitalization, it does not reveal the after-tax effects of a real estate investment. For this type of information a cash flow analysis is required.

## Cash Flow Analysis

In the present context cash flow refers to net operating income remaining after (1) income taxes and (2) mortgage payments. The term is also variously used to describe net operating income after mortgage payments only. For the present purpose this relationship is termed the *net spendable income.* To illustrate cash flow, the following is data for a newly constructed apartment house complex of 160 apartment units:

> Outstanding balance, first mortgage $1,967,250, 8.25 percent, 28 years.
>
> Depreciation method, 40 year building life, double declining balance.

Table 18.3 indicates the cash flow calculations over ten years, assuming an operating income of $225,208. In reviewing these data, note that the property reveals no taxable income until the ninth and tenth year. Assuming a federal income tax rate of 50 percent over the first eight years, the investor may shelter other income to the extent of $57,757 in the first year, and to $6,555 in the eighth year. For persons in upper income tax rate brackets, this would represent a substantial tax savings.[2]

In calculating cash flow as shown in Table 18.3, net spendable income is shown after deducting the annual mortgage payment from annual net operating income, in this instance, $44,861 per year. From this figure other deductions are made to calculate the taxable income. Each year the principal is added back to spendable income since it was deducted originally to calculate net spendable income. This, in effect, is a way of deducting interest which is income tax deductible.

Next, the allowable depreciation, double declining balance, produces the taxable income or tax shelter. Double declining balance depreciation means that ordinary straight line rates may be doubled under this method. That is, a 40-year life building, straight line, would show an annual depreciation deduction of 2.5 percent of the building cost over each year for 40 years which would allow total deduction of the building (40 times 2.5 = 100 percent). If the double declining method is used, 5 percent of the building cost would be deducted during the first

---

2. A 50 percent income tax bracket is reached for taxable income of over $32,000 for a single person and for taxable income of $44,000 for a married couple filing a joint return.

**Table 18.3**

**Calculation of Cash Flow: Year 1 to 10**

| Item | 1 | 2 | 3 | 4 | 5 | 6 | 7 | 8 | 9 | 10 |
|---|---|---|---|---|---|---|---|---|---|---|
| Net operating income | $225,208 | $225,208 | $225,208 | $225,208 | $225,208 | $225,208 | $225,208 | $225,208 | $225,208 | $225,208 |
| Debt Service First Mortgage | | | | | | | | | | |
| Principal | 18,747 | 20,354 | 22,099 | 23,993 | 26,049 | 28,282 | 30,706 | 33,338 | 36,195 | 39,297 |
| Interest | 161,599 | 159,992 | 158,248 | 156,354 | 154,297 | 152,065 | 149,641 | 147,009 | 144,152 | 141,050 |
| Principal + Interest | $180,347 | $180,347 | $180,347 | $180,347 | $180,347 | $180,347 | $180,347 | $180,347 | $180,347 | $180,347 |
| Net spendable income | $ 44,861 | $ 44,861 | $ 44,861 | $ 44,861 | $ 44,861 | $ 44,861 | $ 44,861 | $ 44,861 | $ 44,861 | $ 44,861 |
| Add-Back Principal— First | +18,747 | +20,354 | +22,099 | +23,993 | +26,049 | +28,282 | +30,706 | +33,338 | +36,195 | +39,297 |
| Deduct Depreciation | −121,365 | −115,297 | −109,532 | −104,055 | −98,852 | −93,910 | −89,214 | −84,754 | −80,516 | −76,490 |
| Taxable Income (Shelter) | −$ 57,757 | −$ 50,081 | −$ 42,572 | −$ 35,201 | −$ 27,942 | −$ 20,767 | −$ 13,647 | −$ 6,555 | $ 540 | $ 7,668 |
| Income Tax | | | | | | | | | −270 | −3,834 |
| Income after taxes | | | | | | | | | 270 | 3,834 |
| Add Depreciation | +$121,365 | +$115,297 | +$109,532 | +$104,055 | +$ 98,852 | +$ 93,910 | +$ 89,214 | +$ 84,754 | +$ 80,516 | +$ 76,490 |
| Less Principal— First | −18,747 | −20,354 | −22,099 | −23,993 | −26,049 | −28,282 | −30,706 | −33,338 | −36,195 | −39,297 |
| Cash Flow | $102,618 | $ 94,943 | $ 87,433 | $ 80,062 | $ 72,803 | $ 65,628 | $ 58,508 | $ 51,416 | $ 44,321 | $ 37,193 |

* Totals may not add precisely because cents have been omitted.

387

year. Assuming a $100,000 building, $5,000 would be the allowable depreciation. During the second year, double declining balance depreciation would be 5 percent of $95,000 or $4,750. Each year the double depreciation is calculated on the declining balance.

At this writing all depreciation methods vary according to whether the property is new or existing and according to the type of property. Depreciation allowances must conform to the following summary if the property was acquired after July 25, 1969:

| Type of Building | Residential | Nonresidential |
|---|---|---|
| New Buildings | Straight Line<br>200 percent declining balance<br>150 percent declining balance<br>125 percent declining balance<br>Sum of years digits | Straight Line<br>150 percent declining balance |
| Existing<br>Buildings | Straight Line<br>125 percent declining balance | Straight Line |

Though subject to change, note that double or 200 percent declining balance is only available for new residential buildings (mainly apartments). The sum of years digits is another form of accelerated depreciation. To calculate sum of years depreciation, assuming a ten-year life, total the digits from 1 to 10 which is 55. The first year depreciation would be equal to the fraction, 10/55ths of the building depreciable value; the second year, 9/55ths, and proceeding to the last year, 1/55th of the depreciable value.

It will be noted also that the depreciation deduction represents cash in hand to the investor. For example, the $121,365 shown as the allowable depreciation the first year would be available to the owner. His actual cash flow is this sum plus income after taxes less the principal payment, since this is added in the calculations of Table 18.3 to find taxable income.

Note how double declining balance shifts income tax payments to the later years of the building life. Note further that cash flow varies from $102,618 in the first year to $37,193 during the last year. The declining depreciation allowance and the declining interest payments account for these differences.

The main point is this: For investors subject to high marginal income tax rates, cash flow may be more important than the rate of return calculation illustrated in the first examples of this chapter. If the property is subject to substantial capital gains over the projected investment period, income properties gain added appeal to investors in this category. The amount of cash flow available is largely the result of positive net operating income, annual mortgage requirement, and the depreciation allowance. High loan-to-value ratios, properties with a proportionately greater amount invested in the depreciable buildings relative to the land investment, and properties subject to accelerated depreciation such as new apartment buildings are found in this group.

## Discounted Cash Flow (DCF)

Suppose an investor intends to maximize cash flow. It is then relevant to calculate the *present worth* of anticipated cash flow. Assume, for example, that an investor wanted to compare the cash flow on several properties to select the best alternative investment. Comparing cash flows arithmetically must be discounted since cash flow changes each year. Furthermore, the cash flow cannot be summed since cash flow of $1 in year one is worth more than cash flow of $1 postponed for ten years. Moreover, annuity capitalization used for stabilized incomes is not appropriate. The cash flow for each year must be individually discounted to the present; the sum of their discounted values equals the present worth of cash flow. In other words, cash flow for a given period would be calculated under the formula

$$DCF = \frac{CF_1}{(1 + i)^1} + \frac{CF_2}{(1 + i)^2} + \ldots \frac{CF_n}{(1 + i)^n}$$

The cash flow earned each year is treated as a separate sum discounted by the present worth of one factor. The yield rate (i) is derived from the yield required by the investor or derived from a study of rates of return earned on comparable properties. Algebraically the notation for discounted cash flow for a given time period would be reduced to

$$DCF = \sum_{t = 1}^{n} \frac{CF_t}{(1 + i)^t}$$

Assuming that 10 percent is an appropriate yield rate, cash flow as shown in Table 18.3 is discounted over a ten year term in Table 18.4. Thus, at the end of year one the cash flow of $102,618 has a present worth of $93,289. The cash flow of $37,193 received at the end of year ten a present worth of $14,340. Totaling these amounts gives the discounted cash flow, $461,521.

Investors faced with declining cash flow shown in Table 18.4 would have an incentive to convert the property to cash and select a new investment with a more favorable cash flow. The present worth of the investment, then, must include the present worth of sales proceeds realized after the holding period. For example, if the property is sold at the end of ten years, the amount of cash realized will be less the una-

**Table 18.4**

**Calculation of Discounted Cash Flow**

| Year | Annual Cash Flow | Present Worth of One, 10% | Discounted Cash Flow |
|------|------|------|------|
| 1 | $102,618 | .90909 | $ 93,289 |
| 2 | 94,943 | .82644 | 78,465 |
| 3 | 87,433 | .75131 | 65,689 |
| 4 | 80,062 | .68301 | 54,683 |
| 5 | 72,803 | .62092 | 45,205 |
| 6 | 65,628 | .56447 | 37,045 |
| 7 | 58,508 | .51315 | 30,023 |
| 8 | 51,416 | .46650 | 23,986 |
| 9 | 44,321 | .42409 | 18,796 |
| 10 | 37,193 | .38554 | 14,340 |
| | | Total Discounted Cash Flow | $461,521 |

mortized mortgage and capital gain taxes. With this added qualification the discounted cash flow formula assumes the following form:

$$DCF = \sum_{t=1}^{n} + \frac{CF_t}{(1+i)^t} + \frac{SP-GT-OB}{(1+i)^n}$$

In this case SP equals selling price, GT refers to the capital gain tax, and OB refers to the outstanding balance at the date of sale.

For the same property shown in Table 18.4, suppose then at the end of the ten years the apartment sold for $2,800,000 and was subject to a capital gain tax of $182,000. At this time the original mortgage would show an unpaid balance of $1,688,189. Referring again to the present rate of one factor, 10 percent for ten years is .38554. The factor is derived from the present worth of one formula (or given by a table) —

$$\frac{1}{(1+.10)^{10}}$$

By substituting this formula discounted cash for this example would be equal to—

$$DCF = \$461,521 + \frac{\$2,800,000 - (\$182,000) - (\$1,688,189)}{2.5937}$$

$$= \$461,521 + \frac{\$929,811}{2.5937}$$

$$= \$820,009$$

In comparing the discounted cash flow with other capitalization procedures it will be appreciated that the cash flow is unique to a given investor. The financing terms must be specified, the depreciation method determined, the income tax rate must be assumed for a particular investor, and the discount rate usually refers to the required rate or yield for a particular investor. In the preceding example the discounted cash flow of $820,009 constitutes (1) the present worth of the expected cash flow under a special set of assumptions and (2) the present worth of the proceeds of an assumed sale price.

Since the discounted cash flow in this example presupposes a sale in a relatively short period, the anticipated sale price materially affects the final answer. In addition, the discounted cash flow will change according to the time period of investment. For these reasons the method is more appropriate to analyze a specific investment or investments under circumstances affecting a particular investor.

Indeed the method of analysis appeals to investors generally because of the wide availability of computer programs that make these calculations in a few seconds. In the example cited, figures are drawn from a computer printout of nine pages given the following data:

> Net operating income and expense detail which allows annual expenses and income to be changed by a specific percentage over a ten year term.
>
> Sale proceeds to be realized, assuming a sale at the end of each year over ten years after capital gain taxes and less the unpaid mortgage balance.
>
> Cash flow analysis over ten years.
>
> A valuation page, including mortgage equity capitalization, land residual and property residual valuation techniques.
>
> Thirty-five financial ratios showing the relation between the mortgage, property values, net income and expenses.
>
> Expenses shown per square foot, per room, per apartment and as a percent of gross possible income.
>
> Variations adapted to shopping centers, mobile home parks, office buildings and motels.

Hence, while the discounted cash flow may seem tedious and confusing either programmable calculators or computer facilities provide the many calculations for interpretation by investors and mortgage loan officers alike. The increasing acceptance of these analytical techniques creates a growing demand for personnel equipped with the background to review the more complicated analysis of investment real estate.

## Equity Participation Mortgages

In an earlier chapter it was mentioned that lenders frequently negotiate for a share of gross income, cash flow, net income or capital gains on income property that they finance. If the project is successful, the lender earns not only the mortgage interest but a return or share of the equity interest. Suppose, for example, that a mortgage included a provision that the lender receives 5 percent of the effective gross income—income before expenses less losses from vacancies and bad debts. Assume further that the mortgage will be held in the portfolio for ten years at which time it is anticipated that the mortgage will be refinanced.

Looking at the mortgage as an investment, repayment of the outstanding mortgage balance at the end of ten years would be equivalent to the present worth of a sum postponed for ten years. Payment of the outstanding balance in ten years is similar to the right to a capital sum postponed for ten years. The present value of such a right would be given by multiplying the future outstanding loan balance at the end of ten years times the present worth of one. Furthermore the monthly mortgage payments would be equivalent to an income received over 120 periods discounted at the mortgage interest rate. The value of the participation interest would be given by discounting 5 percent of the expected, effective gross income earned over ten years. In this instance the rate of discount would be considerably higher than the mortgage interest rate to account for the greater uncertainty of receiving this share.

Using the preceding example of Tables 18.3 and 18.4, the value of the mortgage interest would be found by discounting the three shares received by the mortgage lender by the end of ten years. The equity participation of 5 percent of the effective gross income is capitalized at 15 percent. The reversionary value of the remaining mortgage balance and the present worth of monthly payments over ten years (120 periods) are discounted at 8.25 percent, the mortgage interest rate.

1. Reversionary Value of Remaining Mortgage Balance
   $1,688,189 × (Present worth of 1,
   10 years, 8.25%) .4526 . . . . . . . . . . . . . . . . . . . . . . . . . . . . . $ 764,074
2. Present Worth of Monthly Payments
   (120 periods @ 8.25%) $15,028 × 81.53107 . . . . . . . . 1,225,248
3. Present Worth of 5% of Effective Gross Income
   ($439,202 × .05 = $21,960)
   $21,960 × (Present Worth of 1 per period
   10 years @ 15%) 5.01876 . . . . . . . . . . . . . . . . . . . . . . . . 110,212

   Total Value . . . . . . . . . . . . . . . . . . . . . . . . . . . . . . . . . . . . . $2,099,534

Attention should be directed to the special assumptions governing this example. In the first place, the outstanding balance of the mortgage, $1,688,189 is postponed for ten years. The present value of this sum, ten years postponed, discounted at the mortgage interest rate of

8.25 percent, has a current value of $764,074. Next it will be observed that the monthly payments of $15,028 may be considered as an income received over 120 periods, also discounted at the mortgage interest rate. The present worth of $15,028 received over 120 periods, discounted at 8.25 percent, is equal to $1,225,248.

The last calculation, showing the expected $21,960 annually over ten years, representing the "equity kicker" discounted over ten years at 15 percent, has a value of $110,212. Therefore, based on a ten year investment and a projected equity participation annually of $21,960, these assumptions give market value $2,099,534.

The subjective element in this calculation rests on the length of the investment (assumed as ten years), the discount rate used to convert the expected income from the equity interest to present value, and the amount of income to be derived from the effective gross income share. If these questions may be satisfactorily resolved, this type of analysis permits lenders to treat mortgages as capital investments and not merely as a fixed return on capital.

# Appendix to Chapter 18

## The Internal Rate of Return (IRR)

The cash flow example in Chapter 18 emphasized the maximization of cash flow. In other words, given a cash flow from alternative investments, that investment will be selected which will produce the greatest *present value* of cash flow. The method helps determine the feasibility of a proposed project. For example, with a present worth of $821,705, the project would be feasible if cost was equal to or less than the present worth of discounted cash flow. A project costing more than the present worth of discounted cash flow would not be feasible or it would earn a lower rate of return than the rate used in the discounting process.

The internal rate of return also starts with the (1) expected cash flow and (2) the reversion—defined as the expected sale proceeds less the capital gain tax and less the remaining balance of the outstanding loan. With (3) a given proposed cost, the same formula is used, only in this case the unknown factor is the interest rate or the internal rate of return. For example, the same formula would be applied in this way where OC equals original cost.

$$OC = \sum_{t=1}^{n} \frac{Cf_t}{(1 = i)^t} + \frac{SP - GT - OB}{(1 + i)^n}$$

Thus, to apply the internal rate of return suppose an investment costs $875,000. With the facts as given, the internal rate of return would be solved for (i) which is defined here as the internal rate of return. In short, *the internal rate of return is that rate of return that equates the present value of all future net cash benefits with the amount of the original investment.* In the present instance the internal rate of return will be found for that value of (i) that converts the present value of cash flow and the present value of the reversion to $875,000. Using the same formula, the problem would be solved for (i). The value of (i) would be found by a series of successive iterations. To calculate this value, start with the relationship below.

| Rate of Return | Discounted Cash Flow | Original Investment Cost |
|:---:|:---:|:---:|
| .08 | $927,578 | – – – – |
| .09 | $871,422 | – – – – |

If a rate of return of 8 percent were used for the data of Tables 18.3 and 18.4, the present value would be $927,578; under 9 percent, the value would be $871,422. By interpolation the actual rate of return must fall between 8 percent and 9 percent. The calculations shown indicate internal rate of return of 8.94 percent as shown below.

$ 927,578 .08 Rate of Return          $ 871,422 .09 Rate of Return
−875,000 Original Cost              −875,000 Original Cost
$  52,578 Difference            −$    3,578 Difference

The internal rate of return would be given by completing the following calculation.

$$\frac{i - .08}{.09 - .08} = \frac{0 - \$52,578}{-\$3,578 - \$52,578}$$

$$i - .08 = \frac{-\$52,578}{-\$56,156}$$

$$i = 8\% + .9363$$

$$i = 8.94\%$$

Note the main differences between the internal rate of return and cash flow analysis. In the latter example, the proposed investment cost is given, $875,000. Also given is the annual cash flow by year and the reversionary value, which is the projected sale price less capital gain taxes and less the unpaid mortgage balance. The next issue is to find that rate of return which equated present value of both the sum of annual cash flows and the reversionary value with the projected cost.

In practice, the tedious calculations, which here were undertaken by trial and error, are more efficiently calculated by computers. With a given internal rate of return it is presumed that the investor will select that project which earns the maximum internal rate of return. There is an implicit assumption that the return on invested capital is maximized.

The internal rate of return should not be confused with the market rate of capitalization. Actually the internal rate of return is a mathematical calculation which measures the present worth of a proposed investment which is equated with the investment cost.

With these qualifications in mind the internal rate of return has a wide appeal.

1. It is easily calculated; it is accepted by financial institutions that bid on mortgages, bonds and other commercial paper.

2. It provides a rate of return that tests the feasibility of a proposed investment. Such a test provides an objective comparison of the internal rate of return on the investment that earns the highest rate of return.

For the more sophisticated student, it will be appreciated that the internal rate of return is based on an implicit assumption: all cash returns in the early years are assumed to be recovered at the specified rate of return and at the same level of risk. Some investment authorities question this assumption.

# Glossary

**Acceleration.** The right of the lender to collect the full amount of principal if the mortgagee is in default.

**Advance.** Usually this term refers to a partial payment under a construction loan.

**Allocation commitment.** A statement by a national or regional investor to purchase within a specified period a certain volume of mortgages at a given price at a specific location.

**Amortized mortgage.** A mortgage that provides for the periodic repayment of principal and interest.

**Annuity.** A series of periodic payments.

**Assignee.** One to whom an assignment is made.

**Assignment of mortgage.** A written instrument transferring ownership of a mortgage from one party to another.

**Assignor.** One who makes an assignment.

**Assumption fee.** A fee paid to a lender for permitting a third party to assume a mortgage.

**Balloon mortgage.** A mortgage in which instalment payments do not fully amortize the loan. At the end of the term the balance is due in a lump sum or "balloon" payment.

**Band of investment.** A method of deriving capitalization rates by weighting the return on various interests in real estate.

**Bargain and sale deed.** A deed that conveys title with no warranties.

**Basic value.** The worth of rural property derived from earnings under typical operation, and from location and home use features as viewed from the actual, and not previously or properly expressed.

**Basis point.** One one hundredth of one percent which refers to yields in mortgages and other credit instruments.

**Beneficiary.** A person for whose benefit a trust agreement is created or who is designated as the recipient of an interest under an insurance policy.

**Binder.** A downpayment for the purchase of real estate as evidence of good faith on the part of the buyer; includes terms of sale as agreed upon by buyer and seller.

**Blanket mortgage.** A mortgage that covers more than one parcel of real estate.

**Building code.** A local regulation providing for safe buildings by establishing minimum standards of construction and building materials.

**Bundle of rights.** A theory comparing real estate interests as a bundle of sticks which may be bought and sold as sticks in a bundle of sticks.

**Capitalization.** A method of converting an annual net income to a capital value.

**Cash flow analysis.** The amount of money earned after payment of income taxes and annual mortgage payments.

**Certificate of reasonable value.** A statement issued by the Veterans Administration establishing the maximum loan for a VA-guaranteed mortgage.

**Closing statement.** A financial statement given the buyer and seller showing the proration of prepaid expenses, closing expenses, the amount due from the buyer and the amount due to the seller.

**Collateral.** Property pledged as security for a debt, including real estate.

**Commitment.** An agreement between the lender and borrower to lend money in the future subject to stated conditions.

**Common element.** The undivided interest held by a condominium owner in any portion of a condominium other than individual units.

**Community property.** In several states property owned in common by a husband and wife during marriage with no right of survivorship.

**Community shopping center.** A center organized around a junior department or variety store which serves as the leading tenant.

**Construction mortgage.** A form of interim financing over a relatively short period made in anticipation of a long term loan upon completion of construction.

**Constructive notice.** A legal notice provided by the recording of documents in a public office, substituting for actual notice.

**Conventional loan.** A mortgage that is not insured by FHA nor guaranteed by the VA.

**Cooperative apartments.** A form of multiple family ownership in which each apartment owner owns a share in the cooperative with possession of an apartment unit under a proprietary lease.

**Covenant.** A promise by one party to another regarding certain performance or non-performance of certain acts or a promise that certain conditions do or do not exist.

**Curtesy.** The interest of a husband in all real estate owned by the wife during marriage at the time of her death.

**Declaration.** An instrument provided for by state statute that provides for condominium ownership.

**Deeds.** A written instrument that transfers an interest in real estate.

**Default.** Non-performance of a duty.

**Deficiency judgment.** A judgment secured by a lender for the amount of that part of a debt secured by a mortgage not satisfied upon sale of the mortgage property.

**Development mortgage.** A loan for the purpose of developing vacant land for the construction of buildings.

**Discounted cash flow.** A method of calculating the present worth of anticipated cash flow.

**Disintermediation.** The outflow of savings from financial institutions to higher earning stocks and bonds.

**Dominant estate.** The parcel of land whose owner enjoys an easement or privilege to use another parcel of land for a special purpose.

**Dower.** The right which a surviving wife has in real estate owned during the marriage.

**Earnest money.** A deposit given to buy real estate.

**Easement.** The right to use real estate for a special purpose.

**Easement appurtenant.** An easement granted by deed that "runs with the land."

**Easement by prescription.** An easement acquired by the open, continuous and hostile use of real property for a statutorily required time.

**Easement in gross.** The right to use land of another for a special purpose representing a personal right —the easement does not run with the land.

**Economic base analysis.** A study of all economic activities in which people earn their living.

**Effective gross income.** Gross possible income less an allowance for vacancy and bad debts.

**Effective income.** Income which is reasonably certain and less nonrecurring income earned on an infrequent basis.

**Emergency Home Owners Relief Act of 1975.** An act authorizing the Secretary of Housing and Urban Development to make repayable emergency mortgage relief payments on behalf of distressed home owners.

**Eminent domain.** The right of government to take private property for public purposes upon payment of just compensation.

**Encumbrance.** A limitation on the fee simple title to real estate.

**Equity interest.** The difference between market value and debt, representing the owner's cash investment.

**Equity of redemption.** The right of the borrower to recover mortgaged property in default upon payment of the debt plus lender expenses.

**Equity participation mortgages.** The partial ownership of income property conveyed by the owner to the lender as part of the consideration for making the loan.

**Escheat.** The reversion of property to the state in the absence of legal heirs.

**Escrow.** A third party that has a fiduciary duty to the buyer and seller to deliver title on performance of all steps necessary to a real estate closing.

**Estate for years.** A lease that continues for a definite period of time.

**Estates of inheritance.** An estate in which the owner has title during his life which may be passed on to heirs.

**Estoppel certificate.** A statement from a lender showing the remaining balance of an outstanding mortgage.

**Executor deed.** A deed executed under court approval which warrants title only against acts of the executor.

**Federal Home Loan Mortgage Corporation.** A government corporation under regulation by the Federal Home Loan Bank Board that buys and sells conventional mortgages.

**Federal Housing Administration.** An agency of the Department of Housing and Urban Development that insures mortgages on qualified, single-family dwellings.

**Federal National Mortgage Association.** A privately owned, government-regulated corporation that buys and sells government-insured and guaranteed mortgages and conventional mortgages.

**Fee simple determinable.** A fee simple estate that terminates upon the occurrence of a stated event.

**Fee simple estate.** An estate in real property in which the owner is entitled to the entire property free from title restrictions or encumbrances, over which he has an unconditional power of disposition.

**Fee subject to condition subsequent.** A fee simple estate that terminates upon (1) the occurrence of a stated event and (2) action by the owner to reenter and repossess.

**First mortgage.** A mortgage representing a prior lien with respect to subsequent mortgages.

**Flexible payment mortgages.** A mortgage in which the initial monthly payments are below those required by a level payment, amortized mortgage.

**Forbearance.** The act of refraining from foreclosure procedures in the event of a mortgage delinquency.

**Foreclosure by action and a sale.** A method of foreclosure provided by state statute requiring foreclosure by order of the court.

**Foreclosure by entry and possession.** A method of foreclosure under the procedure of peaceable possession or by writ of entry.

**Foreclosure by power of sale.** Foreclosure by a written agreement granting the lender power of a sale in the event of mortgage default.

**Freehold estate.** An interest in real estate for an indeterminate time such as a life estate or a fee simple estate.

**Gap loan.** A temporary loan to finance the difference between a minimum loan and the maximum permanent loan as committed.

**Garden type apartments.** Low rise apartments consisting of three stories or less on landscaped acreage operated under one management.

**General plan.** A statement of local community goals covering the physical development of a community according to social, economic and political objectives.

**Government National Mortgage Association.** A government corporation that operates in the secondary mortgage market, buying and selling government-insured and guaranteed loans, usually involving subsidized government mortgages.

**Grantee.** The person to whom an interest in real estate is conveyed.

**Grantor.** A person that conveys an interest in real property.

**Gross leasable area.** Referring to shopping center operation, gross leasable area is the space available for tenant occupancy, excluding space for central utilities and other space not rented to specific tenants.

**Gross possible income.** The annual gross income assuming 100 percent occupancy.

**High rise elevator apartments.** Apartment buildings with four stories or more with elevators.

**Highest and best use.** That legal use which produces the highest net income to the land which when capitalized gives the highest land value.

**Homeowner's policy.** An insurance policy covering the dwelling and its contents against damage from fire, wind, theft, liability for property damage and personal liability.

**Homestead right.** Rights granted by state statute protecting certain property belonging to a debtor from the claims of creditors.

**Housing codes.** A local regulation which may restrict the number of persons legally permitted in a dwelling, and provide for minimum maintenance, sanitation facilities, ventilation, heating and lighting standards.

**Industrial property.** Buildings used for gainful activity involved in producing, distributing and changing the form of raw materials or assembling components and parts, packaging, warehousing, and transporting finished products.

**Internal rate of return.** The rate of return that equates the present value of future net cash benefits with the amount of the original investment.

**Interstate Land Sales Full Disclosure Act.** Legislation that discourages fraud, misrepresentation and deceit in the sale of subdivision lots over interstate boundaries.

**Junior mortgage.** A mortgage second in priority to a senior mortgage.

**Land contract.** An instalment contract for the purchase of land providing for a deed upon payment of the last instalment.

**Late charge.** A penalty imposed on a delinquent borrower.

**Leased fee.** The interest held by a lessor.

**Leasehold interest.** An interest of the tenant or lessee.

**Leasehold mortgage.** A loan to a lessee secured by his leasehold interest.

**Lessee.** The party (tenant) who holds the exclusive right of possession under a valid lease.

**Lessor.** A party who leases property to a tenant.

**Level payment amortization.** An amortization plan in which mortgage payments are constant but the amount accruing to principal and interest vary with each payment.

**Life estate.** An estate in which title continues only during the life of a person identified as the person whose life determines duration of the title.

**Life tenant.** A person holding a life estate interest.

**Loan submission.** A package consisting of papers and documents required for loan approval.

**Loan-to-value ratio.** A mortgage loan expressed as a percent of the appraised value of real estate.

**Low rise apartments.** Walk-up buildings and elevator buildings of three stories or less.

**Market comparison approach.** A method of appraising property that employs recent sales of similar property.

**Market value.** The highest price in terms of money which a property will bring in the market, neither party acting under distress, and with knowledge of all possible uses to which the property may be put.

**Mechanic's lien.** A lien created by statute that protects persons who have performed work or furnished materials in the erection or repair of buildings.

**Moratorium.** A right granted to the borrower to postpone mortgage payments for a given period.

**Mortgage.** An instrument that pledges real estate as security for a debt.

**Mortgage assumption.** An assignment of the mortgage in which the assignee personally assumes liability for the unpaid debt.

**Mortgage banker.** A party that serves as correspondent between national or regional lenders and individual borrowers.

**Mortgage broker.** A party that earns a commission for serving the lender and borrower; the mortgage broker does not service mortgages.

**Mortgage constant.** Total interest and principal paid annually expressed as a percent of the original mortgage.

**Mortgage discount.** The difference between the mortgage principal and its selling price.

**Mortgage equity capitalization.** A method of capitalizing the net income remaining after mortgage payments including the present worth of the property after sale and mortgage satisfaction.

**Mortgage kicker.** A benefit given the lender above conventional interest payments as an incentive to grant a loan on income property —typically an interest in equity or annual income.

**Mortgage pattern.** A method of rating mortgage risks according to the real estate security, credit of the borrower and terms of the mortgage.

**Mortgagee.** The person who takes a mortgage—the lender.

**Mortgagor.** The person having title to real property who pledges that property as security for a debt.

**Neighborhood.** A portion of a larger community, or an entire community, in which there is a homogeneous grouping of inhabitants, buildings or business enterprises.

**Neighborhood shopping center.** Neighborhood centers specialize in convenience goods, dominated by a leading tenant such as a supermarket or discount drug store.

**Net rentable area.** Usually applying to apartments or office buildings, the term refers to the net square footage of a building rentable to tenants, excluding stair wells, elevator space, maintenance areas, halls and other public areas.

**Open end mortgage.** A privilege granted by the lender allowing the mortgagee to borrow additional money under terms of the original mortgage.

**Operating expenses.** Annual expenses of an income property before income tax depreciation allowances and mortgage payments.

**Option to purchase.** The right to purchase real property within a specified time on stated terms in return for a price.

**Origination fee.** The fee charged for preparation and submission of a proposed mortgage loan.

**Package mortgage.** A mortgage that includes personal property such as kitchen appliances.

**Partially amortized mortgage.** A mortgage that partially amortizes principal, providing for principal repayment down to a given amount with a lump-sum payment of the remaining principal at the date of maturity.

**Participation mortgage.** A mortgage financed by more than one lender.

**Performance standard.** A method of controlling industrial land use by enforcing standards of operation.

**Permanent loan.** A long-term mortgage usually of more than ten years' duration.

**Police power.** The inherent right of government to regulate land use for the protection of the public health, safety, and convenience.

**Power of attorney.** An instrument authorizing a person to act as the agent or attorney of the person granting such power.

**Prepayment penalty.** The amount paid by the borrower for the privilege of prepaying a mortgage before maturity.

**Prepayment privileges.** The right of the borrower to prepay a mortgage debt before the due date.

**Private mortgage insurance.** A private system of mortgage insurance that partially insures a mortgage based on premiums related to the degree of risk.

**Progressively inclusive districts.** A zoning practice that allows land uses of preceding zoning districts; a method of allowing succeeding districts to be used for land uses of the preceding district.

**Promissory note.** A note evidencing a personal promise to pay a debt.

**Property report.** A report required to be issued by the Interstate Land Sales Full Disclosure Act which gives information important to lot buyers in advance of sale.

**Purchase money mortgage.** A mortgage granted by a seller who is willing to accept part of the purchase price in the form of a promissory note from the buyer.

**Quiet enjoyment.** A covenant in a warranty deed that gives the right of possession without disturbance caused by defects in title.

**Quit claim deeds.** A deed that conveys the grantor's interest in real estate.

**Rate of return.** The net income earned on a capital sum expressed as a percent.

**Real estate investment trust.** An organization, that may distribute income to stockholders which is exempt from the corporate net income tax, and organized for the purpose of attracting investment capital into real estate investments.

**Real estate owned.** A term describing property acquired by a lender for investment purposes or as the result of foreclosure.

**Real property.** Land and its attachments. The definition includes buildings, minerals and other products of the soil including the air space above land.

**Realtor.** A member of the National Association of Realtors, formerly the National Association of Real Estate Boards.

**Recording.** The act of making an entry in a public file which places the general public on notice of rights of the parties involved.

**Regional shopping center.** A shopping center dominated by a full-line department store of at least 100,000 square feet of gross leasable area.

**Remainderman.** A party to whom the remainder of an estate passes at the termination of a life estate.

**Satisfaction of mortgage.** A written instrument by the lender evidencing full payment of the mortgage debt.

**Security deed.** A deed used in the state of Georgia that substitutes for a warranty deed and mortgage and includes a statement that the deed secures payment of a debt. The deed establishes a power of attorney authorizing the purchaser or his agent to sell property upon default of a loan.

**Servicing agreement.** A written contract between an investor and a mortgage lender controlling the rights and obligations of the lender in servicing mortgages owned by the investor.

**Servient estate.** An estate limited by the right of the owner of another parcel of land to use it for a special purpose.

**Settlement costs booklet.** A booklet required by the Real Estate Settlement Procedures Act which must be given to a loan applicant at the time of loan application, or within three business days thereafter.

**Settlement statement.** A report that must be given buyer and seller as required under the Real Estate Settlement Procedures Act.

**Sheriff's deed.** A deed conveying title as a result of public sale that includes no warranty or representations of title.

**Special warranty deeds.** A deed that includes warranties of title applying only against acts occurring during the grantor's ownership.

**Stand-by commitment.** A commitment by a long-term lender to purchase a mortgage at above market interest rates for a period longer than the average construction loan.

**Statement of record.** A report required by the developer of a subdivision regulated under the Interstate Land Sales Full Disclosure Act.

**Statute of Frauds.** State laws that require certain contracts to be in writing, such as deeds and other written instruments for the conveyance of real property.

**Statutory right of redemption.** The right of a borrower to redeem mortgaged property after a foreclosure sale.

**Strict foreclosure.** State statutes that terminate a borrower's rights after a given date—the title vests with the lender when the court issues a decree, terminating all rights of the borrower.

**Subject to mortgage.** The assignment of a mortgage to an assignee that assumes no personal liability for the debt.

**Subordination.** A written instrument stating that a debt is inferior to the interest of another in the same property.

**Take-out commitment.** A binding letter or agreement between a permanent investor and mortgage banker, agreeing to purchase a mortgage prior to a specific time at a designated price subject to approval of the borrower and mortgage loan documentation.

**Tandem loans.** A program in which GNMA agrees to purchase government insured or guaranteed mortgages from sellers usually at subsidized terms to low income borrowers.

**Tenancy at sufferance.** A tenant who continues to occupy premises without permission of the owner.

**Tenancy at will.** A tenancy of uncertain duration that may be cancelled upon proper notice by either party.

**Tenancy by the entirety.** Ownership during marriage conveyed to a husband and wife as a single estate with the right of survivorship.

**Tenancy from period to period.** A tenancy that continues from period to period, continuing automatically until legal notice of termination is given.

**Term mortgage.** A mortgage that provides no periodic payment of principal which is due at the end of the term.

**Trust deed.** A deed that conveys title to a third party, a trustee, who holds title for the benefit of a lender, the beneficiary of the trust.

**Usury laws.** State statutes that establish maximum interest rates.

**Variable payment mortgage.** A mortgage calling for a periodic, constant payment to principal.

**Variable rate mortgage.** A mortgage in which a mortgage interest rate varies according to changes in the price index.

**Veterans Administration mortgage.** A mortgage guaranteed by the Veterans Administration.

**Warehousing operations.** The borrowing of funds on a short term basis using permanent mortgage loans as collateral.

**Warranty deed.** A deed that contains covenants by the grantor warranting title to the grantee.

**Wrap around mortgage.** Actually a second mortgage, granted to a borrower with a first mortgage that is continued by the second lender who makes payments on the first mortgage from payments on the second mortgage.

**Zoning ordinance.** A local ordinance that establishes land use districts, controls building bulk and height and other minimum property standards.

# INDEX

## A

Acceleration clauses, 82–83
Advantages of condominium ownership, 167–71
Allocation commitment, 59
Amortized mortgages, 67, 89–91
Analysis of building improvements,
320
Analyzing borrower ability to pay,
298–304
anticipated income, 298–304
assets and liabilities, 299–302
housing expenses, 303–04
willingness to pay, 302
Analyzing net income statements, 196–
200
apartment operating expenses, 198–
99
gross possible income, 197–98
operating expense ratios, 200
vacancy allowance, 198
Analyzing portfolio yields, 371–73
interest income, 371–72
origination fees, 371
warehousing operations, 372–73
Anticipated income, 298–304
current income, 298
effective income, 298
net effective income, 299
stability of income, 299
Apartment locations, 190–91
intermediate locations, 190–91
suburban apartments, 190
Apartment operating expenses, 198–99
Apartment types, 189–90
garden-type apartments, 189
high-rise elevator buildings, 189
low-rise apartments, 190
Apartments, 196
gross floor area, 196
income and expense ratios, 205–06
number of rooms, 196
rentable floor area, 196
standards of comparison, 195

Appraisal for farm mortgages, 231–40
appraisal process, 233
comparable sales approach, 236
evaluating farm buildings, 239–40
income approach, 233–36
Appraisal process, 233
Appraising the mortgage security, 177–
82
amenities, 177
bylaws, condominiums, 177
declaration, condominiums, 177
income technique, 182
location, 177
sale comparisons, 179–82
services, 177
Assets and liabilities, 299–302
Assignment of mortgages, 84
Assumption of mortgages, 83–84

## B

Balloon mortgage, 91
Band of investment, 202
Bargain and sale deeds, 34
Basic requirements of RESPA, 289–95
advance disclosure settlement costs,
290
settlement costs booklet, 289–90
Blanket mortgages, 86
Borrower data, 319
Borrowers credit status, 147
Building codes, 38

## C

Capitalization in perpetuity, 377–78
Capitalization of net income, 201–03
band of investment, 202
market value, 202–03
Cash flow analysis, 312–15, 386–93
discounted cash flow (DCF), 389–
91
equity participation mortgages, 391–
93
Causes of mortgage delinquency, 368–
69

407

Appraisal for farm mortgages, 231–40
  appraisal process, 233
Certificate of eligibility, 134
Characteristics of apartment houses, 189–92
  apartment locations, 190
  apartment types, 189–90
  locational characteristics, 191–92
    access, 192
    employment centers, 192
    government services, 192
    land use controls, 192
    shopping facilities, 192
Characteristics of real estate, 93–100
  estate, 98–100
  immobility, 99
  indestructibility, 98–99
  modification, 100
  short run supply, 99–100
  stratified markets, 99
Class B participation program, 110
Clean Air Act Amendments of 1970, 248
Closing the construction loan, 322–23
Coastal Zone Mangament Act of 1972, 247–48
Collection efficiency, 358
Collection management, 357–58
  collection efficiency, 358
  individual account review, 358
  monthly reports, 357–58
Commercial banks, 53–57
  commercial banks since World War II, 56–57
  early mortgage activity, 54–56
Commerical land, 256–57
Community centers, 270
Community property, 26
Comparable sales approach, 236
Condominium bylaws, 164–65
Condominium construction mortgages, 173–74
Condominiums, 162–82
  appraising the mortgage security, 177–82
    income technique, 182
    sale comparisons, 179–82
  evaluation of condominium ownership, 167–72
    advantages of condominium ownership, 167–71

disadvantages of condominium ownership, 171–72
  legal aspects of condominiums, 163–67
    condominium bylaws, 164–65
    elements of the declaration, 163–64
    percentage ownership of common elements, 165–67
  mortgage financing of the condominium, 172–76
    condominium construction mortgages, 173–74
    financing condominium conversions, 175–76
    financing new units, 172
    mortgage financing techniques, 174
Construction costs, 281
Construction loan, 9
Construction loan administration, 316–34
  loan agreement, 321–30
    closing the construction loan, 322–23
    contract administration, 323–27
    establishing priority of claims by recording, 328–30
  loan application, 317–20
    analysis of building improvements, 320
    borrower data, 319
    contractor data, 319
    loan details, 318–319
    other requirements, 320
    site data, 320
  loan documentation, 321
  loan requirements, 316–17
  residential construction loans, 330–34
    scattered lot development, 330–33
    subdivision construction loans, 333–34
Construction loan details, 318–19
Construction loan documentation, 321
Construction loan requirements, 316–17
Construction mortgages, 88
Contract administration, 323–27
Contractor data, 319
Conventional rate of return estimates, 376–79
  capitalization in perpetuity, 377–78

limitations of rate of return calculations, 378–79
Conversion of an existing apartment, 183
Cooperative apartments, 182–86
bylaws, 184
conversion of an existing apartment, 183
financing new developments, 183–84
financing techniques, 186
limitations of cooperative ownership, 185–86
ownership, 184–85
Cooperative bylaws, 184
Cooperative ownership, 184–86
Correction deeds, 34
Credit analysis for single family dwelling loans, 127, 295–308
analyzing borrower ability to pay, 298–304
anticipated income, 298–99
assets and liabilities, 299–302
willingness to pay, 302
housing expenses, 303–04
Equal Credit Opportunity Act, 296–98
loan application, 296–98
Credit of the borrower, 97
Current role of FNMA, 104–06
mortgage credit market, 104–05
periods of credit ease, 106
periods of tight credit, 105–06
Current assets, 221
Curtesy, 25

**D**

Deed restrictions, 365
Deliberate delinquent, 339
Demand analysis, 193–94
Demand for farm mortgages, 225–26
Demand for land, 254–55
Determinants of farm land value, 230–31
Development of savings and loan associations since 1932, 43–44
Disadvantages of condominium ownership, 167–71
Disclosure Settlement Statement, 290–92
Discounted cash flow, (DCF), 389–91

Dominant estate, 29
Dower interest, 25
Downtown retail stores, 274–75

**E**

Early development of mortgage lending for banks, 66–70
Early development of savings and loan associations, 42–47
Early mortgage activity, 54–56
Easement appurtenant, 29
Easement by prescription, 31
Easement rights, 29–31
Economic base analysis, 140–41
Effective gross income, 198
Effects of disintermediation, 46–47
Elements of a mortgage, 80 81
Elements of the declaration, 163–64
Emergency Home Finance Act of 1970, 109
Emergency Price Control Act of 1942, 188
Employee Retirement Income Security Act of 1974, 61
Employment centers, 192
Environmental controls, 38–40
air quality, 39
Flood Disaster Protection Act of 1973, 40
management of coastal zones, 40
national environmental policy, 38–39
water quality, 40
Environmental Impact Statement, 39
Equal Credit Opportunity Act Amendments of 1976, 296–98
Equity participation mortgages, 391–93
Equity of redemption, 81
Establishing priority of claims by recording, 328–30
Estate for years; 28
Estates not of inheritance, 23–27
Estates of inheritance, 21–23
Estate *pur autre vie*, 24
Estimating the feasibility of land developments, 258–61
Evaluating credit of the borrower, 220–22
Evaluating farm buildings, 239–40

Evaluating mortgage risks on single family dwellings, 139–49
  judging borrower credit, 147–49
    borrower's credit status, 147
    housing expenditure patterns, 148
    rules of thumb, 148–49
    source of income, 147–48
  real estate security, 140–47
    economic base analysis, 140–41
    neighborhood analysis, 142–44
    personal income, 141–42
    population characteristics, 141
    site analysis, 144–45
    valuation data, 146
Evaluation of condominium ownership, 167–72
  advantages of condominium ownership, 167–71
  disadvantages of condominium ownership, 171–72
Executor's deed, 34

# F

Farm Credit Act of 1971, 226
Farm land value trends, 227–28
Farm loan policy, 228–31
  determinants of farm land value, 230–31
  historical definition of value, 228–30
Farmers Home Administration, 16
Federal Assistance in mortgage markets, 101–36
  Federal Housing Administration, 111–33
    FHA programs, 117–23
    Housing and Community Development Act of 1974, 123–26
    Mutual mortgage insurance, 117
    Title I, community development, 123
    Title II, assisted housing, 124
    Title III, mortgage credit assistance, 124–25
    Title V, rural housing, 125
    Title VII, consumer home mortgage assistance, 125–26
    Title VIII, miscellaneous authority, 126

Federal Home Loan Mortgage Corporation, 109–11
  guaranteed mortgage certificates, 111
  mortgage participation certificates, 110–11
Federal National Mortgage Association, 102–08
  current role of FNMA, 104–06
  FNMA Charter Act of 1968, 104
  FNMA operations, 106
  GNMA programs administered by FNMA, 106–08
    Program 16, 107
    Program 17, 107
    Program 18, 107
    Program 19, 107
    Program 20, 107
    Programs 21 and 22, 108
  Government National Mortgage Association, 108–09
    security regulations, 108–09
    types of securities, 109
  Impact of federal programs, 101–02
  Veterans Administration guaranteed loans, 134–36
    insurance and direct loans, 136
    loan procedures, 134–36
Federal Home Loan Bank System, 43–44
Federal Home Loan Mortgage Corportion, 11, 17, 19, 109–11
  guaranteed mortgage certificates, 111
  mortgage participation certificates, 110–11
Federal Housing Administration, 111–33
  FHA programs, 117–23
  mutual mortgage insurance, 117
Federal National Mortgage Association, 11, 15, 102–08
  current role of FNMA, 104–06
    mortgage credit market, 104–05
    periods of credit ease, 106
    periods of tight credit, 105–06
  FNMA Charter Act of 1968, 104
  FNMA operations, 106
  GNMA programs administered by FNMA, 106–08
    Program 16, 107
    Program 17, 107
    Program 18, 107

Program, 20, 107
Programs 21 and 22, 108
Origin, 103–05
Fee simple determinable, 23
Fee simple estate, 21–23
  exclusive possession, 21–22
  exclusive possession, 22
  quiet enjoyment, 22
Fee subject to condition subsequent, 23
FHA requirements, 351–52
FHA mortgage forms, 127–33
  credit analysis, 127
  mortgage application, 127
  property appraisal, 127
FHA mortgage insurance programs, 118–22
FHA rating system, 152–54
Financial analysis of the borrower, 310–12
Financial causes of mortgage default, 364–67
Financial causes of mortgage default and delinquency, 364–69
Financial ratios, 204–06
Financing agricultural property, 224–44
  appraisal for farm mortgages, 231–40
    appraisal process, 233
    comparable sales approach, 236
    evaluating farm buildings, 239–40
    income approach, 233–36
  farm land value trends, 227–28
  farm loan policy, 228–31
    determinants of farm land value, 230–31
    historical definition of value, 228–30
    judging the mortgage security, 240–44
  market for agricultural mortgages, 224–27
  market for farm real estate loans, 225–27
    demand for farm mortgages, 225–26
    supply of farm mortgage credit, 226–27
Financing condominium conversions, 175–76
Financing industrial property, 207–23

industrial building analysis, 217–19
  industrial buildings classified by plant layout, 217–18
  industrial building standards, 219
  single story buildings, 218
judging industrial credit, 219–22
  company standing in the industry, 219–20
  evaluating credit of the borrower, 220–22
location analysis, 208–17
  industries location requirements, 209
    footloose industries, 210
    industries oriented to labor, 210
    industries oriented to markets, 209
    industries oriented to raw materials, 209–10
  industrial site requirements, 210–17
    industrial zoning, 215–17
    judging industrial land, 211–13
  site analysis, 213–15
sale leaseback financing, 222–23
Financing Methods, 280–86
  construction costs, 281
  financing techniques, 283–86
  land acquisition, 280–81
  presentation of the loan proposal, 281–83
  shopping center leases, 286–87
Financing multiple family dwellings, 187–206
  analyzing net income statements, 196–200
    apartment operating expenses, 198–99
    gross possible income, 197–98
    operating expense ratios, 200
    vacancy allowance, 198
  characteristics of apartment houses, 189–92
    apartment locations, 190
    apartment types, 189–90
    locational characteristics, 191–92
      access, 192
      employment centers, 192
      government services, 192
      land use controls, 192
      shopping facilities, 192

rental structure, 191
impact of rent control, 187–89
investment analysis, 200–05
  capitalization of net income, 201–03
    band of investment, 202
    market value 202–03
  cash flow analysis, 203–04
  financial ratios, 204–06
rent control rationale, 188–89
rental housing market, 193–96
  demand analysis, 193–94
  standards of comparison, 195–96
  supply analysis, 194
Financing new developments, 183–84
Financing new units, 172
Financing plans, 263–64
  first mortgage financing, 265
  land contracts, 263–64
  option to purchase, 264–65
  purchase money mortgages, 264
Financing Single Family Dwellings, 137–61
  evaluating mortgage risks, 139–49
    judging borrower credit, 147–49
      borrower's credit status, 147
      housing expenditure patterns, 148
      rules of thumb, 148–49
      source of income, 147–48
    real estate security, 140–41
      economic base analysis, 140–41
      neighborhood analysis, 142–44
      personal income, 141–42
      population characteristics, 141
      site analysis, 144–45
      valuation data, 146
  judging the mortgage pattern, 149–57
    conventional appraisal report forms, 149–52
    FHA rating system, 152–54
    private mortgage insurance (PMI), 155–57
    statistical tests of the mortgage pattern, 154–55
    veterans administration appraisal report, 152

single family dwelling mortgage application, 157–61
Financing techniques, 186, 283–86
First mortgage financing, 265
Flexible payment mortgages, 92
Flood Disaster Protection Act of 1973, 40
Flow of funds into real estate mortgages, 6–8
  indicators of mortgage flows, 11–13
  mortgage origination, 9
  secondary market agencies, 11
  secondary mortgage markets, 10
FNMA Charter Act of 1968, 104
FNMA operations, 106
FNMA origin, 103–05
Forbearance, 355–56
Foreclosure by action and sale, 260–61
Foreclosure by entry and possession, 361
Foreclosure by power of sale, 362
Foreclosure, strict, 360
Freehold estates, 21–27
  estates not of inheritance, 23–27
  estates of inheritance, 21–23

# G

General characteristics of mortgages, 95–100
  credit of the borrower, 97
  interest rates on government-insured and guaranteed loans, 96
  mortgage foreclosure regulations, 98
  mortgages subject to loan-to-value ratios, 97
  real estate valuation, 97
  usury laws, 96
General plan, 36
Government National Mortgage Association, 11, 15–17, 108–09
  security regulations, 108–09
  types of securities, 109
GNMA programs administered by FNMA, 106–08
  programs 16, 107
  programs 17, 107
  programs 18, 107

programs 19, 107
programs 20, 107
programs 21 and 22, 108.
Grant deed, 34
Gross leasable area, 269
Gross possible income, 197–98
Guaranteed mortgage certificates, 110–11

# H

IIistorical definition of value, 228–30
Home loan program, 110
Home Mortgage Disclosure Act of 1975, 370
Housing and Rent Act of 1947, 188
Housing expenditure patterns, 148
  acquisition costs, 148
  monthly costs, 148
Housing expenses, 303–04
Housing and Urban Development Act of 1968, 104
Housing and Community Development Act of 1974, 74, 116–17, 123–26
  Title I, community development, 123
  Title II, assisted housing, 124
  Title III, mortgage credit assistance, 124–25
  Title V, rural housing, 125
  Title VII, consumer home mortgage assistance, 125–26
  Title VIII, miscellaneous authority, 126
HUD rating system, 304–06
Homestead rights, 26

# I

Impact of federal programs, 101–02
Impact of rent control, 187–89
Income approach, 182, 233-36
Indicators of mortgage flows, 11–13
Indifferent borrower, 336–37
Individual account review, 358
Industrial building analysis, 217–19
  industrial buildings classified by plant layout, 217–18
    process layout, 217–18
    product layout, 217

industrial building standards, 219
  single story buildings, 218
Industrial building standards, 219
Industrial land, 256–57
  centrally located land, 256–57
  industrial acreage, 256–57
  planned industrial districts, 256–57
  redeveloped urban renewal land, 256–57
Industrial location requirements, 209
  footloose industries, 210
  industries oriented to labor, 210
  industries oriented to markets, 209
  industries oriented to raw materials, 209–10
Industrial site requirements, 210–17
  industrial zoning, 215–17
  judging industrial land, 211–13
  site analysis, 213–15
Industrial zoning, 215–17
  performance standards, 216
  progressively inclusive districts, 216–17
  prohibited industries, 216
Industries oriented to labor, 210
Industries oriented to markets, 209
Industries oriented to raw materials, 209–10
Industry, judging industrial sites, 213–15
  community analysis, 215
  regional analysis, 215
Industry, judging industrial land, 211–13
  centrally located industrial sites, 211
  industrial acreage, 212
  organized industrial districts, 212–13
  redeveloped land, 213
Interest income, 371-72
Interest Rate Adjustment Act of 1966, 46
Interest rates on government-insured and guaranteed loans, 96
Internal rate of return (IRR), 394–96
Interstate Land Sales Full Disclosure Act, 248–51
Investment analysis, 200–05
  capitalization of net income, 201–03
    band of investment, 202
    market value, 202–03
  cash flow analysis, 203–04
  financial ratios, 204–06

# J

Judging borrower credit, 147–49
  borrower's credit status, 147
  housing expenditure patterns, 148
  rules of thumb, 148–49
  source of income, 147–48
Judging industrial credit, 219–22
  company standing in the industry, 219–20
  evaluating credit of the borrower, 220–22
Judging industrial land, 211–13
Judging the mortgage pattern, 149–57
  conventional appraisal report forms, 149–52
  FHA rating system, 152–54
  private mortgage insurance (PMI), 155–57
  statistical tests of the mortgage pattern, 154–55
  Veterans Administration appraisal report, 152
Judging mortgage security, 240–44, 275–80
  merchant association, 278–79
  retail sales forecasts, 276–77
  shopping center management, 277–78
  site characteristics, 277
  tenant restrictions, 278
  tenant selection, 279–80

# L

Land acquisition, 280–81
Land contracts, 263–64
Land development loans, 245–67
  land financing techniques, 261–67
    financing plans, 263–67
      first mortgage financing, 265
      land contracts, 263–64
      option to purchase, 264–65
      purchase money mortgages, 264
    reducing risks in land development loans, 261–63
  land use regulations, 245–54
    federal land use controls, 246–51
      Clean Air Act Amendments of 1970, 248
      Coastal Zone Management Act of 1972, 247–48
      Interstate Land Sales Full Disclosure Act, 248–51
      National Environmental Policies Act of 1969, 246–47
      Noise Control Act of 1972, 248
    local regulations, 252–54
    state administered land use controls, 251–52
  market for developed land, 254–57
    commercial land, 256–57
    demand for land, 254–55
    residential land, 255–56
  subdivison development, 257–61
    developments, 258–61
    estimating the feasibility of land developments, 258–61
    site suitability, 258
Land Use controls, 192
Land Use regulations, 245–67
  Clean Air Act Amendments of 1970, 248
  Coastal Zone Management Act of 1972, 247–48
  Interstate Land Sales Full Disclosure Act, 248–51
  National Environment Policies Act of 1969, 246–47
  Noise Control Act of 1972, 248
Leased fee, 27
Leasehold interest, 27
Legal aspects of condominiums, 163–67
  condominium bylaws, 164–65
  elements of the declaration, 163–64
  percentage ownership of common elements, 165–67
Less than freehold estates, 27–29
  estate for years, 28
  tenancy at sufferance, 29
  tenancy at will, 28
  tenancy from period to period, 28
Lessee, 27
Lessor, 27
Level payment amortization, 90
Lien theory states, 85
Life estates, 21
Life insurance companies, 51–53
Life tenant, 24
Limitations of cooperative ownership, 185–86
Limitation on escrow deposits, 290–91

Limitations of rate of return calculations, 278–79
Loan application, 295–310
Local regulations, 252–54
Location analysis, 208–17
  industrial location requirements, 209
    footloose industries, 210
    industries oriented to labor, 210
    industries oriented to markets, 209
    industries oriented to raw materials, 209–10
  industrial site requirements, 210–17
    industrial zoning, 215–17
    judging industrial land, 211–13
    site analysis, 213–15
Locational characteristics, 191–92
  access, 192
  employment centers, 192
  government services, 192
  land use controls, 192
  shopping facilities, 192

# M

Management of costal zones, 40
Market for agricultural mortgages, 224–27
  demand for farm mortgages, 225–26
  market for farm real estate loans, 225–27
  supply of farm mortgage credit, 226–27
Market for developed land, 254–57
  commercial land, 256–57
  demand for land, 254–55
  residential land, 255–56
Market value, 202–03
Mechanics' lien, 327–28
Merchant association, 278–79
Mortgage application, 127
Mortgage-backed securities program, 16
Mortgage Bankers Association of America, 335
Mortgage bankers, 57–60
Mortgages classified by purpose, 86–88
  blanket mortgages, 86
  construction mortgages, 88
  open-end mortgages, 86
  package mortgages, 87
  participation mortgages, 87

  purchase money mortgages, 87
  wraparound mortgages, 87–88
Mortgages classified by type of payment, 88–93
  amortized mortgages, 89–91
  flexible payment mortgages, 92
  partially amorized mortgages, 91–92
  term mortgage, 88–89
  variable rate mortgages, 93–95
Mortgage collection policies, 335–58
  collection management, 357–58
    collection efficiency, 358
    individual account review, 358
    monthly reports, 357–58
  FHA and VA requirements, 351–52
  main reasons for delinquencies, 336–40
    deliberate delinquent, 339
    delinquencies unknown to spouse, 337–38
    divorce or separation, 337–38
    family debts, 337–38
    family sickness, 337–38
    indifferent borrower, 336–37
    personal emergencies, 337–38
    poor personal spending habits, 337–38
    property in process of sale, 337–38
    reduction of income, 337–38
    seasonal loss of income, 337–38
    short-term strike, 337–38
    temporary unemployment, 339
    unemployment, 337–38
  prevention of delinquencies, 340–43
    initial payment period, 341–43
    other administrative measures, 343
    preparing the borrower, 340–41
  recommended collection procedures, 343–51
    routine procedures, 344–48
    follow-up records, 348
    personal conferences, 347–48
    special collection procedures, 348–51
    telephone interviews, 345–47
  recommending foreclosure, 352–57
Mortgage Corporation, 110
Mortgage characteristics, 95–100
  characteristics of real estate, 98–100
    immobility, 99

indestructibility, 98–99
modification, 100
short run supply, 99–100
stratified markets, 99
credit of the borrower, 97
interest rates on government-insured and guaranteed loans, 96
mortgage foreclosure regulations, 98
mortgages subject to loan-to-value ratios, 97
real estate valuation, 97
usury laws, 96
Mortgage credit analysis, 288–315
credit analysis for single family dwelling loans, 295–308
analyzing borrower ability to pay, 298–304
anticipated income, 298–99
assets and liabilities, 299–302
housing expenses, 303–04
willingness to pay, 302
Equal Credit Opportunity Act, 296–98
HUD rating system, 304–06
loan application, 295–96
mortgage pattern, 306–08
mortgage credit analysis for income properties, 308–15
cash flow analysis, 312–15
financial analysis of the borrower, 310–12
loan application, 309–10
real estate settlement procedures, 289–95
basic requirements of RESPA, 289–95
impact on lenders, 295
Mortgage credit market, 104–05
Mortgage delinquencies, 336–40
deliberate delinquent, 339
indifferent borrower, 336–37
personal emergencies, 337–38
temporary unemployment, 339
Mortgage equity capitalization, 379–86
Mortgage financing by commercial banks, 66–78
early development, 66–70
national bank lending authority, 70–77
continued prudence and careful evaluations, 77

existing loan authority extended, 76–77
increase in available mortgage funds, 71–76
new loans permitted, 76
related financing activities, 78
Mortgage financing of condominiums, 172–74
condominium construction mortgages, 173–74
financing new units, 172
mortgage financing techniques, 174
Mortgage foreclosure regulations, 98
Mortgage instruments, 79–85
elements of a mortgage, 80–81
other finance instruments, 93–95
security deeds, 95
trust deeds, 94–95
other legal aspects, 85
lien theory states, 85
title theory states, 85
recording mortgages, 84–85
rights of the mortgagee, 82–84
acceleration clauses, 82–83
assignment of mortgages, 84
assumption of mortgages, 83–84
rights of the mortgagor, 81
equity of redemption, 81
prepayment privileges, 82
statutory right of redemption, 82
types of mortgages, 85–95
mortgages classified by purpose, 86–88
blanket, 86
construction, 88
open-end, 86
package, 87
participation, 87
purchase money, 87
wraparound, 87–88
mortgages classified by type of payment, 88–93
amortized, 89–91
flexible payment, 92
partially amortized, 91–92
term, 88–89
variable rate, 92–93
Mortgage loan activity, 44–45
Mortgage origination, 9
Mortgage participation certificates, 110–11

Mortgage pattern, 306–08
Mortgage pools, 16
Mortgage portfolio administration, 359–74
  analyzing portfolio yields, 371–73
    interest income, 371–72
    origination fees, 371
    warehousing operations, 372–73
  forecloure procedures, 359–62
    foreclosure by action and sale, 360–61
    foreclosure by entry and possession, 361
    foreclosure by power of sale, 362
    strict foreclosure, 360
  mortgage portfolio policy, 373–74
  mortgage risk analysis, 362–70
    financial causes of mortgage default and delinquency, 364–69
    causes of mortgage delinquency, 368–69
    financial causes of mortgage default, 364–67
    property characteristics associated with default, 369–70
    geopraphic diversification, 369–70
    property types, 370
Mutual mortgage insurance, 117
Mutual savings banks, 47–51
  competition for savings, 50–51
  current development, 48–50
  early development, 47–48

# N

National Bank Act of 1863, 63
National environmental policy, 38–39
National Environmental Policies Act of 1969, 246–47
National Housing Act of 1934, 54, 67
National private debt, 5
Neighborhood analysis, 142–44
  location analysis, 143
  physical adaptability, 143
  utility services, 144
Neighborhood centers, 270–71
Net fixed assets, 221
Net quick asset position, 221
Net spendable income, 386
Noise Control Act of 1972, 248

# O

Open-end mortgages, 86
Operating expense ratios, 200
Operations of secondary mortgage market, 13–19
  Federal Home Loan Mortgage Corporation, 17–19
  Federal National Mortgage Association, 15
  Government National Mortgage Association, 15–17
Option to purchase, 264–65
Ordinary life estates, 23–24
Origination fees, 371
Ownership interests, 21–30
  easement rights, 29–31
  freehold estates, 21–27
    estates not of inheritance, 23–27
    estates of inheritance, 21–23
  less than freehold estates, 27–29
    estate for years, 28
    tenancy at sufferance, 29
    tenancy at will, 28
    tenancy from period to period, 28

# P

Package mortgages, 87
Partially amortized mortgages, 91–92, 294
Participation mortgages, 87
Pension funds, 61–62
Percentage ownership of common elements, 165–67
Performance bonds, 332
Periods of credit ease, 106
Periods of tight credit, 105–06
Personal conferences, 347–48
Personal emergencies, 337–38
Personal income, 141–42
Physical changes, 175
Planned unit developments, 37
Population characteristics, 141
Prepayment privileges, 82
Presentation of the loan proposal, 281–83
Prevention of delinquencies, 340–43
  initial payment period, 341–43

other administrative measures, 343
preparing the borrower, 340–41
Primary lenders, 12
Private mortgage insurance (PMI), 155–57
Primary mortgage market, 10
Private property rights, 20–40
  environmental controls, 38–40
    air quality, 39
    Flood Disaster Protection Act of 1973, 40
    management of coastal zones, 40
    national environmental policy, 38–39
    water quality, 40
  ownership interests, 21–30
    easement rights, 29–31
    freehold estates, 21–27
      estates not of inheritance, 23–27
      estates of inheritance, 21–23
    less than freehold estates, 27–29
      estate for years, 28
      tenancy at sufferance, 29
      tenancy at will, 28
      tenancy from period to period, 28
  public land use controls, 35–38
    building codes, 37
    general plan, 36
    housing codes, 38
    zoning ordinances, 36–37
  real estate conveyance instruments, 31–35
    types of deeds, 31–35
    bargain and sale deeds, 34
    quit claim deeds, 34
    special warranty deeds, 33
    specialized deeds, 34–35
    warranty deeds, 32–33
Property appraisal, 127
Property report, 249–51
Public land use controls, 35–38
  building codes, 38
  general plan, 36
  zoning ordinances, 36–37
Purchase money mortgages, 87, 264

# Q

Quit claim deeds, 34

# R

Real estate credit, 1–19
  flow of funds into real estate mortgages, 6–8
  brief overview of secondary mortgage markets, 10
    indicators of mortgage flows, 11–13
    secondary market agencies, 11
  mortgage origination, 9
  operations of secondary mortgage market, 13–19
    Federal National Mortgage Association, 15
    Government National Mortgage Association, 15–17
  role of real estate finance, 2–6
    mortgages held by institutions, 6
    real estate as source of income, 3
    significance of real estate debt, 4–6
Real estate deeds, 31–35
  bargain and sale, 34
  quit claim, 34
  special warranty, 33
  specialized, 34–35
  warranty, 32–33
Real estate investment trusts, 62–64
Real estate investment yields, 375–96
  cash flow analysis, 386–93
    discounted cash flow (DCF), 389–91
    equity participation mortgages, 391–93
    conventional rate of return estimates, 376–79
    capitalization in perpetuity, 377–78
    limitations of rate of return calculations, 378–79
    internal rate of return (IRR), 394–96
    mortgage equity capitalization, 379–86
Real estate security, 140–47
  economic base analysis, 140–41
  neighborhood analysis, 142–44
  personal income, 141–42
  population characteristics, 141

site analysis, 144–45
valuation data, 146
Real estate settlement procedures, 289–95
basic requirements of RESPA, 289–95
impact on lenders, 295
Real Estate Settlement Procedures Act Amendments of 1975, 289
Real Estate Settlement Procedures Act of 1974 (RESPA), 289–94
Real estate valuation, 97
Recommended collection procedures, 343–51
follow-up records, 348
personal conferences, 347–48
routine procedures, 344–48
special collection procedures, 348–51
telephone interviews, 345–47
Reconstruction Finance Corporation, 103
Reconstruction Finance Corporation Mortgage Company, 13
Recording, 328–30
notice statutes, 329
race-notice statutes, 329–30
race type statutes, 329
Recording mortgages, 84–85
Regional shopping centers, 269–70
Regulation B, Federal Reserve Board, 296–97
Regulation Q, 46
Remainderman, 24–25
Rent control rationale, 188–89
Rental housing market, 193–96
demand analysis, 193–94
standards of comparison, 195–96
supply analysis, 194
Residential construction loans, 330–34
scattered lot development, 330–33
subdivision construction loans, 333–34
Residential land, 255–56
Retail sales forecasts, 276–77
Rights of the mortgagee, 82–84
acceleration clauses, 82–83
assignment of mortgages, 84
assumption of mortgages, 83–84
Rights of the mortgagor, 81
equity of redemption, 81
prepayment privileges, 82
statutory right of redemption, 82
Rules of thumb, 148–49

## S

Sales comparisons, 179–82
Sale leaseback financing, 222–23
Savings and loan associations, 42–47
developments since 1932, 43–44
early development, 43
effects of disintermediation, 46–47
mortgage loan activity, 44–45
Scattered lot development, 330–33
Secondary mortgage markets, 10
indicators of mortgage flows, 11–13
secondary market agencies, 11
Security deeds, 95
Security regulations, 108–09
Servient estate, 29
Sheriff's deed, 34
Shopping center management, 277–78
Shopping center mortgages, 268–87
financing methods, 280–86
construction costs, 281
financing techniques, 283–86
land acquisition, 280–81
presentation of the loan proposal, 281–83
judging mortgage security, 275–80
merchant association, 278–79
retail sales forecasts, 276–77
shopping center management, 277–78
site characteristics, 277
tenant restrictions, 278
tenant selection, 279–80
nature of shopping centers, 268–75
downtown retail stores, 274–75
shopping center operations, 271–74
types of shopping centers, 269–70
community centers, 270
neighborhood centers, 270–71
regional centers, 269–70
shopping centers classified by design, 271
shopping center leases, 286-87
Shopping facilities, 192
Short run supply, 99–100
Significance of real estate debt, 4–6

Single family dwelling mortgage application, 157–61
Single story buildings, 218
Site analysis, 144–47, 213–15
   land use restrictions, 144–45
   physical site characteristics, 145
   surface characteristics, 145
   surrounding encroachments, 145
Site characteristics, 277
Site suitability, 258
Sources of mortgage credit, 41–65
   commercial banks, 53–57
      commercial banks since World War II, 56–57
      early mortgage activity, 54–56
   life insurance companies, 51–53
   mortgage bankers, 57–60
   mutual savings banks, 47–51
      competition for savings, 50–51
      current development, 48–50
      early development, 47–48
   other financial sources, 60–65
      individuals and other credit sources, 64–65
      pension funds, 61–62
      real estate investment trusts, 62–64
   savings and loan associations, 42–47
      developments since 1932, 43–44
      early development, 43
      effects of disintermediation, 46–47
      mortgage loan activity, 44–45
Special assistance program, 16
Special warranty deeds, 33
Specialized deeds, 34
   correction deeds, 34
   executor's deeds, 34
   sheriff's deeds, 34
   trust deeds, 34
Split borrowings, 331
Stand-by purchase commitment, 60
Standards of comparison, 195–96
State administered land use controls, 251–52
Statement of record, 249
Statistical tests of the mortgage pattern, 154–55
Statutory right of redemption, 82
Stratified markets, 99
Strict foreclosure, 360
Subdivision construction loans, 333–34

Subdivision development, 257–61
   developments, 258–61
   estimating the feasibility of land site suitability, 258
Subject to mortgages, 83
Supply analysis, 194
Supply of farm mortgage credit, 226–27

## T

Take-out commitment, 59
Tandem plan, 17
Tangible wealth, 4
Telephone interviews, 345–47
Temporary unemployment, 339
Tenancy at sufferance, 29
Tenancy at will, 28
Tenancy by the entirety, 26
Tenancy from period to period, 28
Tenant restrictions, 278
Tenant selection, 279–80
Term mortgage, 88–89
Title I, community development, 123
Title II, assisted housing, 124
Title III, mortgage credit assistance, 124–25
Title V, rural housing, 125
Title VII, consumer home mortgage assistance, 125–26
Title VIII, miscellaneous authority, 126
Title theory states, 85
Trust deeds, 34, 94–95
   beneficiary, 94
   trustee, 94
   trustor, 94
Types of deeds, 31–35
   bargain and sale deeds, 34
   quit claim deeds, 34
   special warranty deeds, 33
   specialized deeds, 34–35
   warranty deeds, 32–33
Types of mortgages classified by purpose, 86–88
   blanket, 86
   construction, 88
   open-end, 86
   package, 87
   participation, 87

purchase money, 87
  wraparound, 87–88
Types of securities, 109
Types of shopping centers, 269–71
  community centers, 270
  neighborhood centers, 270–71
  regional centers, 269–70
  shopping centers classified by design,
    271

## U

Uniform settlement statement, 290
Usury laws, 96

## V

Vacancy allowance, 198
Valuation data, 146
Variable payment mortgage, 89

Variable rate mortgages, 93–95
Veterans Administration appraisal report, 152

## W

Warehousing operations, 372–73
Warranty deeds, 32–33
  covenant against encumbrances, 33
  covenant of further assurances, 33
  covenant of quiet enjoyment, 33
  convenant of seizin, 33
  covenant of warranty of title, 33
Water quality, 40
Willingness to pay, 303–04
Wraparound mortgages, 87–88

## Z

Zoning ordinances, 36–37

------------------------------------------------------------------------

# BUSINESS REPLY MAIL
No Postage Stamp Necessary If Mailed in the United States

Postage Will Be Paid by

Education Policy & Development Group
**American Bankers Association**
1120 Connecticut Avenue
Washington, D.C. 20036

# I. REAL ESTATE FINANCE
### Date_____

**A.** Indicate your perception of specific chapters by placing checkmarks in appropriate squares. You need not comment on every chapter.

| Chapter Number | Especially Relevant | Irrelevant to My Needs | Too Much Depth | Not Enough Depth | Difficult to Understand | Charts/Graphs Unclear | Outdated/Errors | Other | Make comments on specific topics/pages to which characteristic applies. (If more than one square is checked, please use letters to categorize comments). |
|---|---|---|---|---|---|---|---|---|---|
| | | | | | | | | | |
| | | | | | | | | | |
| | | | | | | | | | |
| | | | | | | | | | |
| | | | | | | | | | |
| | | | | | | | | | |
| | | | | | | | | | |
| | | | | | | | | | |

**B. What additional subject areas should be included in the textbook?**

_____

_____

**C.** Please indicate your overall perception of the text in relation to the following characteristics: (by checking the appropriate box or number)

1. Practicality ☐ too theoretical ☐ about right ☐ too practical
2. Readability ☐ too difficult ☐ about right ☐ too easy
3. Prior knowledge assumed ☐ too much ☐ about right ☐ too little
4. Scope and depth of content ☐ too much ☐ about right ☐ insufficient
5. Content currency    5    4    3    2    1
   up to date        out dated
6. Organization of subject matter    5    4    3    2    1
   excellent        poor
7. Interest level    5    4    3    2    1
   interesting        boring

**D. Indicate other suggestions for improving this textbook not covered:**

_____

_____

# II. YOUR PURPOSES

**A.** What was (were) your purposes in reading this material? (Check those which apply)

1. ☐ Obtain overall knowledge of subject
2. ☐ Learn specific information
3. ☐ Perform job better
4. ☐ Improve promotion potential
5. ☐ Work toward AIB certificate
6. ☐ Directed to do so by superior
7. ☐ Other (specify)

**B.** How well did the textbook meet your purposes? (circle one)

5    4    3    2    1
Extremely well        Inadequately

# III. YOU

A. I am a(n) _____ Instructor _____ Student

B. Name of Bank (Institution) _____

C. My Name _____

D. If a banker, asset size of Bank is $_____

E. Highest formal education: ☐ High School ☐ College ☐ AB Degree ☐ Advanced Degree

F. I am a(n) ☐ Officer ☐ Non-Officer

G. My job function is_____

H. I have worked in banking for:
   ☐ more than 5 years    ☐ 3-5 years
   ☐ 1-3 years    ☐ under 1 year

I. This Textbook was used in:
   ☐ AIB classroom course    ☐ Correspondence course